BECAUSE I'M THE GODDESS

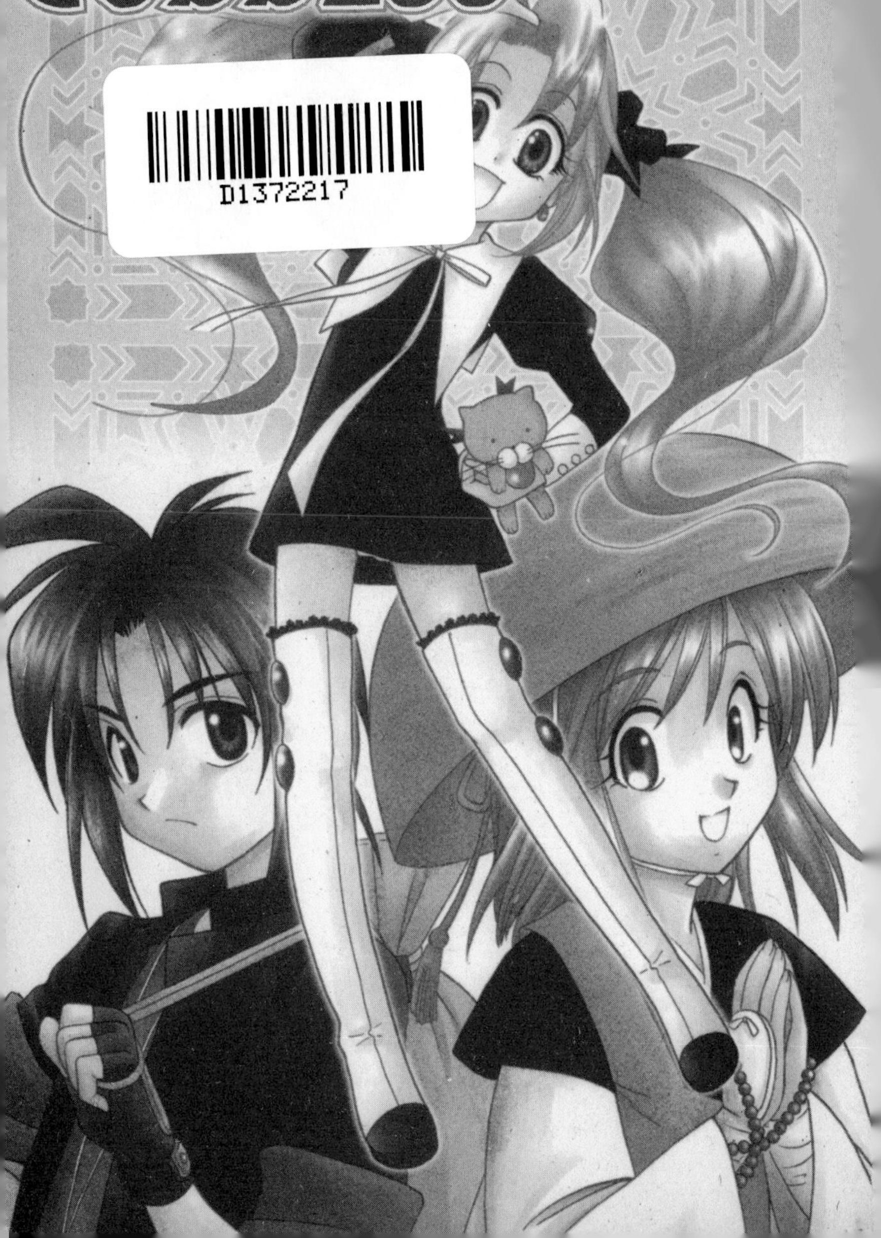

Because I'm the Goddess Vol. 1
Created by Shamneko

Translation - Mike Kiefl
English Adaptation - Jamie S. Rich
Copy Editor - Hope Donovan
Retouch and Lettering - Erika "skooter" Terriquez
Graphic Designer - Jose Macasocol, Jr.

Editor - Rob Valois
Digital Imaging Manager - Chris Buford
Production Manager - Elisabeth Brizzi
Managing Editor - Sheldon Drzka
VP of Production - Ron Klamert
Editor-in-Chief - Rob Tokar
Publisher - Mike Kiley
President and C.O.O. - John Parker
C.E.O. and Chief Creative Officer - Stuart Levy

A  Manga

TOKYOPOP Inc.
5900 Wilshire Blvd. Suite 2000
Los Angeles, CA 90036

E-mail: info@TOKYOPOP.com
Come visit us online at www.TOKYOPOP.com

ISBN: 1-59816-488-0

First TOKYOPOP printing: August 2006
10 9 8 7 6 5 4 3 2
Printed in the USA

BECAUSE I'M THE GODDESS

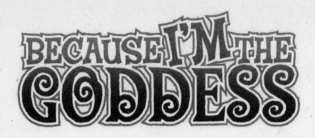

Volume 1

by:
Shamneko

TOKYOPOP®

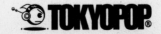

HAMBURG // LONDON // LOS ANGELES // TOKYO

Table of Contents

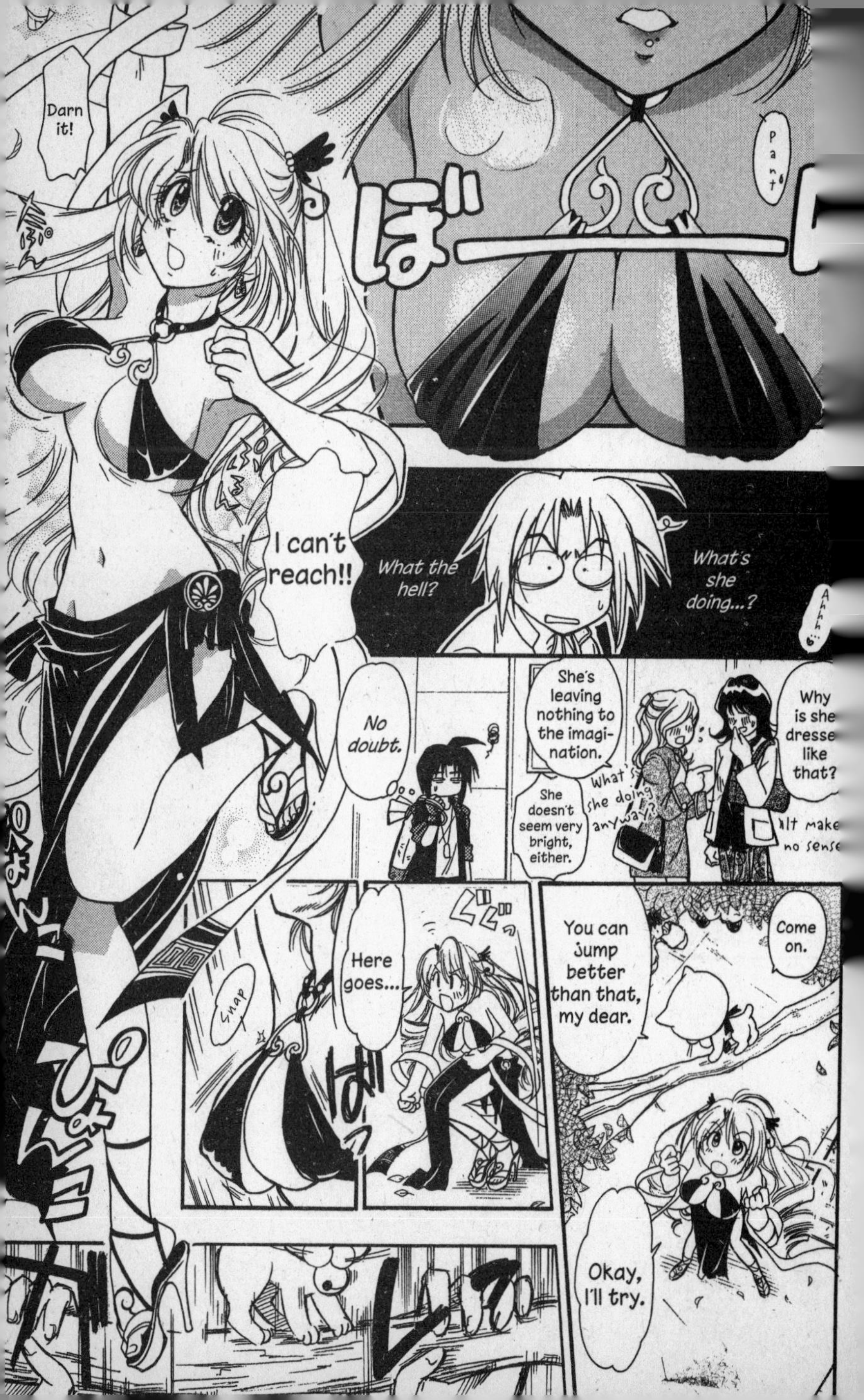

Pant
ぼーッ
What's she doing...?
What the hell?
Ahhh...
Why is she dresse like that?
It make no sense
She's leaving nothing to the imagination.
What's she doing anyway!?
She doesn't seem very bright, either.
No doubt.
Come on.
You can jump better than that, my dear.
Okay, I'll try.
Here goes...
Snap
Darn it!
I can't reach!!

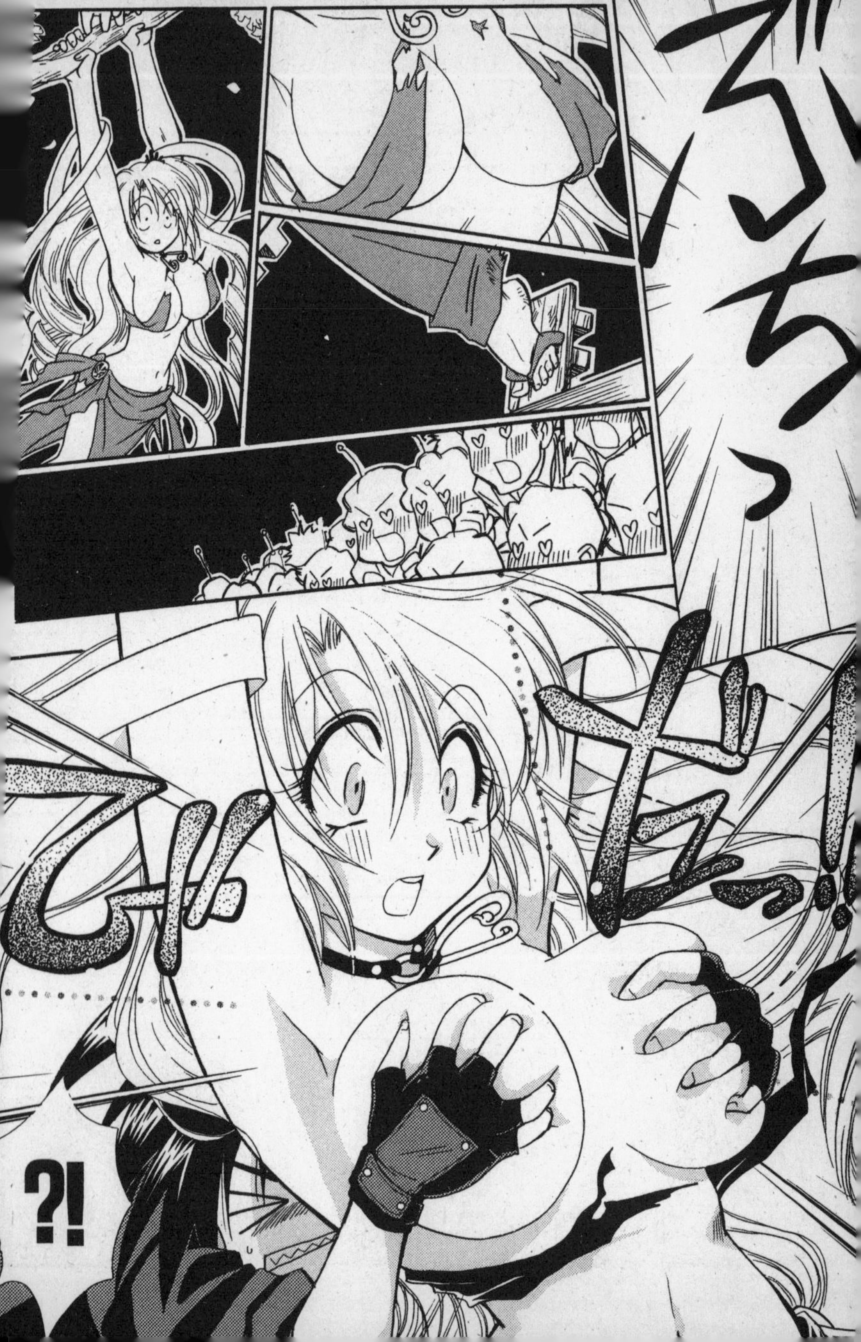
?!

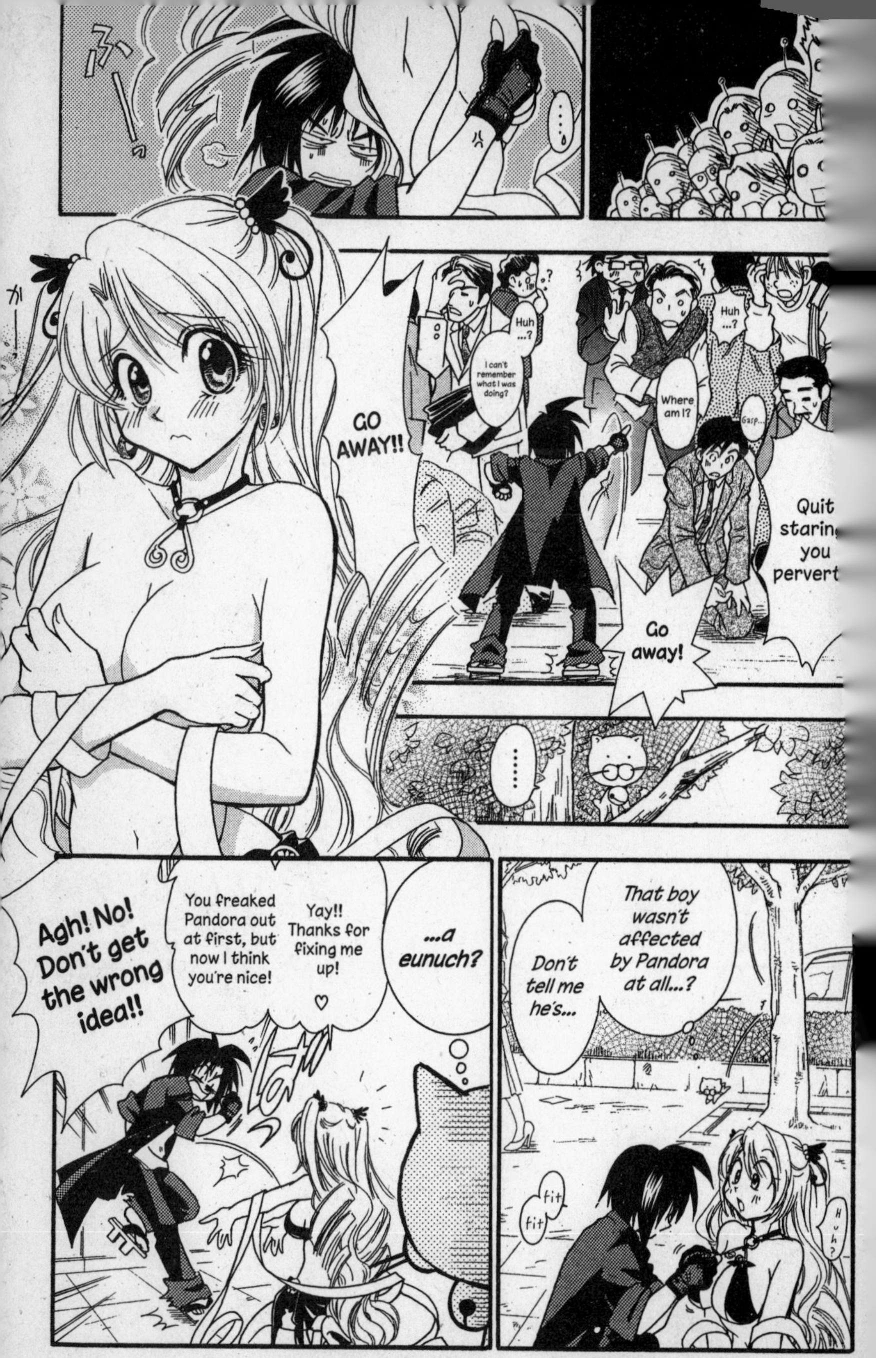
Huh ...?
Gasp...
Where am I?
Quit starin you pervert
Huh ...?
I can't remember what I was doing?
GO AWAY!!
Go away!
......
That boy wasn't affected by Pandora at all...?
Don't tell me he's...
fit fit
Huh?
...a eunuch?
Yay!! Thanks for fixing me up! ♡
You freaked Pandora out at first, but now I think you're nice!
Agh! No! Don't get the wrong idea!!

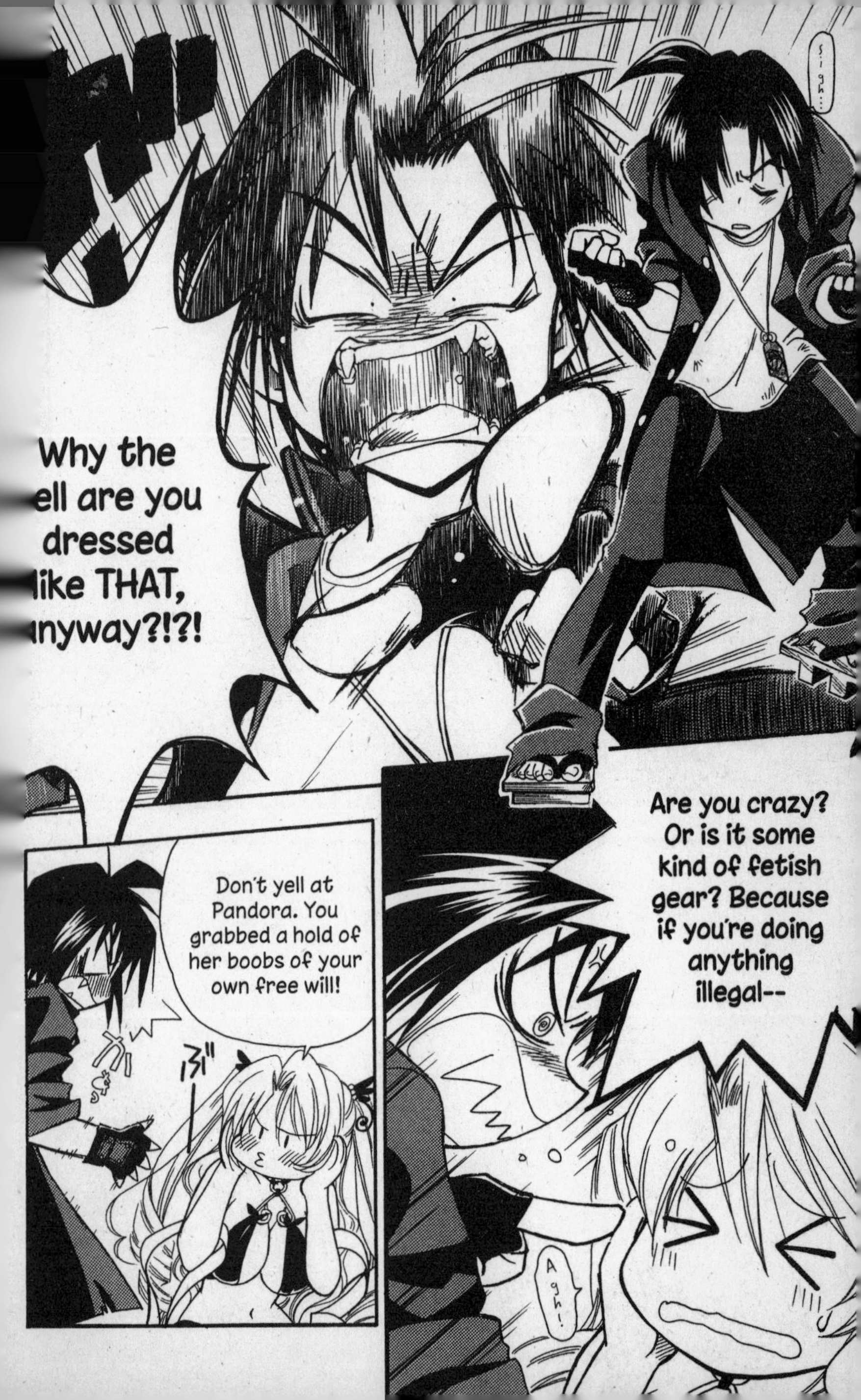

Sigh...
Why the ell are you dressed like THAT, nyway?!?!
Are you crazy? Or is it some kind of fetish gear? Because if you're doing anything illegal--
Agh!
Don't yell at Pandora. You grabbed a hold of her boobs of your own free will!

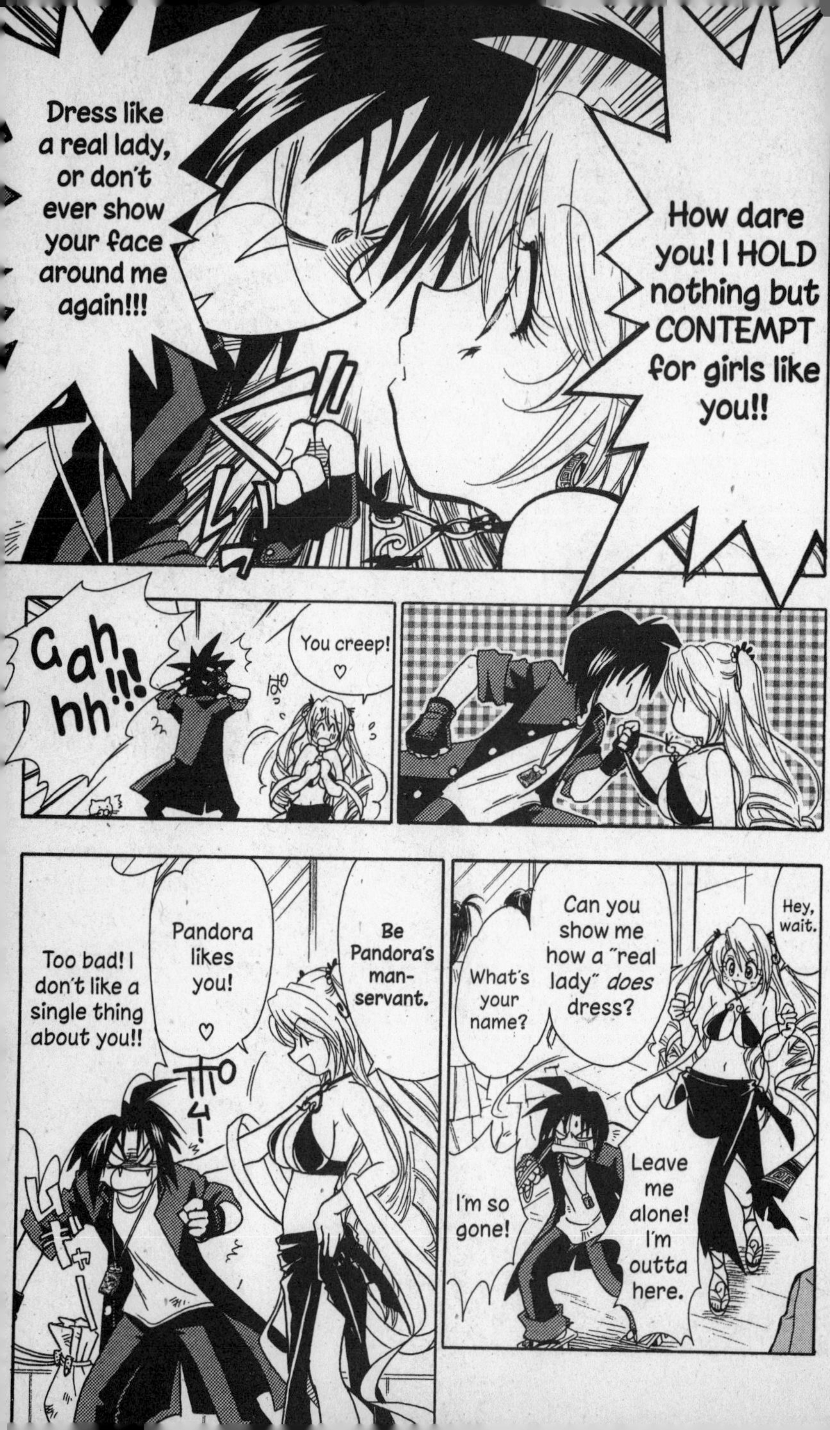

How dare you! I HOLD nothing but CONTEMPT for girls like you!!
Dress like a real lady, or don't ever show your face around me again!!!
You creep! ♡
Gahhh!!!
Hey, wait.
Can you show me how a "real lady" *does* dress?
What's your name?
Leave me alone! I'm outta here.
I'm so gone!
Be Pandora's man-servant.
Pandora likes you! ♡
Too bad! I don't like a single thing about you!!

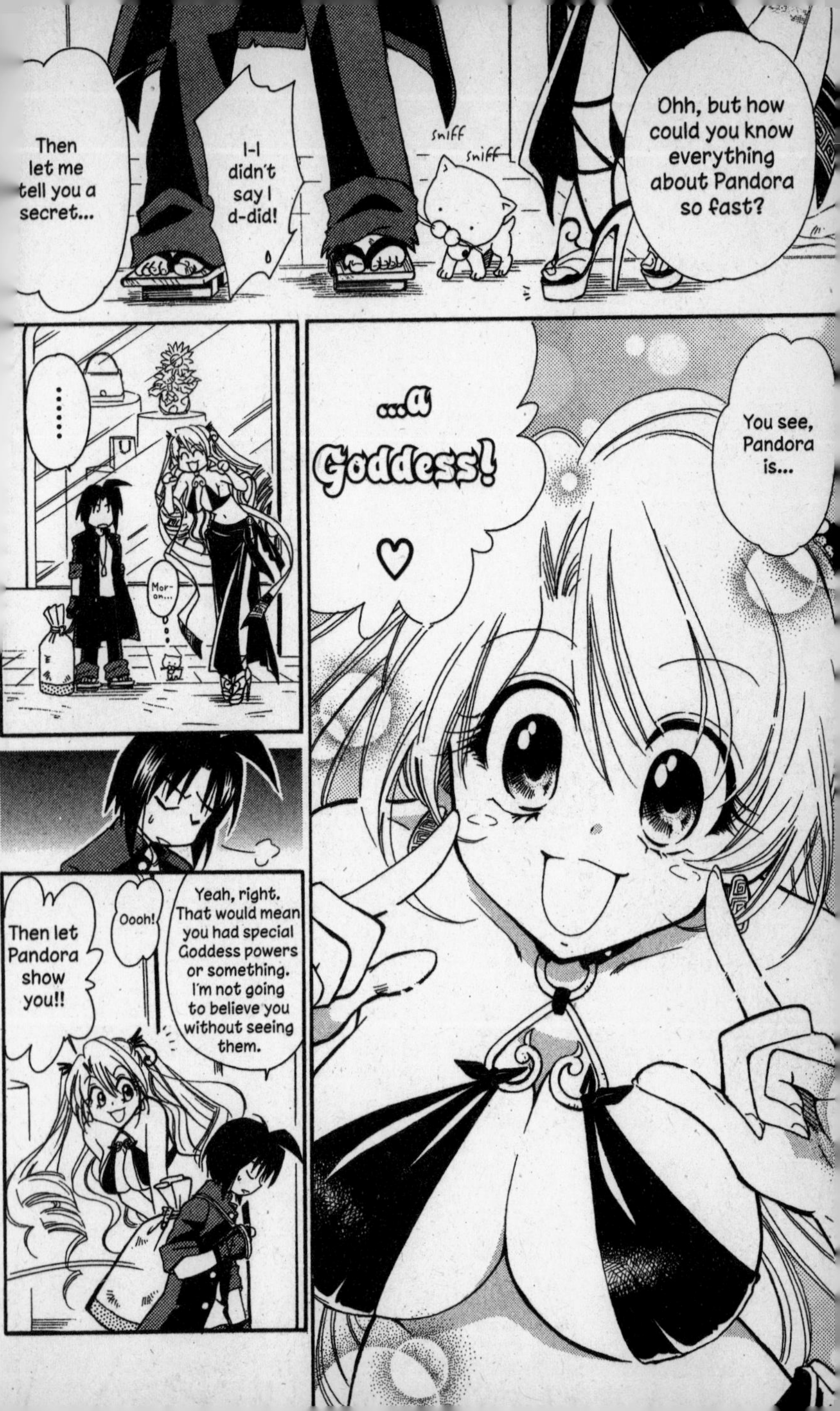
Ohh, but how could you know everything about Pandora so fast?
sniff
sniff
I-I didn't say I d-did!
Then let me tell you a secret...
You see, Pandora is...
...a Goddess! ♥
......
Mor-on...
Yeah, right. That would mean you had special Goddess powers or something. I'm not going to believe you without seeing them.
Oooh!
Then let Pandora show you!!

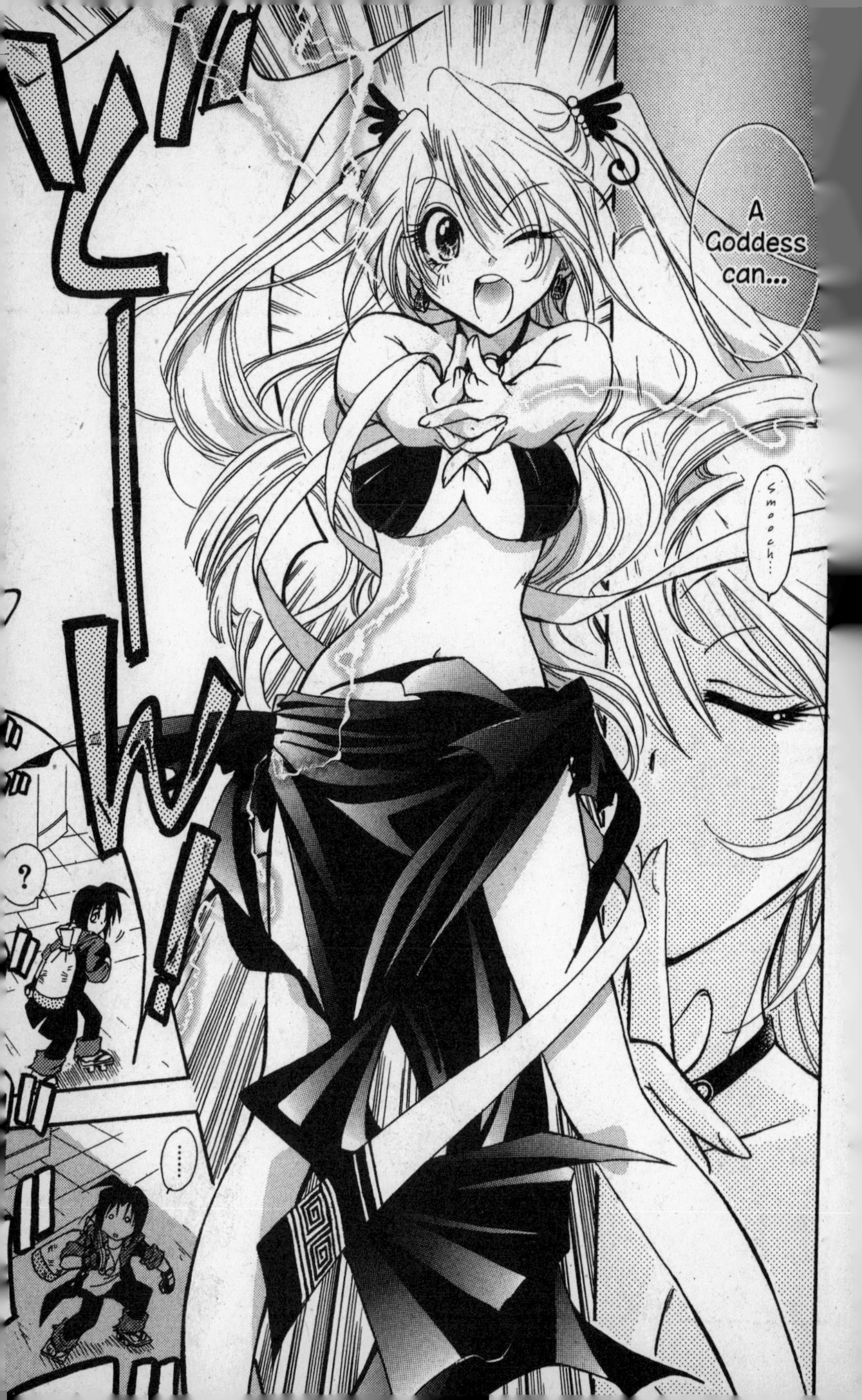
A Goddess can...
Smooch...
?
......

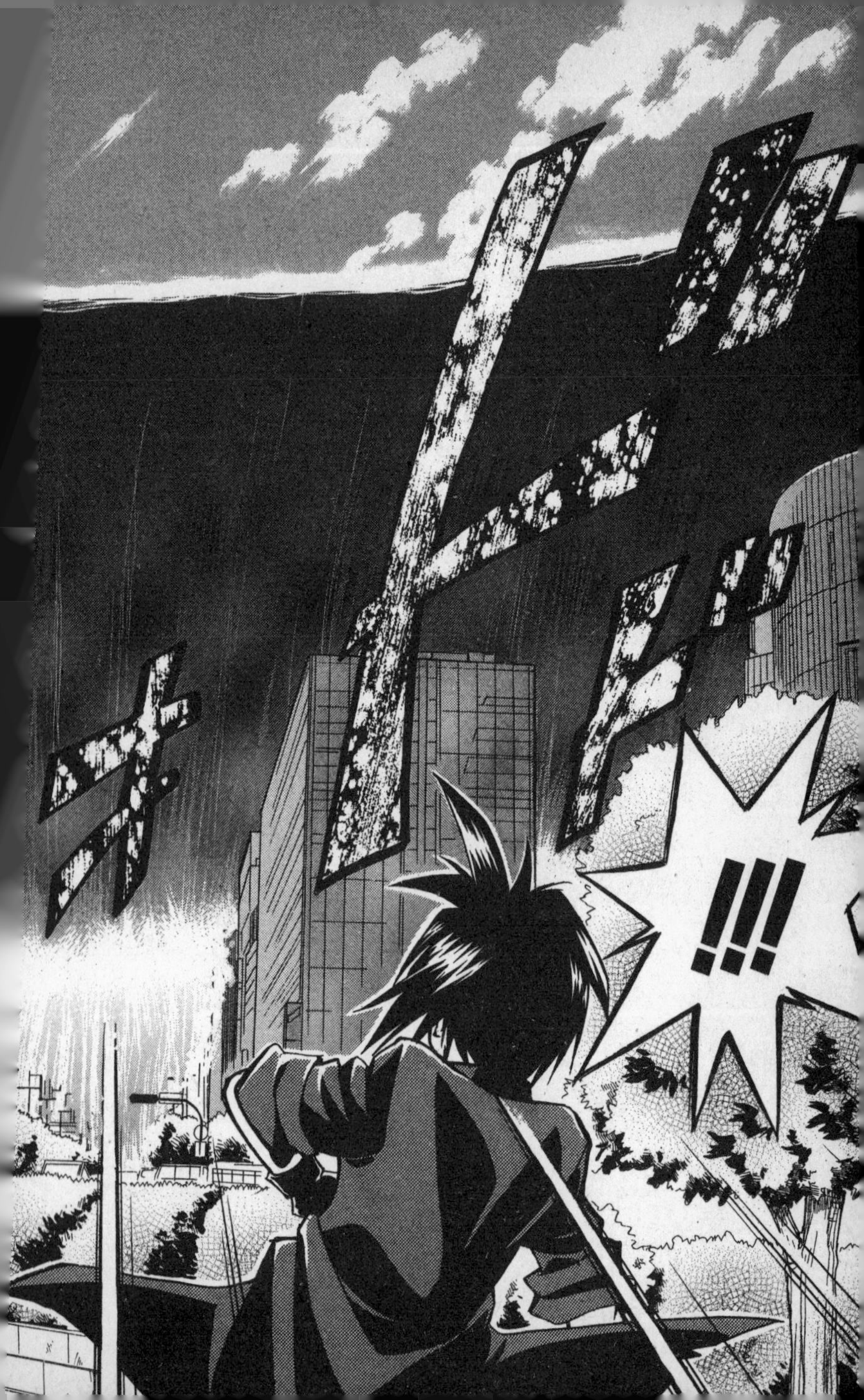
!!!

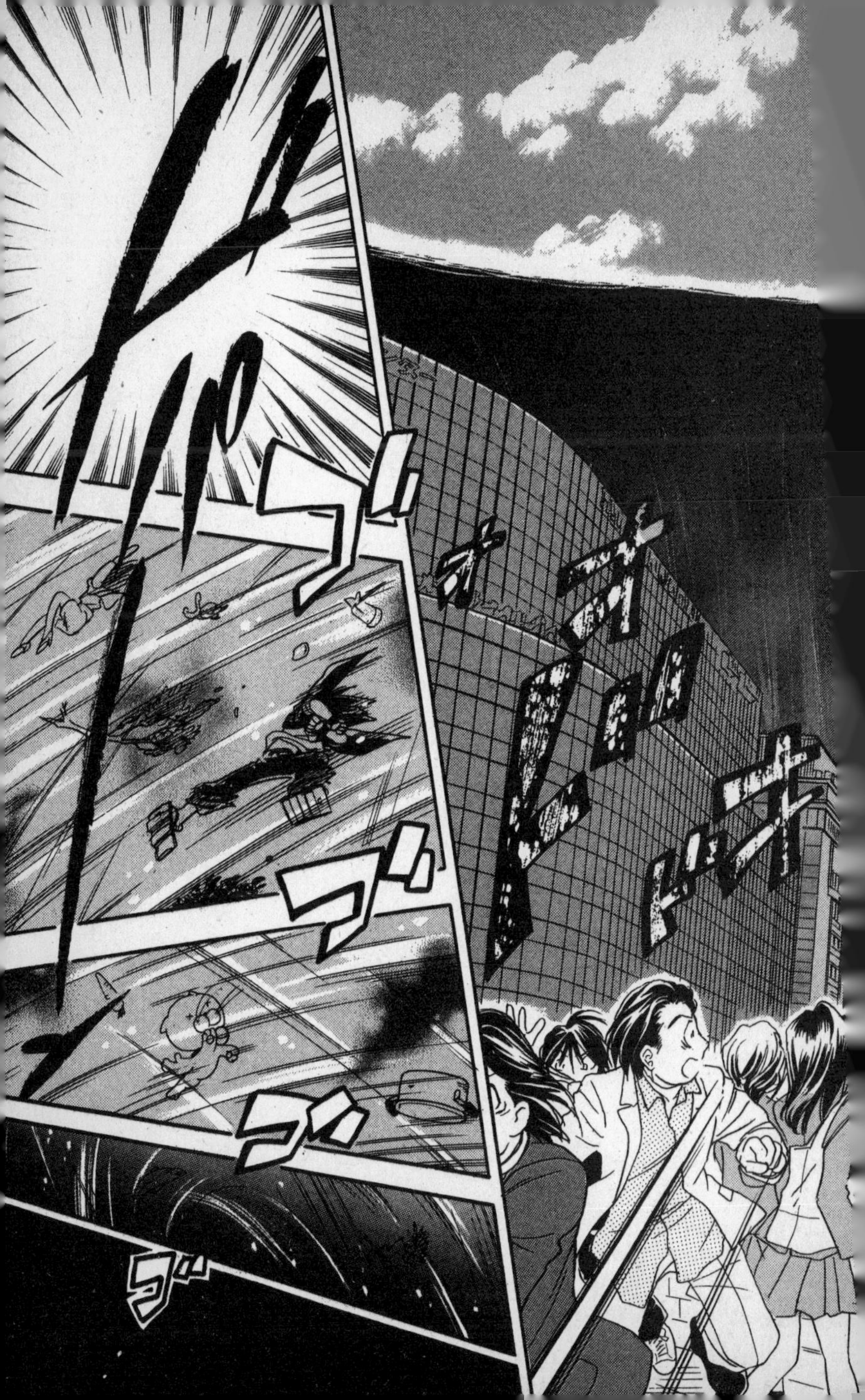
ゴ
ゴ
ゴ
ゴ

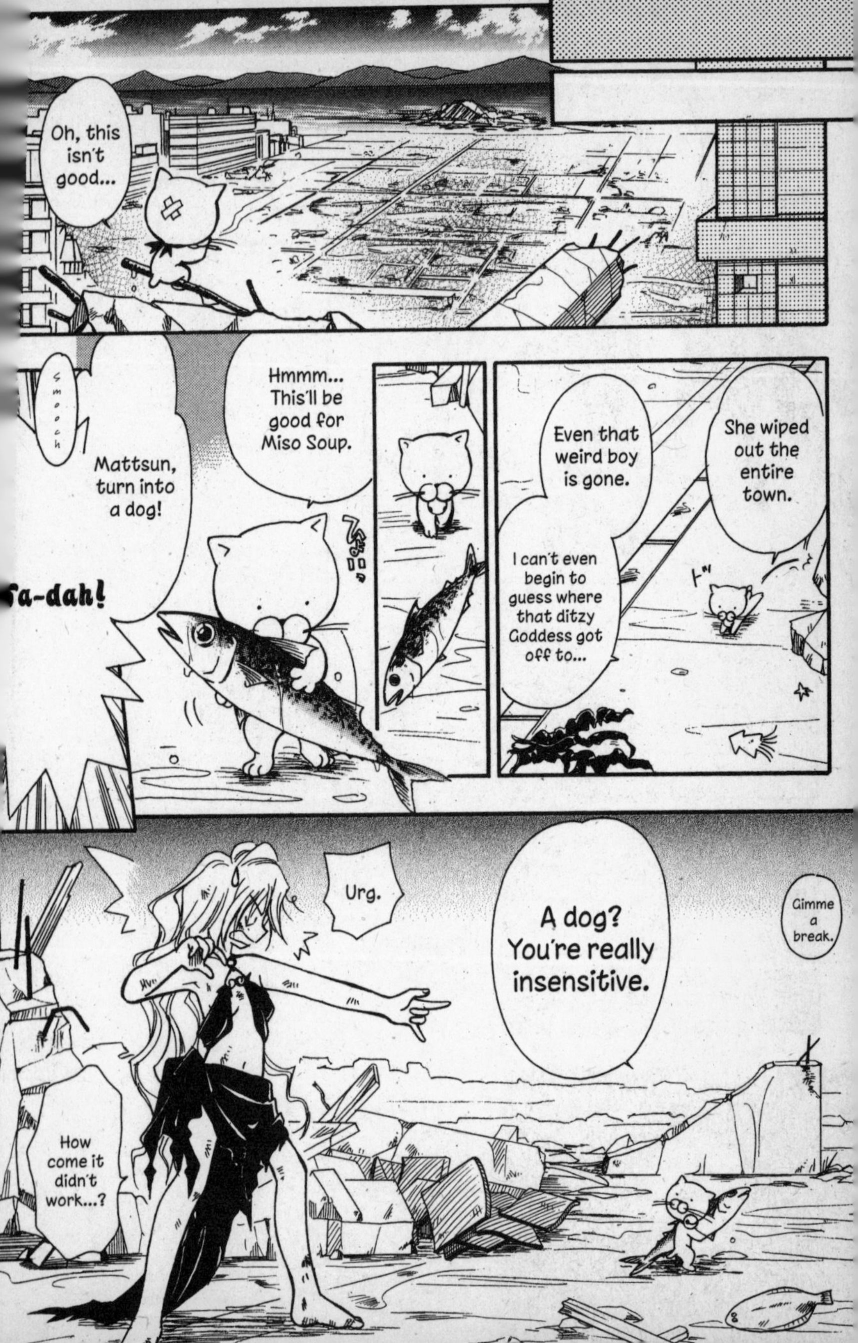

Oh, this isn't good...
She wiped out the entire town.
Even that weird boy is gone.
I can't even begin to guess where that ditzy Goddess got off to...
Hmmm... This'll be good for Miso Soup.
Mattsun, turn into a dog!
smooch
Ta-dah!
Gimme a break.
A dog? You're really insensitive.
Urg.
How come it didn't work...?

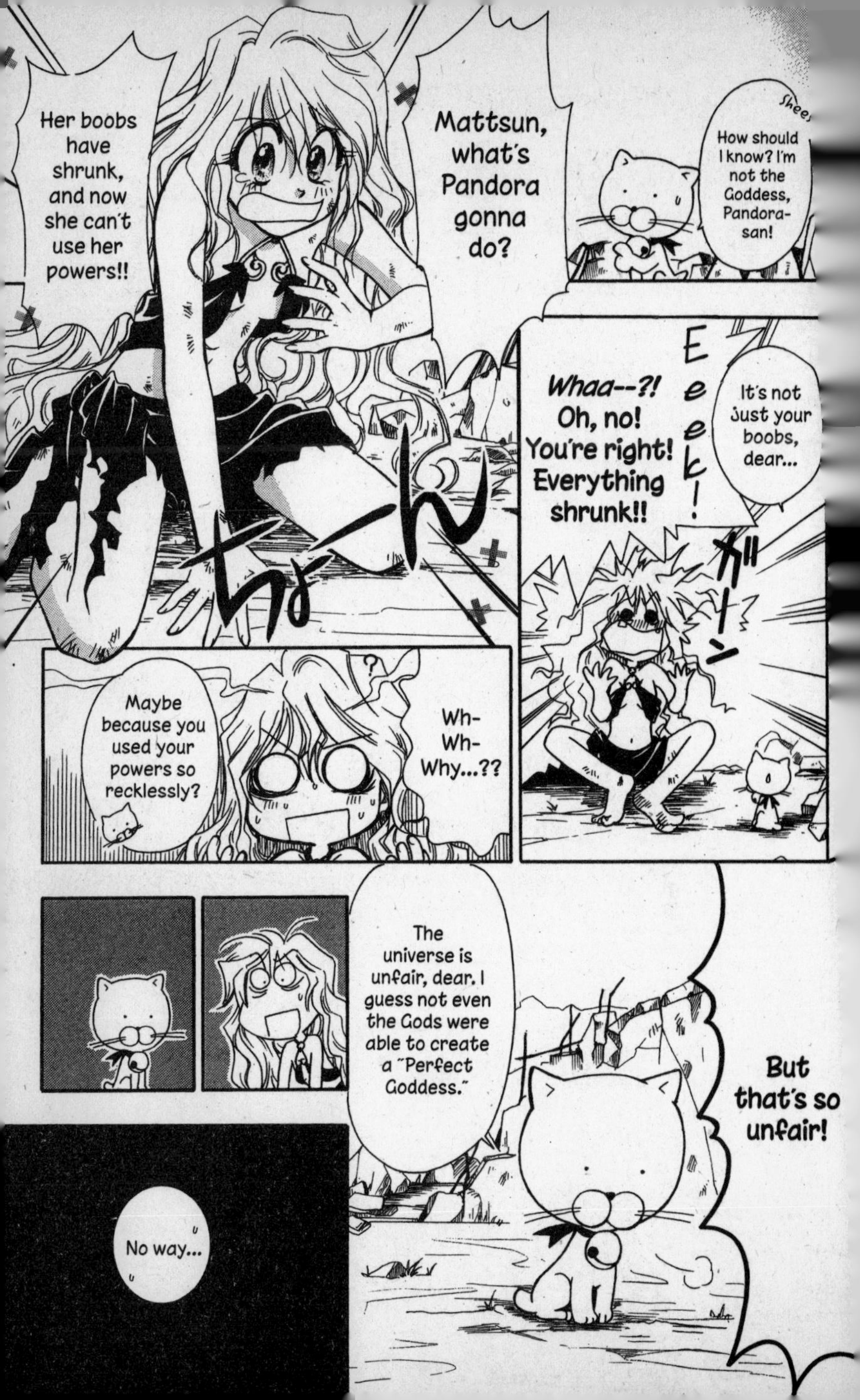
Mattsun, what's Pandora gonna do?
Her boobs have shrunk, and now she can't use her powers!!
Shees
How should I know? I'm not the Goddess, Pandora-san!
It's not just your boobs, dear...
Eeek!
Whaa--?! Oh, no! You're right! Everything shrunk!!
ガーン
Wh-Wh-Why...??
Maybe because you used your powers so recklessly?
But that's so unfair!
The universe is unfair, dear. I guess not even the Gods were able to create a "Perfect Goddess."
No way...

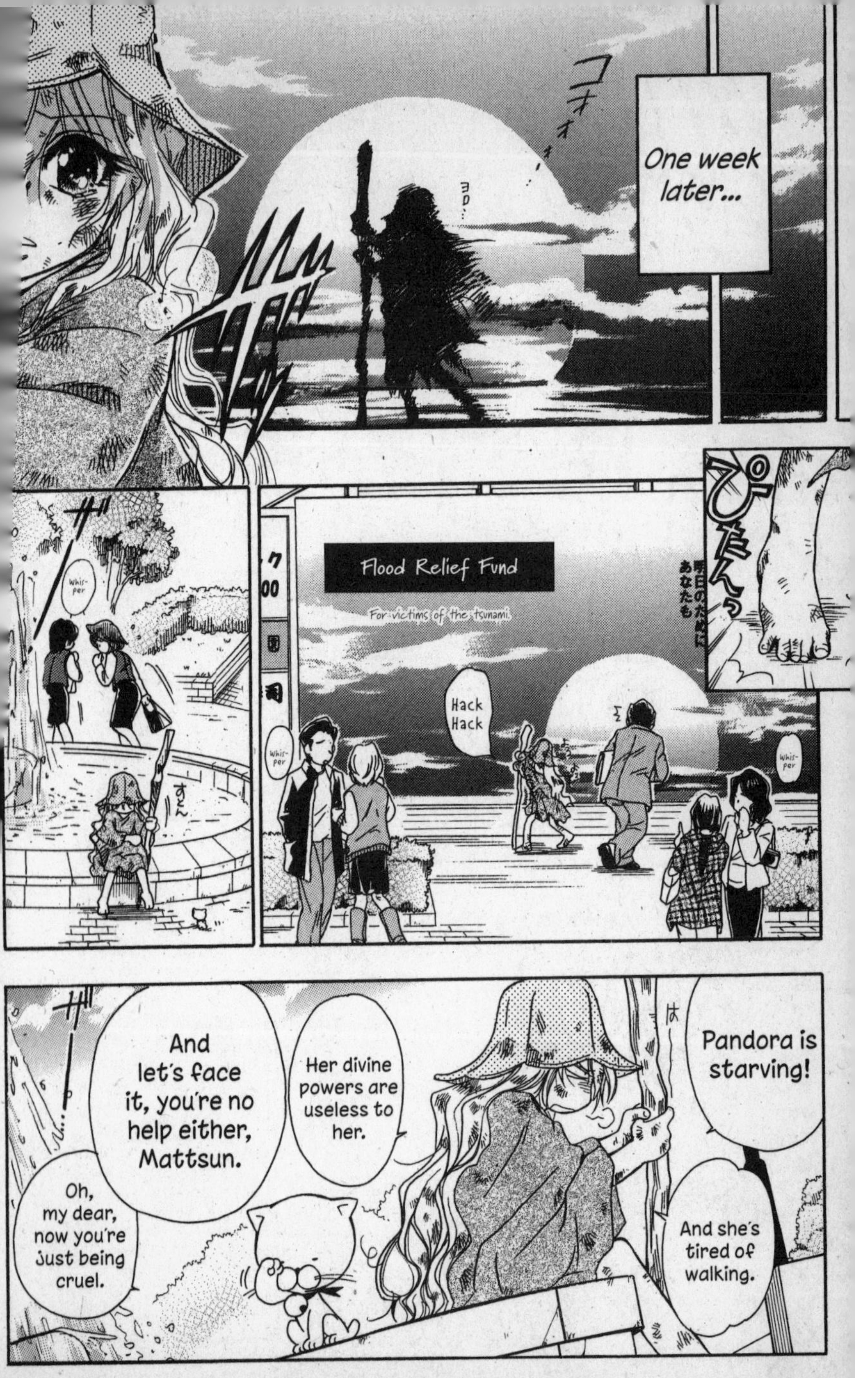
コオオォ
One week later...
ヨロ…
ぴたんっ
明日のために
あなたも
Flood Relief Fund
For victims of the tsunami.
Whis-per
Hack Hack
Whis-per
Whis-per
すとん
Pandora is starving!
And she's tired of walking.
Her divine powers are useless to her.
And let's face it, you're no help either, Mattsun.
Oh, my dear, now you're just being cruel.

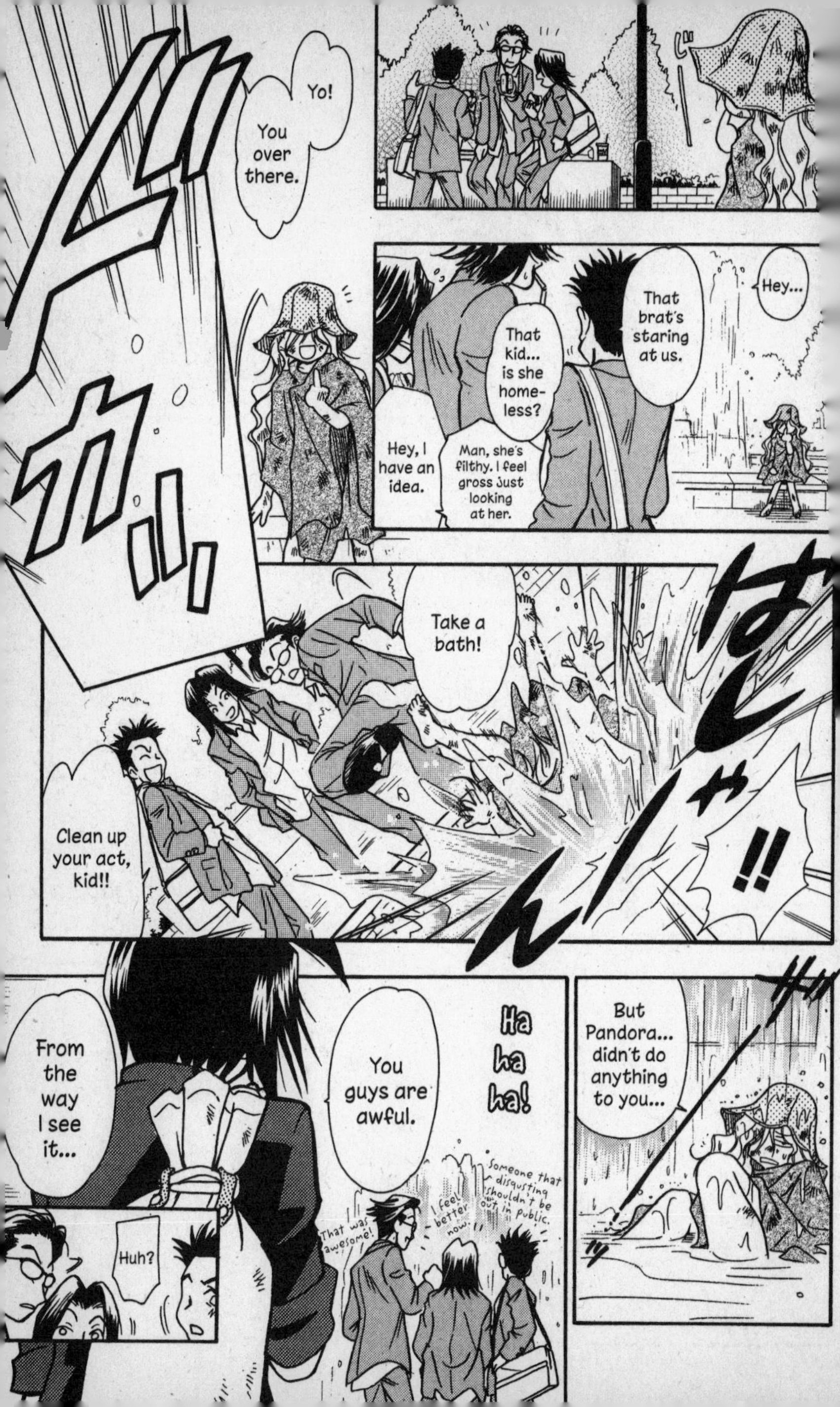

Hey...
That brat's staring at us.
That kid... is she homeless?
Man, she's filthy. I feel gross just looking at her.
Hey, I have an idea.
Yo!
You over there.
Take a bath!
Clean up your act, kid!!
But Pandora... didn't do anything to you...
Ha ha ha!
You guys are awful.
Someone that disgusting shouldn't be out in public.
I feel better now.
That was awesome!
From the way I see it...
Huh?

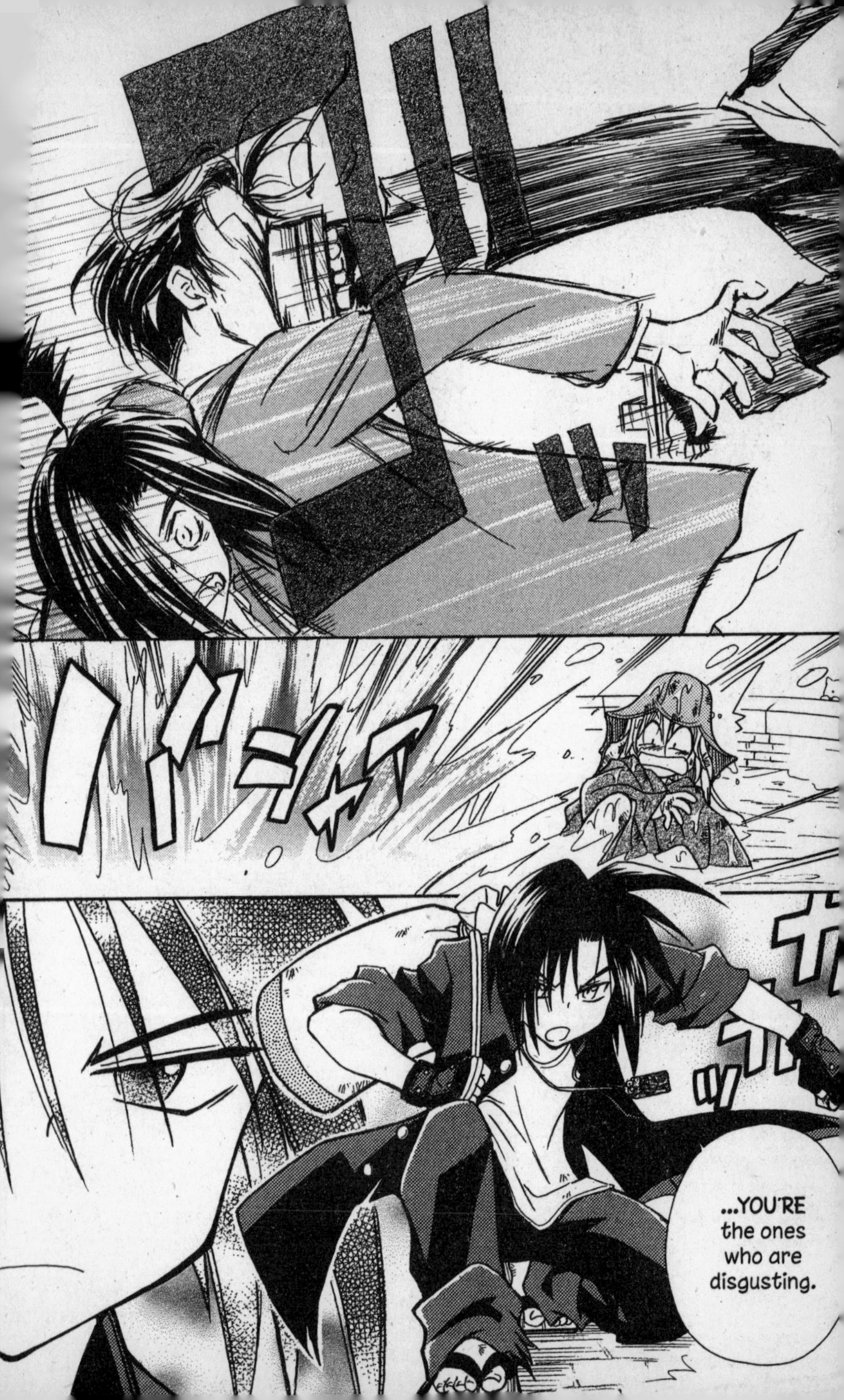
...YOU'RE the ones who are disgusting.

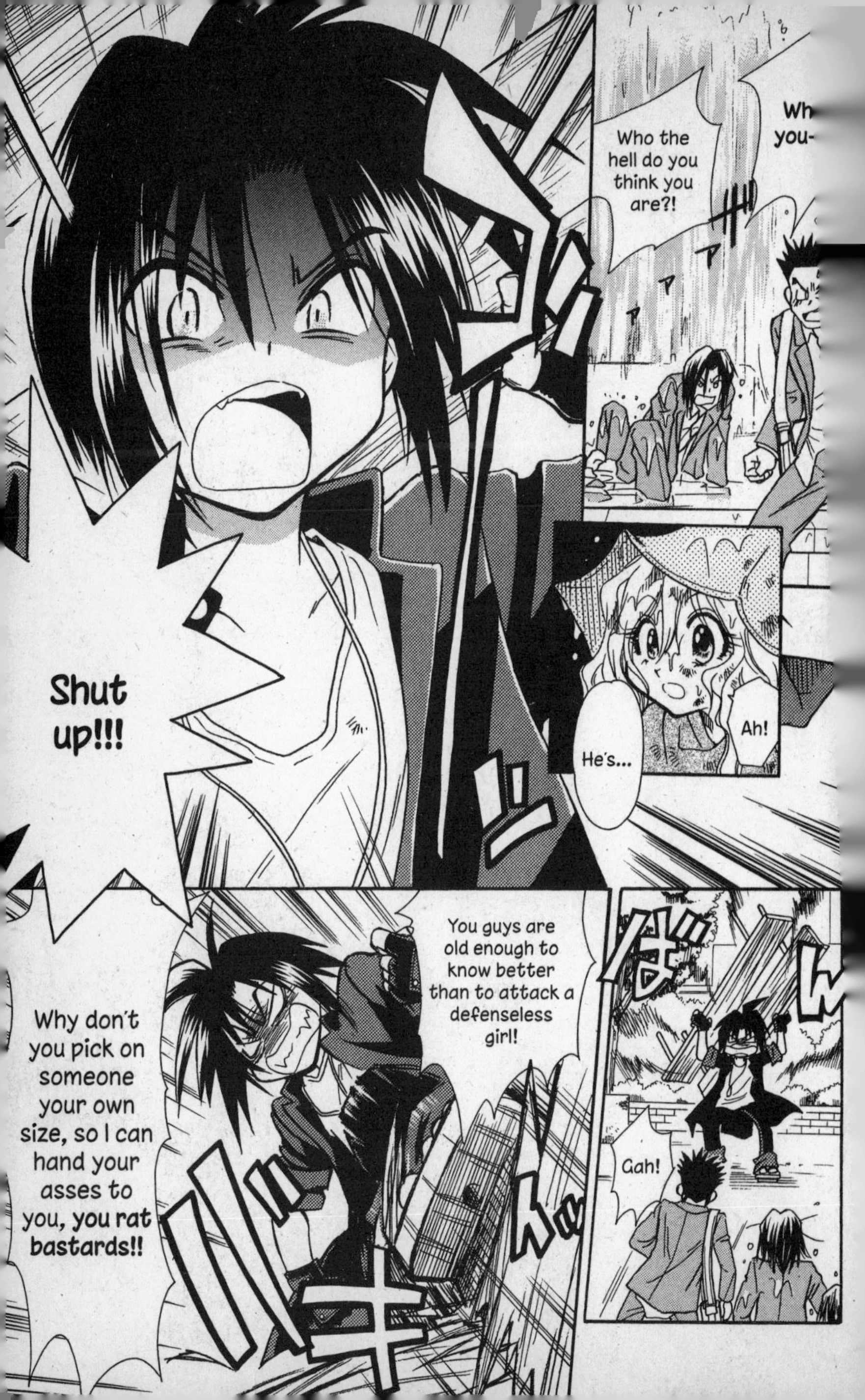
Wh
you-
Who the hell do you think you are?!
Ah!
He's...
Shut up!!!
Gah!
You guys are old enough to know better than to attack a defenseless girl!
Why don't you pick on someone your own size, so I can hand your asses to you, you rat bastards!!

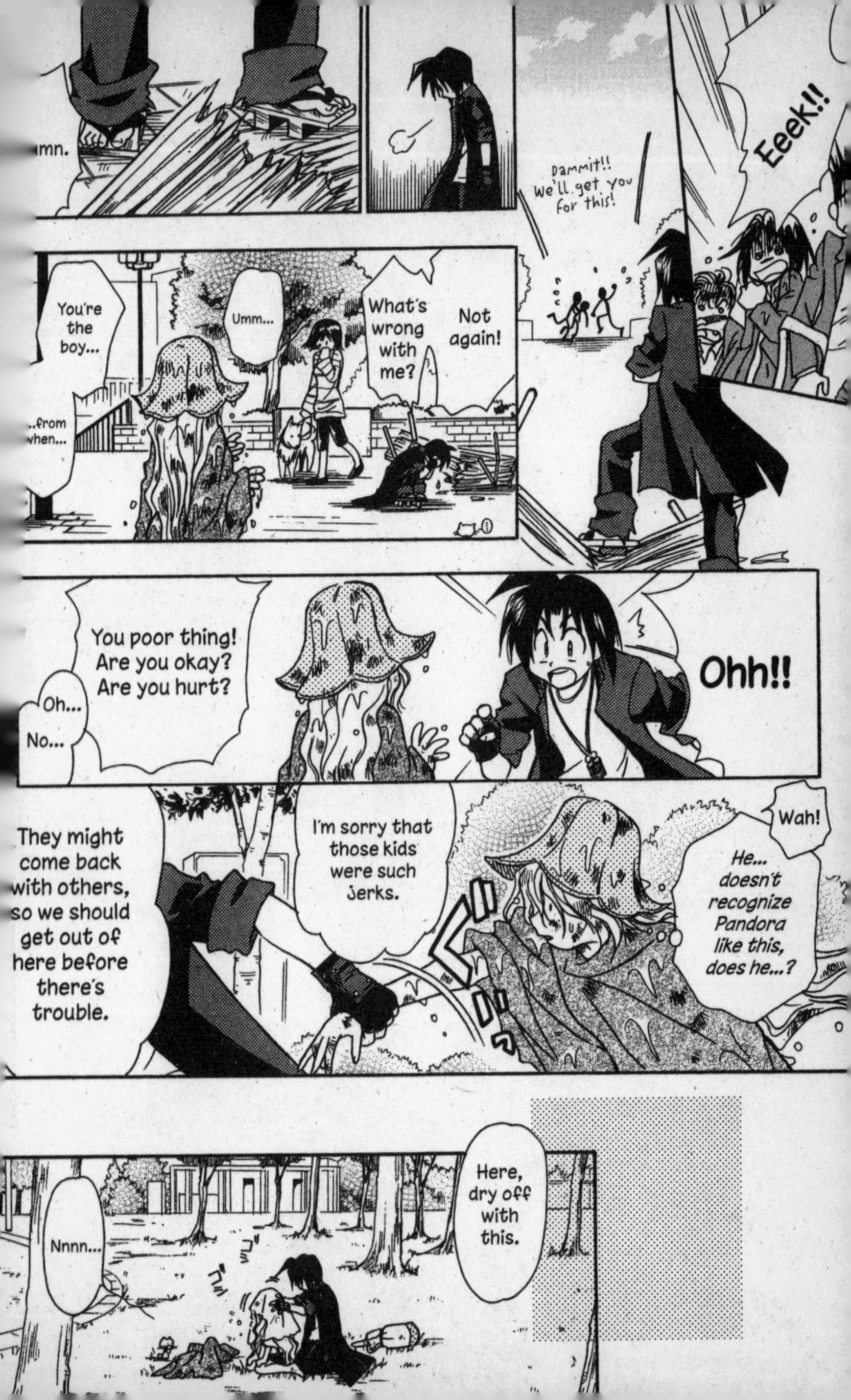
Eeek!!
Dammit!! We'll get you for this!
..mn.
Not again!
What's wrong with me?
Umm...
You're the boy...
..from when...
Ohh!!
You poor thing! Are you okay? Are you hurt?
Oh...
No...
Wah!
He... doesn't recognize Pandora like this, does he...?
I'm sorry that those kids were such jerks.
They might come back with others, so we should get out of here before there's trouble.
Here, dry off with this.
Nnnn...

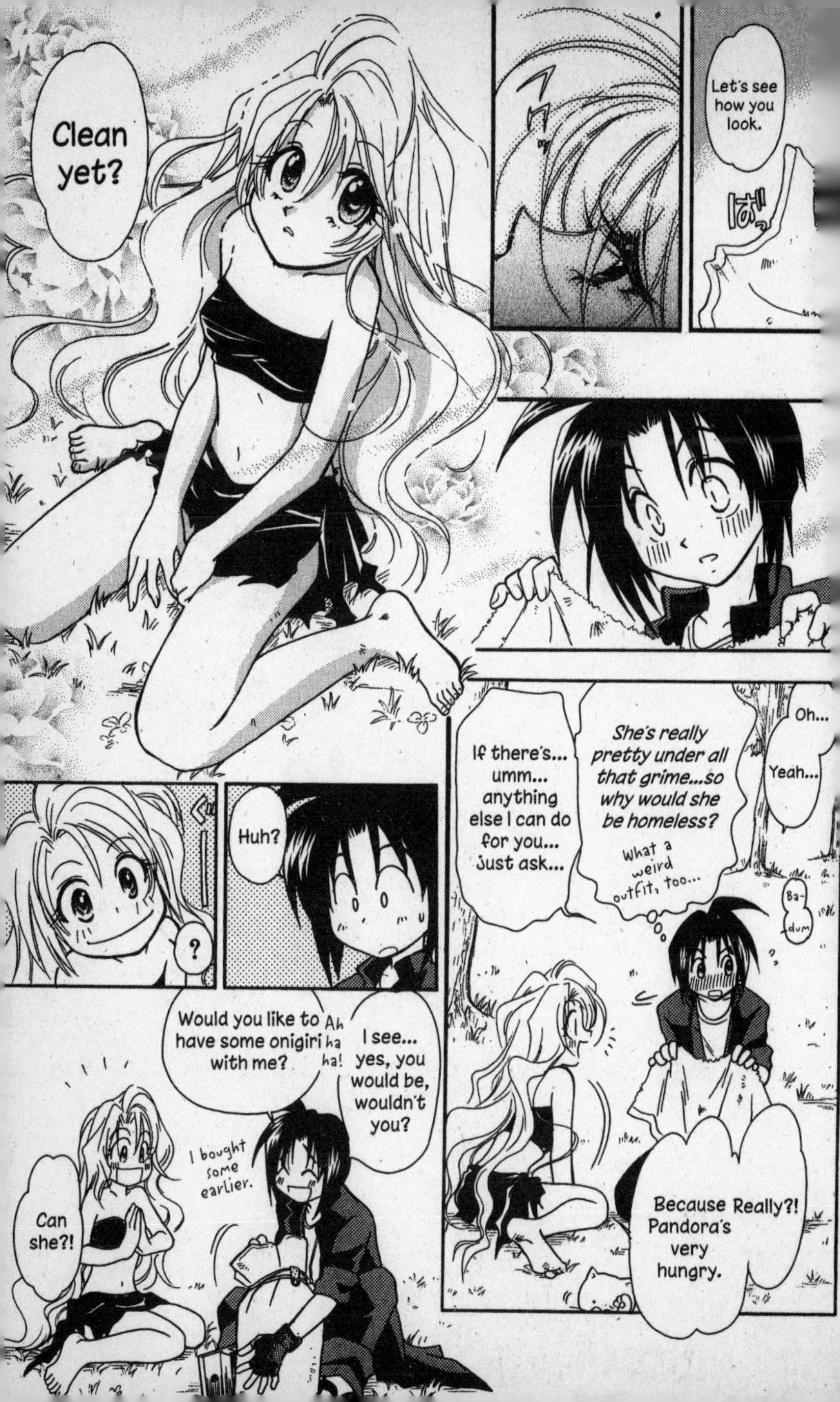
Let's see how you look.
ばっ
Clean yet?
Oh...
Yeah...
She's really pretty under all that grime...so why would she be homeless?
What a weird outfit, too...
If there's... umm... anything else I can do for you... just ask...
Ba-dum
Really?!
Because Pandora's very hungry.
Huh?
?
I see... yes, you would be, wouldn't you?
Ah ha ha!
Would you like to have some onigiri with me?
I bought some earlier.
Can she?!

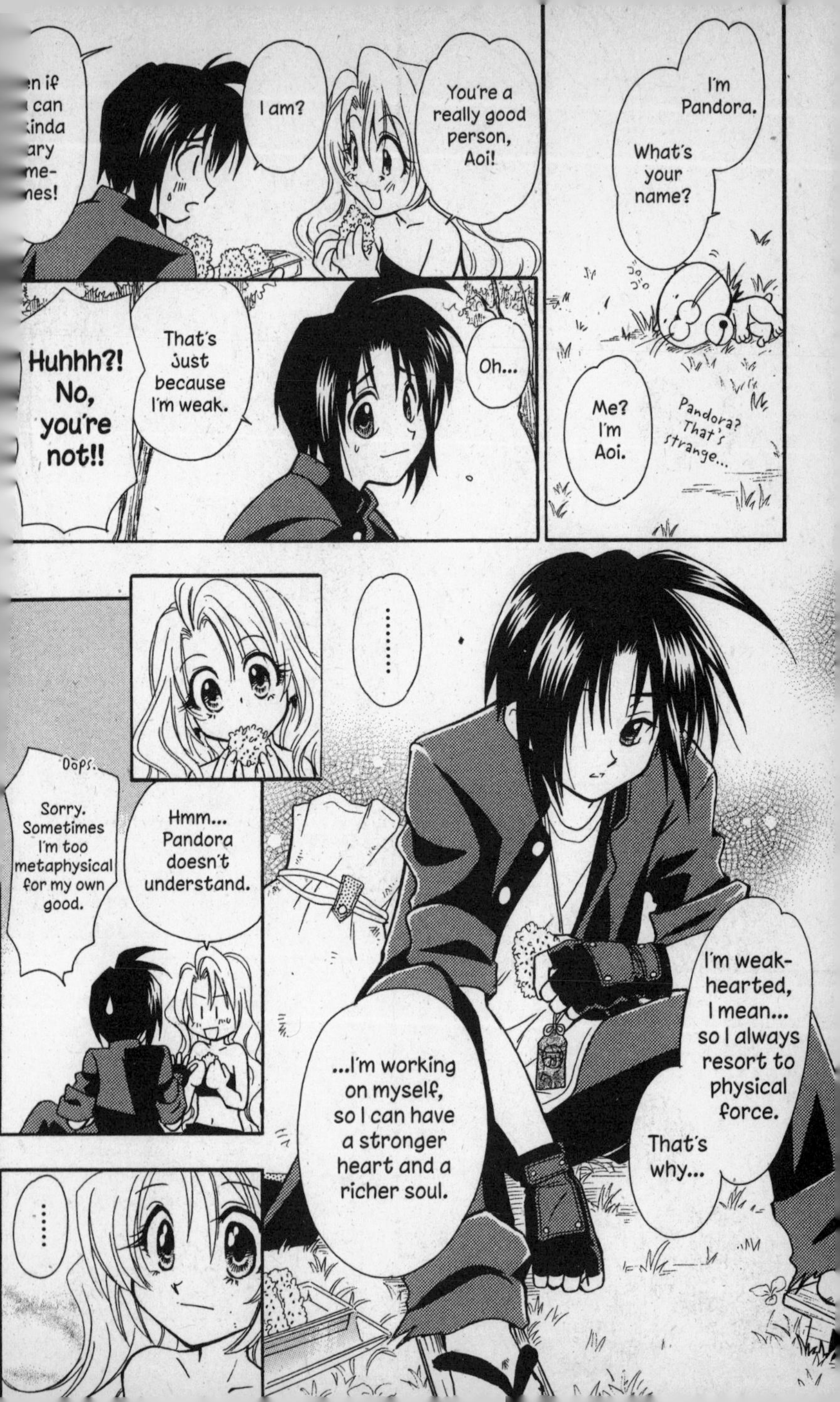
I'm Pandora.
What's your name?
Me? I'm Aoi.
Pandora? That's strange...
You're a really good person, Aoi!
I am?
en if can kinda ary me- nes!
Oh...
That's just because I'm weak.
Huhhh?! No, you're not!!
I'm weak-hearted, I mean... so I always resort to physical force.
That's why...
...I'm working on myself, so I can have a stronger heart and a richer soul.
......
Hmm... Pandora doesn't understand.
Oops.
Sorry. Sometimes I'm too metaphysical for my own good.
......

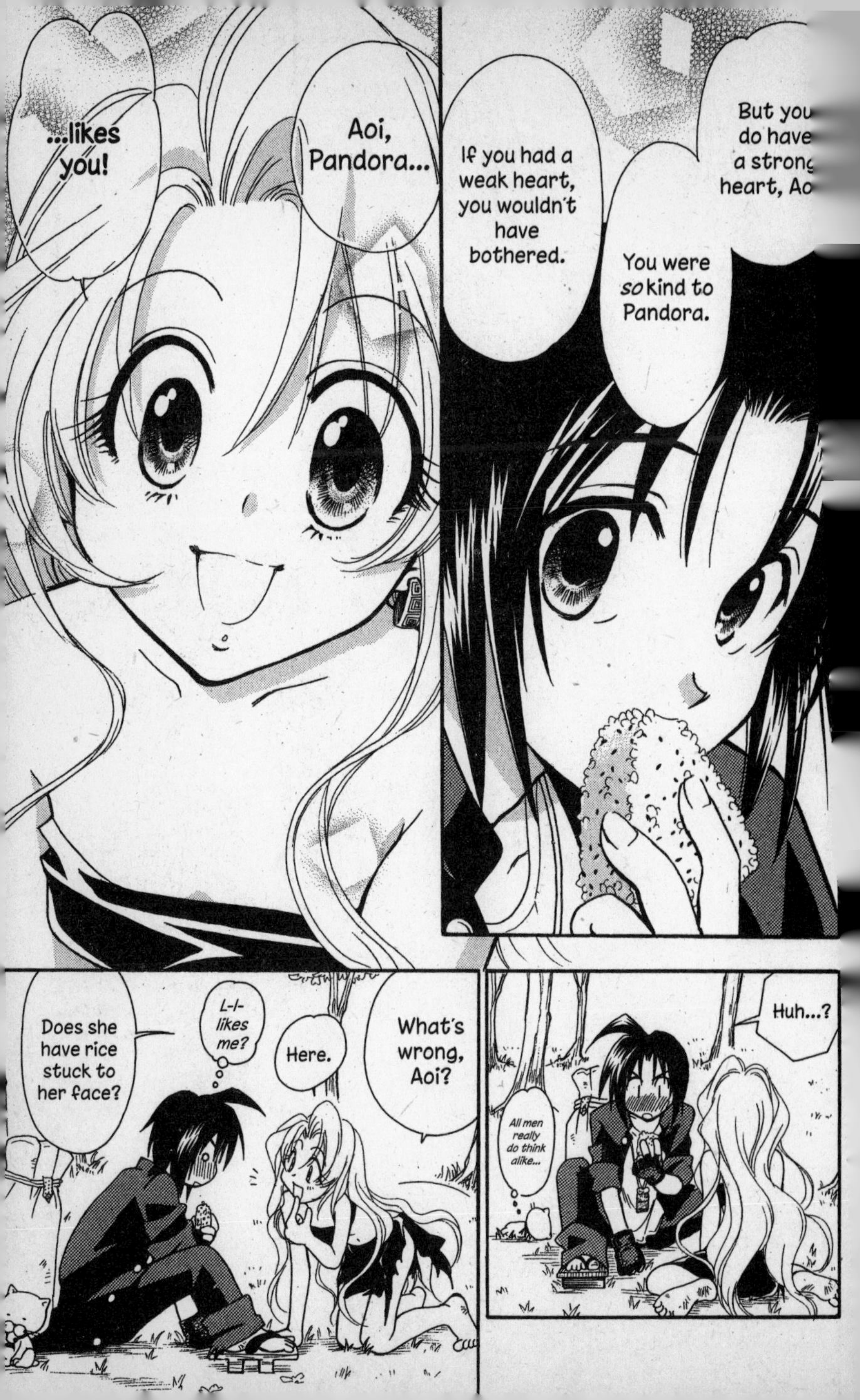

But you do have a strong heart, Ao
You were *so* kind to Pandora.
If you had a weak heart, you wouldn't have bothered.
Aoi, Pandora...
...likes you!
Huh...?
All men really do think alike...
What's wrong, Aoi?
Here.
L-l-likes me?
Does she have rice stuck to her face?

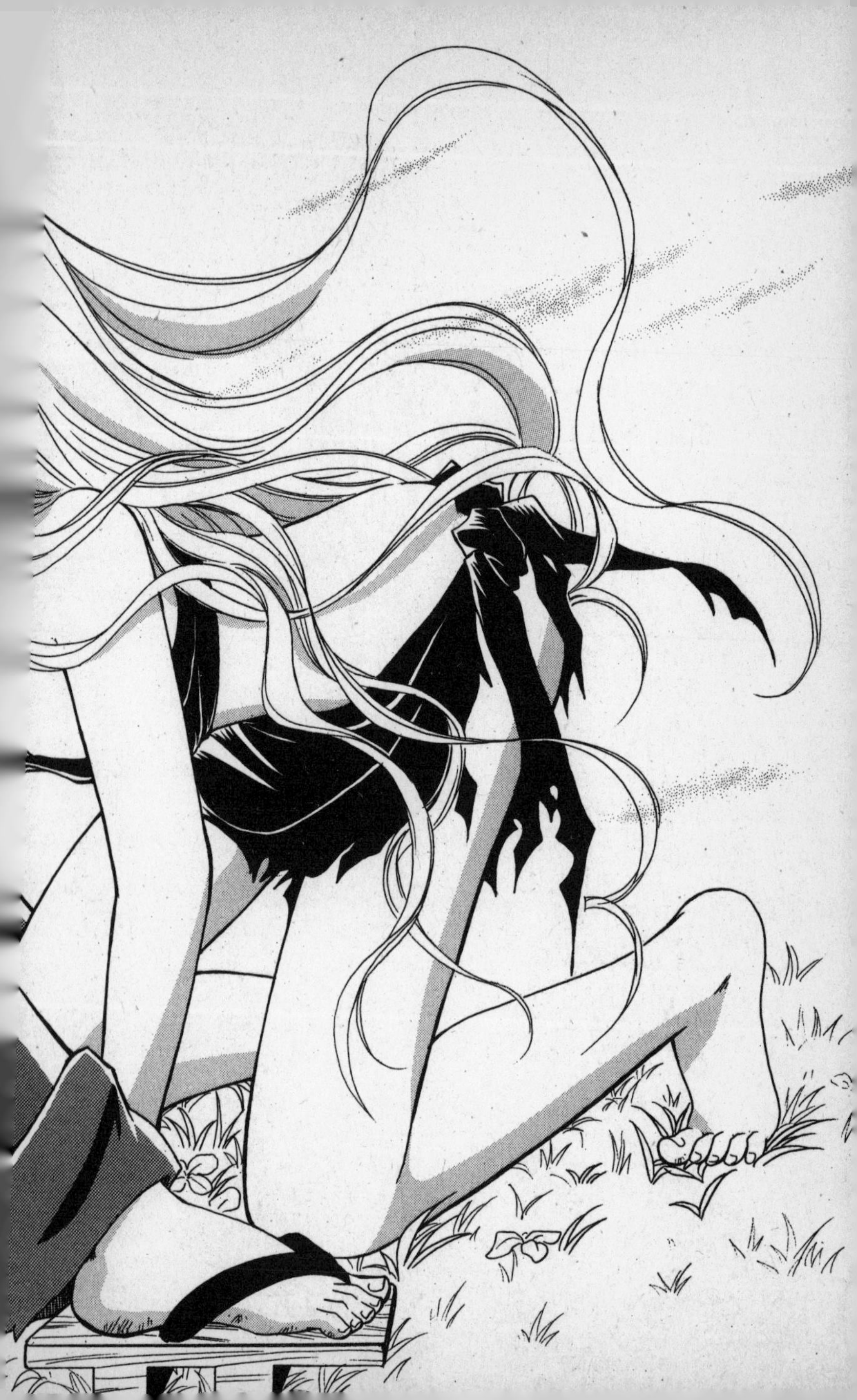

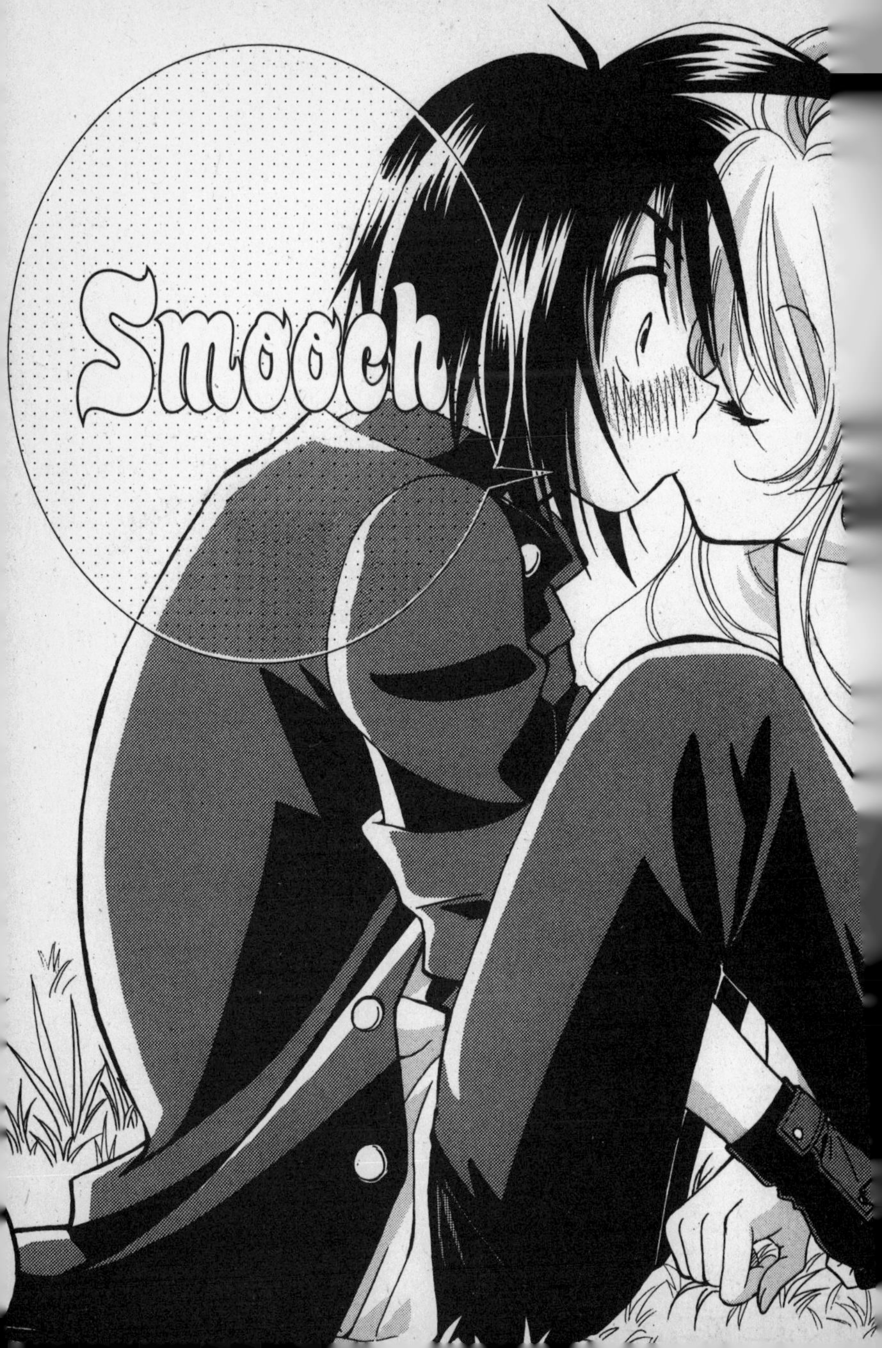
Smooch

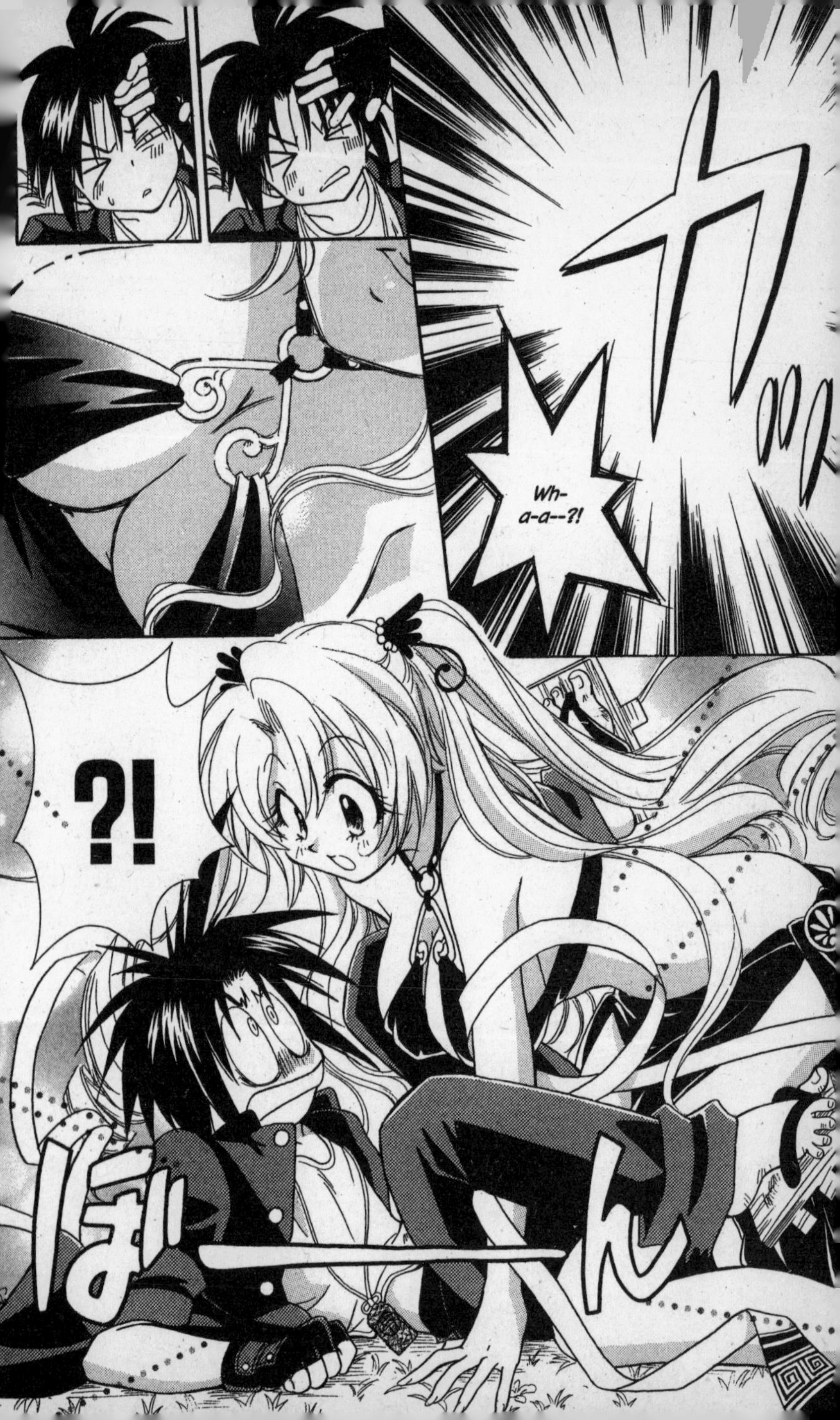
Wh-a-a--?!
?!

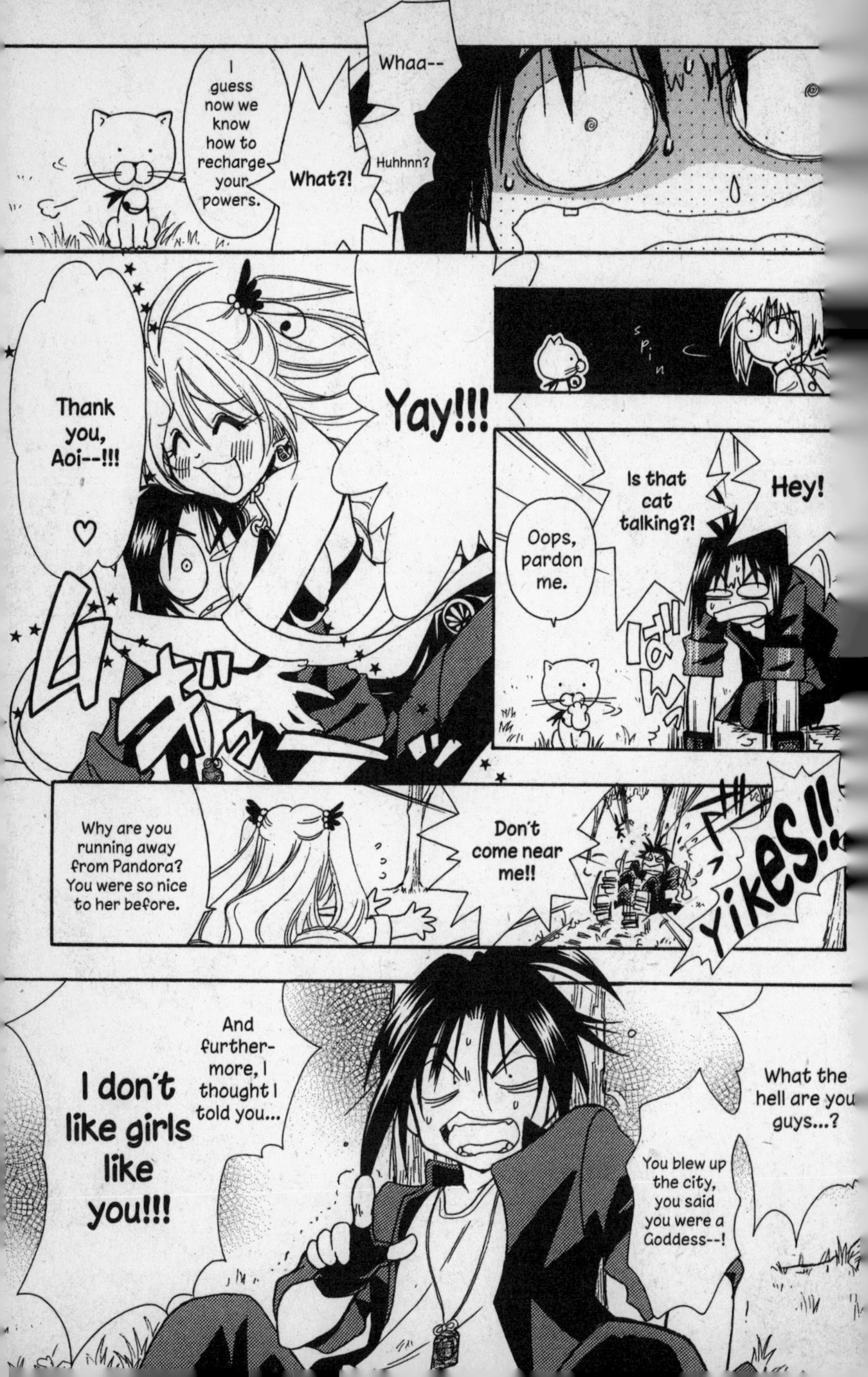
Whaa--
Huhhnn?
What?!
I guess now we know how to recharge your powers.
spin
Hey!
Is that cat talking?!
Oops, pardon me.
Yay!!!
Thank you, Aoi--!!!
YIKES!!
Don't come near me!!
Why are you running away from Pandora? You were so nice to her before.
What the hell are you guys...?
You blew up the city, you said you were a Goddess--!
And furthermore, I thought I told you...
I don't like girls like you!!!

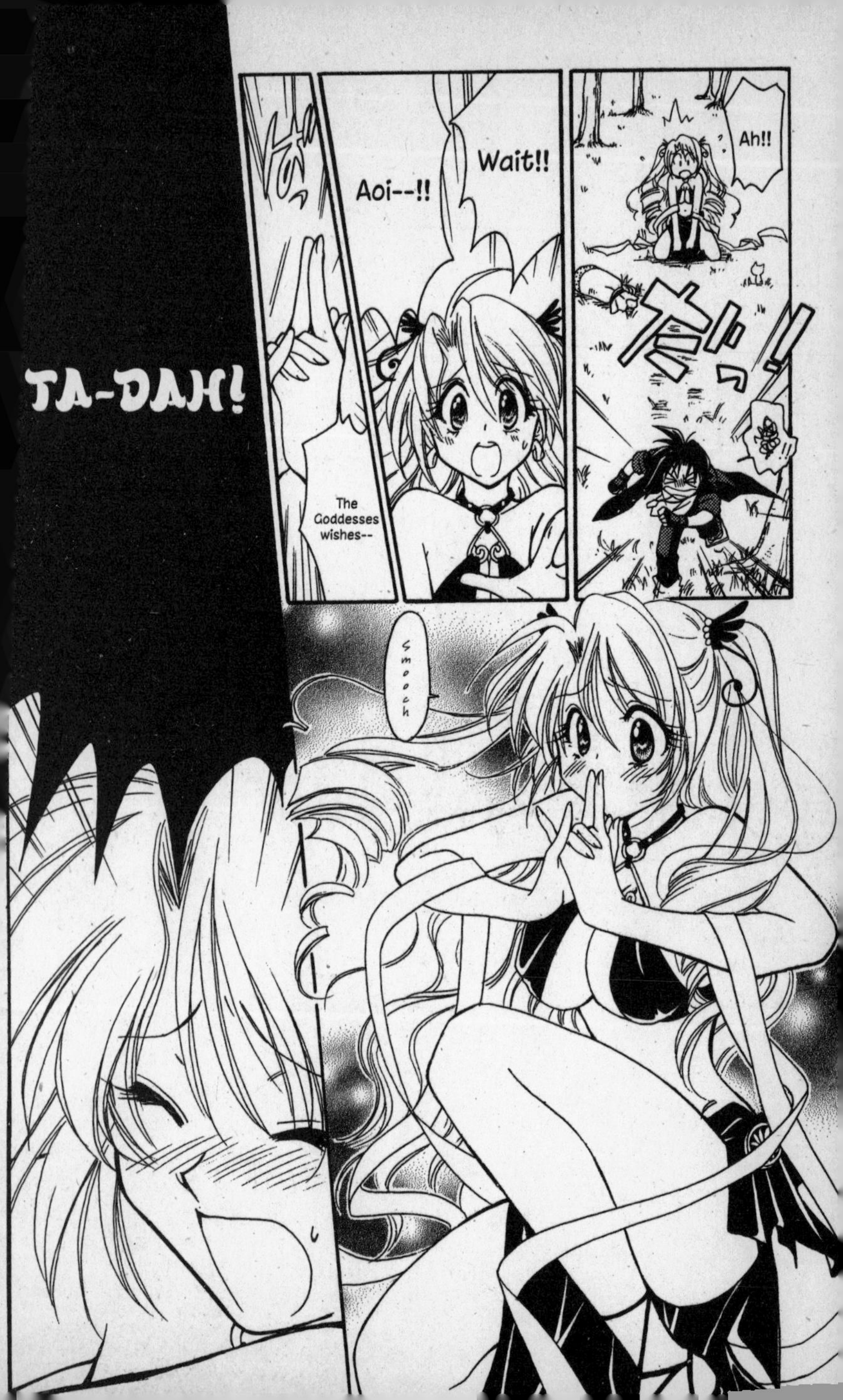
Ah!!
Wait!!
Aoi--!!
The Goddesses wishes--
Smooch
TA-DAH!

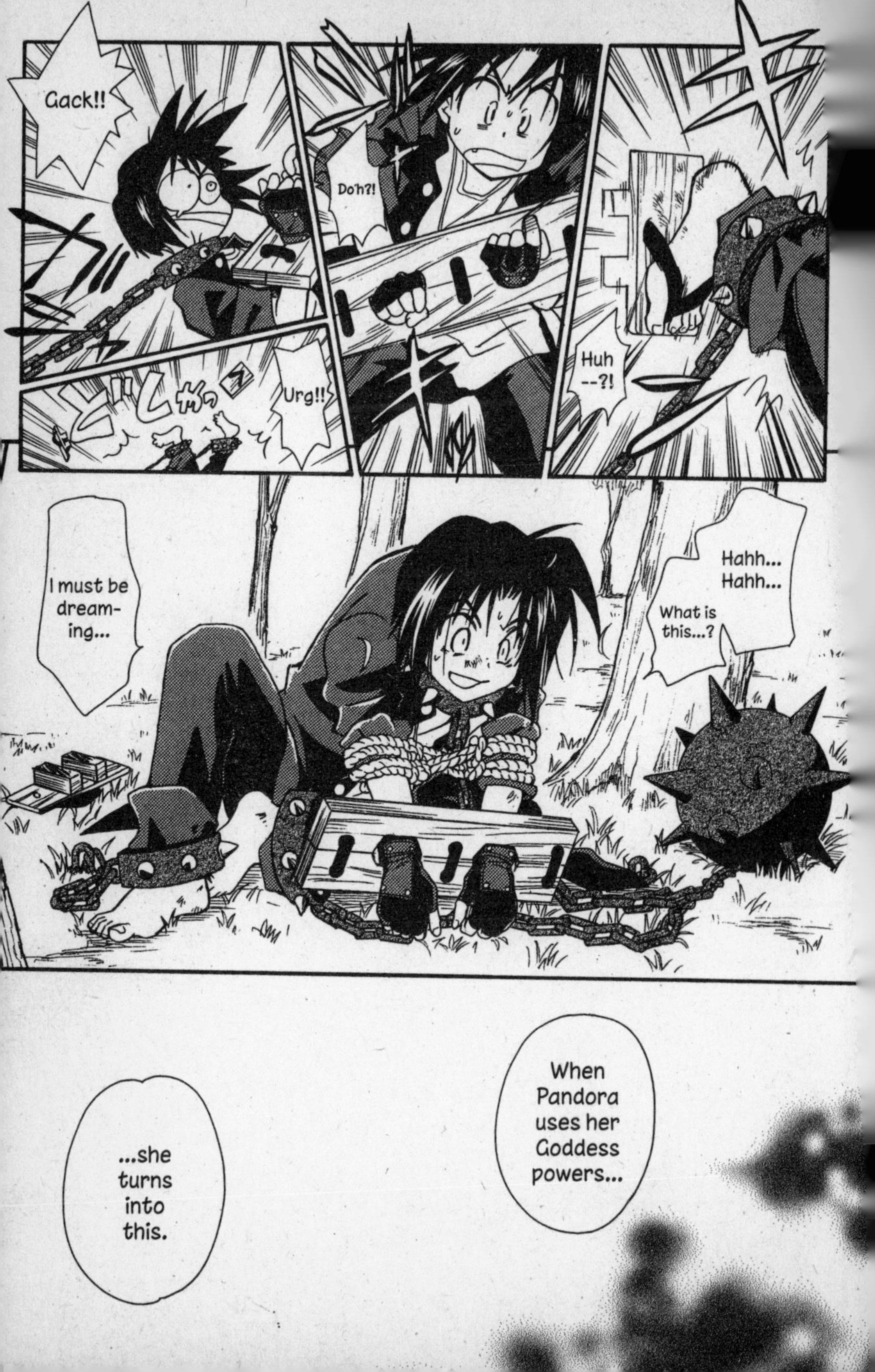
Huh --?!
Do'h?!
Gack!!
Urg!!
Hahh... Hahh...
What is this...?
I must be dreaming...
When Pandora uses her Goddess powers...
...she turns into this.

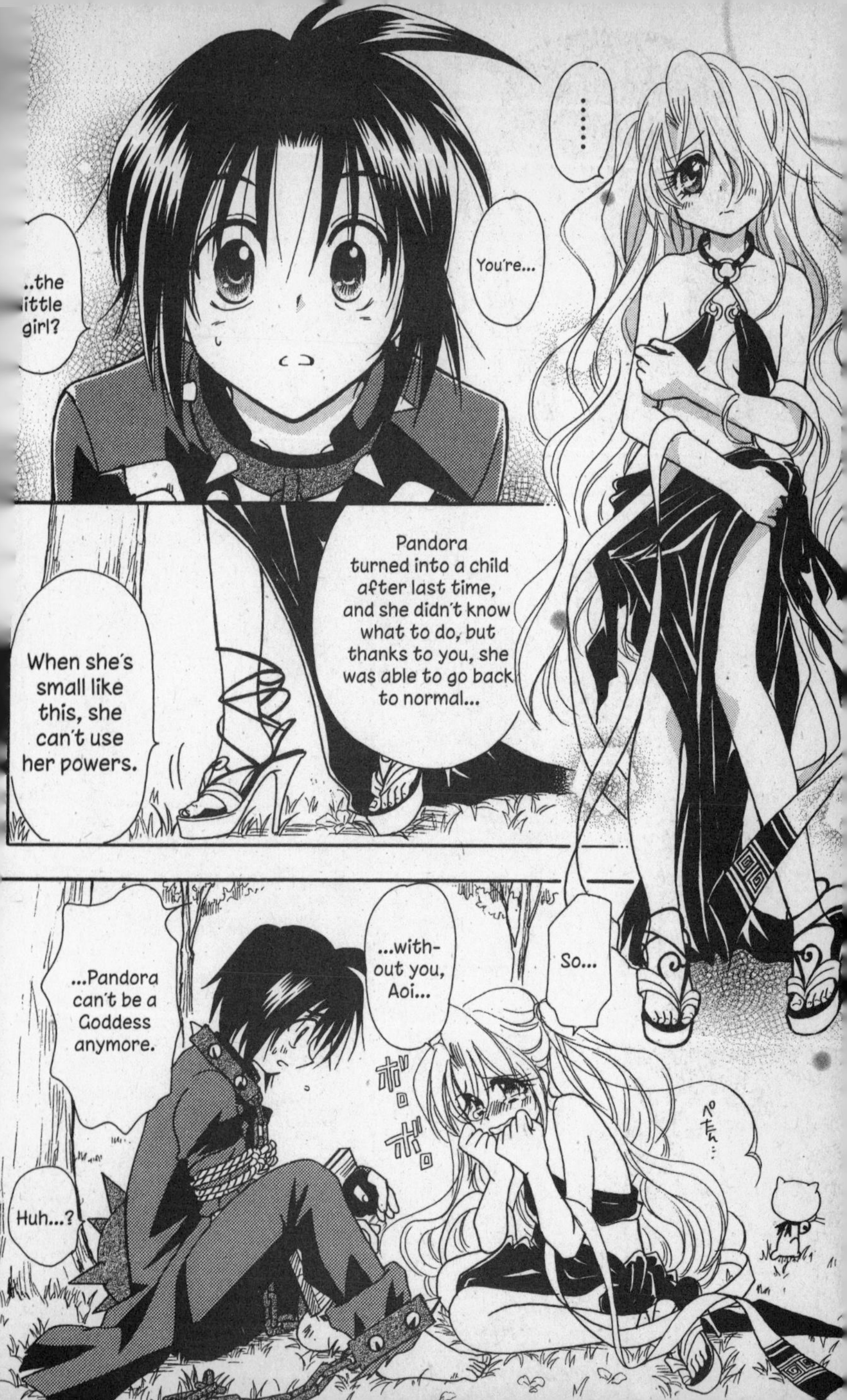
……
You're...
..the ittle girl?
Pandora turned into a child after last time, and she didn't know what to do, but thanks to you, she was able to go back to normal...
When she's small like this, she can't use her powers.
So...
...with-out you, Aoi...
...Pandora can't be a Goddess anymore.
ぺたん…
ボロボロ
Huh...?

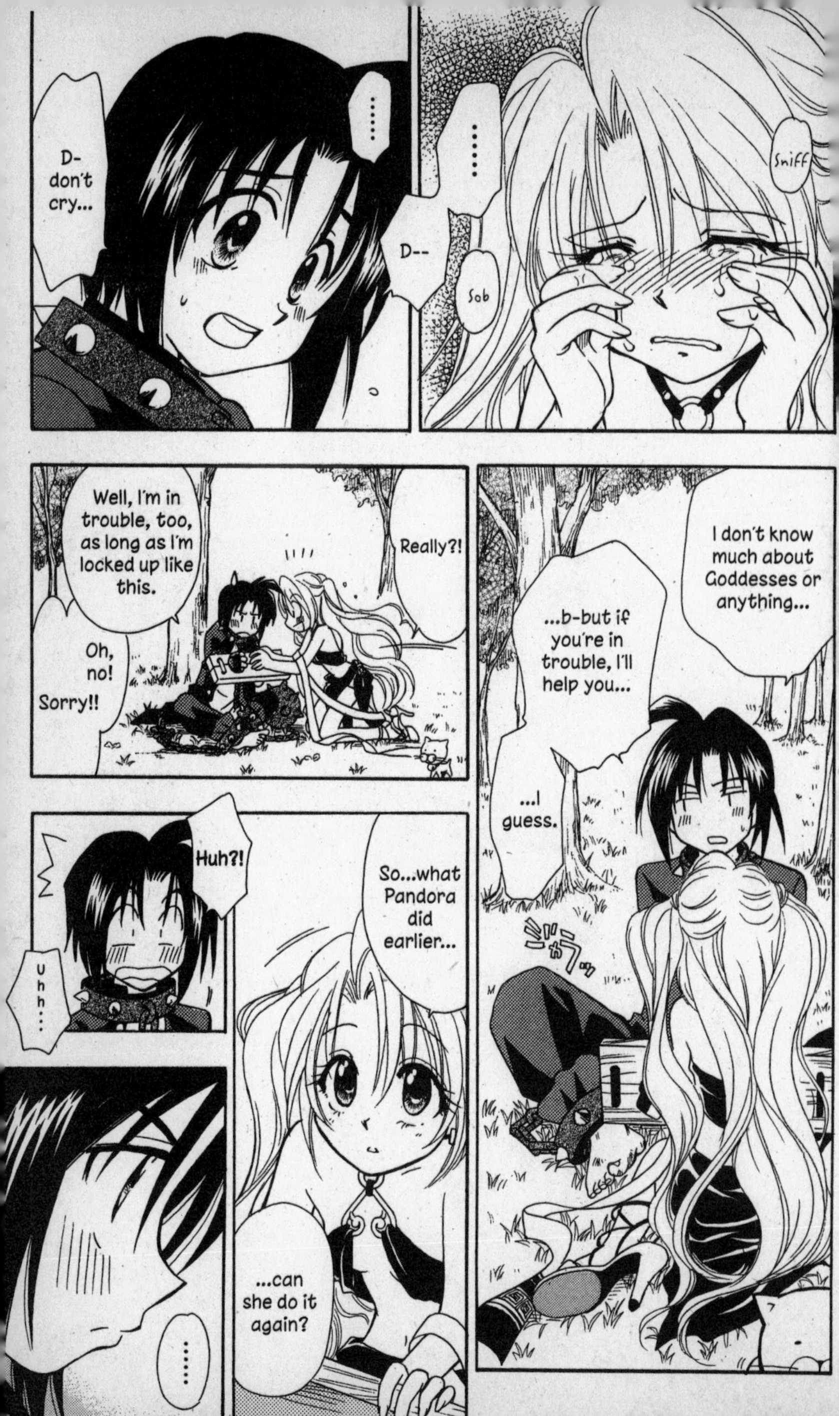
......
Sniff
D--
Sob
......
D- don't cry...
I don't know much about Goddesses or anything...
...b-but if you're in trouble, I'll help you...
...I guess.
ジャラッ
Really?!
Well, I'm in trouble, too, as long as I'm locked up like this.
Oh, no! Sorry!!
So...what Pandora did earlier...
...can she do it again?
Huh?!
Uhh...
......

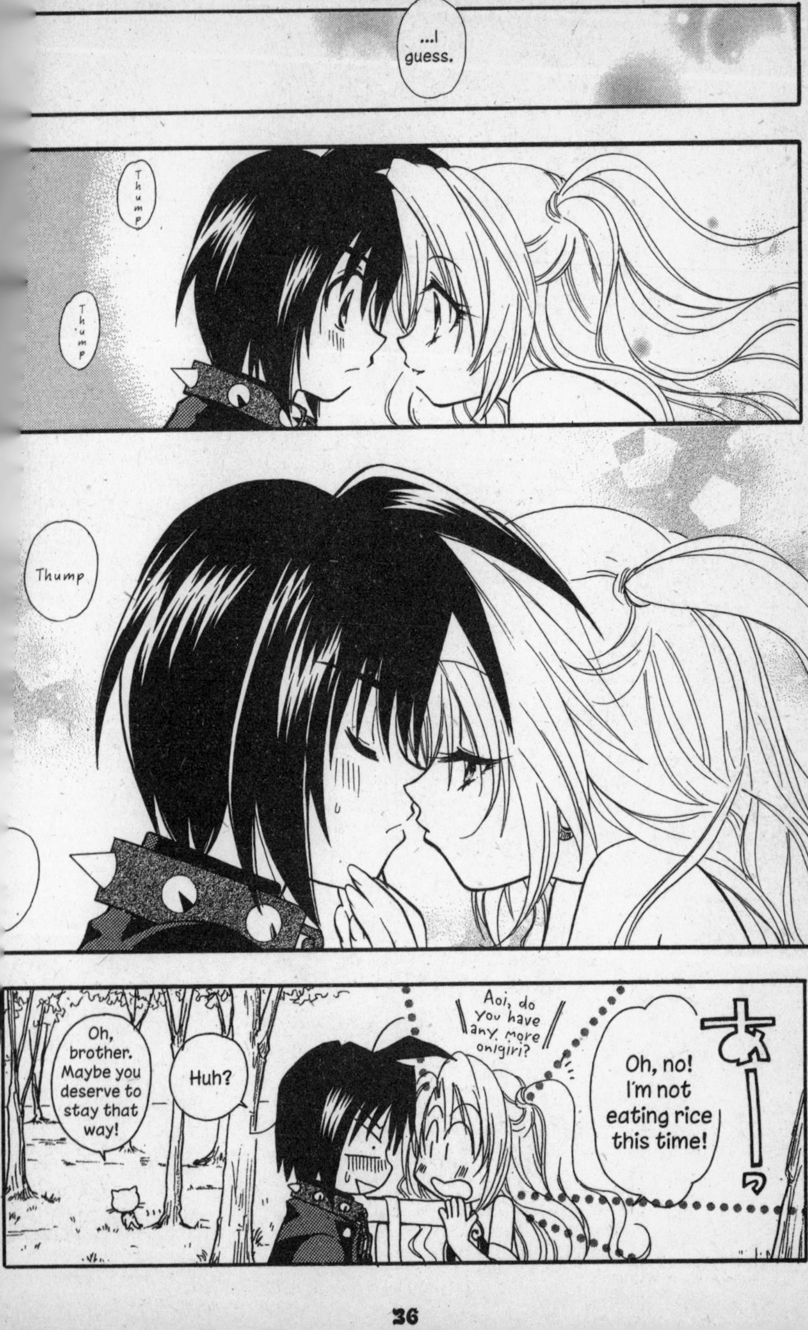

...I guess.
Thump
Thump
Thump
Oh, no! I'm not eating rice this time!
Aoi, do you have any more onigiri?
Huh?
Oh, brother. Maybe you deserve to stay that way!

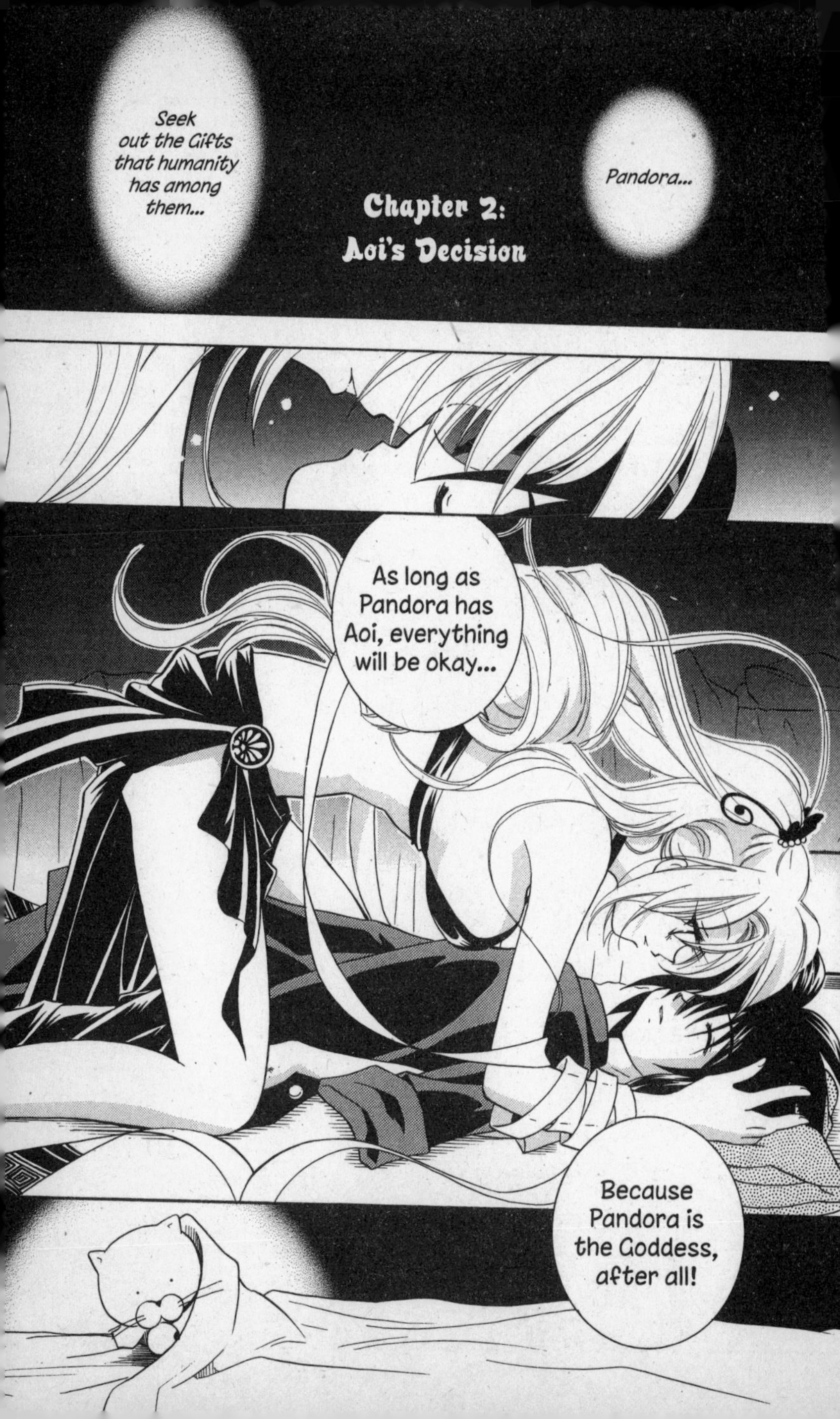
Pandora...
Chapter 2: Aoi's Decision
Seek out the Gifts that humanity has among them...
As long as Pandora has Aoi, everything will be okay...
Because Pandora is the Goddess, after all!

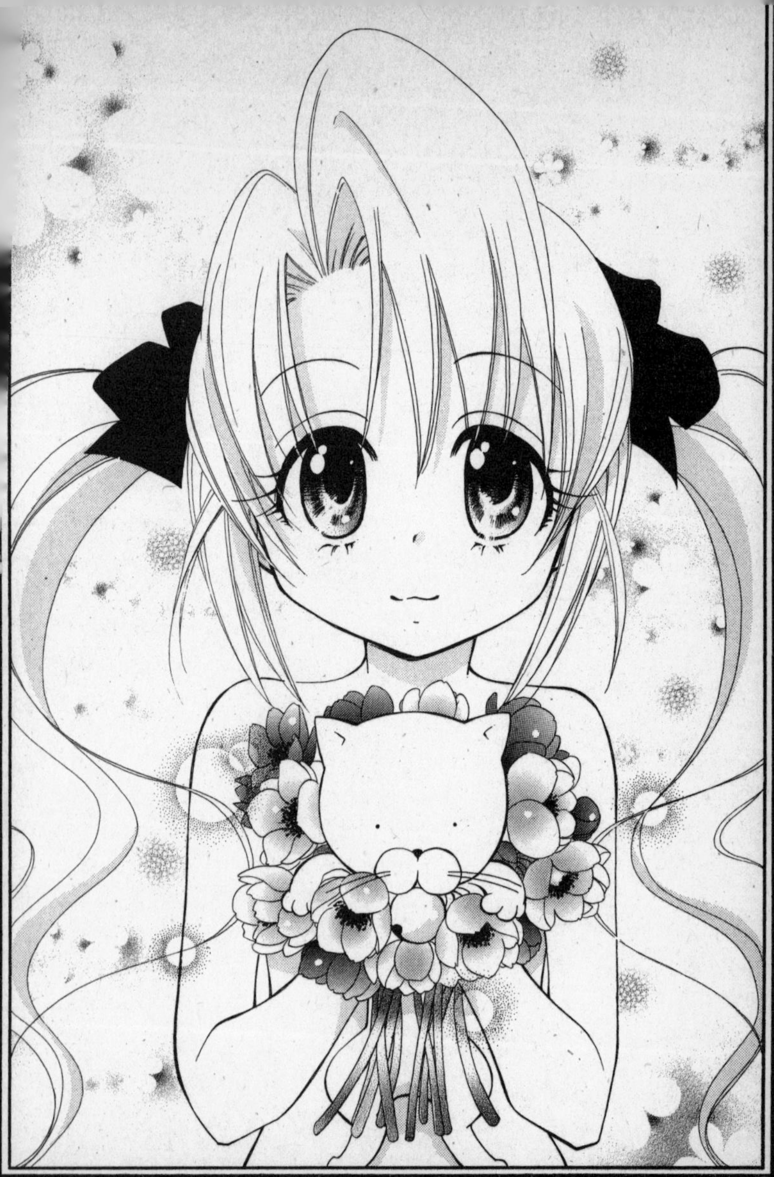

Chapter 2: Aoi's Decision

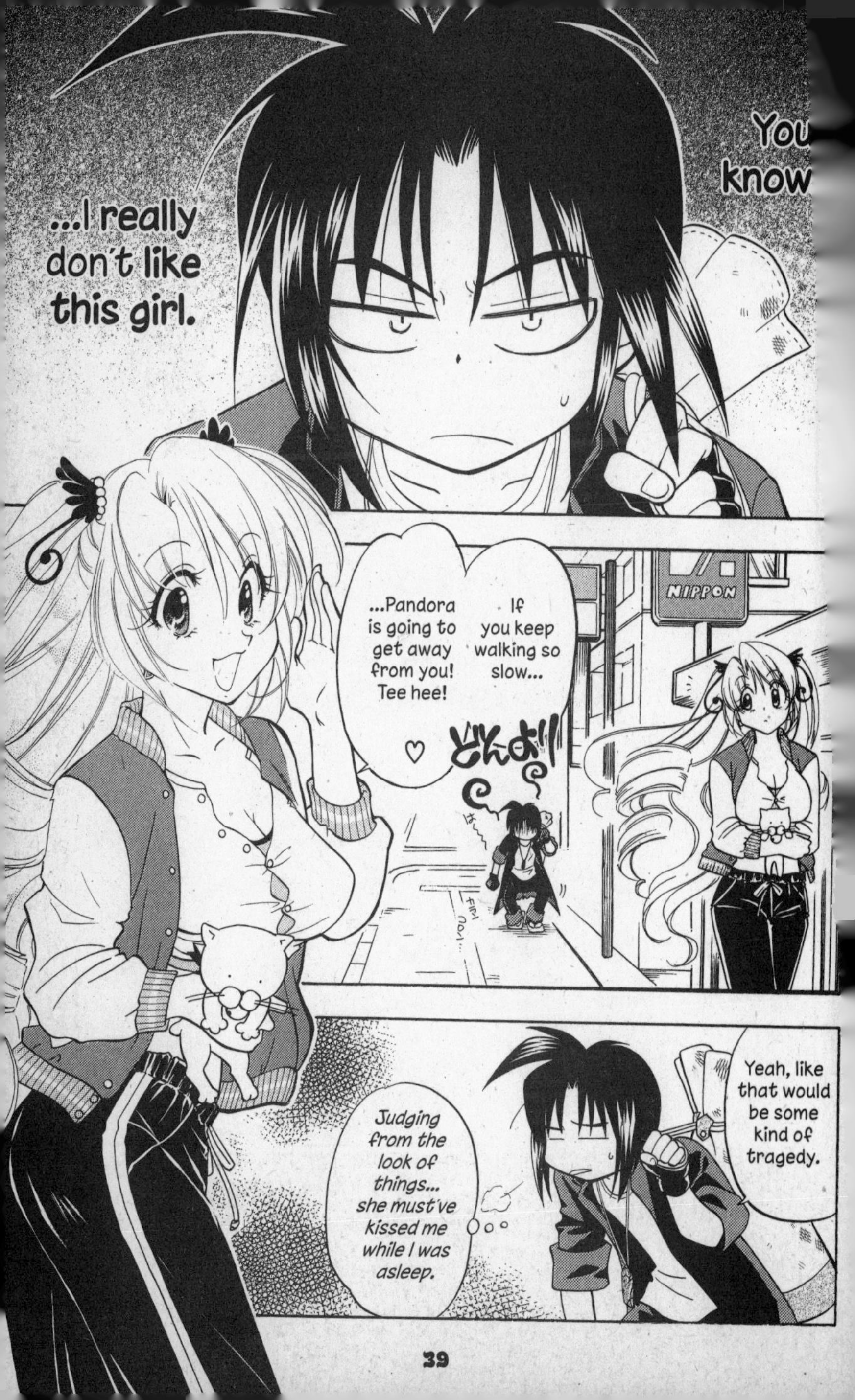
You know
...I really don't like this girl.
If you keep walking so slow...
...Pandora is going to get away from you! Tee hee!
どんより!!
Yeah, like that would be some kind of tragedy.
Judging from the look of things... she must've kissed me while I was asleep.

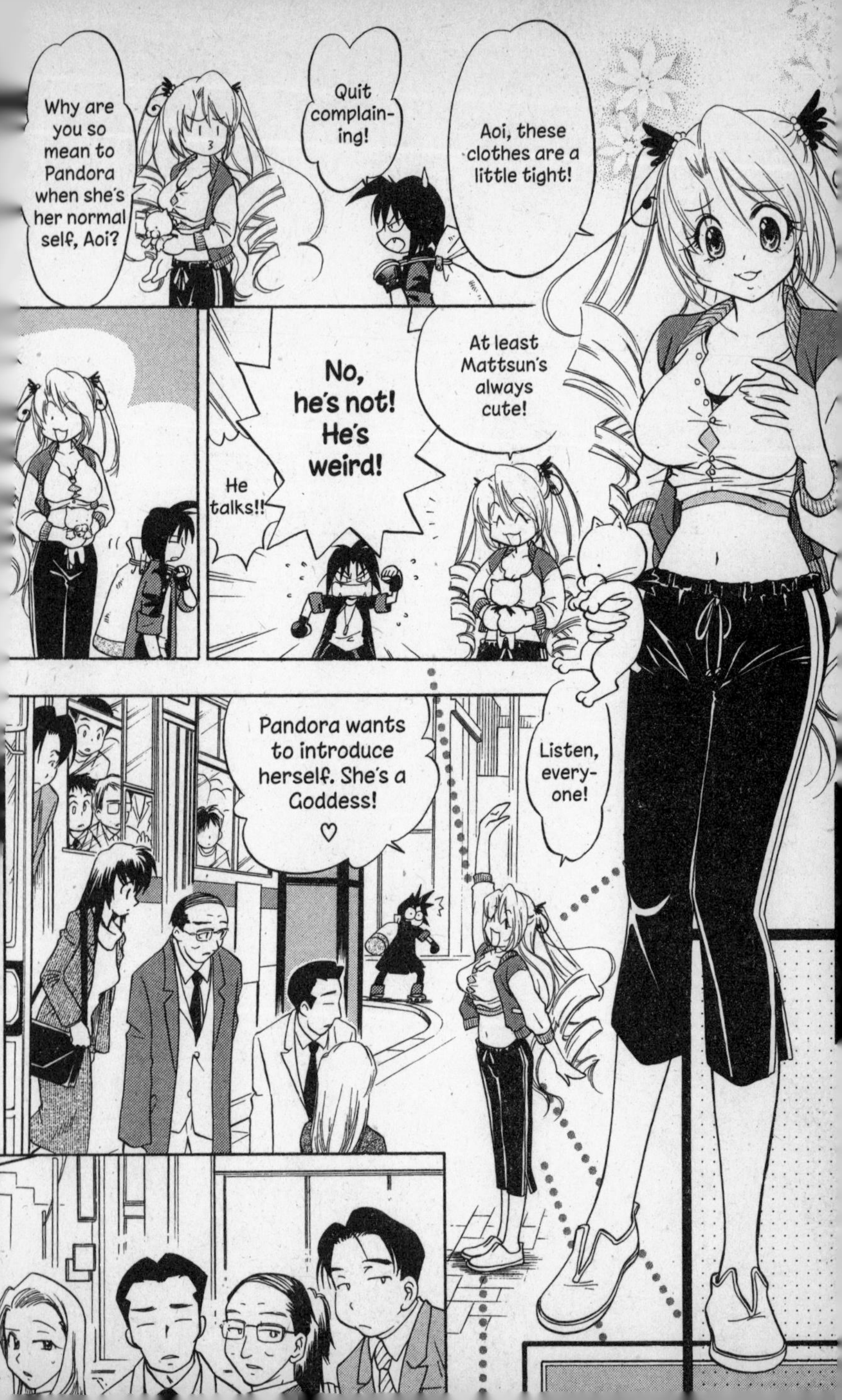

Aoi, these clothes are a little tight!
Quit complain-ing!
Why are you so mean to Pandora when she's her normal self, Aoi?
At least Mattsun's always cute!
No, he's not! He's weird!
He talks!!
Listen, every-one!
Pandora wants to introduce herself. She's a Goddess! ♡

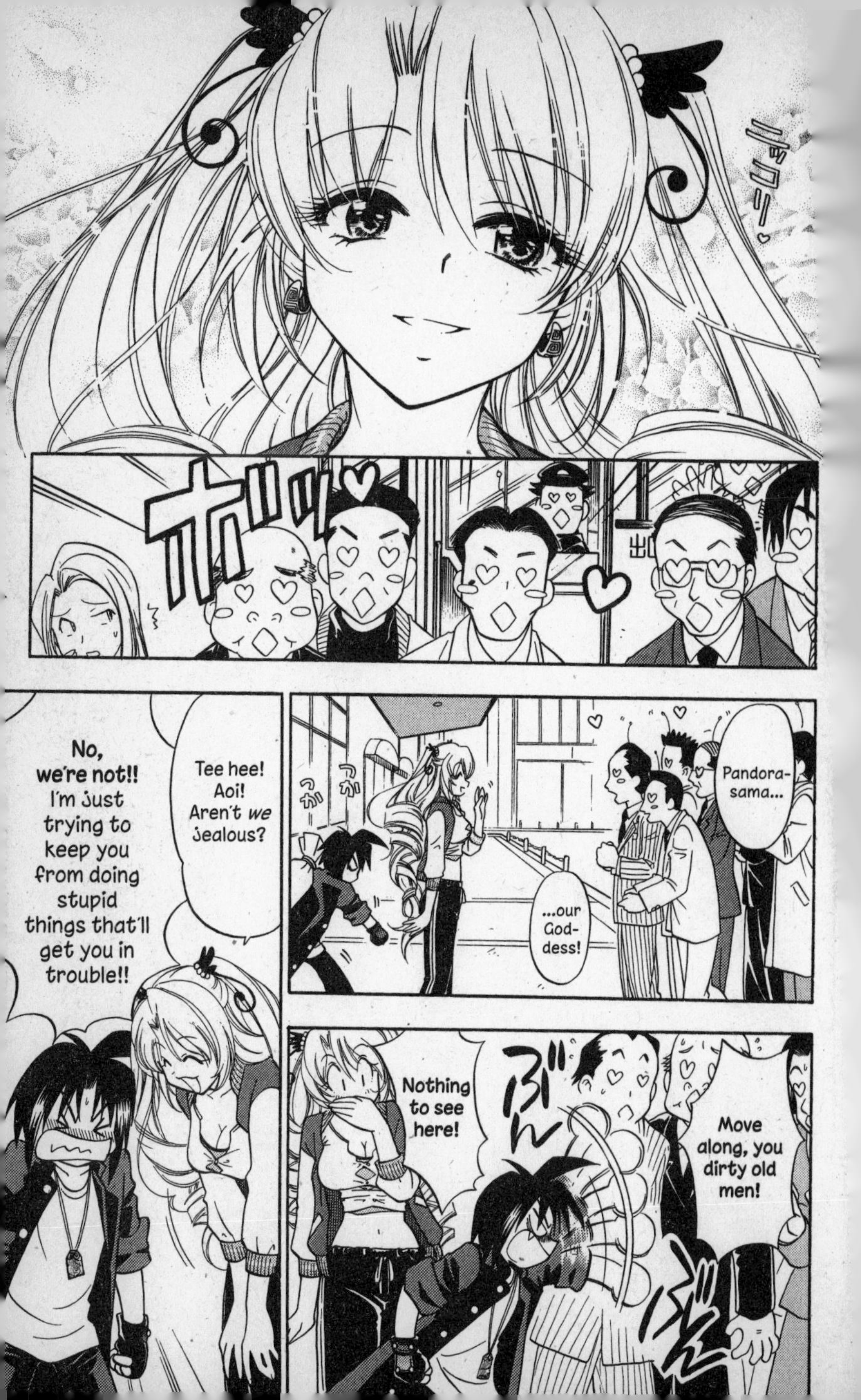

ニッコリ
ボッ
Pandora-sama...
...our God-dess!
つか つか
Move along, you dirty old men!
Nothing to see here!
ぶん
Tee hee! Aoi! Aren't *we* jealous?
No, we're not!! I'm just trying to keep you from doing stupid things that'll get you in trouble!!

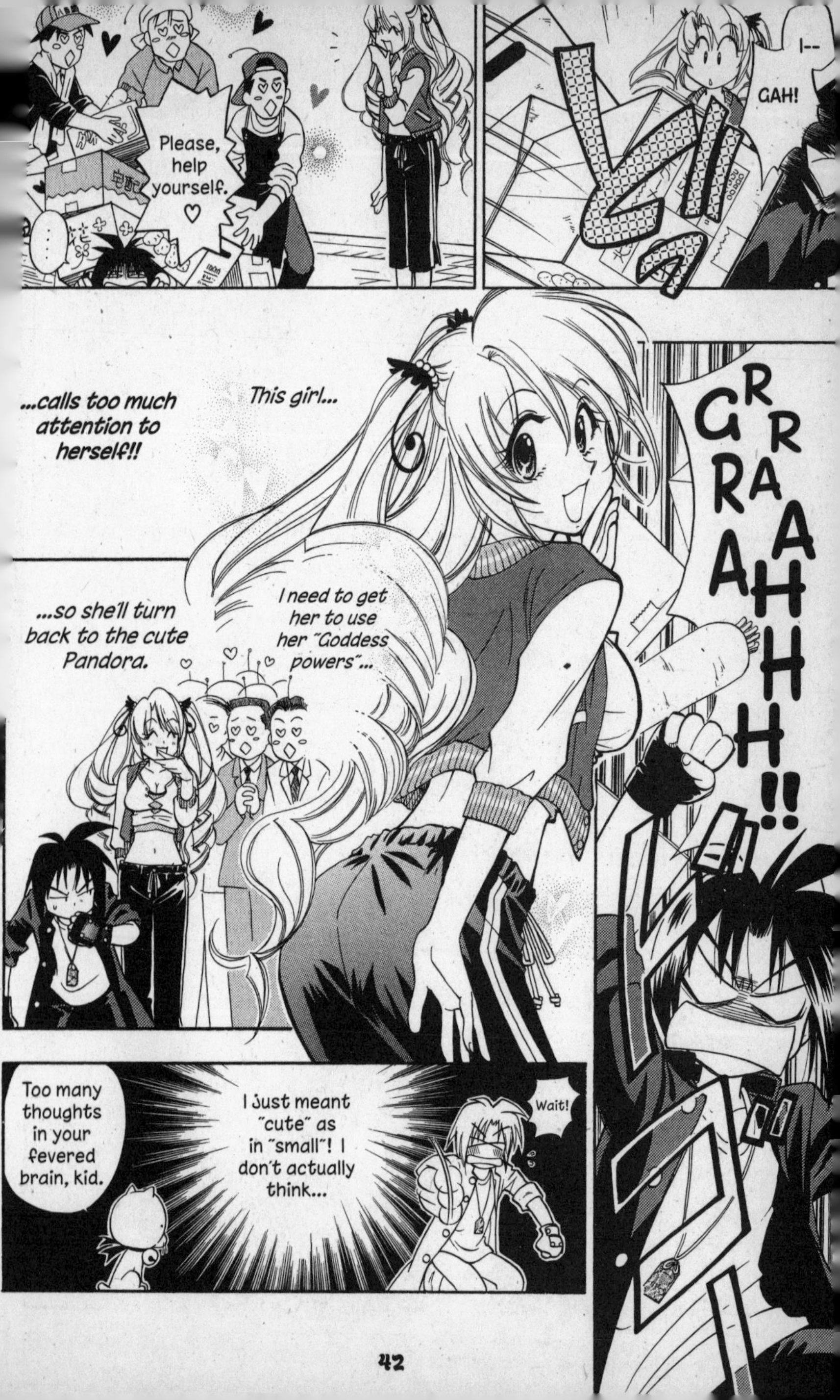
I--
GAH!
Please, help yourself. ♡
...
GRRRAAAHHHH!!
This girl...
...calls too much attention to herself!!
I need to get her to use her "Goddess powers"...
...so she'll turn back to the cute Pandora.
Wait!
I just meant "cute" as in "small"! I don't actually think...
Too many thoughts in your fevered brain, kid.

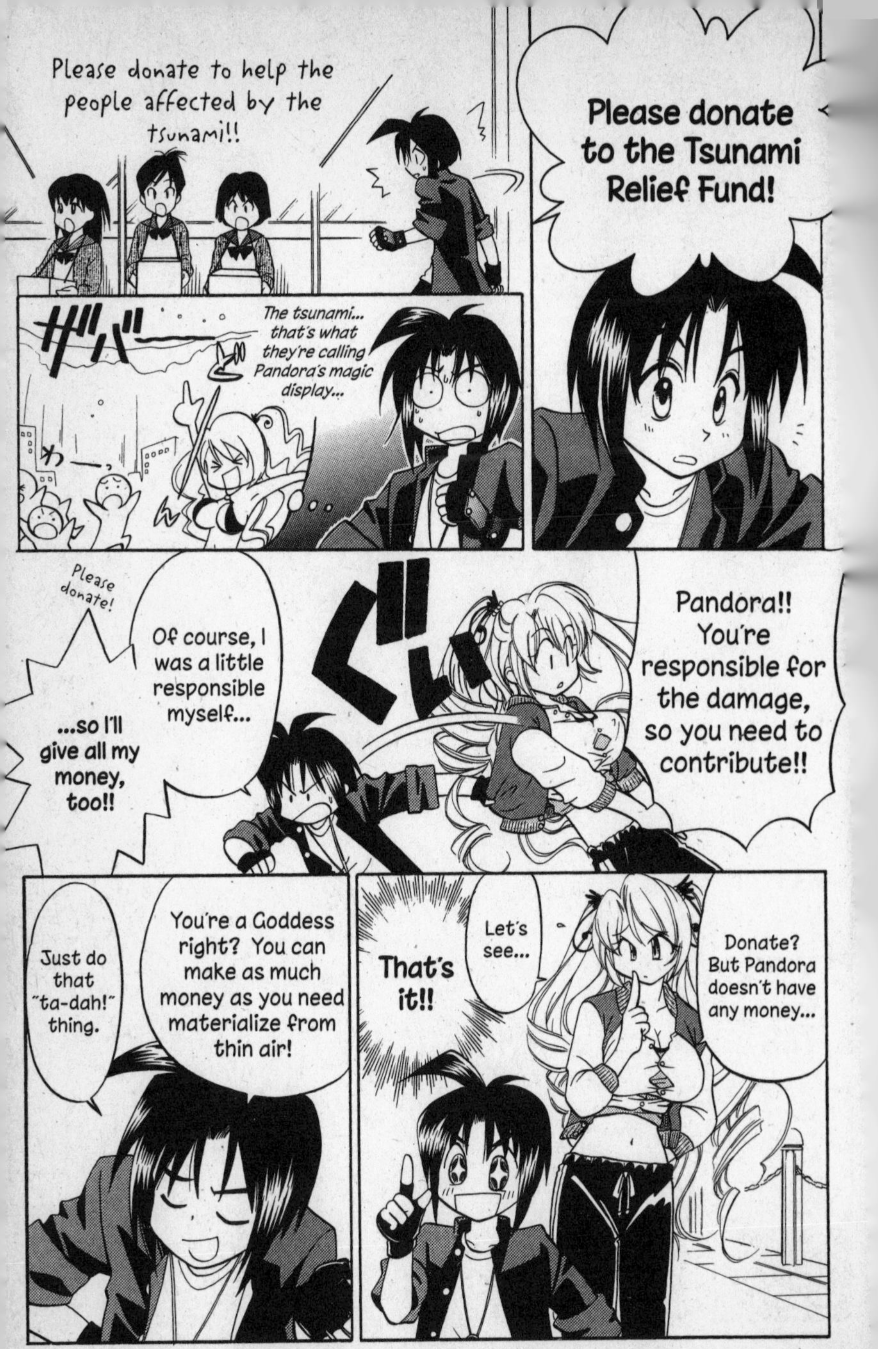

Please donate to the Tsunami Relief Fund!
Please donate to help the people affected by the tsunami!!
ザバー
The tsunami... that's what they're calling Pandora's magic display...
わー
Pandora!! You're responsible for the damage, so you need to contribute!!
ぐい
Of course, I was a little responsible myself...
...so I'll give all my money, too!!
Please donate!
Donate? But Pandora doesn't have any money...
Let's see...
That's it!!
You're a Goddess right? You can make as much money as you need materialize from thin air!
Just do that "ta-dah!" thing.

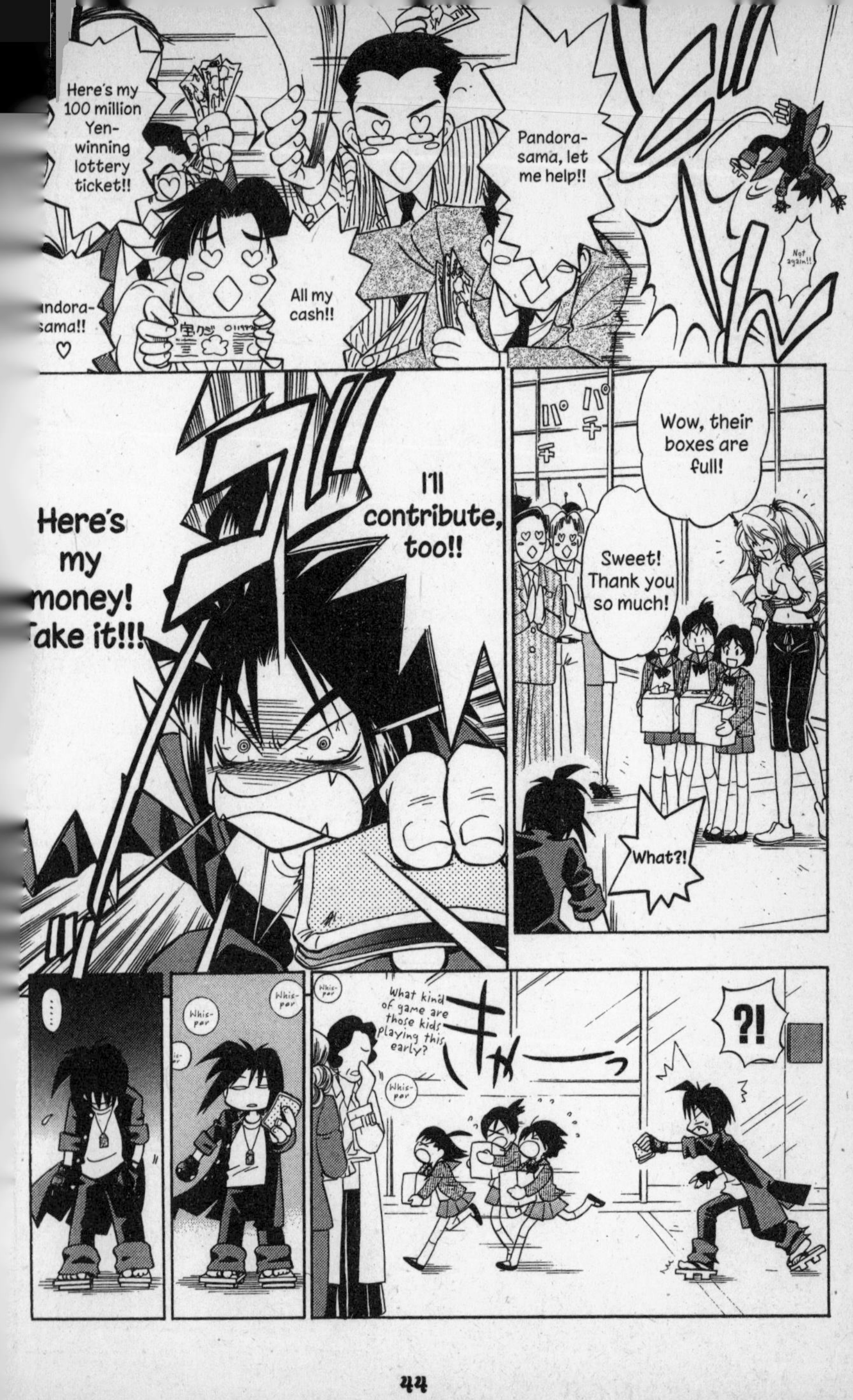
Not again!!
Pandora-sama, let me help!!
All my cash!!
Here's my 100 million Yen-winning lottery ticket!!
andora-sama!! ♡
パチ パチ
Wow, their boxes are full!
Sweet! Thank you so much!
What?!
I'll contribute, too!!
Here's my money! Take it!!!
?!
キャーっ
What kind of game are those kids playing this early?
Whis-per
Whis-per
Whis-per
Whis-per
......

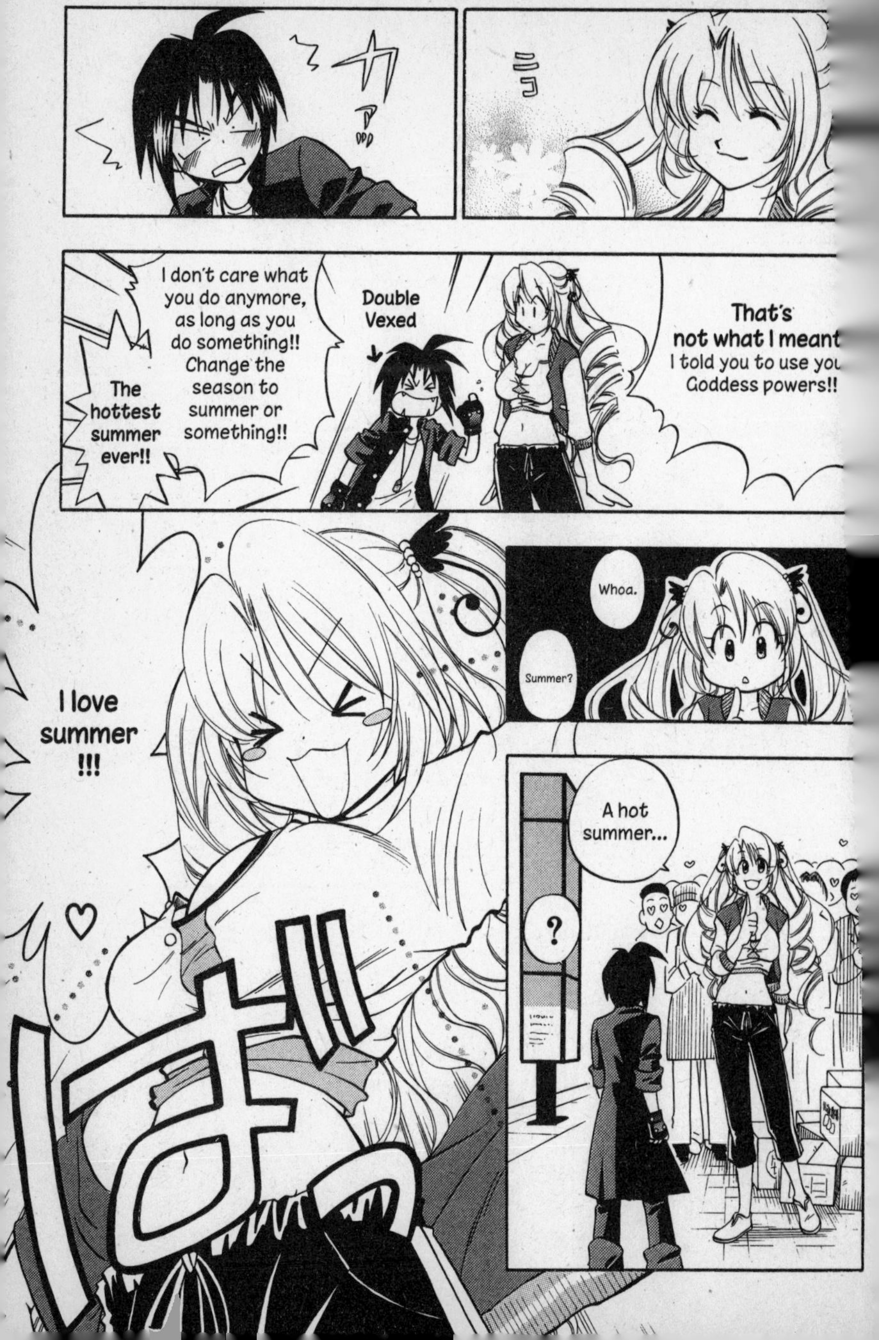
ニコ
That's not what I meant
I told you to use you
Goddess powers!!
Double Vexed
I don't care what you do anymore, as long as you do something!! Change the season to summer or something!!
The hottest summer ever!!
Whoa.
Summer?
A hot summer...
?
I love summer !!!

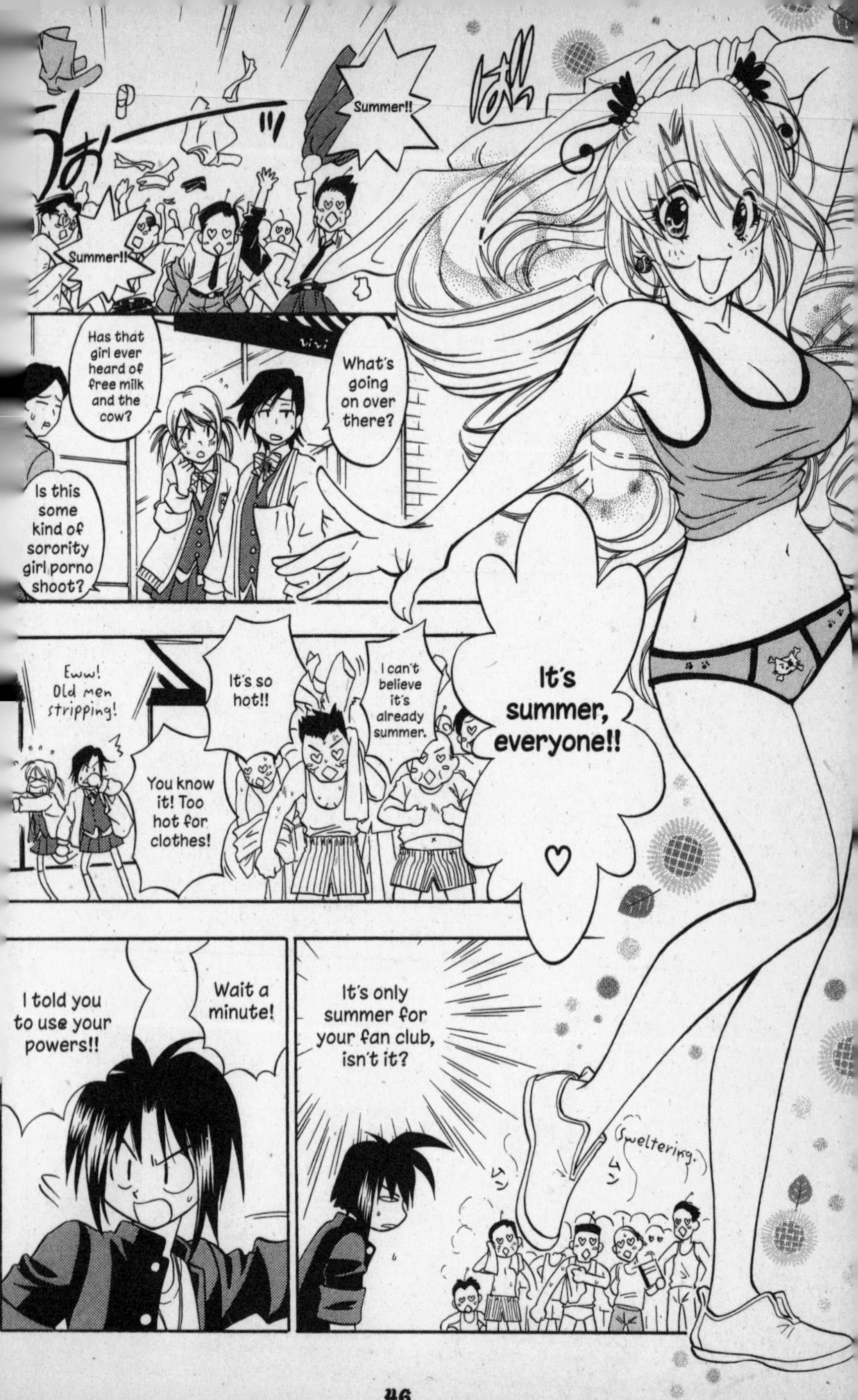
It's summer, everyone!!
(Sweltering.)
Summer!!
Summer!!
What's going on over there?
Has that girl ever heard of free milk and the cow?
Is this some kind of sorority girl porno shoot?
I can't believe it's already summer.
It's so hot!!
Eww! Old men stripping!
You know it! Too hot for clothes!
It's only summer for your fan club, isn't it?
Wait a minute!
I told you to use your powers!!

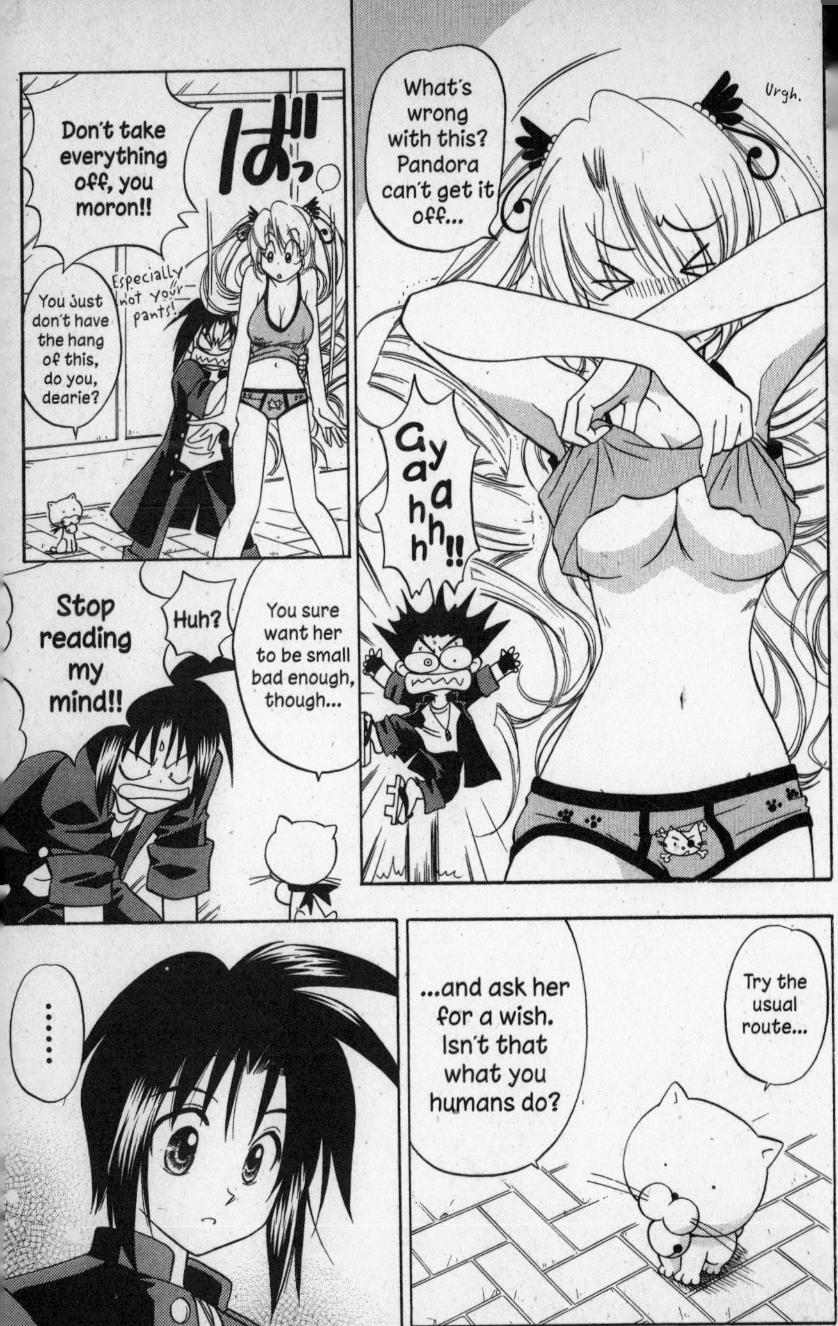

Urgh.
What's wrong with this? Pandora can't get it off...
Gyaahhh!!
ぱっ
Don't take everything off, you moron!!
Especially not your pants!
You just don't have the hang of this, do you, dearie?
You sure want her to be small bad enough, though...
Huh?
Stop reading my mind!!
Try the usual route...
...and ask her for a wish. Isn't that what you humans do?
......

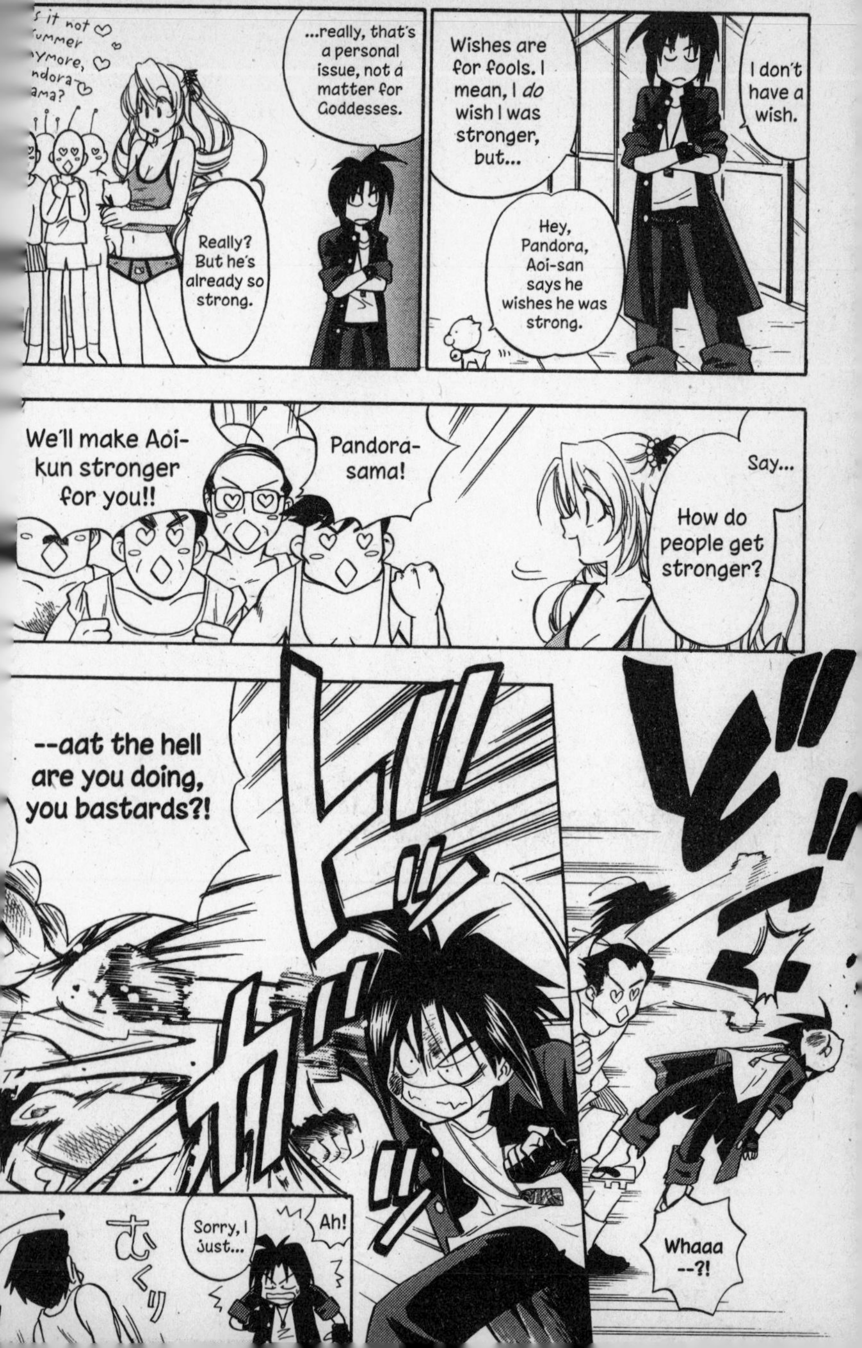
I don't have a wish.
Wishes are for fools. I mean, I *do* wish I was stronger, but...
Hey, Pandora, Aoi-san says he wishes he was strong.
...really, that's a personal issue, not a matter for Goddesses.
s it not ummer ymore, ndora- ama?
Really? But he's already so strong.
Say...
How do people get stronger?
Pandora-sama!
We'll make Aoi-kun stronger for you!!
--aat the hell are you doing, you bastards?!
Whaaa --?!
Ah!
Sorry, I just...

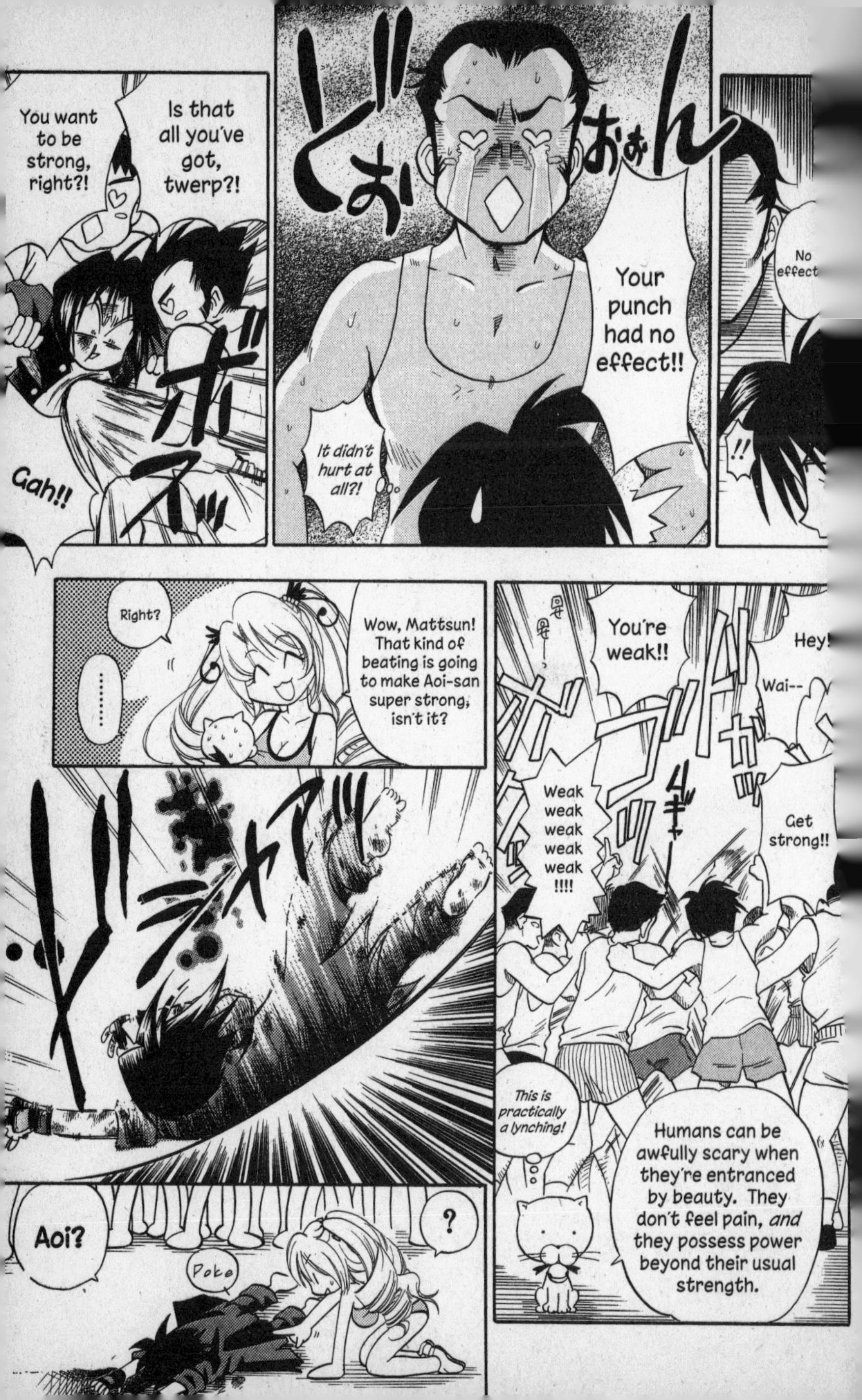
No effect
!!
Your punch had no effect!!
It didn't hurt at all?!
Is that all you've got, twerp?!
You want to be strong, right?!
Gah!!
Hey!
Wai--
You're weak!!
Weak weak weak weak weak !!!!
Get strong!!
This is practically a lynching!
Humans can be awfully scary when they're entranced by beauty. They don't feel pain, *and* they possess power beyond their usual strength.
Wow, Mattsun! That kind of beating is going to make Aoi-san super strong, isn't it?
Right?
......
?
Aoi?
Poke

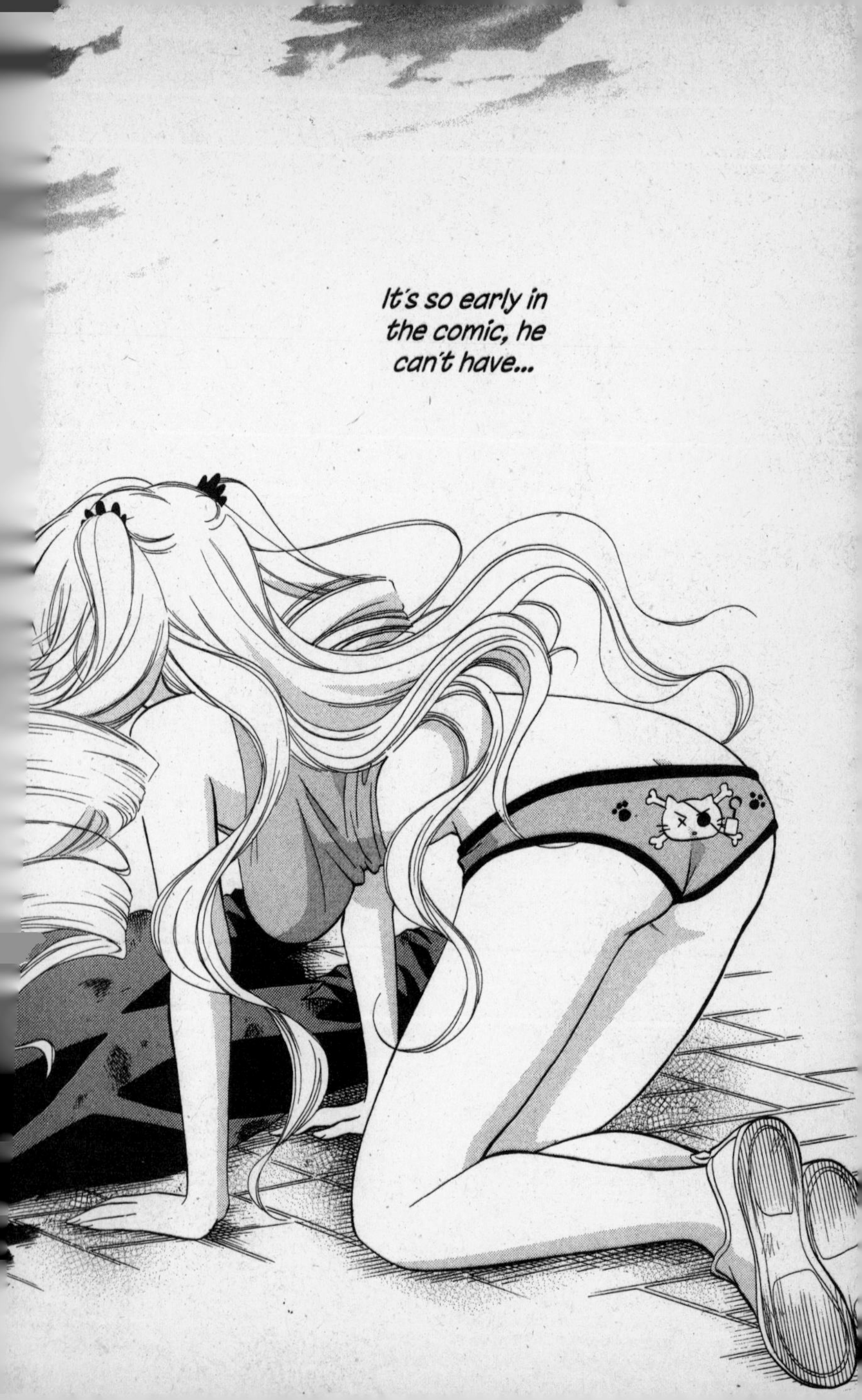
It's so early in the comic, he can't have...

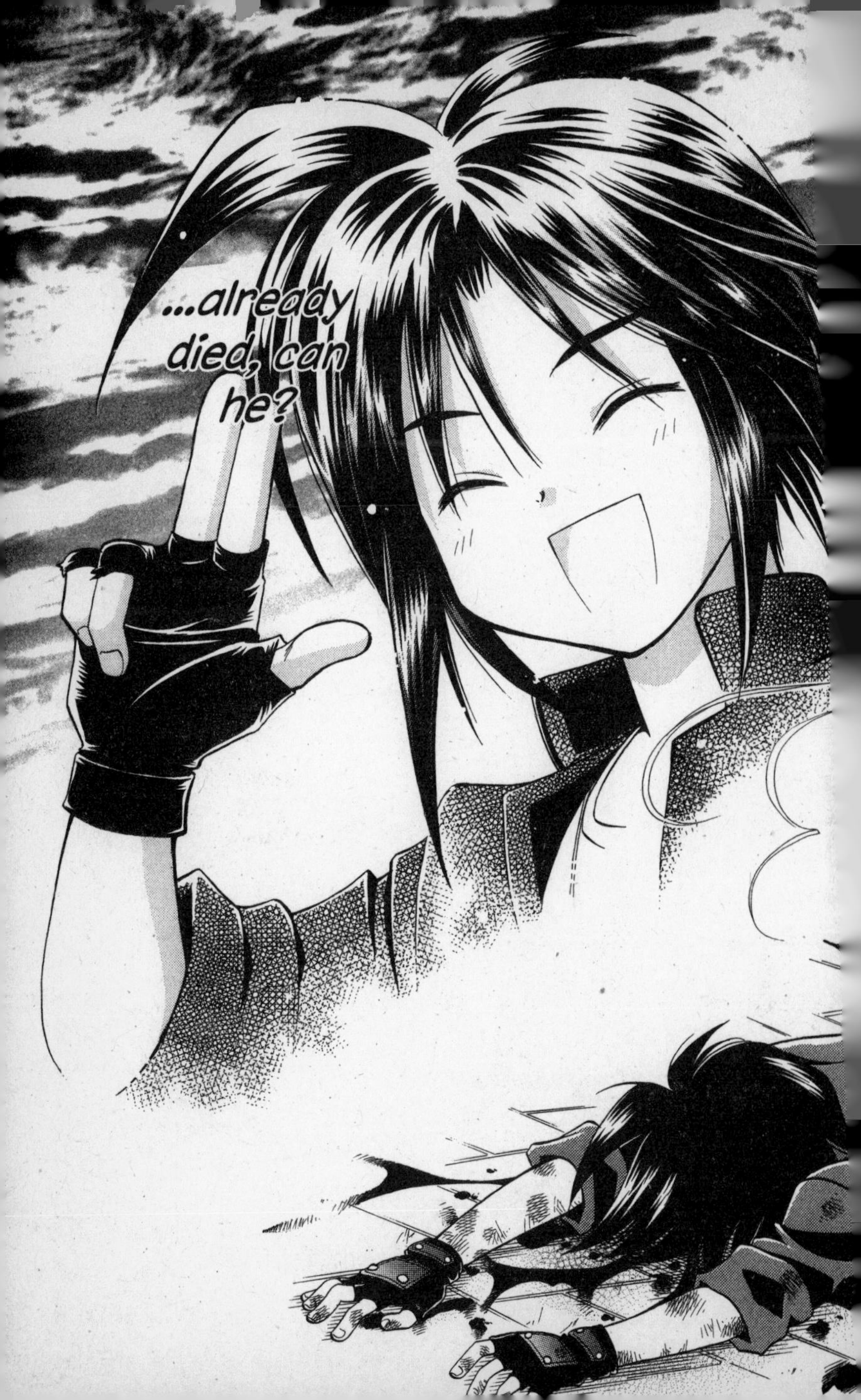
...already died, can he?

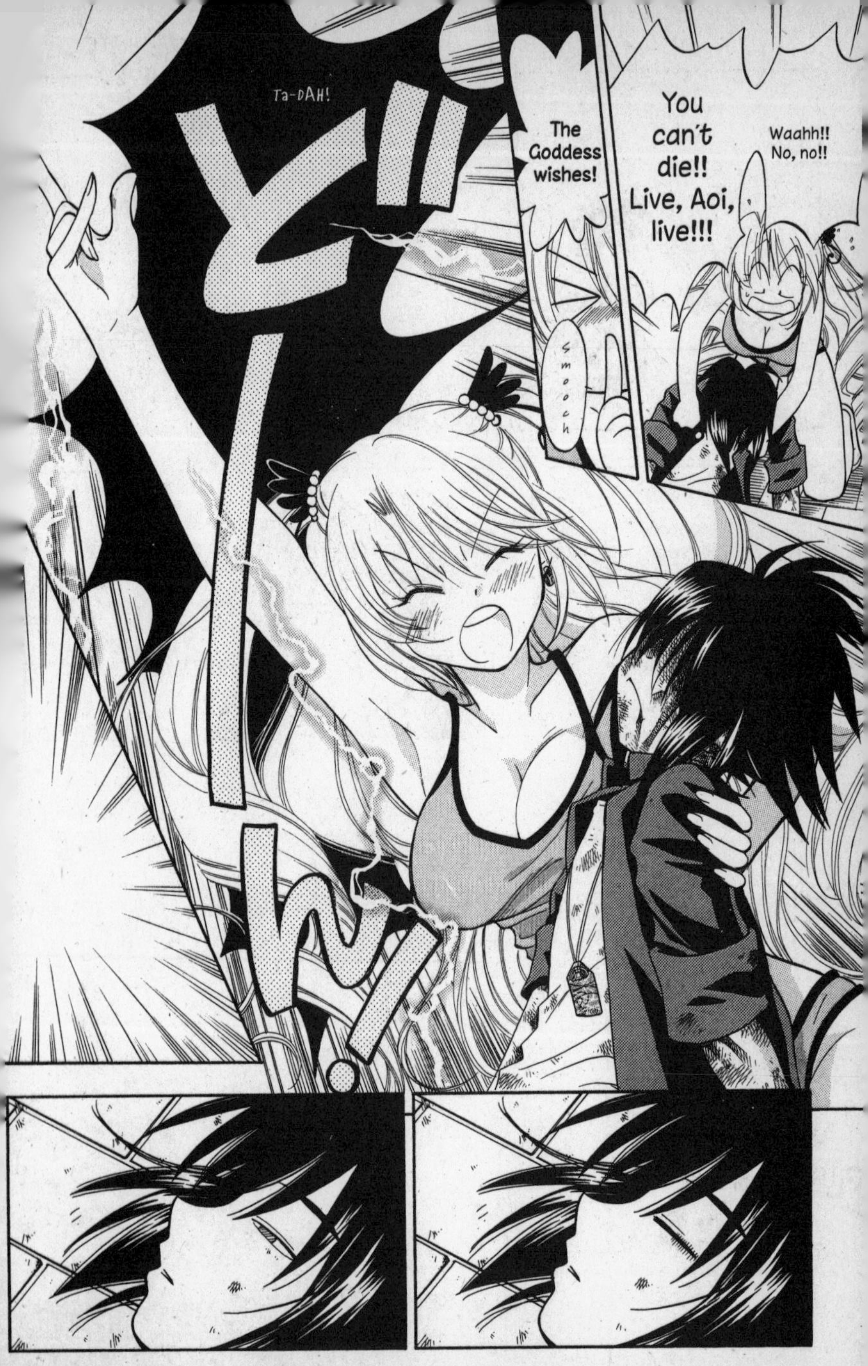
Waahh!! No, no!!
You can't die!! Live, Aoi, live!!!
The Goddess wishes!
smooch
Ta-DAH!

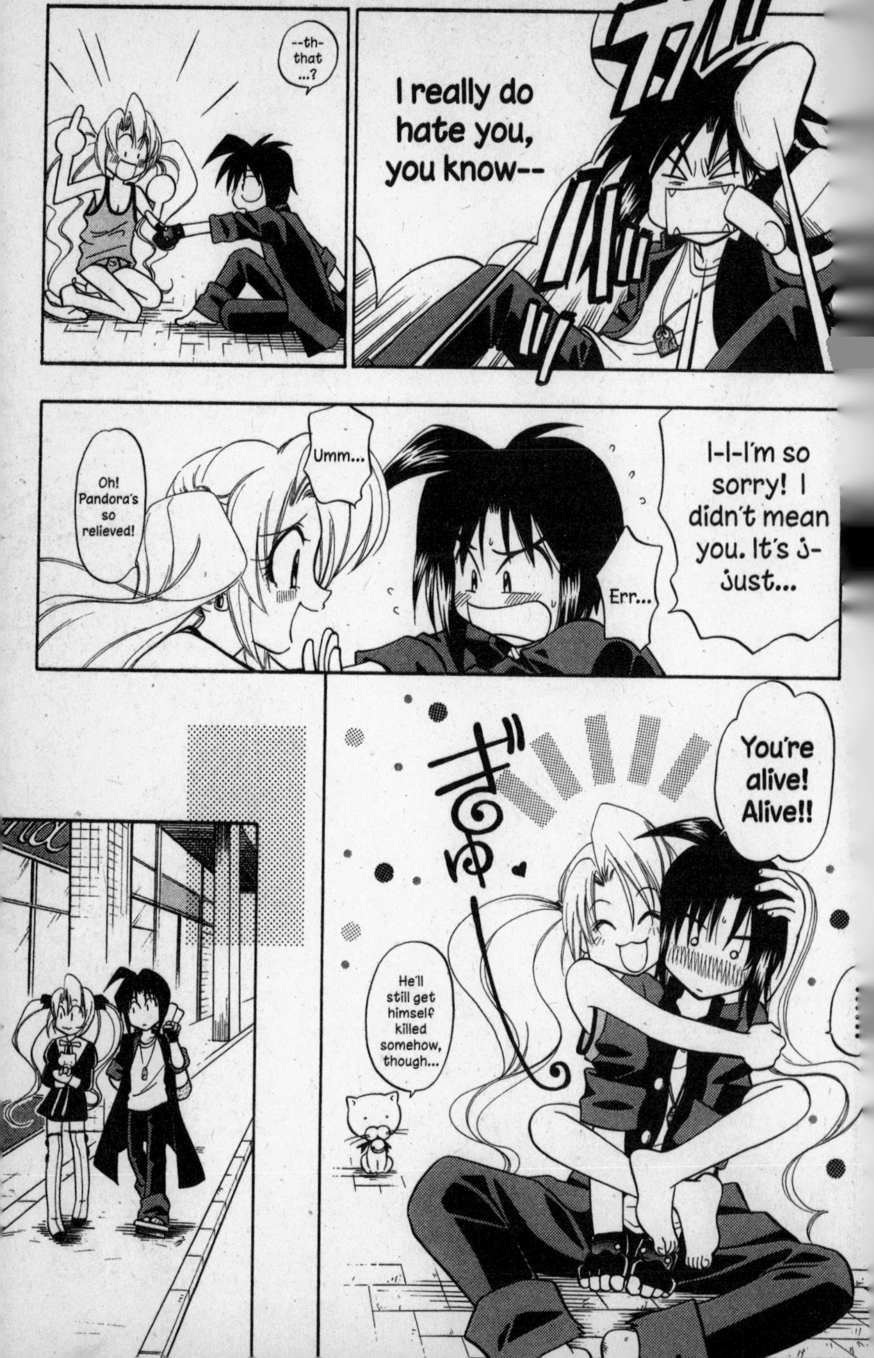
I really do hate you, you know--
--th- that ...?
I-I-I'm so sorry! I didn't mean you. It's j-just...
Err...
Umm...
Oh! Pandora's so relieved!
You're alive! Alive!!
He'll still get himself killed somehow, though...

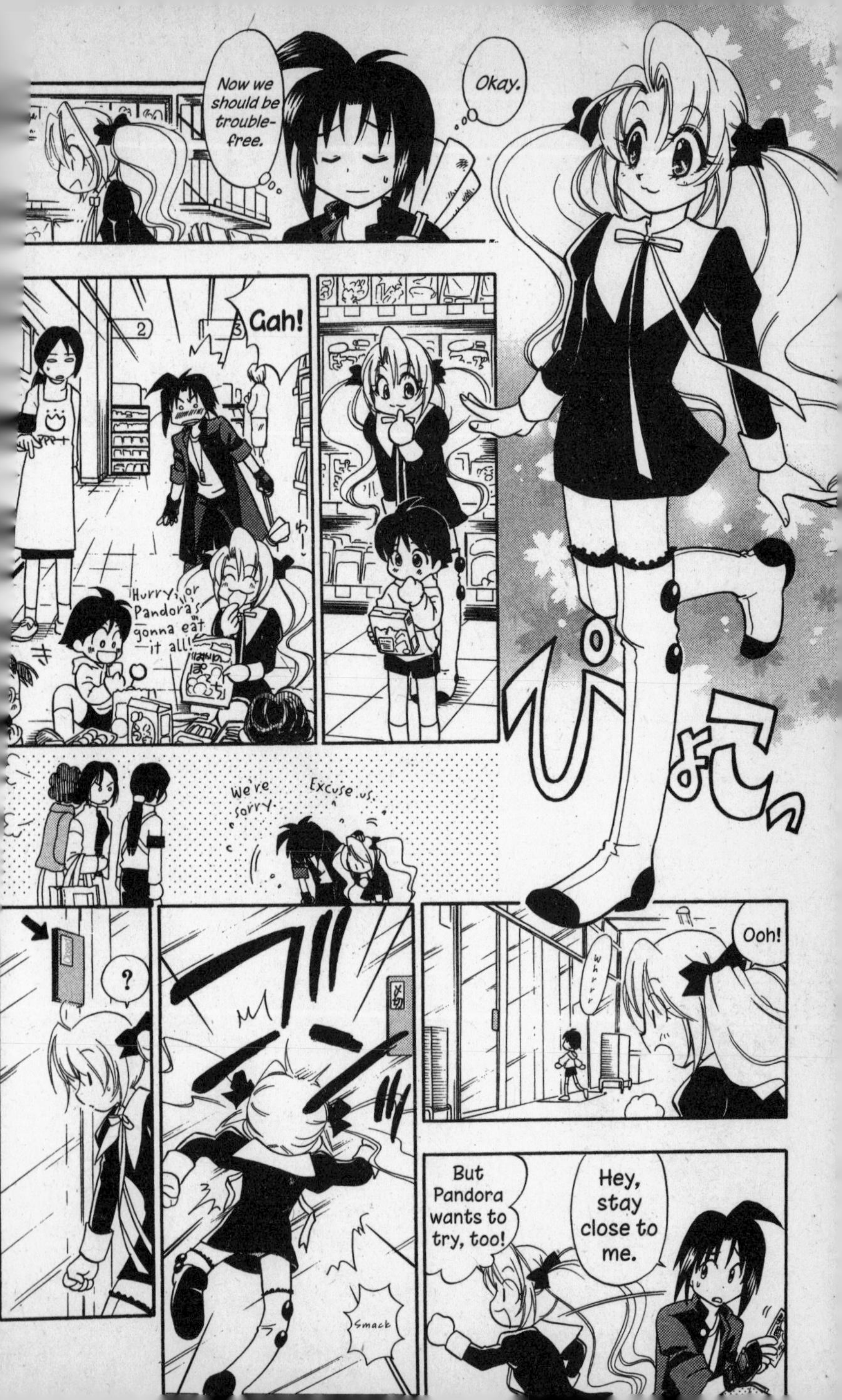
ぴょこっ
Now we should be trouble-free.
Okay.
Gah!
Hurry, or Pandora's gonna eat it all!
Excuse us.
We're sorry.
Ooh!
Whrrr
Hey, stay close to me.
But Pandora wants to try, too!
Smack
?

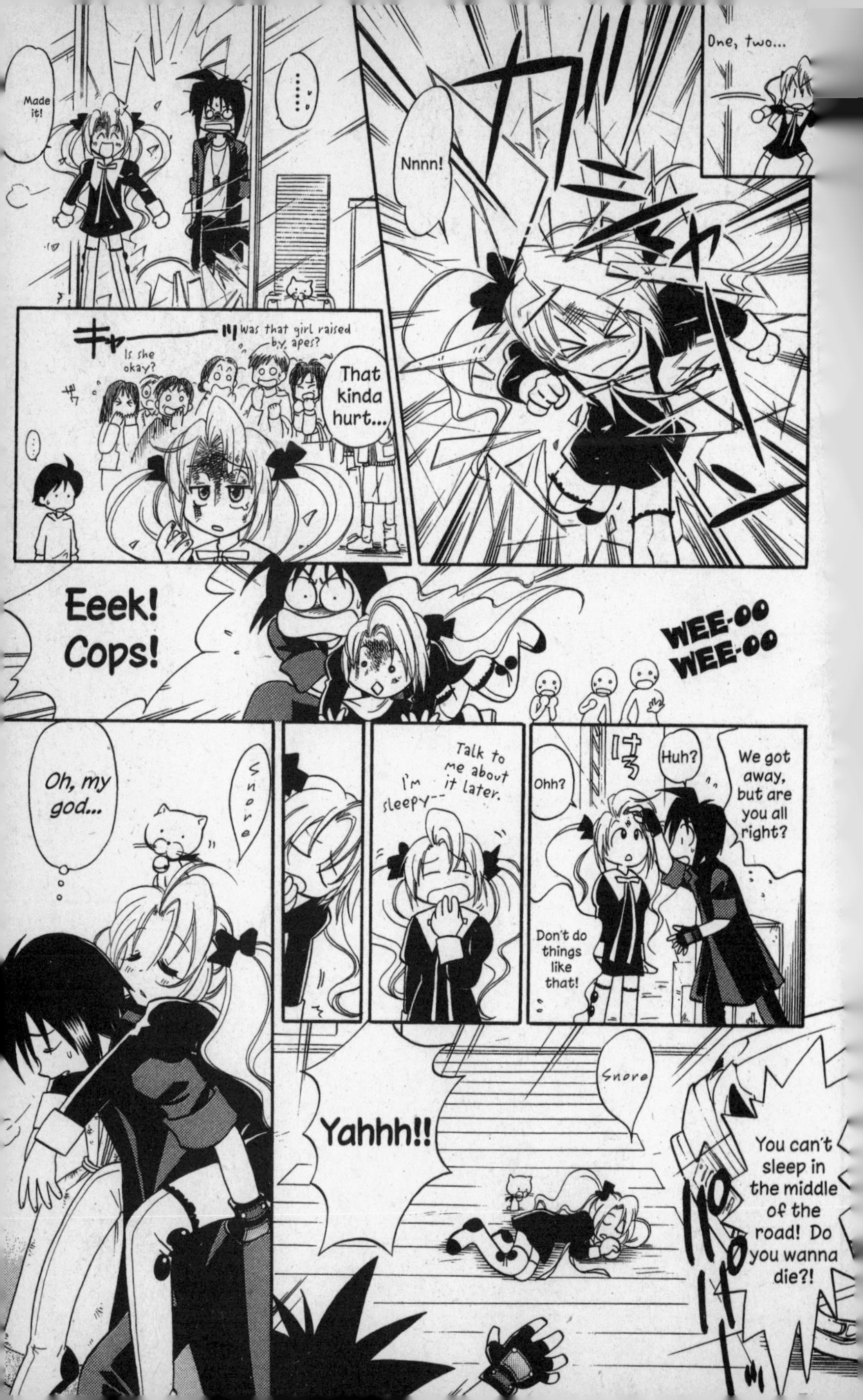

One, two...
Nnnn!
Made it!
......
キャー
Was that girl raised by apes?
Is she okay?
That kinda hurt...
...
WEE-OO WEE-OO
Eeek! Cops!
We got away, but are you all right?
Huh?
Ohh?
Don't do things like that!
Talk to me about it later.
I'm sleepy--
Snore
Oh, my god...
You can't sleep in the middle of the road! Do you wanna die?!
Snore
Yahhh!!

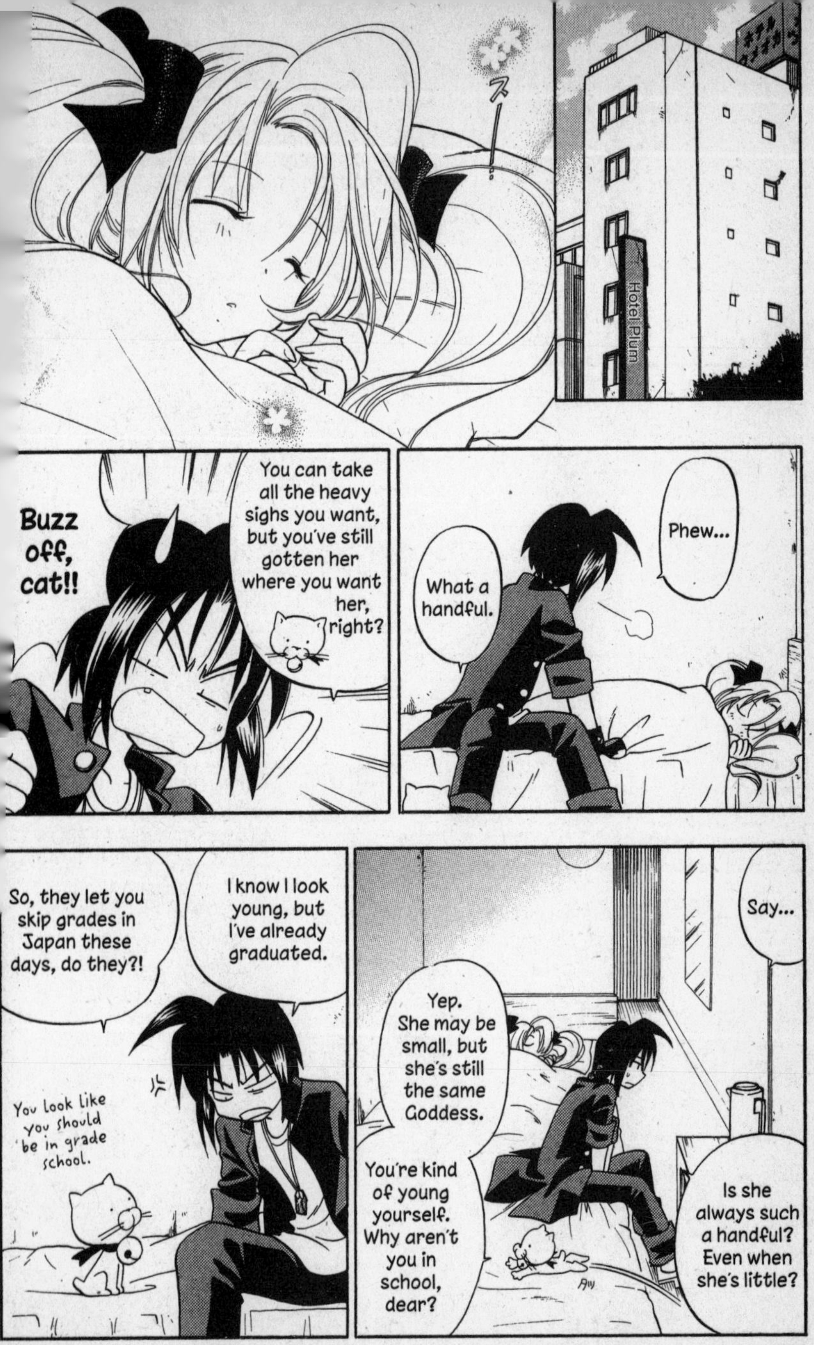
Hotel Plum
Phew...
What a handful.
You can take all the heavy sighs you want, but you've still gotten her where you want her, right?
Buzz off, cat!!
Say...
Is she always such a handful? Even when she's little?
Yep. She may be small, but she's still the same Goddess.
You're kind of young yourself. Why aren't you in school, dear?
I know I look young, but I've already graduated.
So, they let you skip grades in Japan these days, do they?!
You look like you should be in grade school.

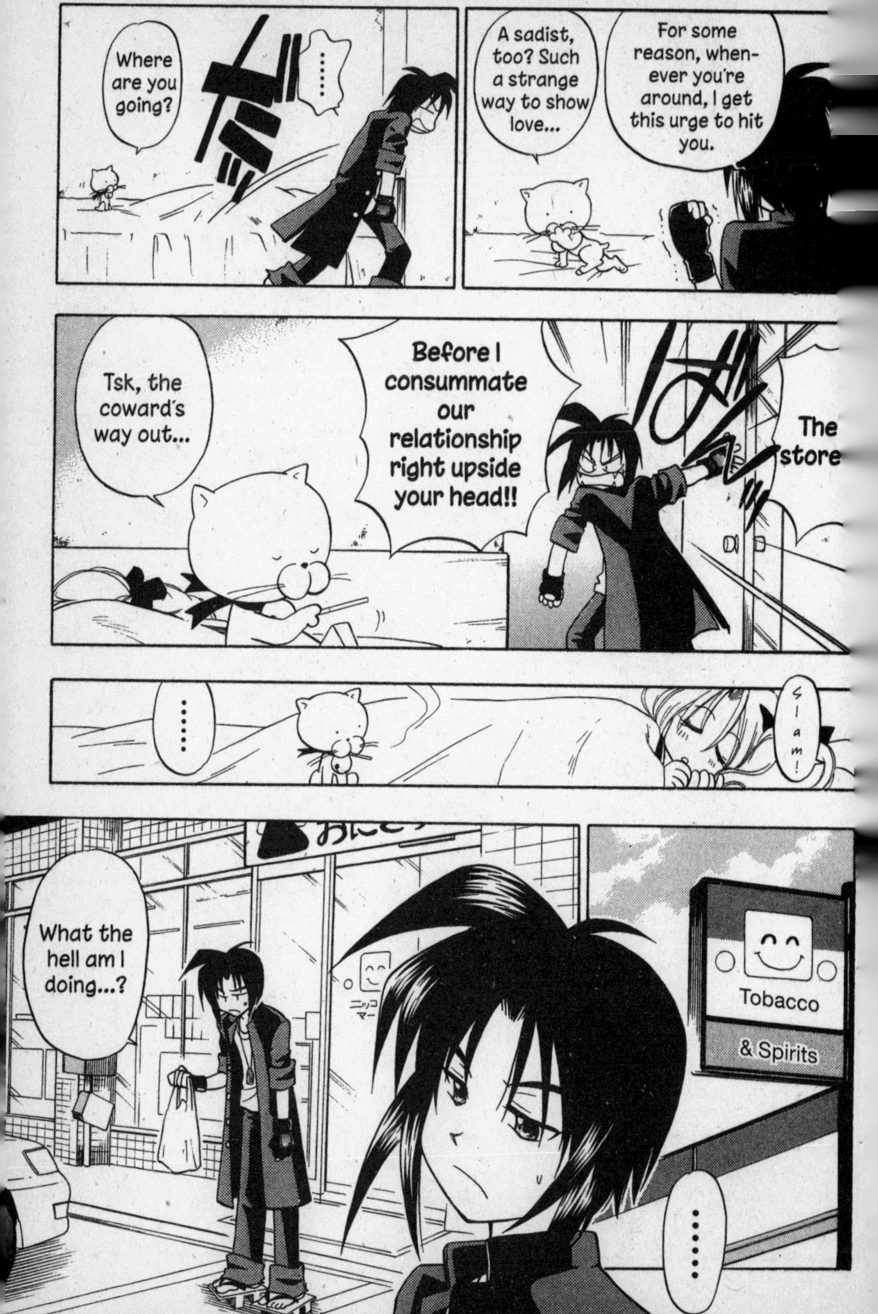
For some reason, when-ever you're around, I get this urge to hit you.
A sadist, too? Such a strange way to show love...
......
Where are you going?
The store
Before I consummate our relationship right upside your head!!
Tsk, the coward's way out...
Slam!
......
Tobacco
& Spirits
......
What the hell am I doing...?

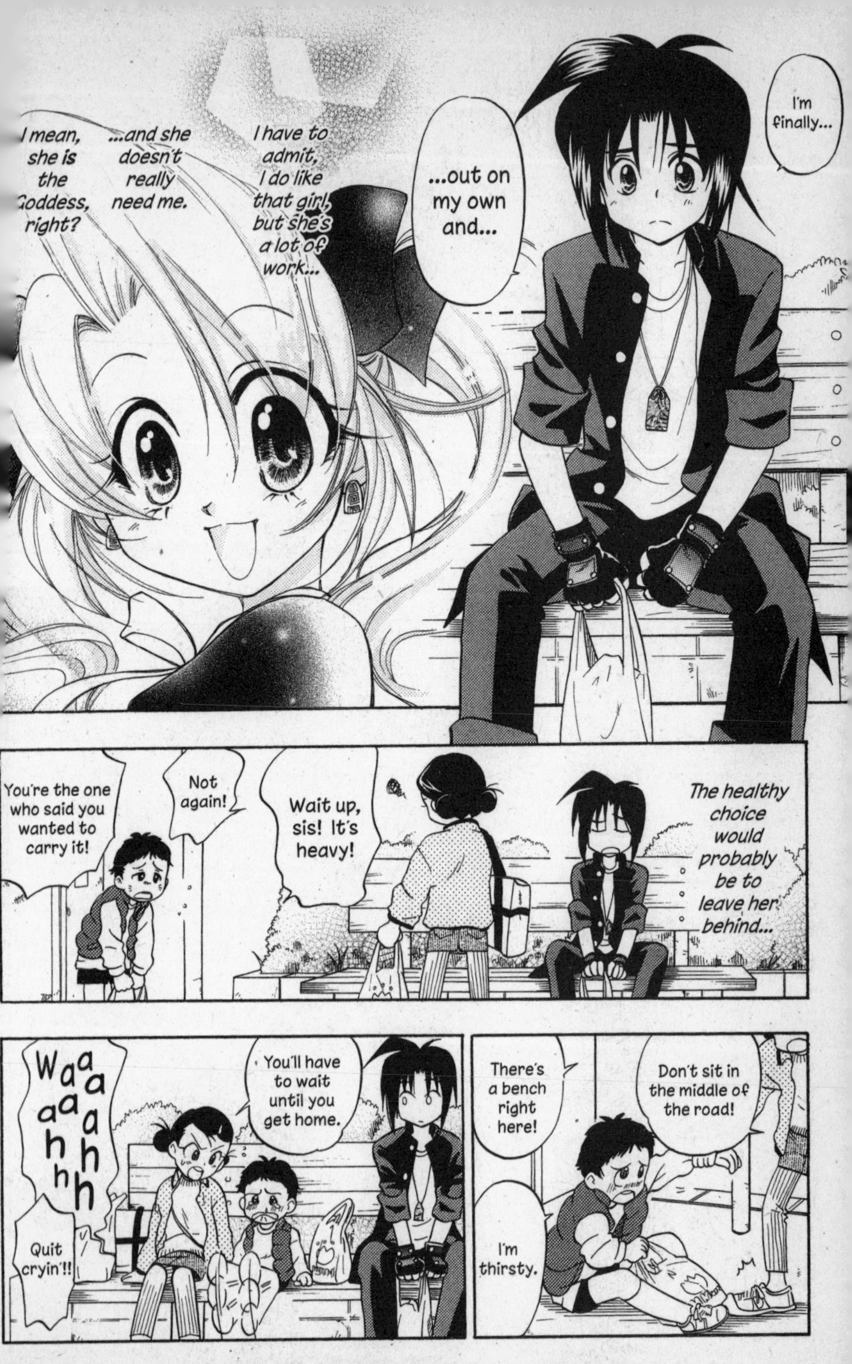
I'm finally...
...out on my own and...
I have to admit, I do like that girl, but she's a lot of work...
...and she doesn't really need me.
I mean, she is the Goddess, right?
The healthy choice would probably be to leave her behind...
Wait up, sis! It's heavy!
Not again!
You're the one who said you wanted to carry it!
Don't sit in the middle of the road!
There's a bench right here!
I'm thirsty.
You'll have to wait until you get home.
Waaaaaaahhhh
Quit cryin'!!

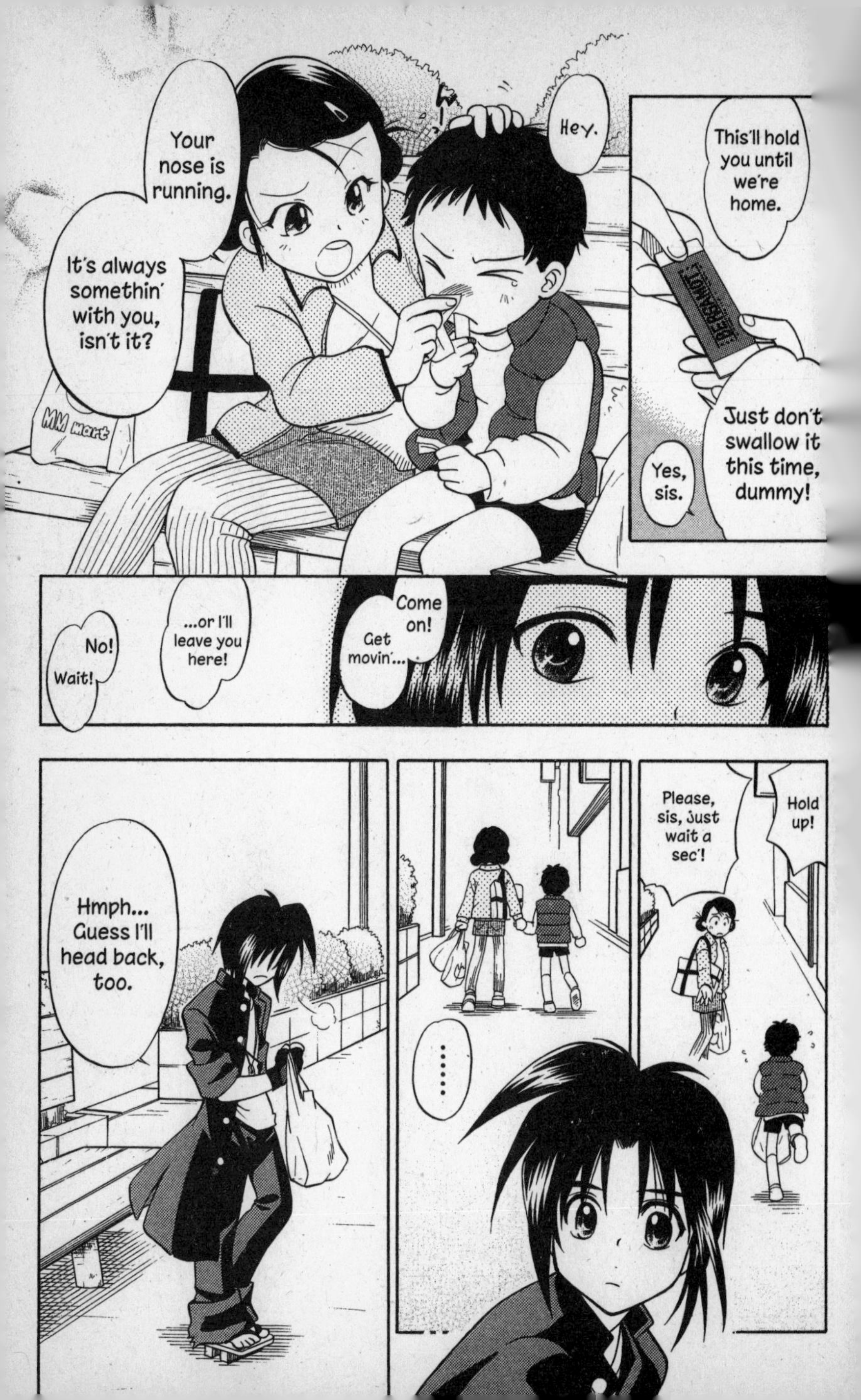
This'll hold you until we're home.
Just don't swallow it this time, dummy!
Yes, sis.
Hey.
Your nose is running.
It's always somethin' with you, isn't it?
MM mart
Come on!
Get movin'...
...or I'll leave you here!
No!
Wait!
Please, sis, just wait a sec'!
Hold up!
......
Hmph... Guess I'll head back, too.

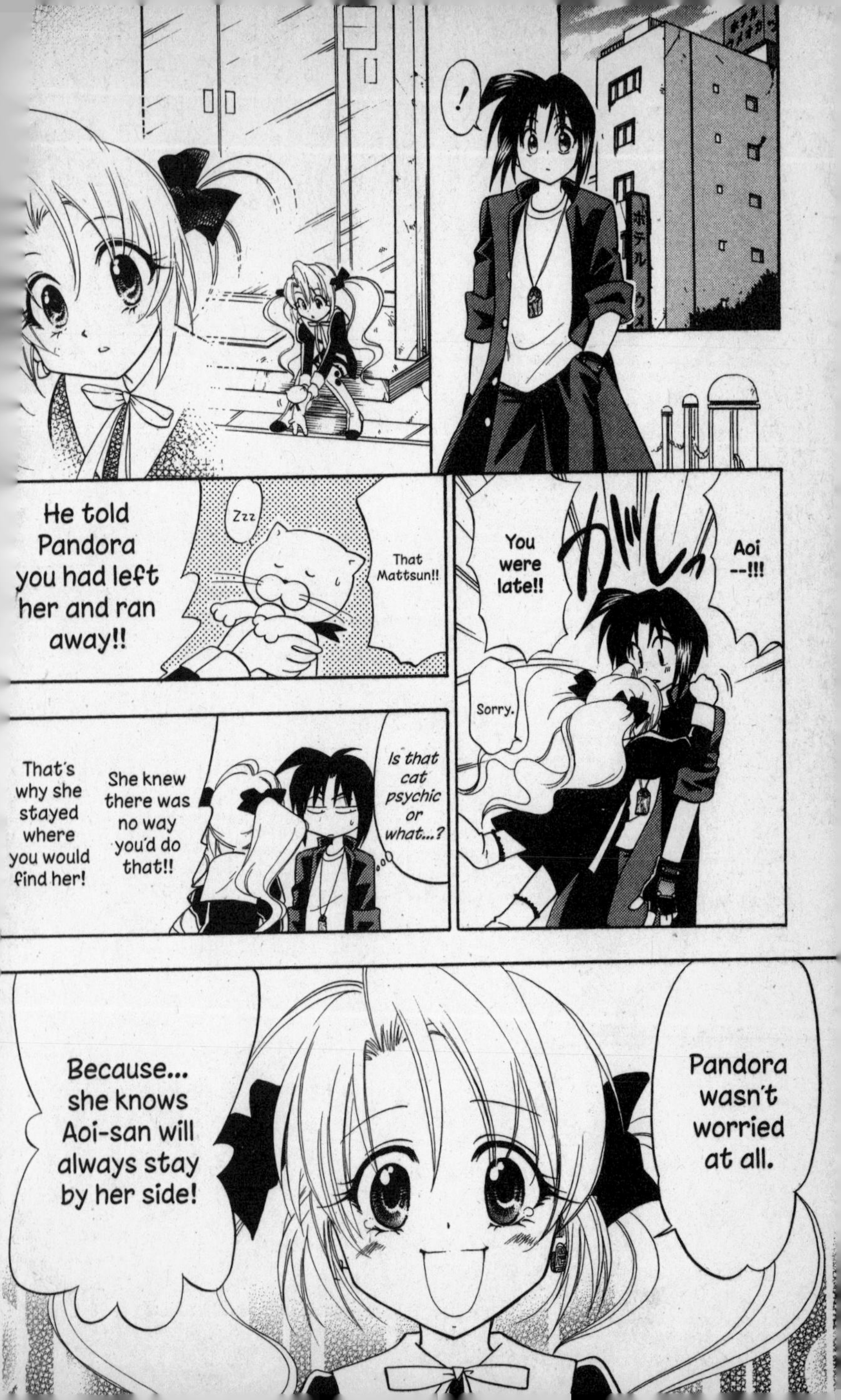
!
Aoi --!!!
You were late!!
Sorry.
That Mattsun!!
Zzz
He told Pandora you had left her and ran away!!
Is that cat psychic or what...?
She knew there was no way you'd do that!!
That's why she stayed where you would find her!
Pandora wasn't worried at all.
Because... she knows Aoi-san will always stay by her side!

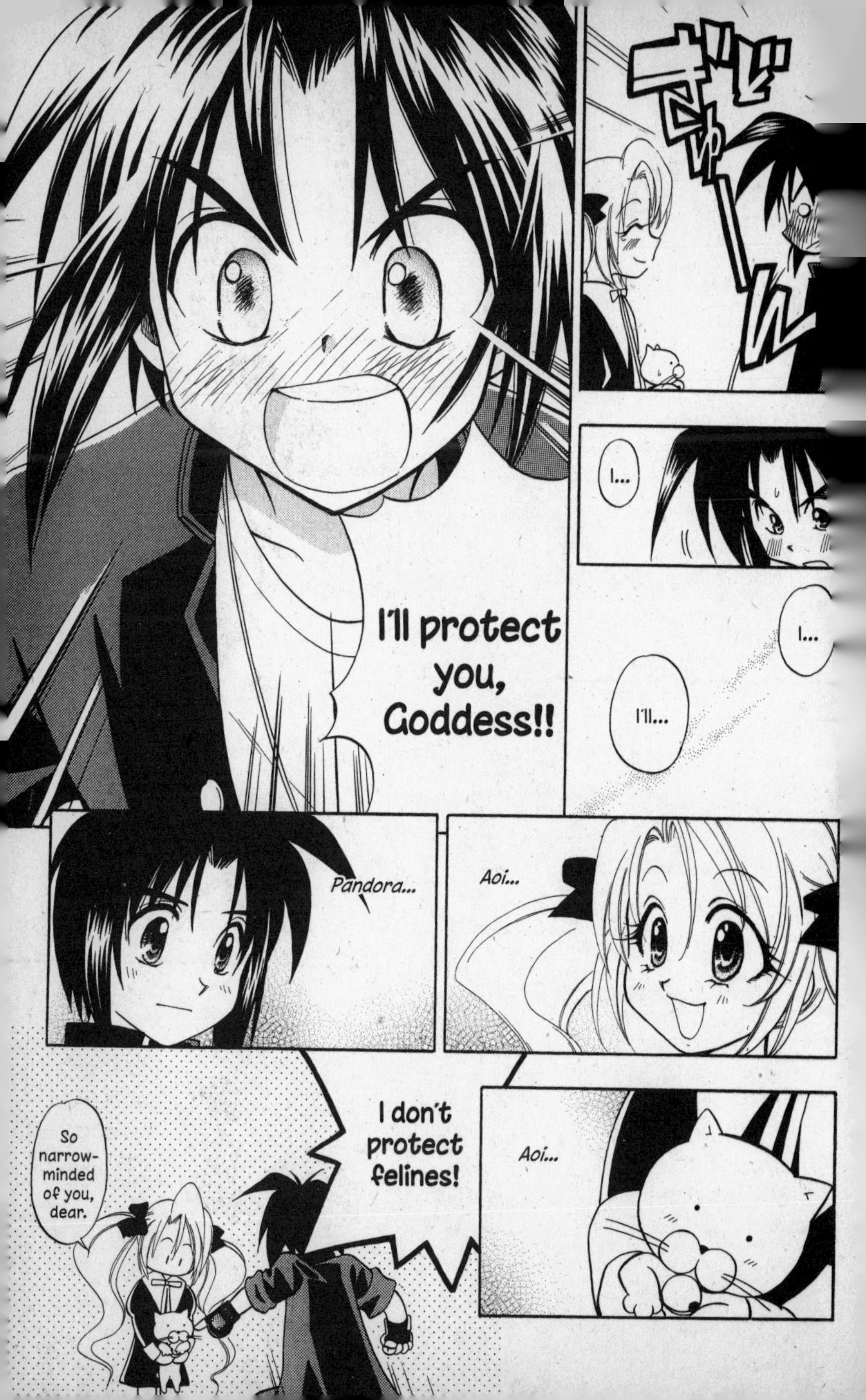
ぎゅーん
I...
I...
I'll...
I'll protect you, Goddess!!
Aoi...
Pandora...
Aoi...
I don't protect felines!
So narrow-minded of you, dear.

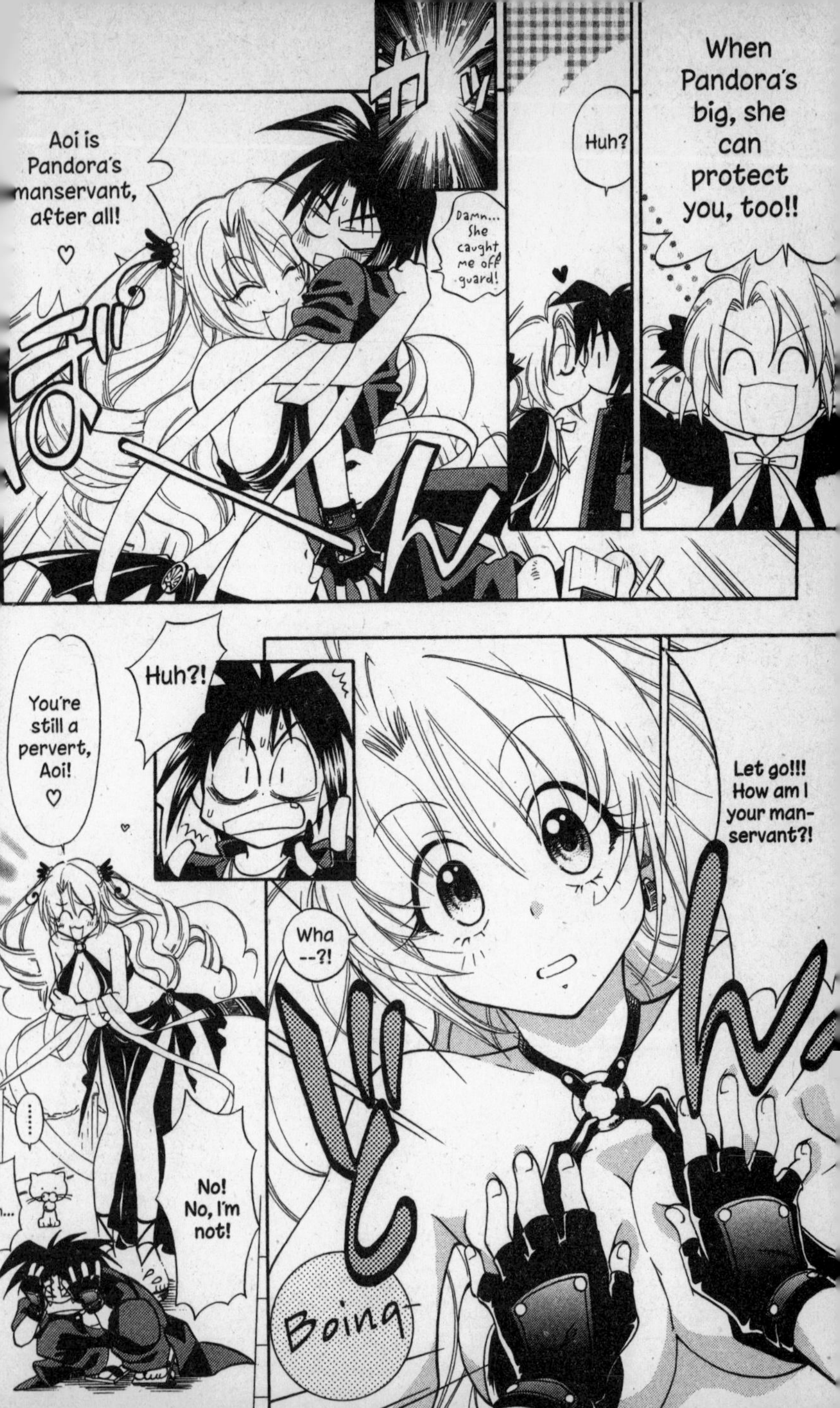
When Pandora's big, she can protect you, too!!
Huh?
Damn... She caught me off guard!
Aoi is Pandora's manservant, after all! ♡
Let go!!! How am I your man-servant?!
Wha --?!
Boing
Huh?!
You're still a pervert, Aoi! ♡
......
I'm...
No! No, I'm not!

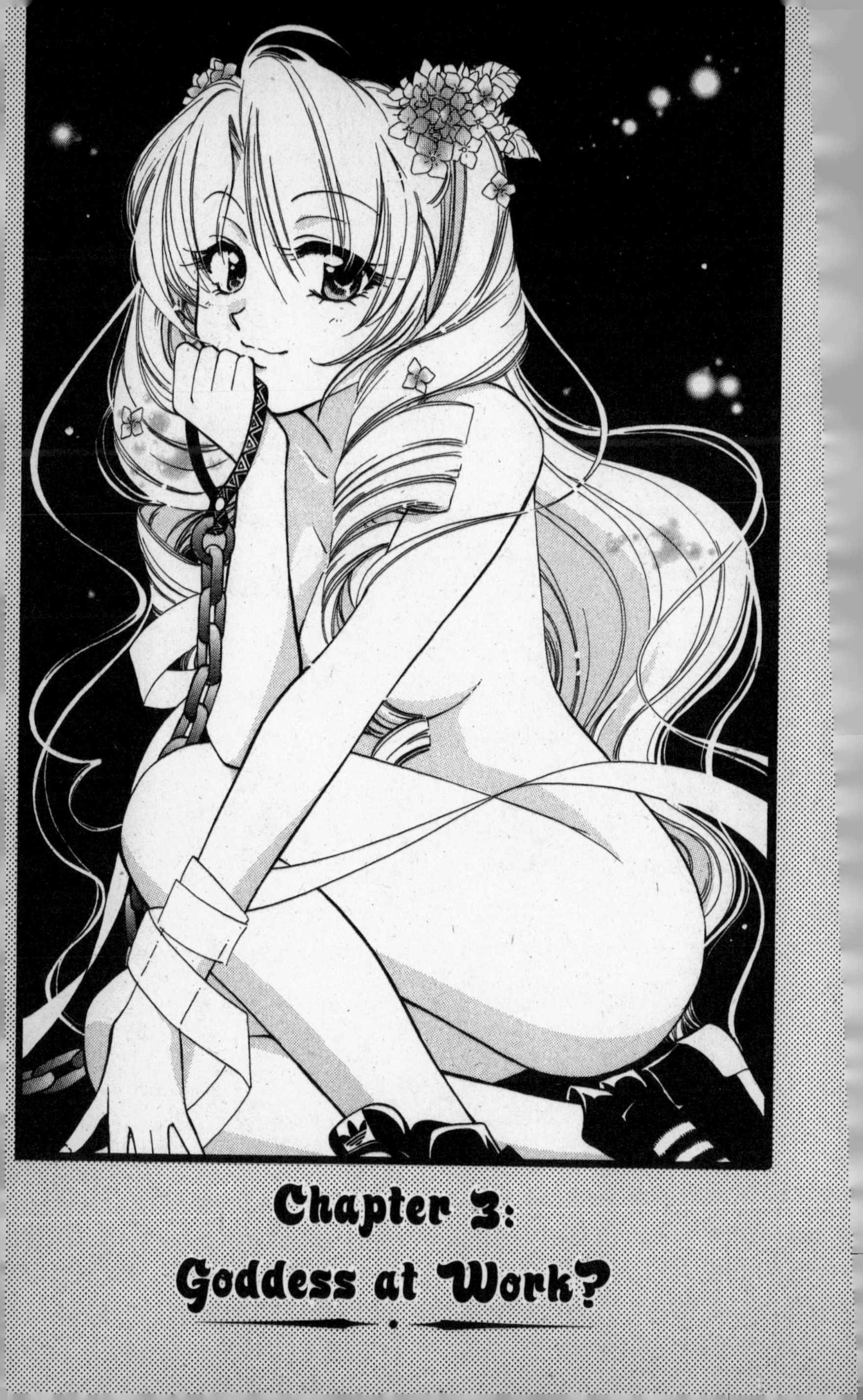

Chapter 3: Goddess at Work?

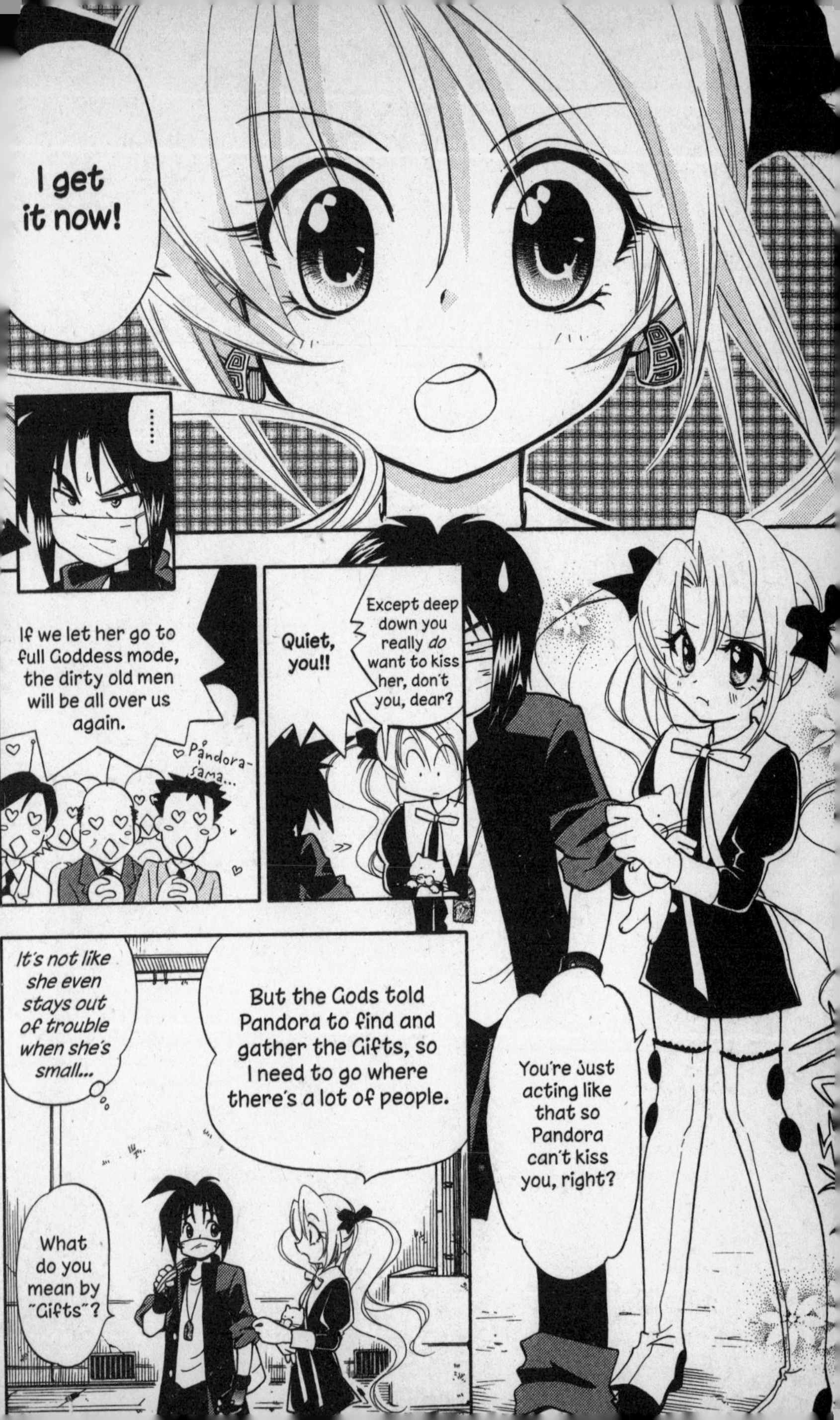

I get it now!
......
You're just acting like that so Pandora can't kiss you, right?
Except deep down you really *do* want to kiss her, don't you, dear?
Quiet, you!!
If we let her go to full Goddess mode, the dirty old men will be all over us again.
Pandora-sama...
But the Gods told Pandora to find and gather the Gifts, so I need to go where there's a lot of people.
It's not like she even stays out of trouble when she's small...
What do you mean by "Gifts"?

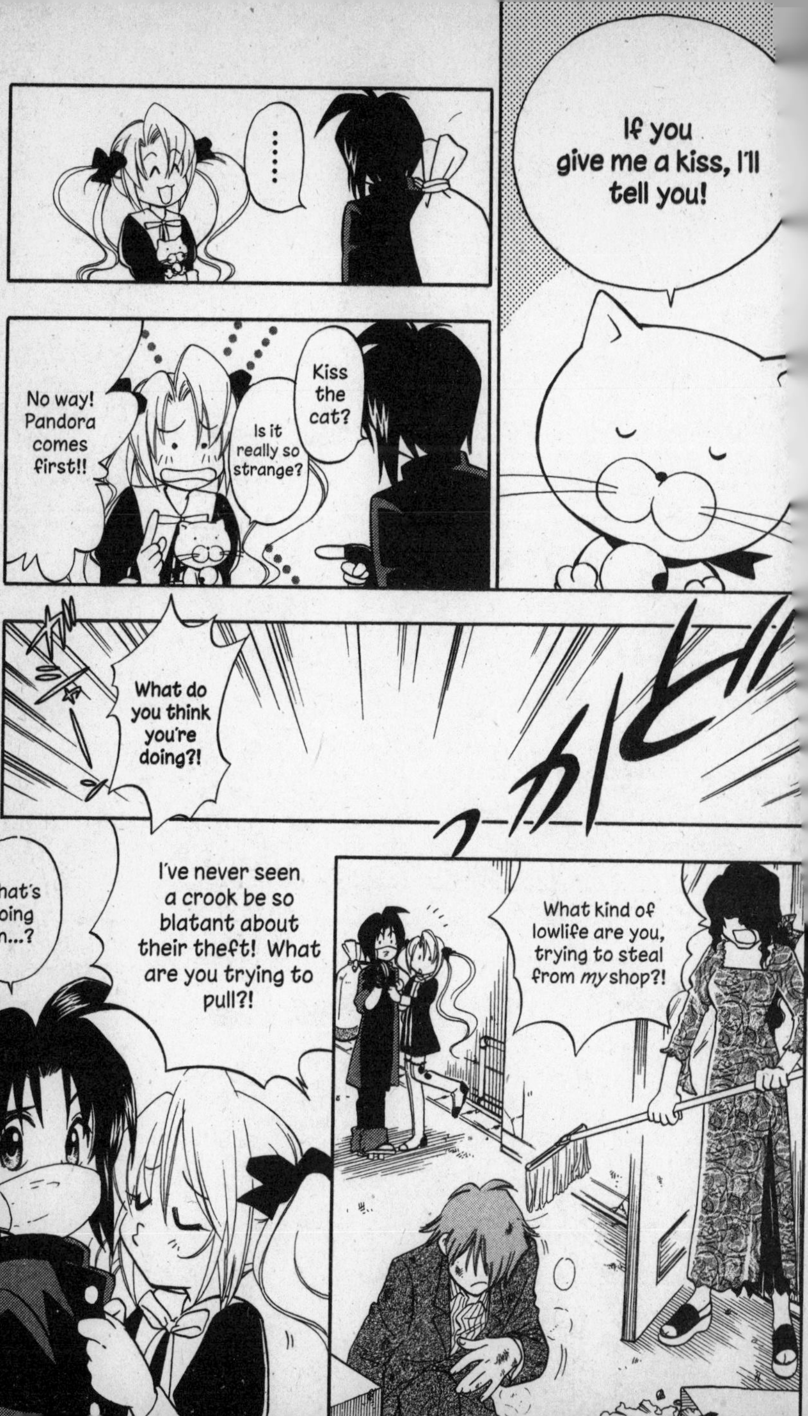
If you give me a kiss, I'll tell you!
......
Kiss the cat?
Is it really so strange?
No way! Pandora comes first!!
What do you think you're doing?!
What kind of lowlife are you, trying to steal from *my* shop?!
I've never seen a crook be so blatant about their theft! What are you trying to pull?!
What's going on...?

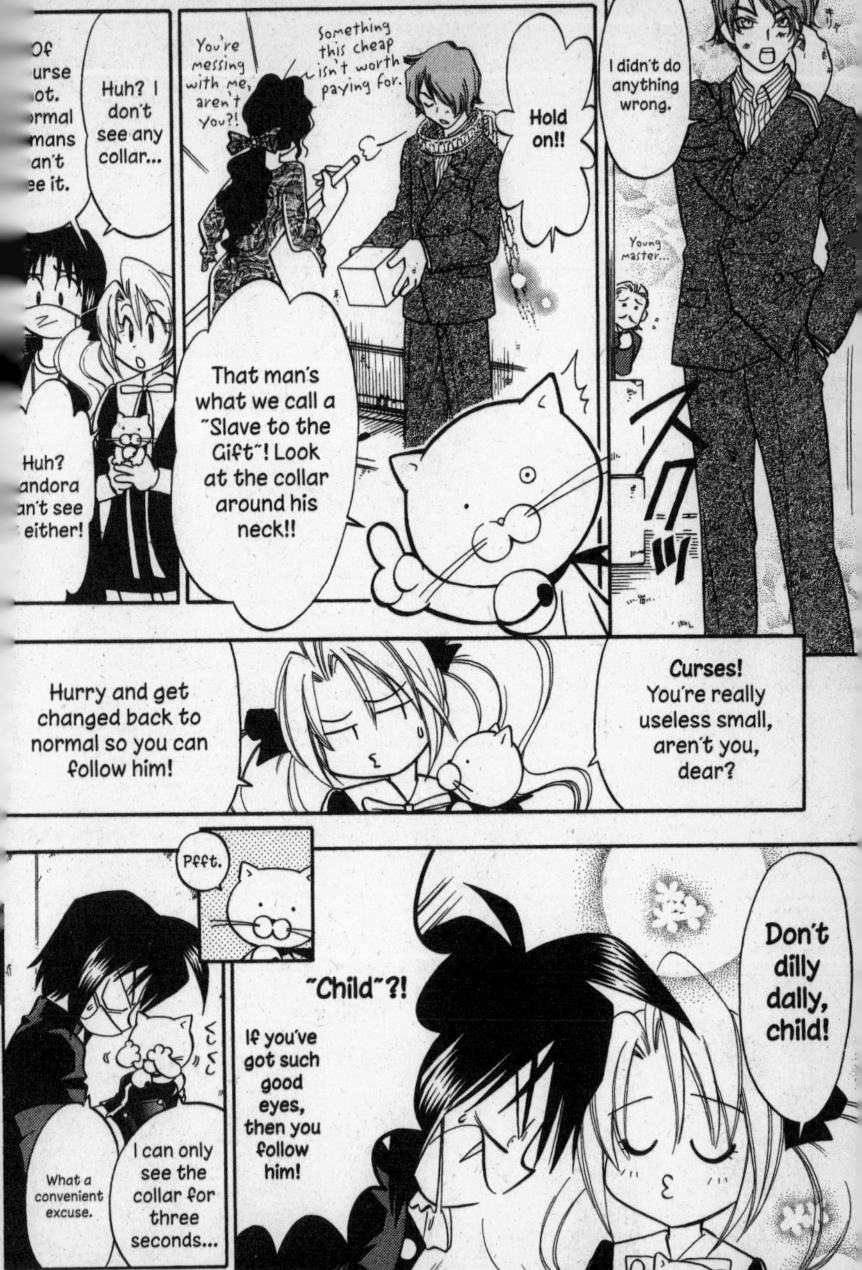
I didn't do anything wrong.
Young master...
Hold on!!
Something this cheap isn't worth paying for.
You're messing with me, aren't you?!
That man's what we call a "Slave to the Gift"! Look at the collar around his neck!!
Huh? I don't see any collar...
Of ...urse ...ot. ...ormal ...mans ...an't ...ee it.
Huh? ...andora ...an't see ... either!
Curses! You're really useless small, aren't you, dear?
Hurry and get changed back to normal so you can follow him!
Don't dilly dally, child!
"Child"?!
If you've got such good eyes, then you follow him!
Pfft.
I can only see the collar for three seconds...
What a convenient excuse.

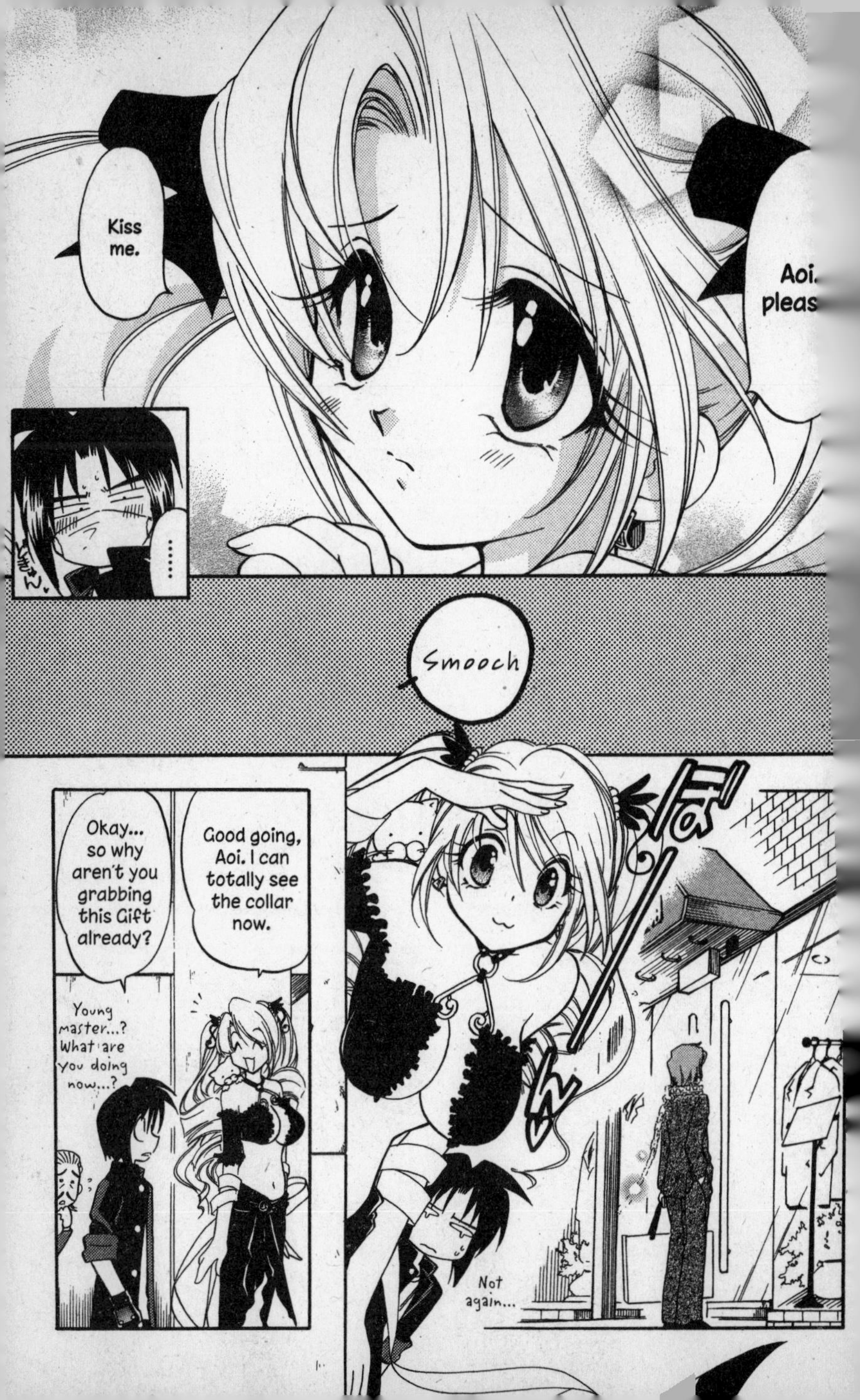
Aoi. pleas
Kiss me.
......
Smooch
Not again...
Good going, Aoi. I can totally see the collar now.
Okay... so why aren't you grabbing this Gift already?
Young master...? What are you doing now...?

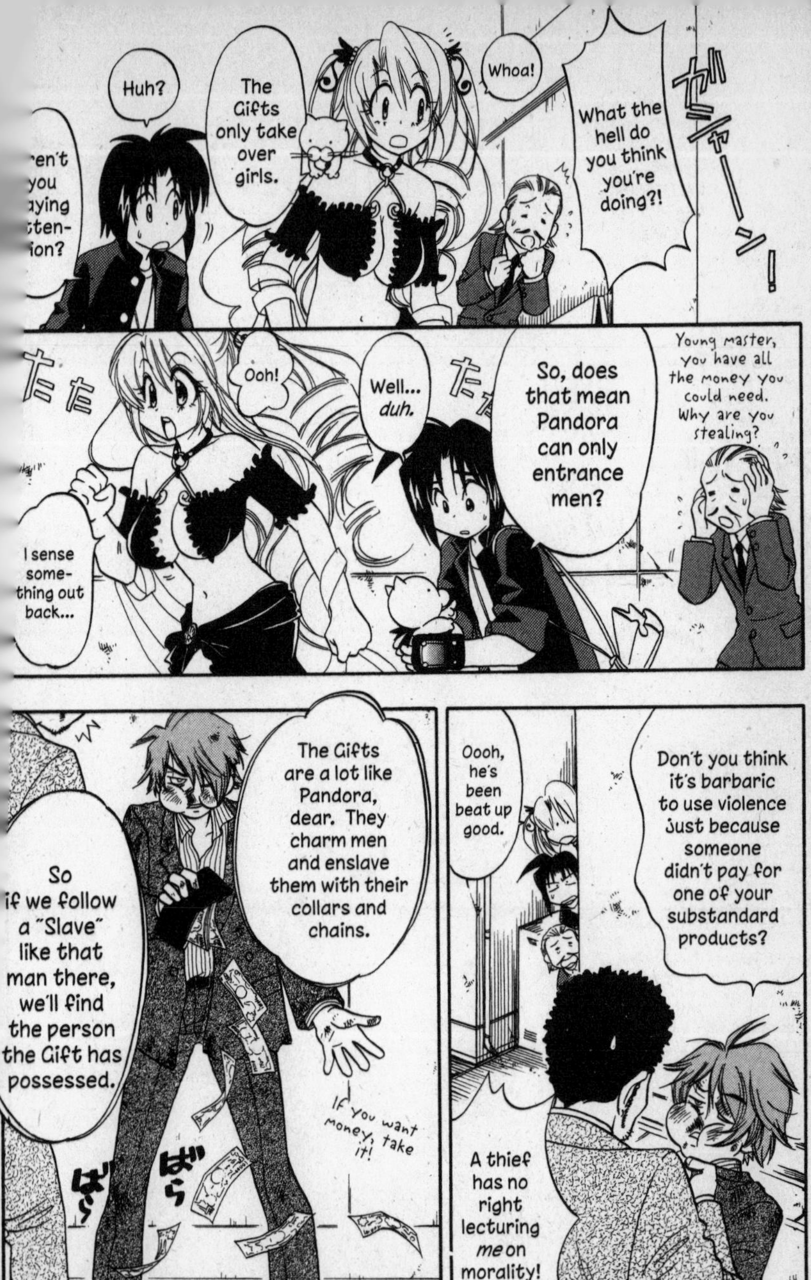

What the hell do you think you're doing?!
ガシャーン!
Whoa!
The Gifts only take over girls.
Huh?
ren't you aying tten- ion?
Young master, you have all the money you could need. Why are you stealing?
So, does that mean Pandora can only entrance men?
たた
Well... *duh.*
Ooh!
たた
I sense something out back...
Don't you think it's barbaric to use violence just because someone didn't pay for one of your substandard products?
Oooh, he's been beat up good.
A thief has no right lecturing *me* on morality!
The Gifts are a lot like Pandora, dear. They charm men and enslave them with their collars and chains.
So if we follow a "Slave" like that man there, we'll find the person the Gift has possessed.
If you want money, take it!
ばら
ばら

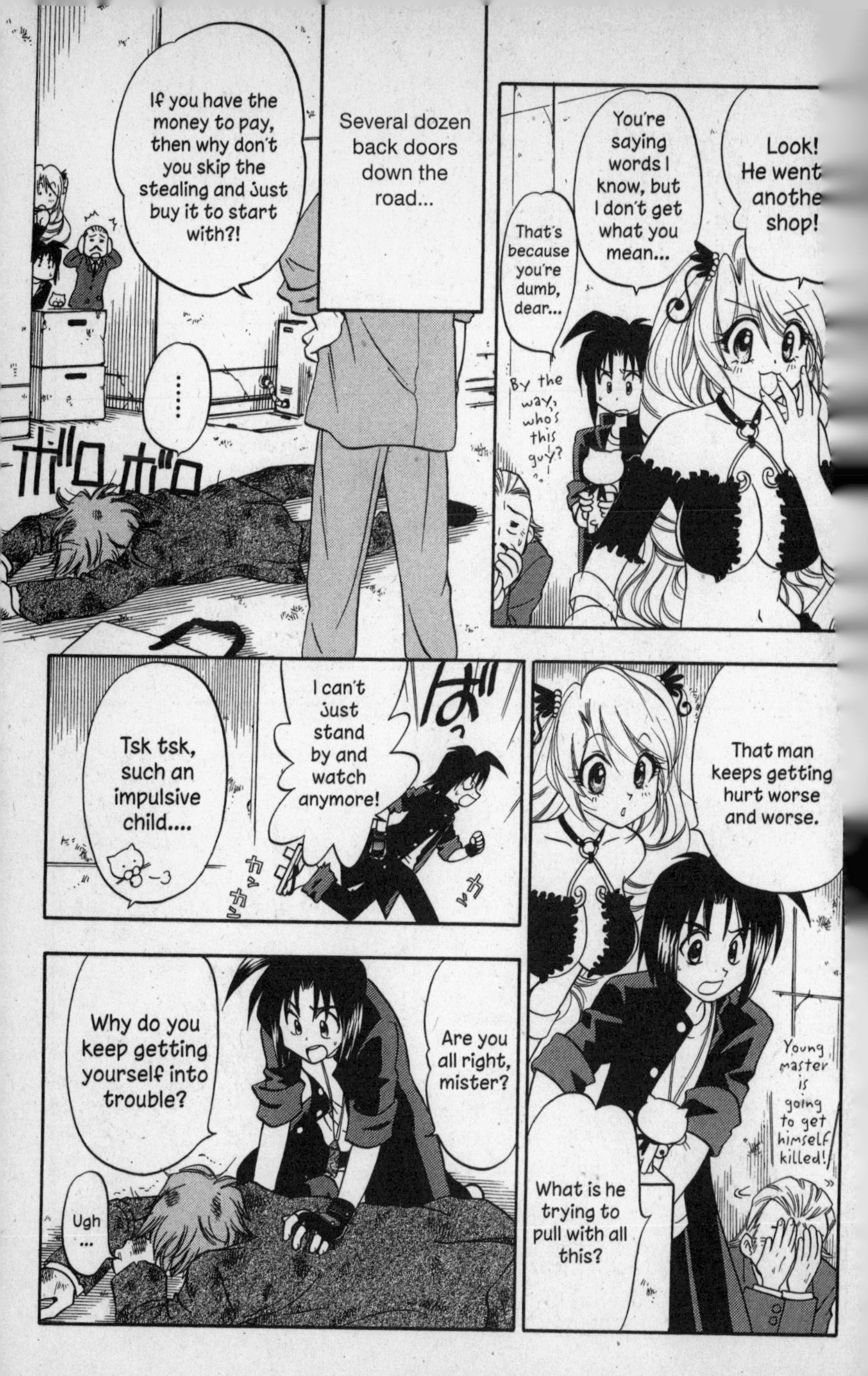
Look! He went another shop!
You're saying words I know, but I don't get what you mean...
That's because you're dumb, dear...
By the way, who's this guy?
Several dozen back doors down the road...
If you have the money to pay, then why don't you skip the stealing and just buy it to start with?!
......
ボロボロ
That man keeps getting hurt worse and worse.
Young master is going to get himself killed!
What is he trying to pull with all this?
ばっ
I can't just stand by and watch anymore!
Tsk tsk, such an impulsive child....
Are you all right, mister?
Why do you keep getting yourself into trouble?
Ugh ...

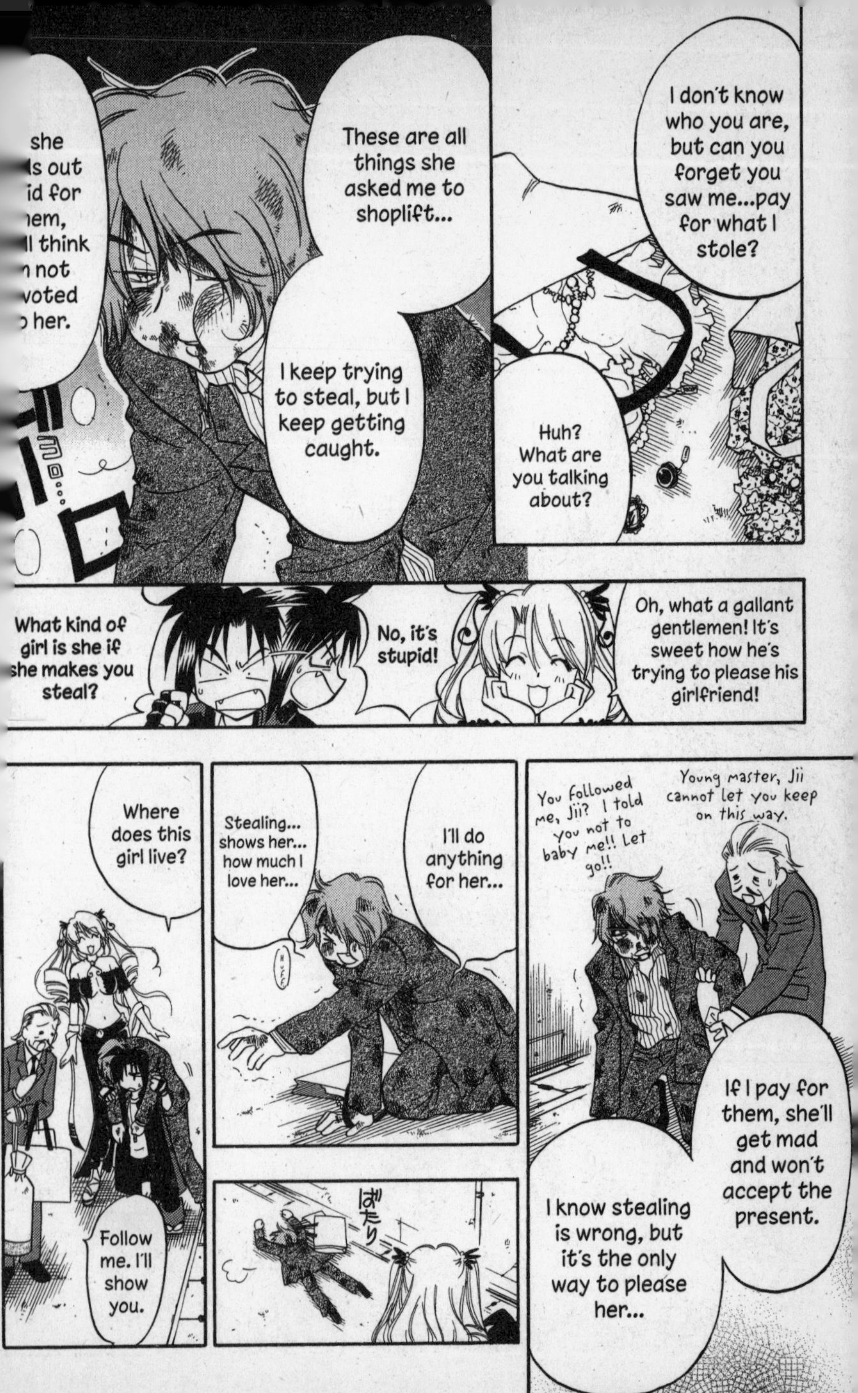
I don't know who you are, but can you forget you saw me...pay for what I stole?
Huh? What are you talking about?
These are all things she asked me to shoplift...
I keep trying to steal, but I keep getting caught.
she
ds out
id for
hem,
ll think
n not
voted
o her.
Oh, what a gallant gentlemen! It's sweet how he's trying to please his girlfriend!
No, it's stupid!
What kind of girl is she if she makes you steal?
Young master, Jii cannot let you keep on this way.
You followed me, Jii? I told you not to baby me!! Let go!!
If I pay for them, she'll get mad and won't accept the present.
I know stealing is wrong, but it's the only way to please her...
I'll do anything for her...
Stealing... shows her... how much I love her...
ばたり
Where does this girl live?
Follow me. I'll show you.

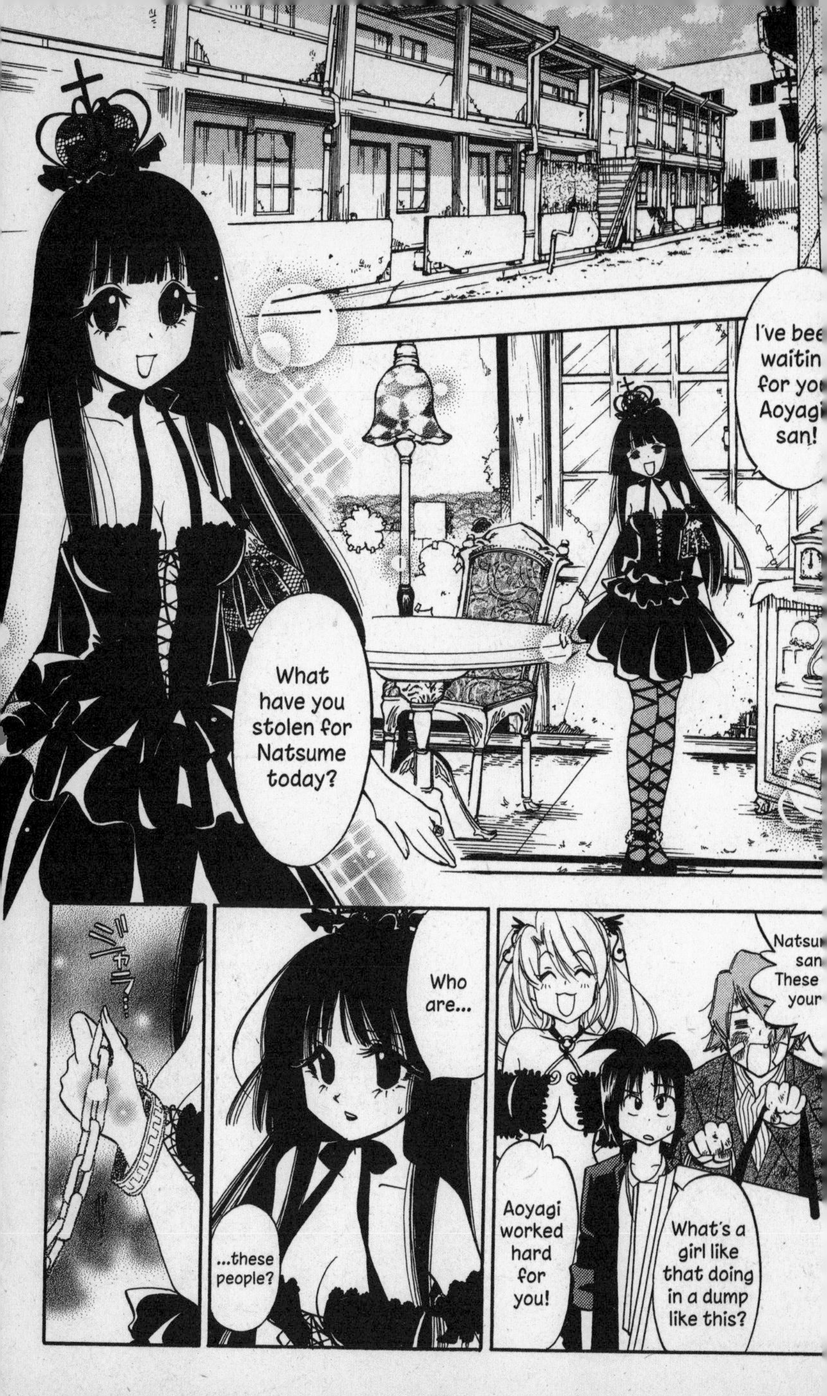
I've bee waitin for yo Aoyagi san!
What have you stolen for Natsume today?
Natsu san These your
What's a girl like that doing in a dump like this?
Aoyagi worked hard for you!
Who are...
...these people?
ジャラ…

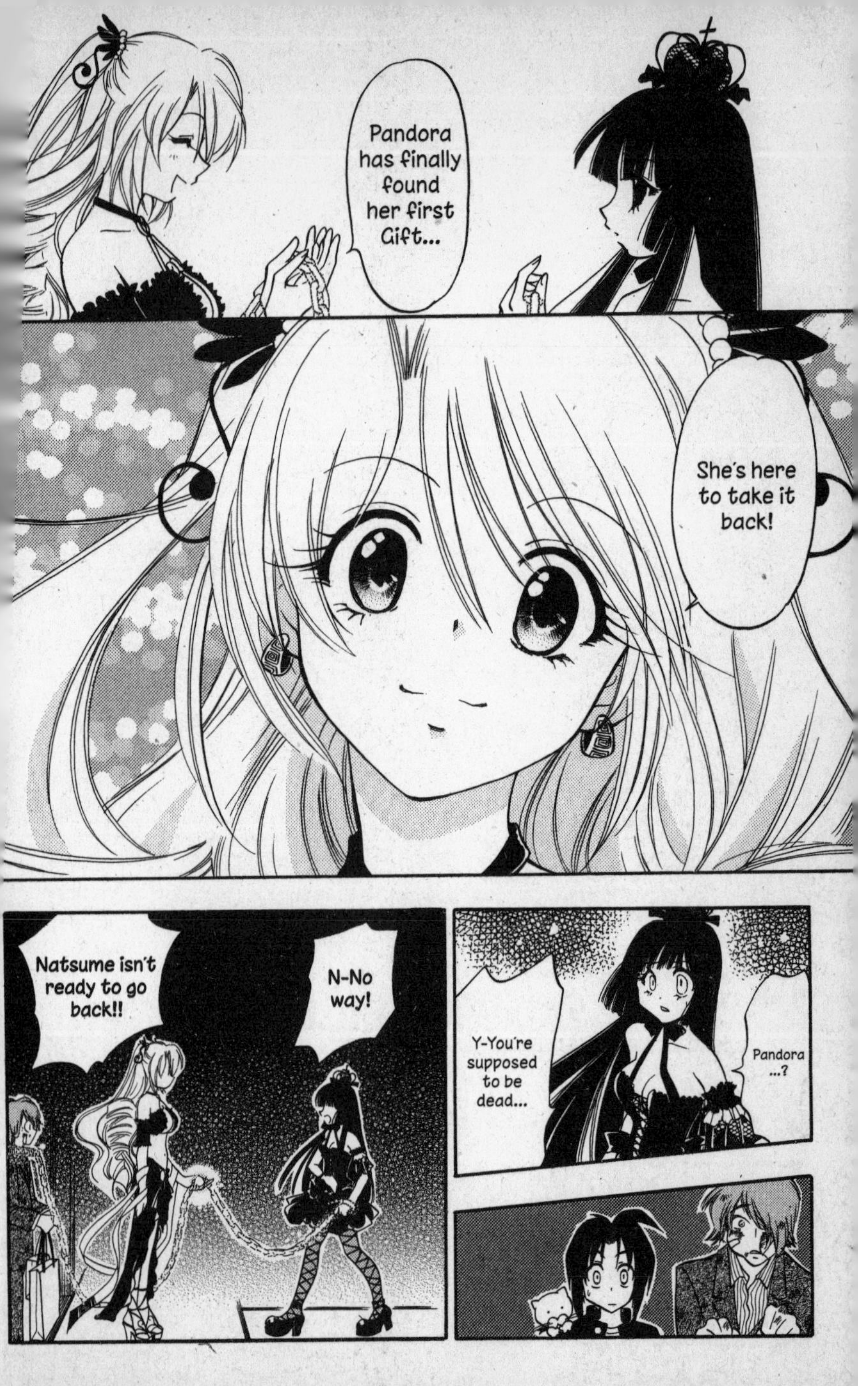

Pandora has finally found her first Gift...
She's here to take it back!
Pandora ...?
Y-You're supposed to be dead...
N-No way!
Natsume isn't ready to go back!!

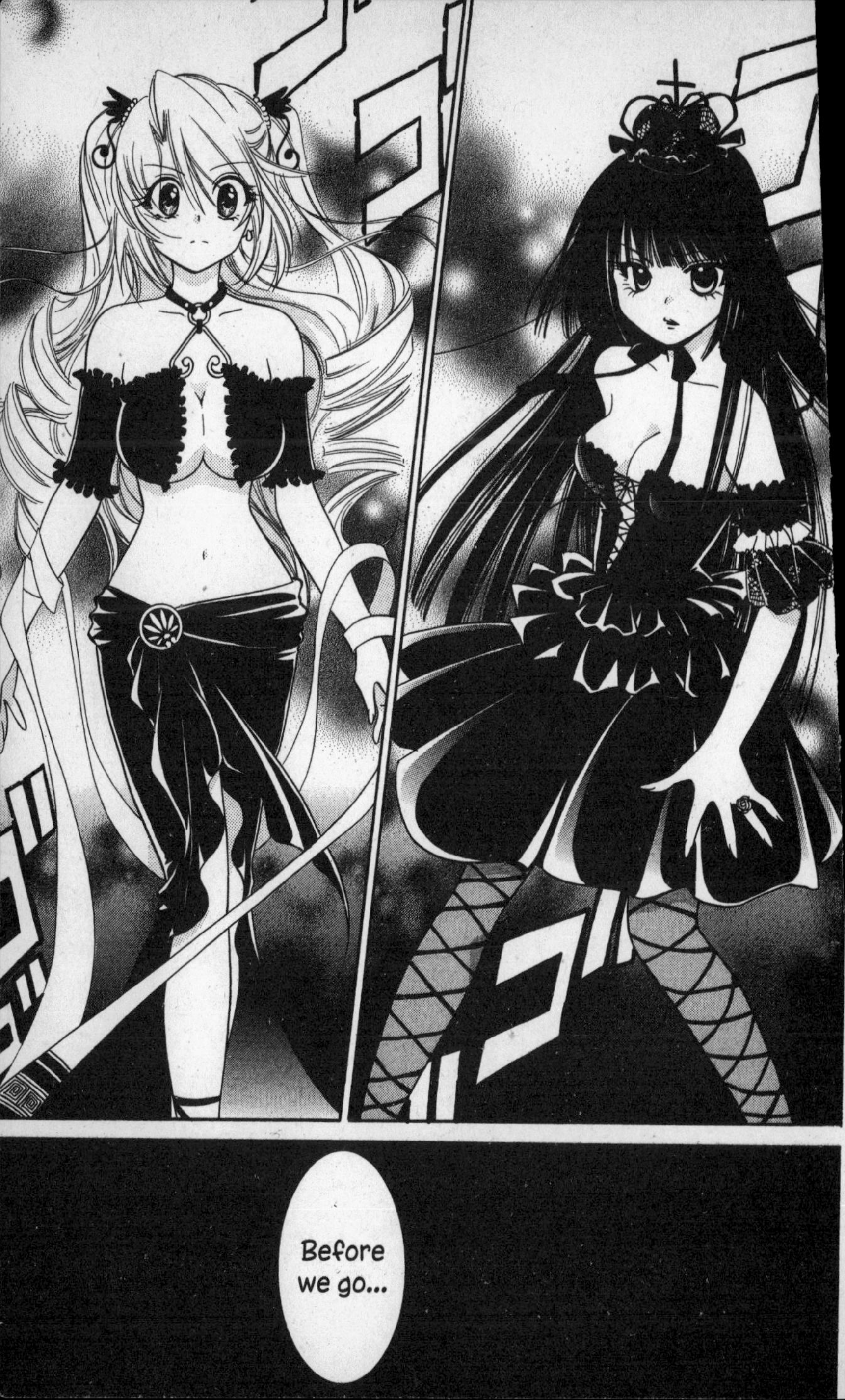
Before we go...

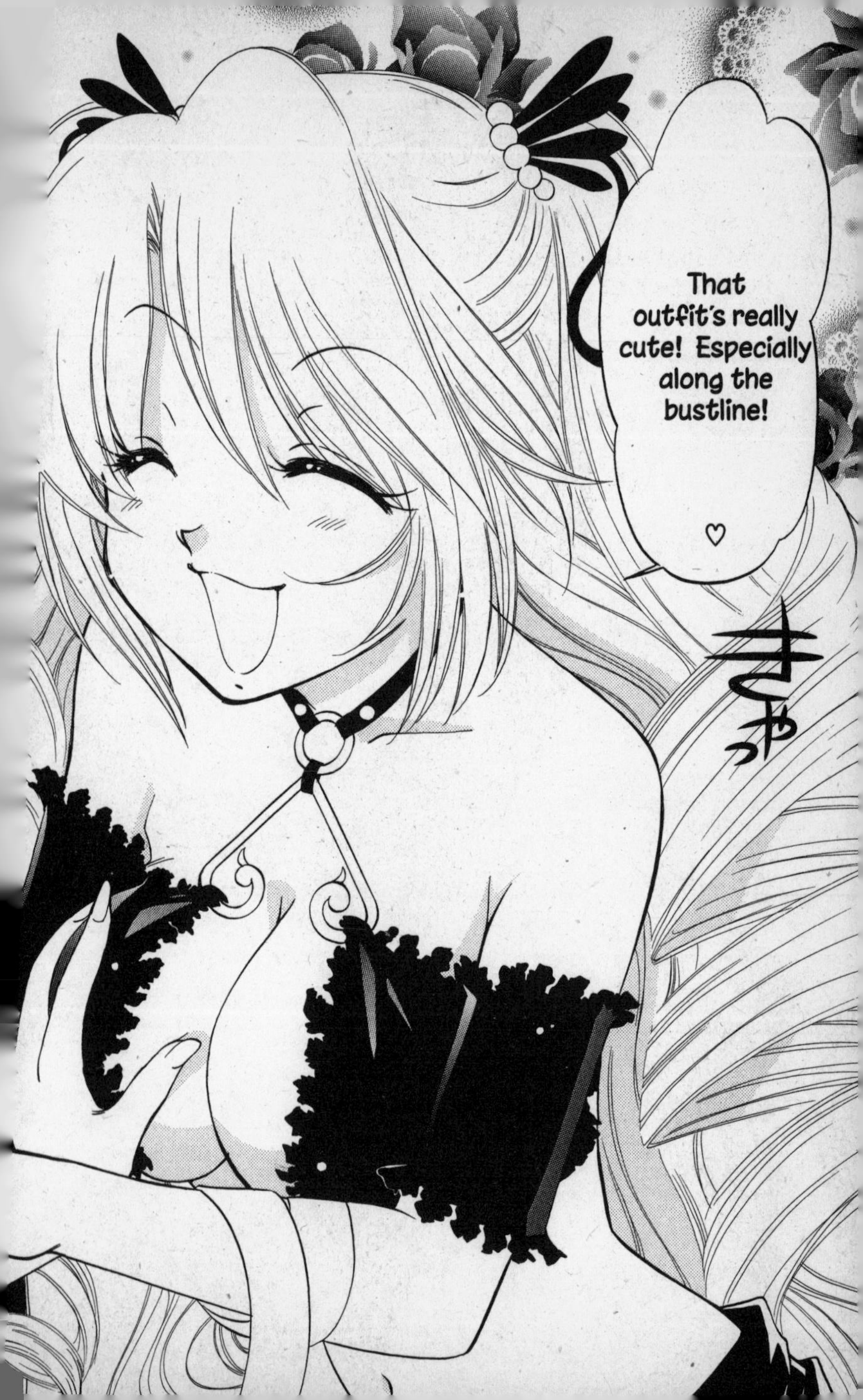
That outfit's really cute! Especially along the bustline! ♡
きゃっ

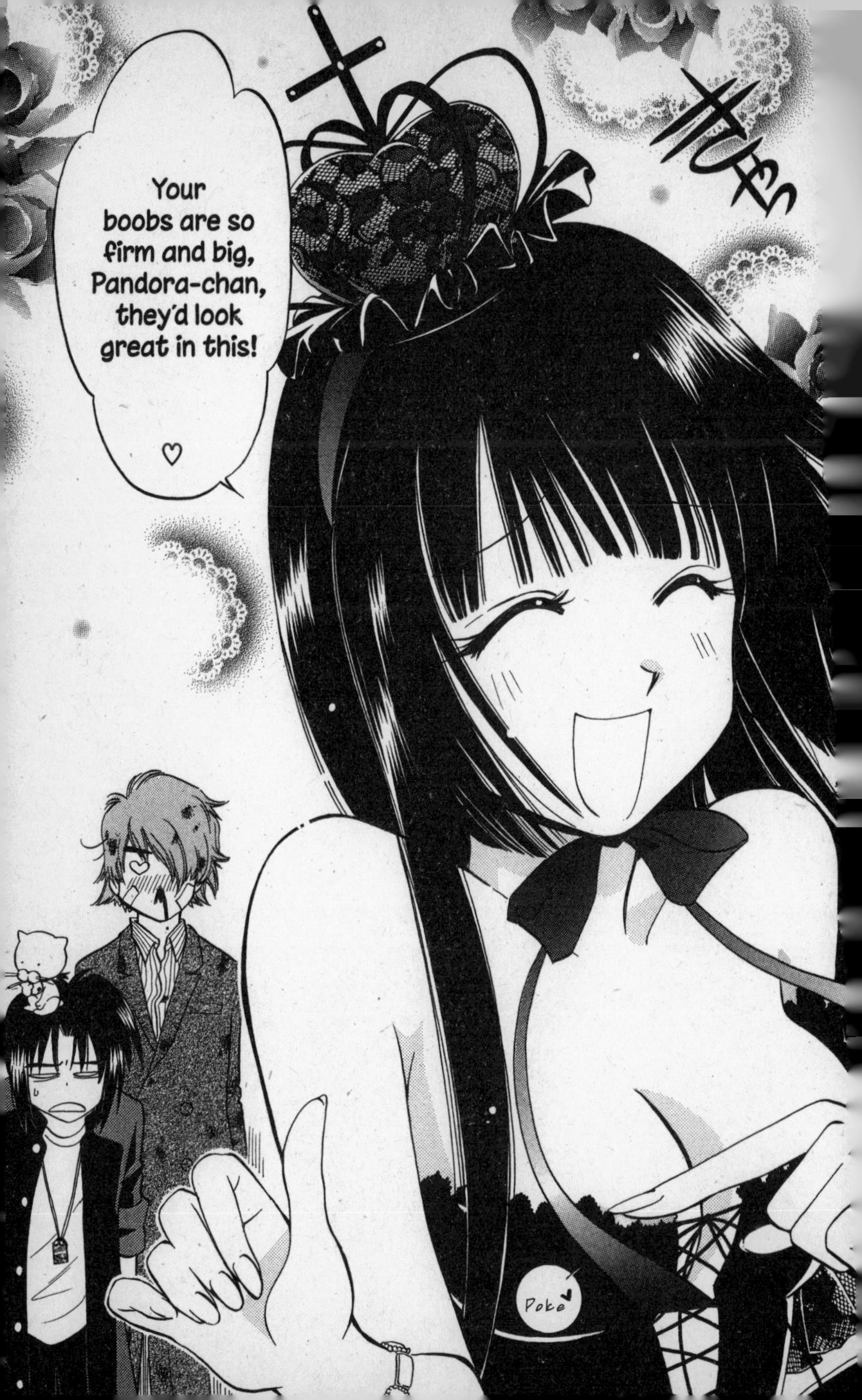
Your boobs are so firm and big, Pandora-chan, they'd look great in this! ♡
Poke♥

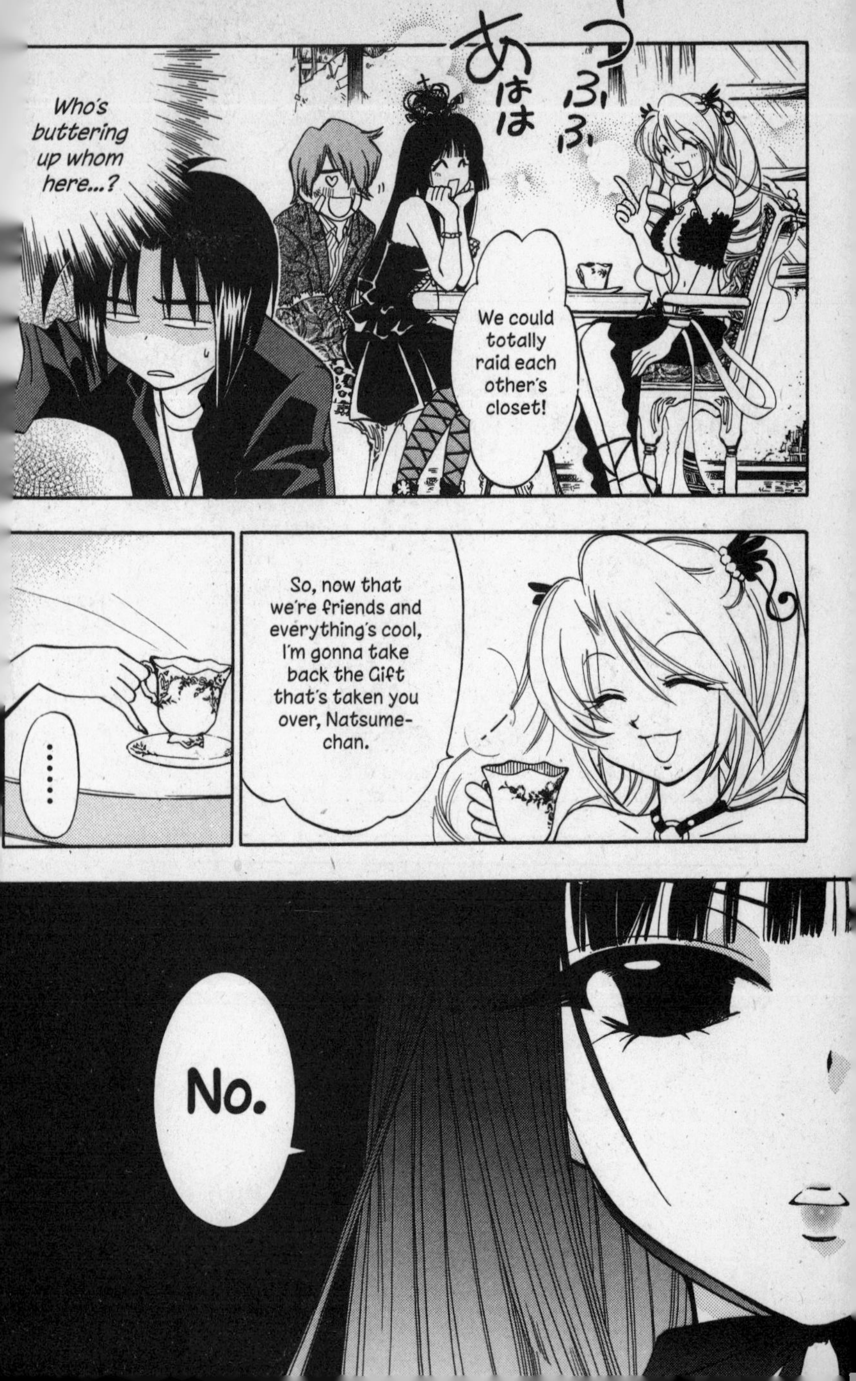
うふふ
あはは
We could totally raid each other's closet!
Who's buttering up whom here...?
So, now that we're friends and everything's cool, I'm gonna take back the Gift that's taken you over, Natsume-chan.
......
No.

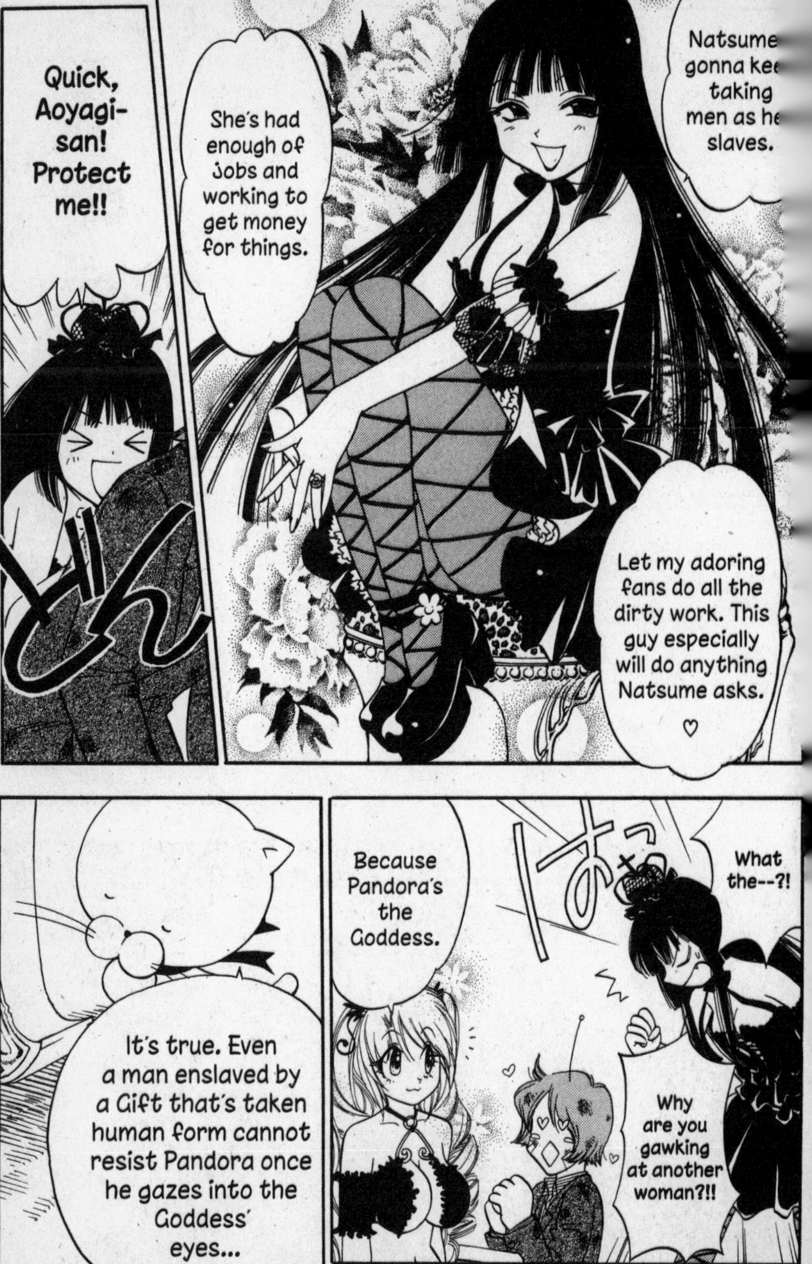

Natsume gonna kee taking men as he slaves.
She's had enough of jobs and working to get money for things.
Let my adoring fans do all the dirty work. This guy especially will do anything Natsume asks. ♡
Quick, Aoyagi-san! Protect me!!
What the--?!
Because Pandora's the Goddess.
Why are you gawking at another woman?!!
It's true. Even a man enslaved by a Gift that's taken human form cannot resist Pandora once he gazes into the Goddess' eyes...

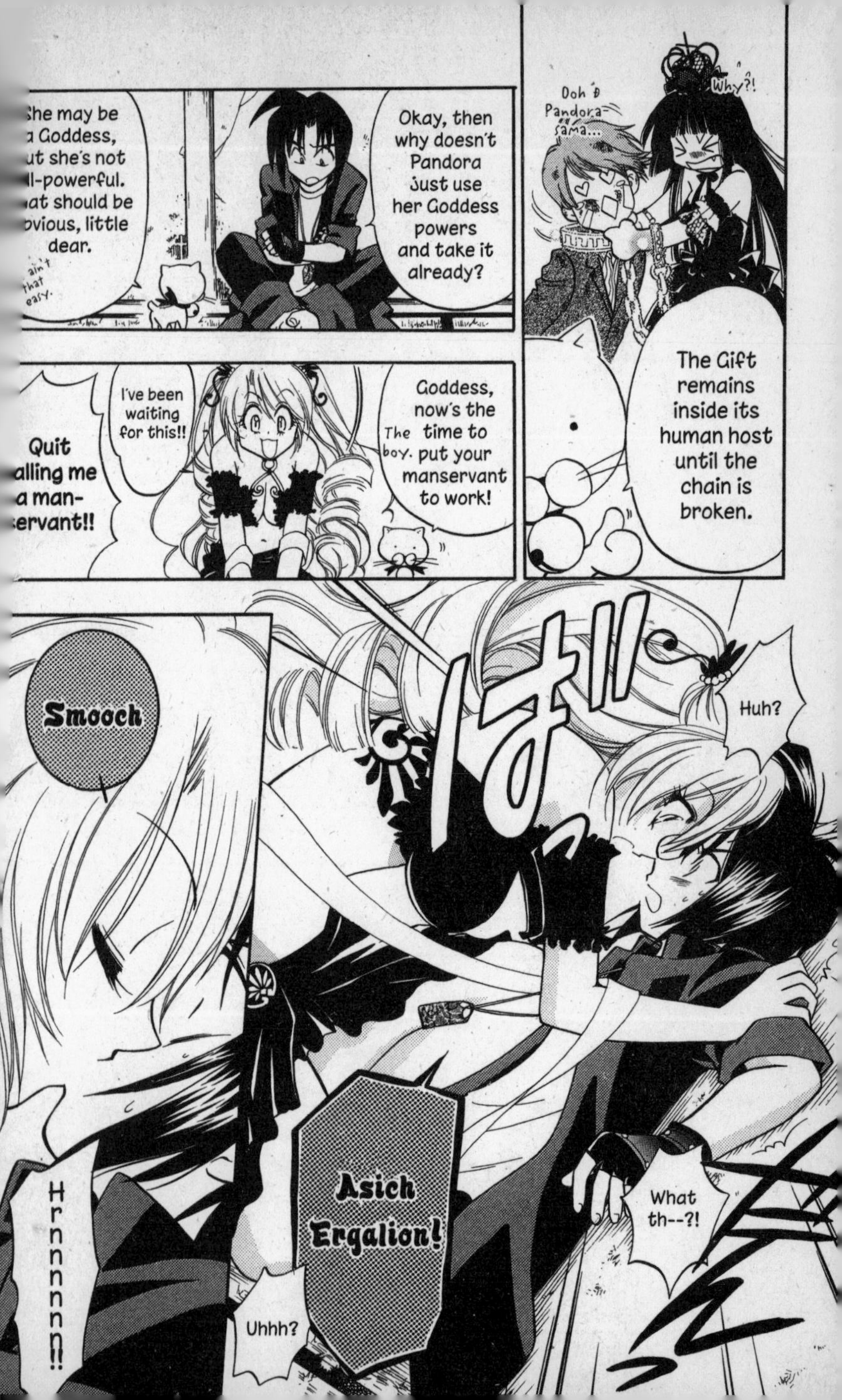

Doh ♪ Pandora-sama...
Why?!
The Gift remains inside its human host until the chain is broken.
Okay, then why doesn't Pandora just use her Goddess powers and take it already?
he may be a Goddess, ut she's not ll-powerful. at should be bvious, little dear.
ain't that easy.
Goddess, now's the time to put your manservant to work!
The boy.
I've been waiting for this!!
Quit alling me a man-ervant!!
Huh?
はっ
Smooch
What th--?!
Asich Ergalion!
Uhhh?
Hrnnnnnn!!

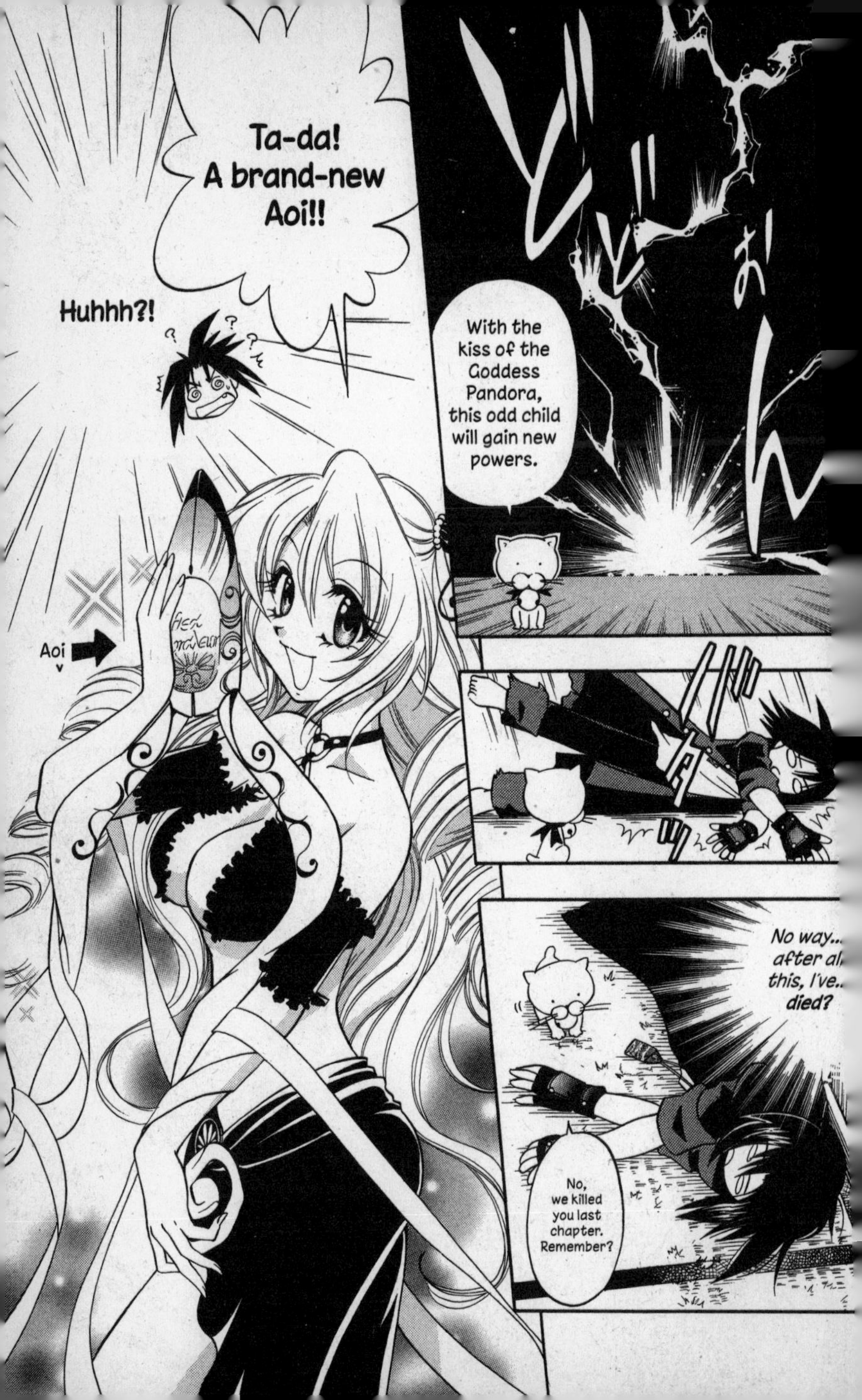
With the kiss of the Goddess Pandora, this odd child will gain new powers.
No way... after al this, I've... died?
No, we killed you last chapter. Remember?
Ta-da! A brand-new Aoi!!
Huhhh?!
Aoi

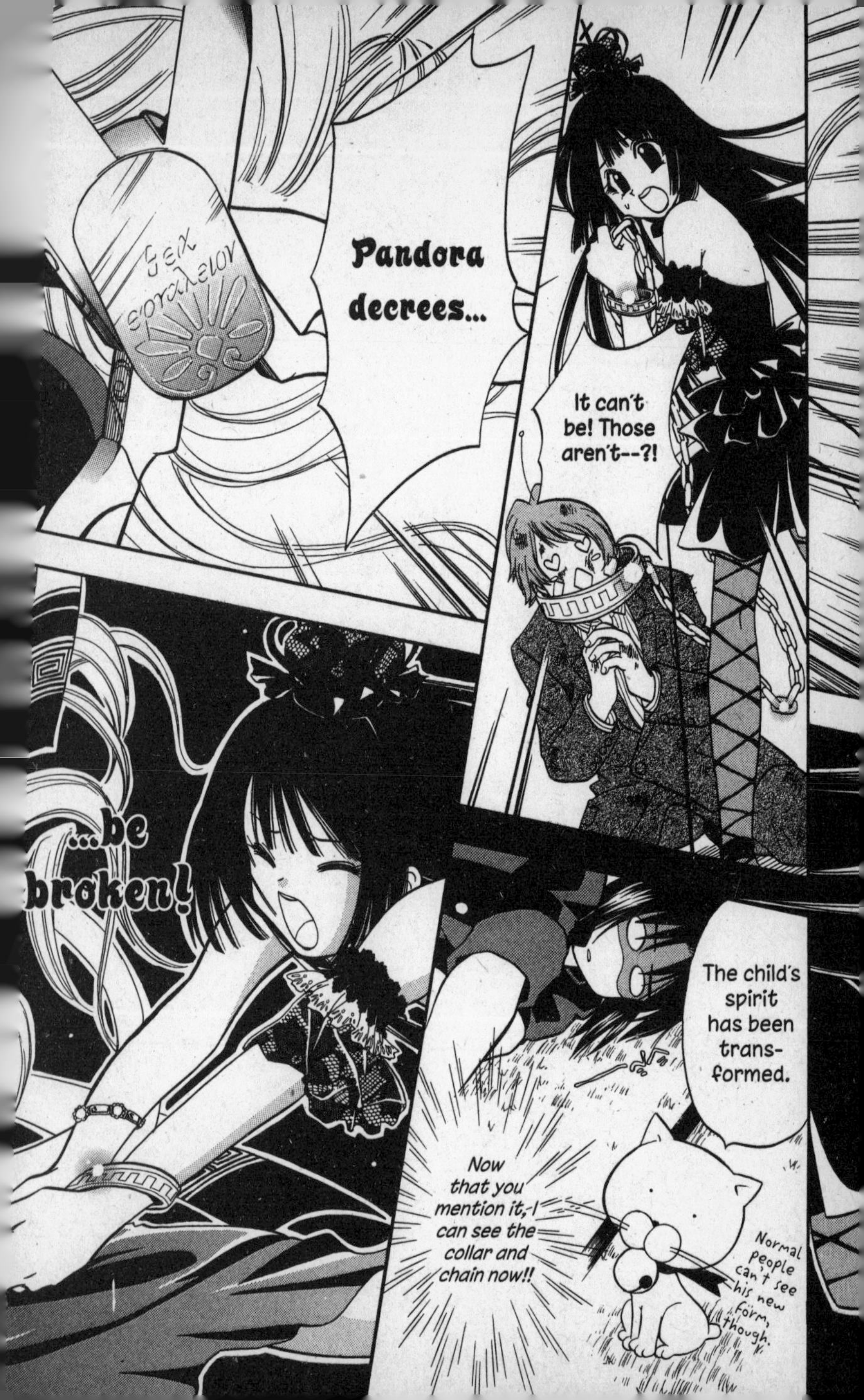
Pandora decrees...
...be broken!
It can't be! Those aren't--?!
The child's spirit has been transformed.
Now that you mention it, I can see the collar and chain now!!
Normal people can't see his new form, though.

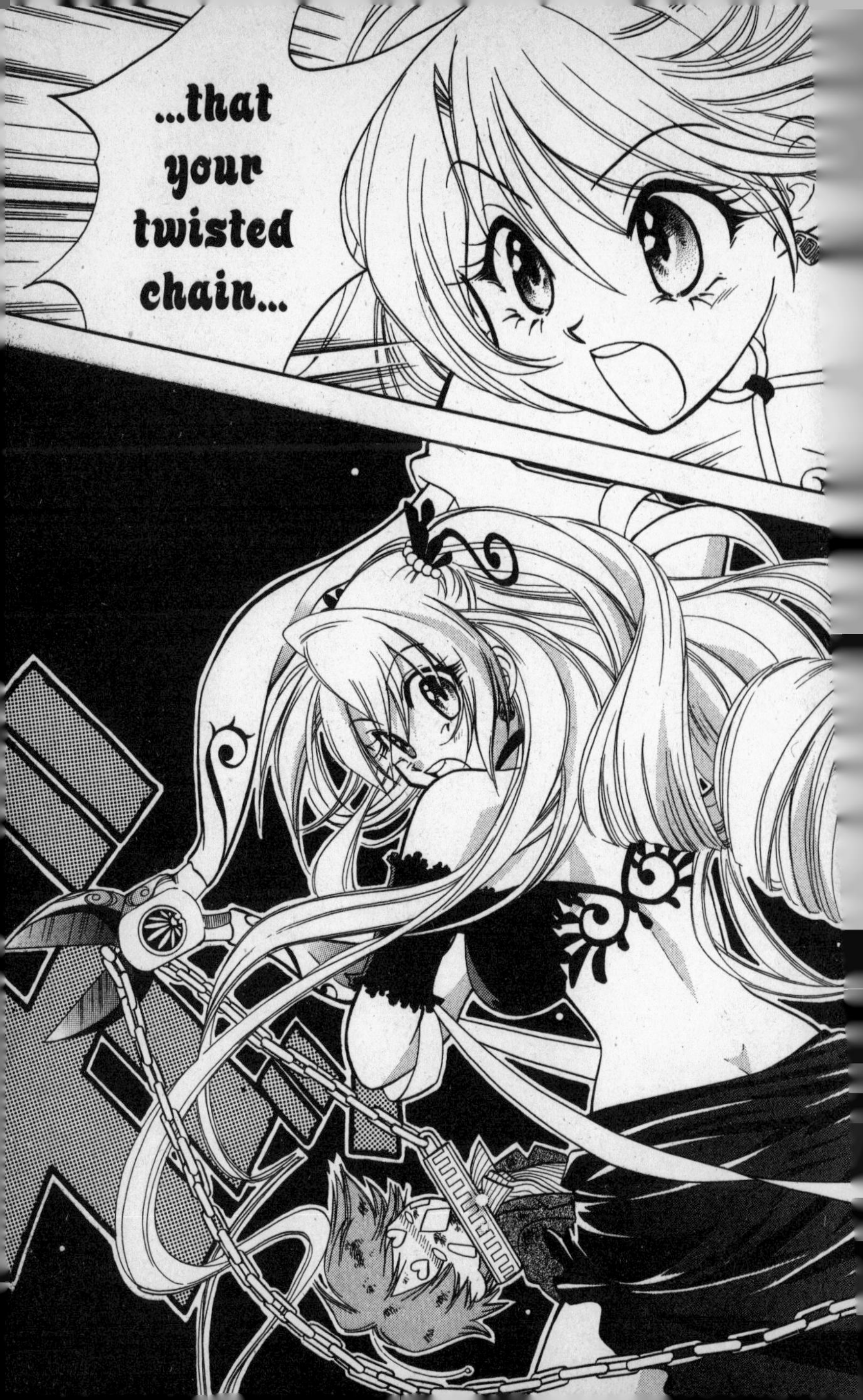
...that your twisted chain...

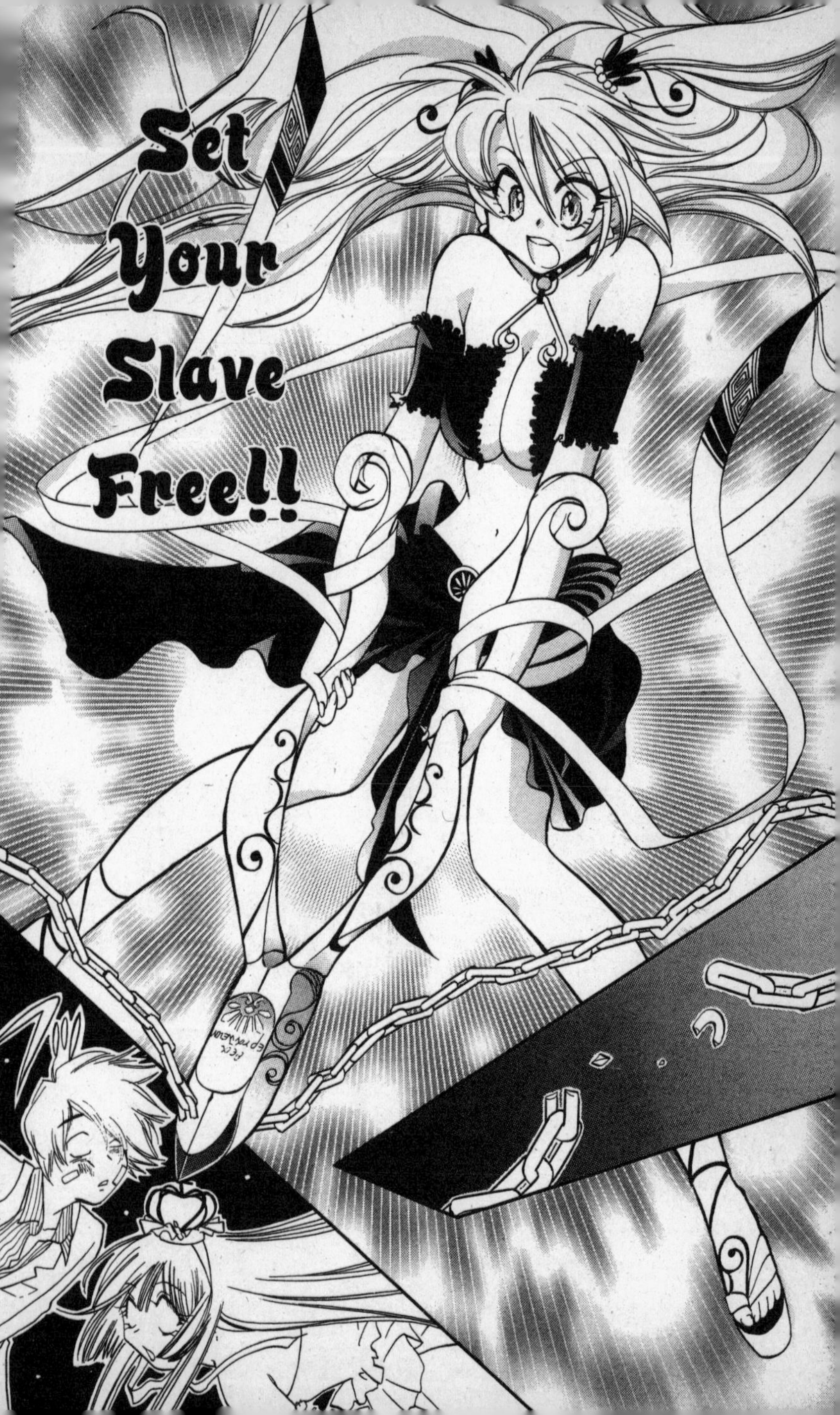
Set Your Slave Free!!

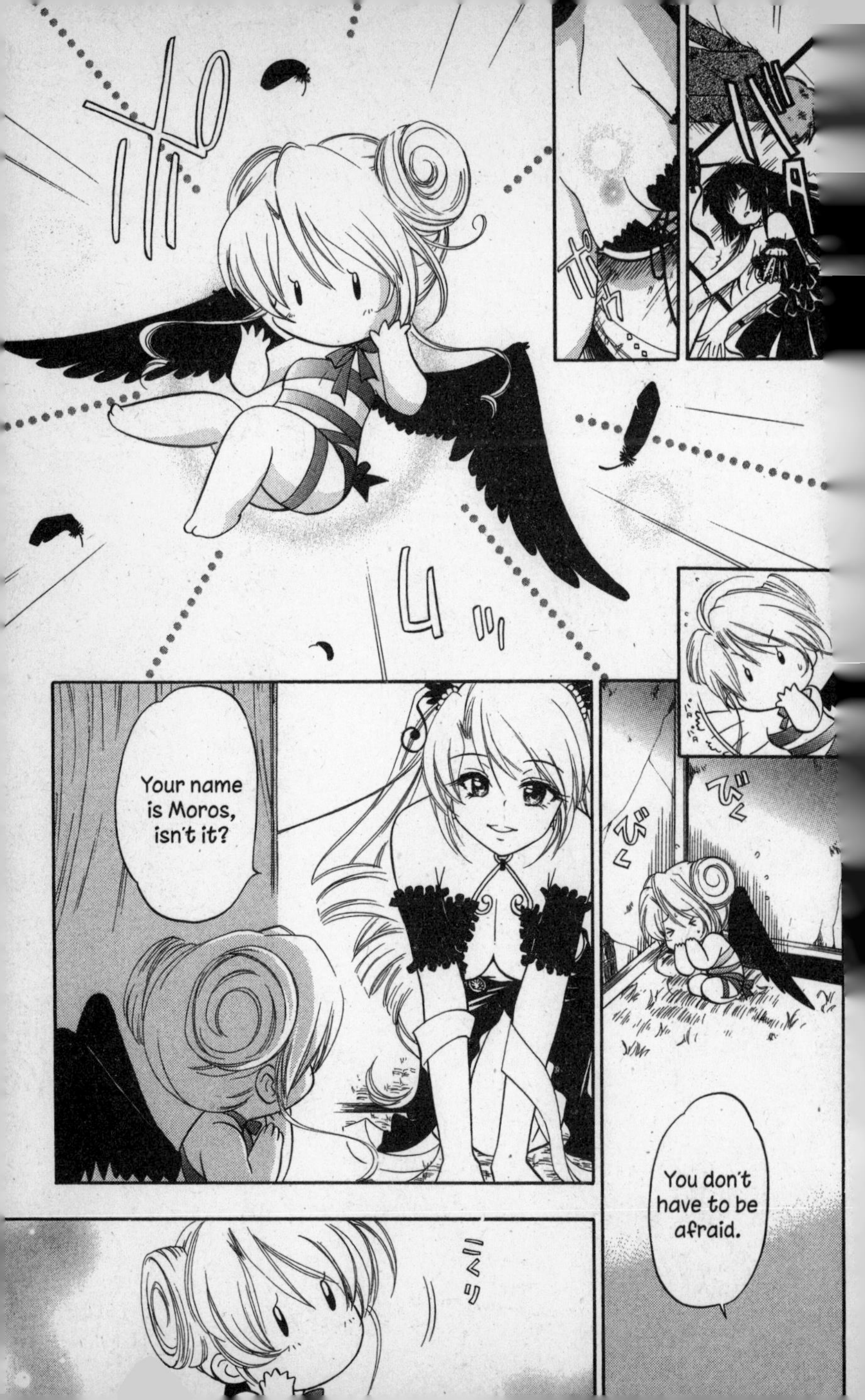
You don't have to be afraid.
Your name is Moros, isn't it?

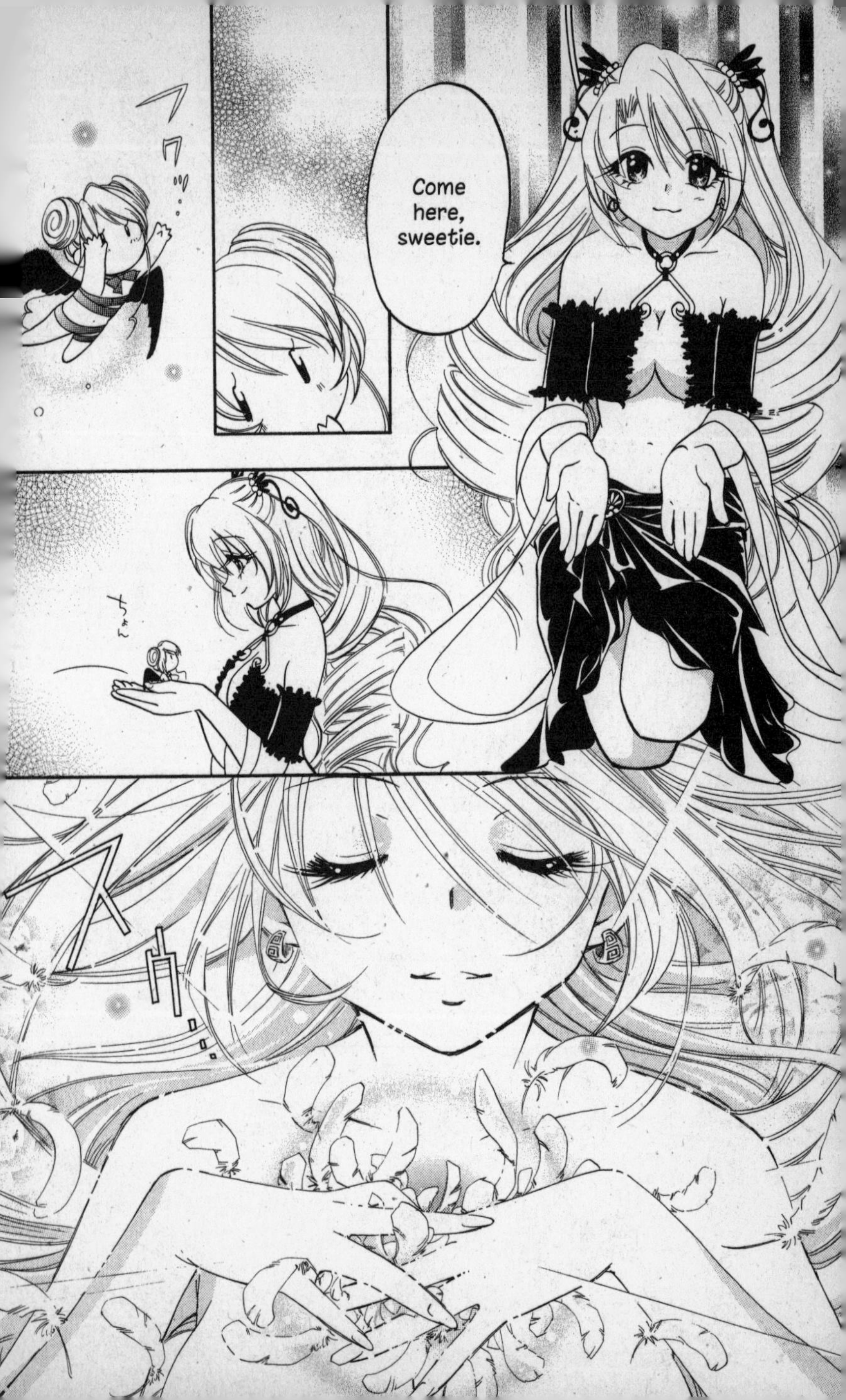
Come here, sweetie.
フワッ...
ちょん

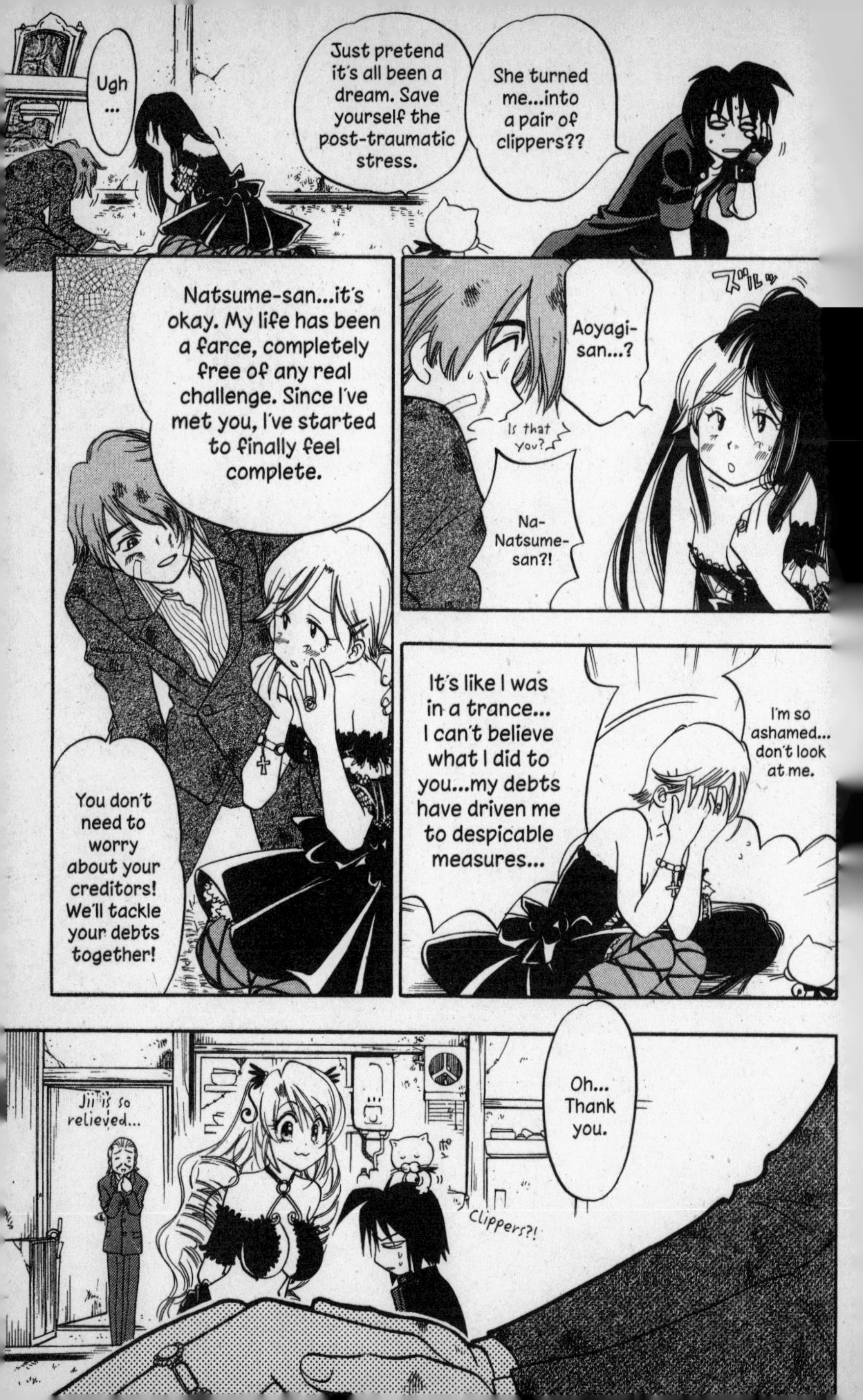
She turned me...into a pair of clippers??
Just pretend it's all been a dream. Save yourself the post-traumatic stress.
Ugh ...
ズルッ
Aoyagi-san...?
Is that you?
Na-Natsume-san?!
I'm so ashamed... don't look at me.
It's like I was in a trance... I can't believe what I did to you...my debts have driven me to despicable measures...
Natsume-san...it's okay. My life has been a farce, completely free of any real challenge. Since I've met you, I've started to finally feel complete.
You don't need to worry about your creditors! We'll tackle your debts together!
Oh... Thank you.
Clippers?!
Jii is so relieved...

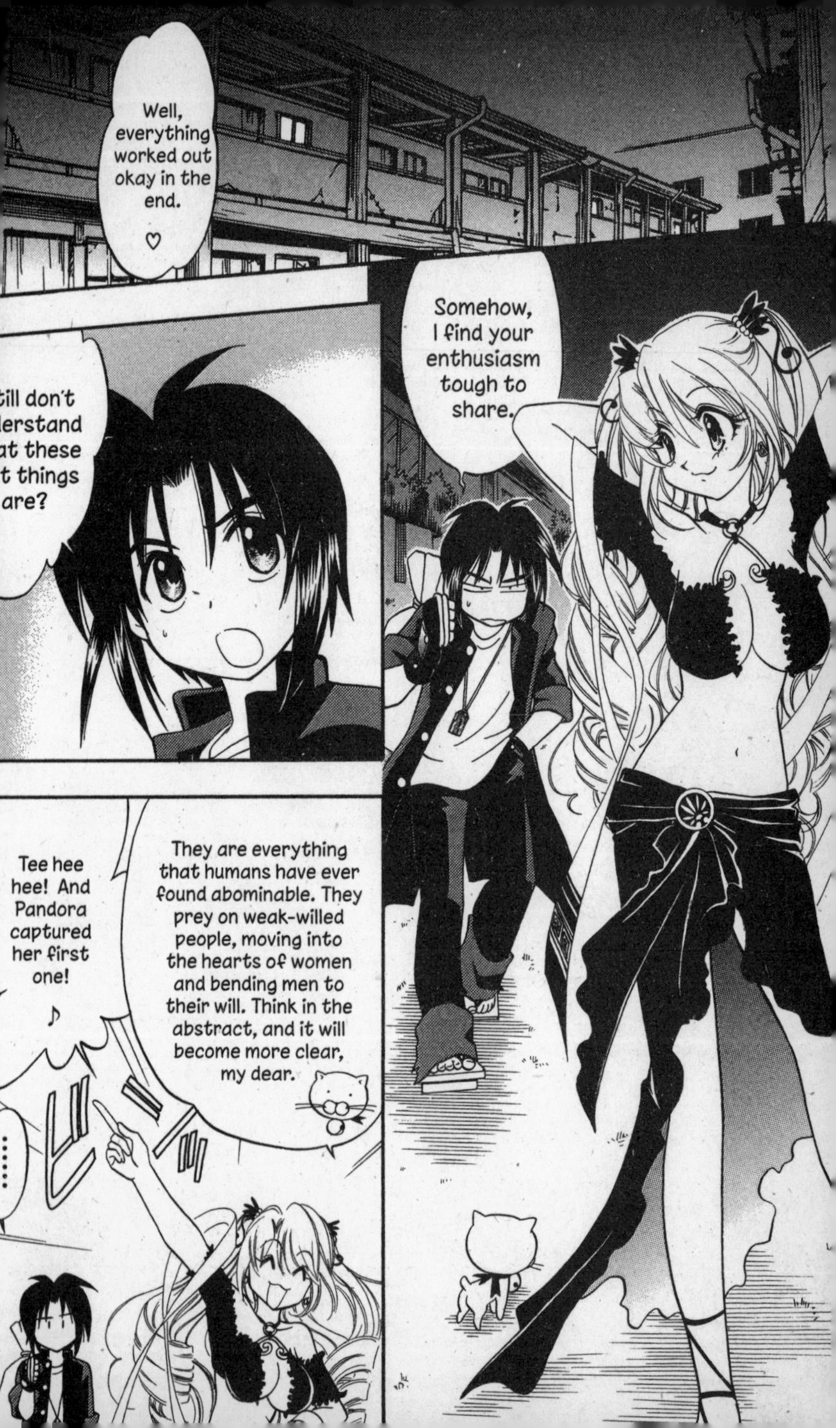

Well, everything worked out okay in the end. ♡
Somehow, I find your enthusiasm tough to share.
till don't derstand at these ft things are?
They are everything that humans have ever found abominable. They prey on weak-willed people, moving into the hearts of women and bending men to their will. Think in the abstract, and it will become more clear, my dear.
Tee hee hee! And Pandora captured her first one! ♪
......

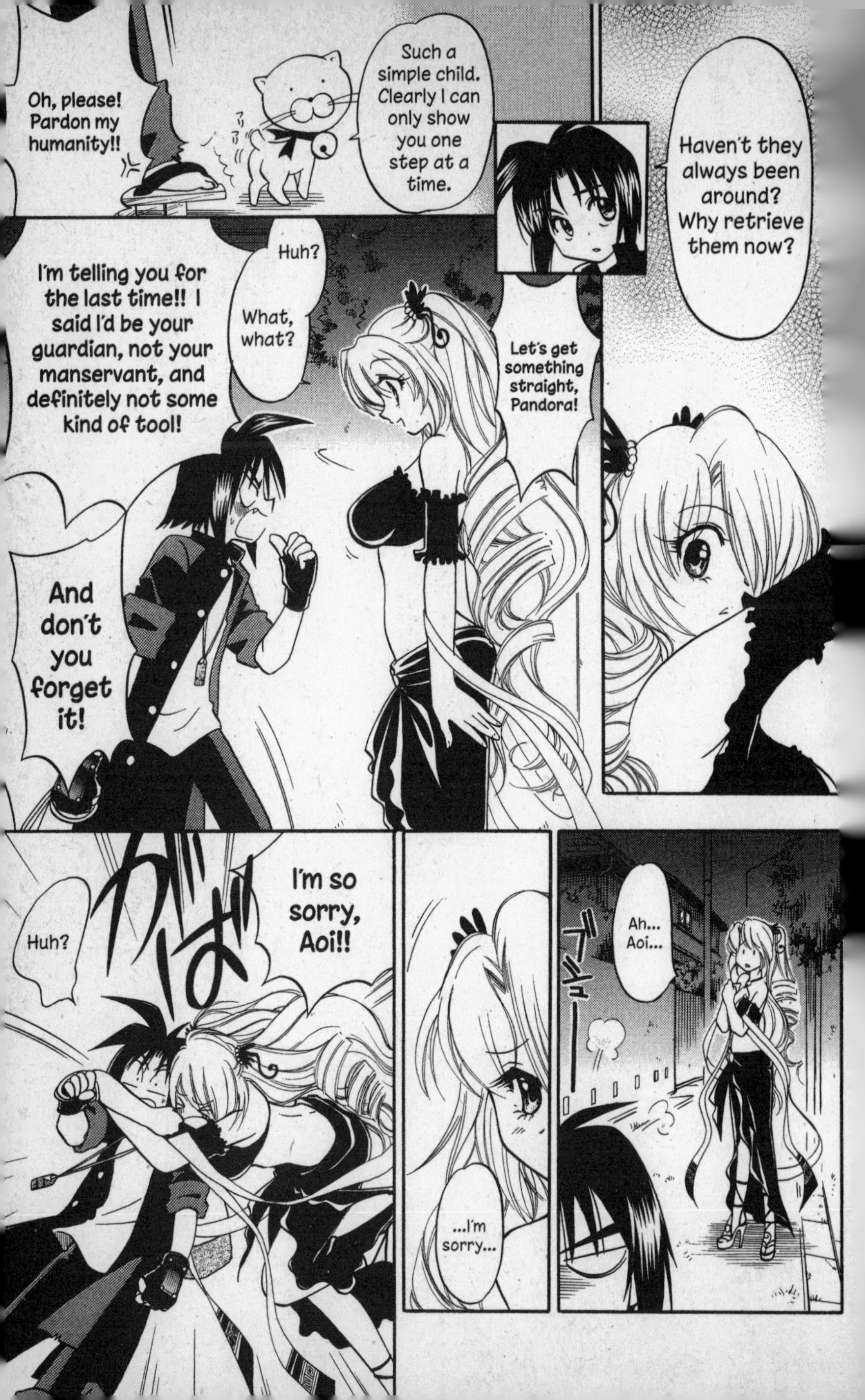
Haven't they always been around? Why retrieve them now?
Such a simple child. Clearly I can only show you one step at a time.
Oh, please! Pardon my humanity!!
Let's get something straight, Pandora!
Huh?
What, what?
I'm telling you for the last time!! I said I'd be your guardian, not your manservant, and definitely not some kind of tool!
And don't you forget it!
Ah... Aoi...
...I'm sorry...
I'm so sorry, Aoi!!
Huh?

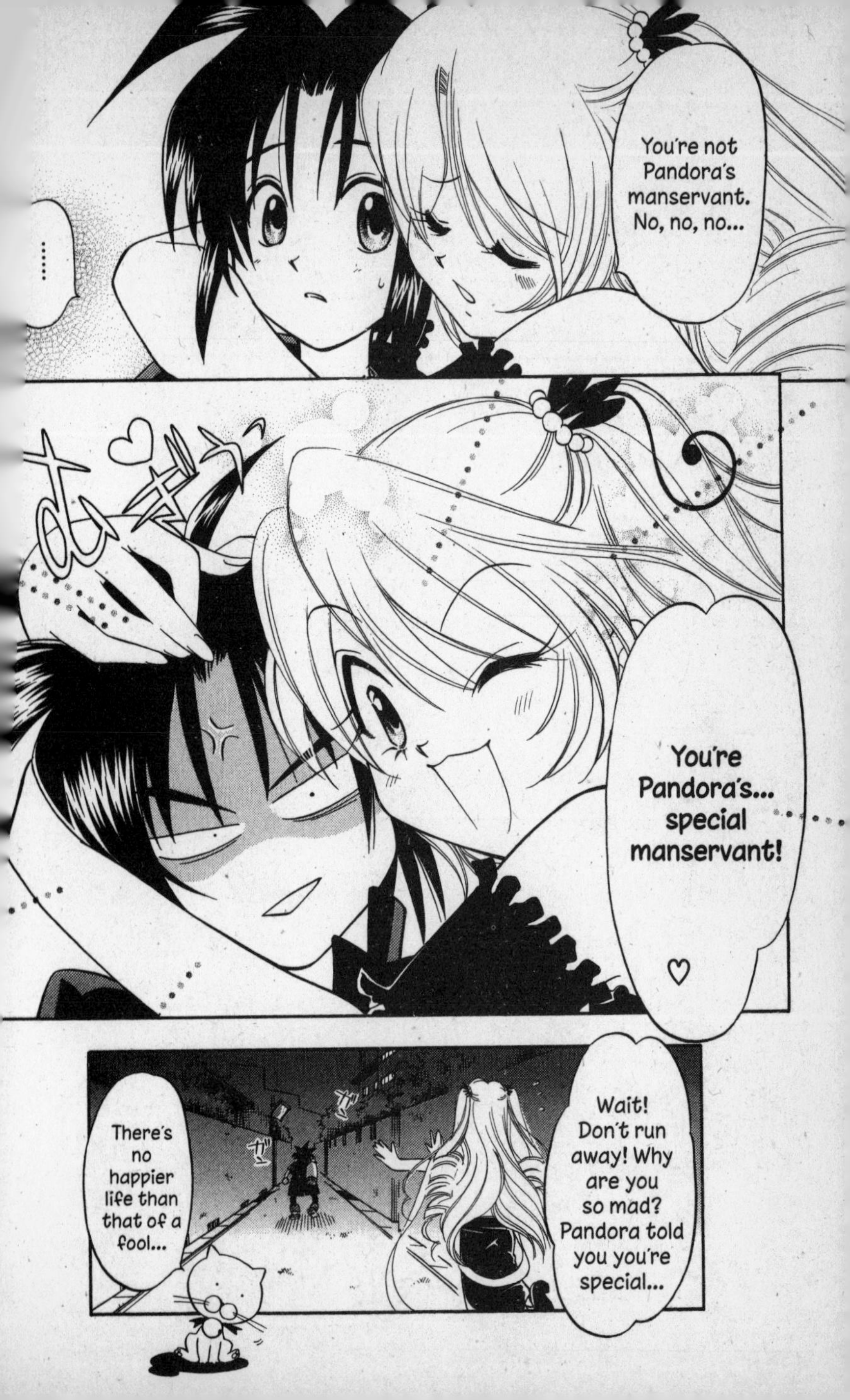
You're not Pandora's manservant. No, no, no...
......
You're Pandora's... special manservant! ♡
Wait! Don't run away! Why are you so mad? Pandora told you you're special...
There's no happier life than that of a fool...

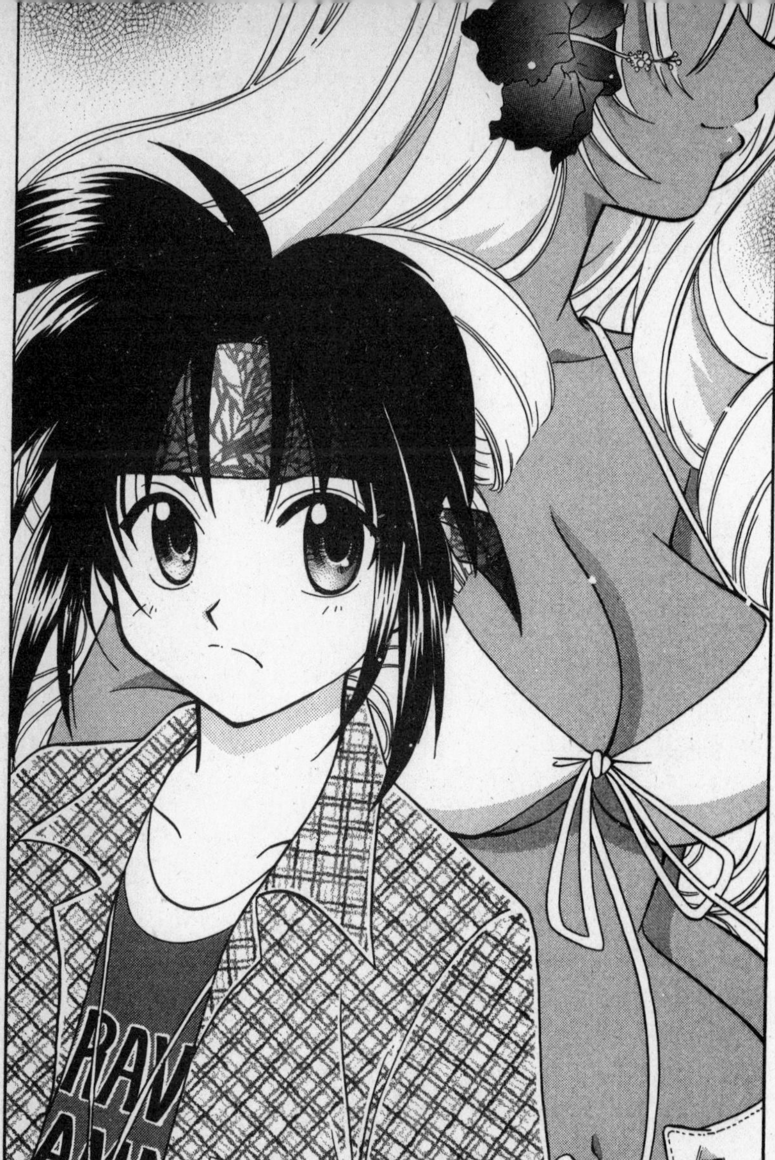

Chapter 4: An Unusual Slave

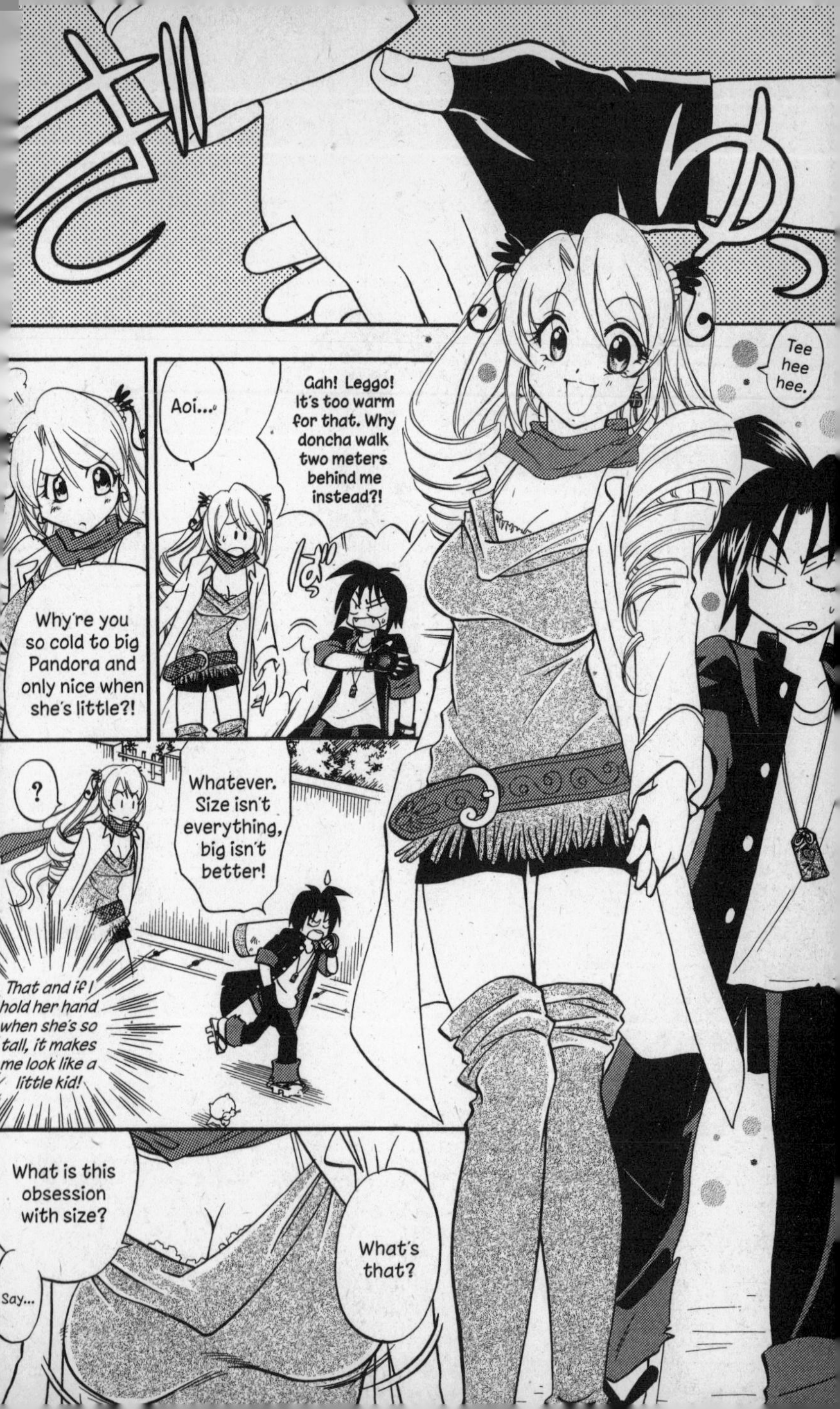
Tee hee hee.
Gah! Leggo! It's too warm for that. Why doncha walk two meters behind me instead?!
Aoi...
Why're you so cold to big Pandora and only nice when she's little?!
Whatever. Size isn't everything, big isn't better!
?
That and if I hold her hand when she's so tall, it makes me look like a little kid!
What is this obsession with size?
Say...
What's that?

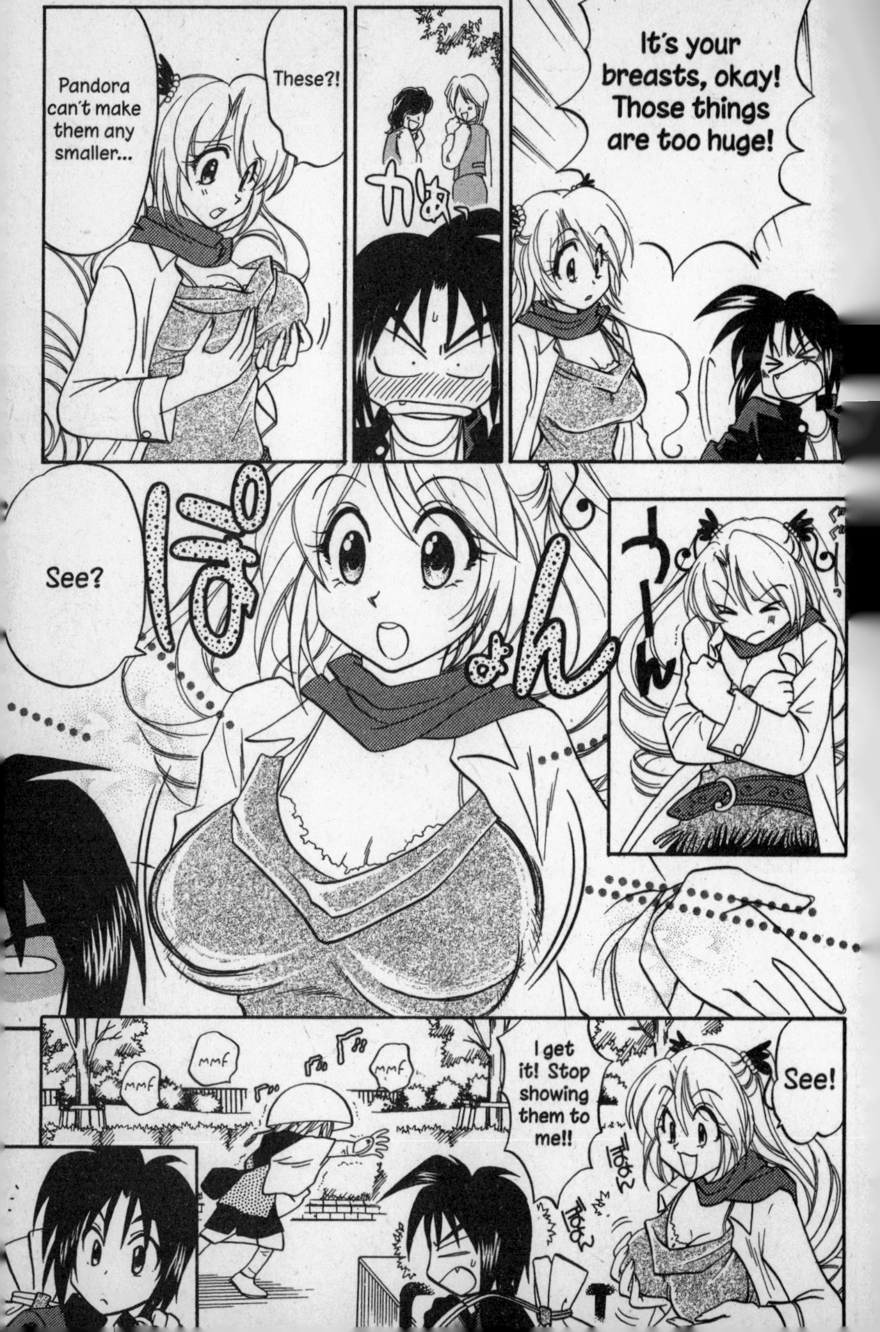
It's your breasts, okay! Those things are too huge!
These?!
Pandora can't make them any smaller...
See?
See!
I get it! Stop showing them to me!!
mmf
mmf
mmf

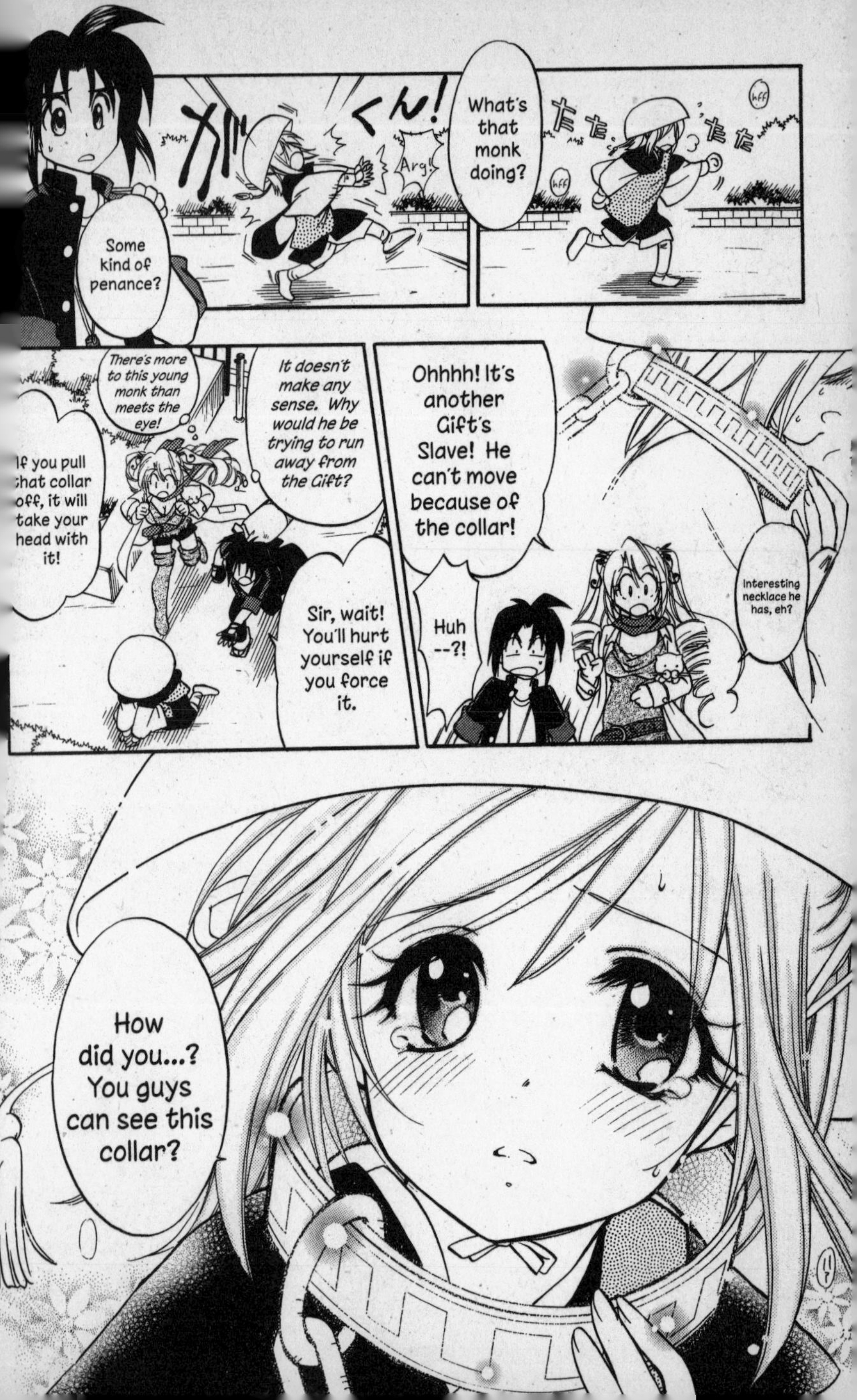

たた
hff
たた
hff
What's that monk doing?
くん!
Arg!
Some kind of penance?
Interesting necklace he has, eh?
Ohhhh! It's another Gift's Slave! He can't move because of the collar!
Huh --?!
It doesn't make any sense. Why would he be trying to run away from the Gift?
There's more to this young monk than meets the eye!
Sir, wait! You'll hurt yourself if you force it.
If you pull that collar off, it will take your head with it!
How did you...? You guys can see this collar?

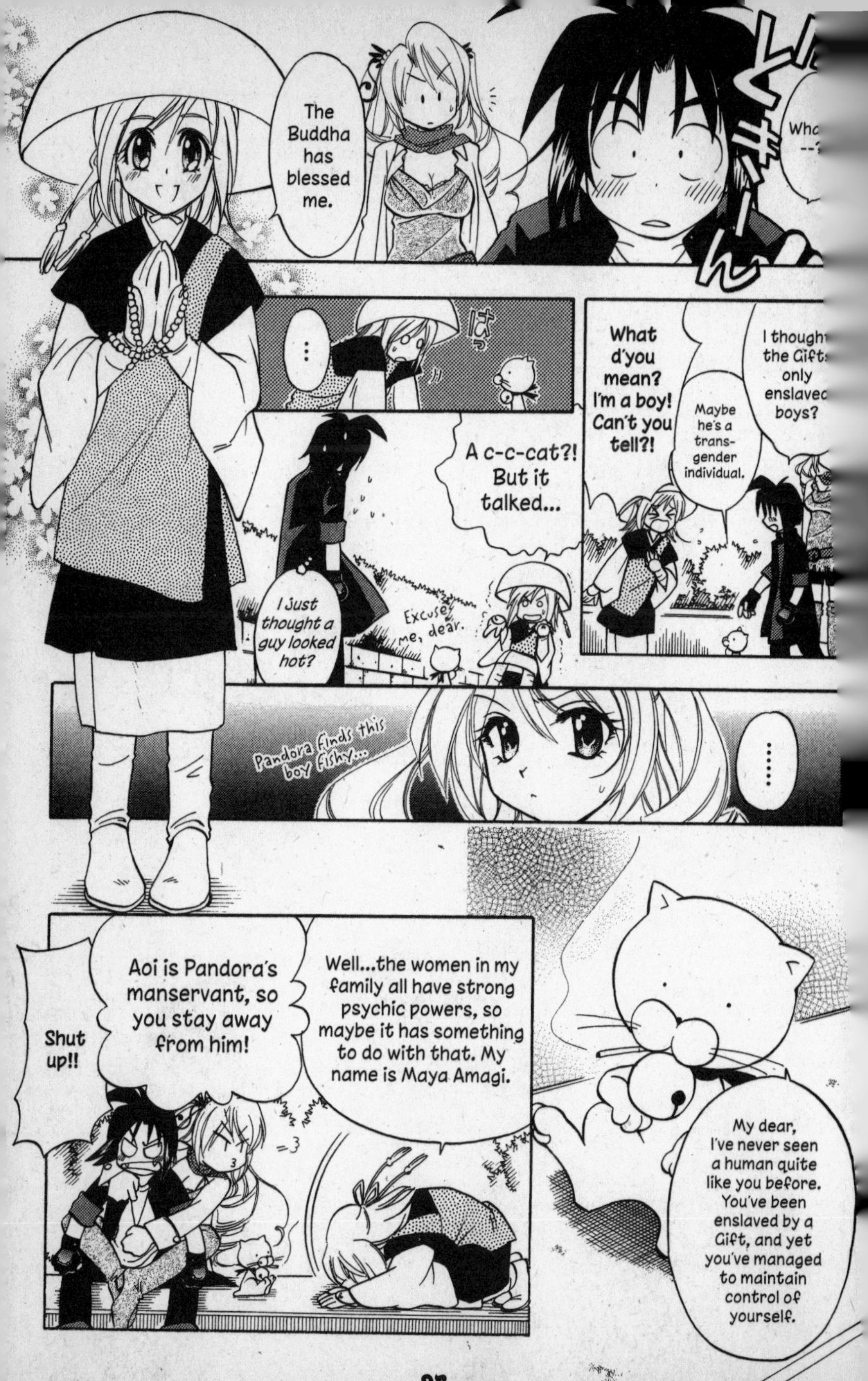

Wha --
The Buddha has blessed me.
I thought the Gifts only enslaved boys?
What d'you mean? I'm a boy! Can't you tell?!
Maybe he's a transgender individual.
...
はっ
A c-c-cat?! But it talked...
Excuse me, dear.
I just thought a guy looked hot?
......
Pandora finds this boy fishy...
My dear, I've never seen a human quite like you before. You've been enslaved by a Gift, and yet you've managed to maintain control of yourself.
Well...the women in my family all have strong psychic powers, so maybe it has something to do with that. My name is Maya Amagi.
Aoi is Pandora's manservant, so you stay away from him!
Shut up!!

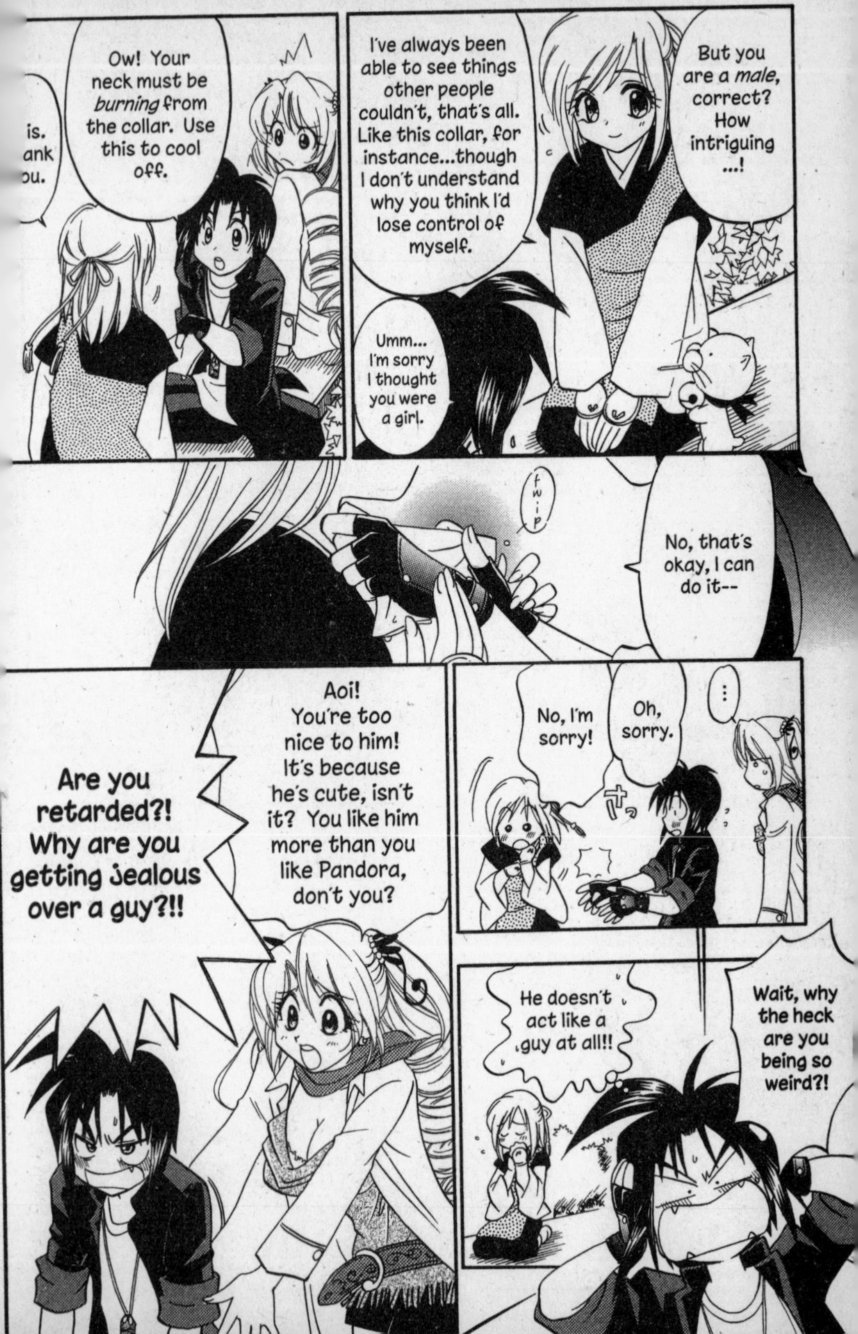

But you are a *male*, correct? How intriguing ...!
I've always been able to see things other people couldn't, that's all. Like this collar, for instance...though I don't understand why you think I'd lose control of myself.
Umm... I'm sorry I thought you were a girl.
Ow! Your neck must be *burning* from the collar. Use this to cool off.
is. ank ou.
fwip
No, that's okay, I can do it--
...
Oh, sorry.
No, I'm sorry!
Wait, why the heck are you being so weird?!
He doesn't act like a guy at all!!
Aoi! You're too nice to him! It's because he's cute, isn't it? You like him more than you like Pandora, don't you?
Are you retarded?! Why are you getting jealous over a guy?!!

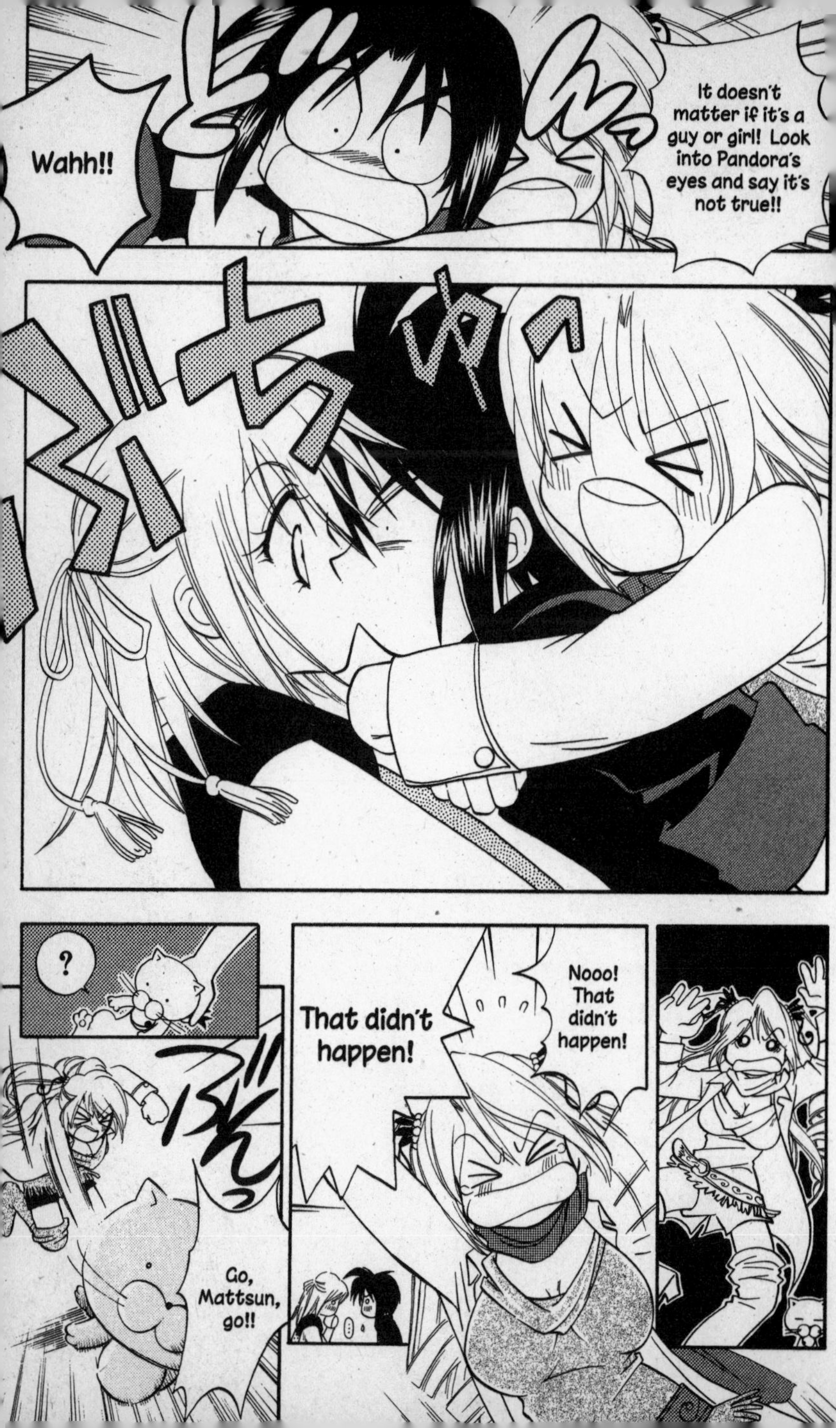

It doesn't matter if it's a guy or girl! Look into Pandora's eyes and say it's not true!!
Wahh!!
Nooo! That didn't happen!
That didn't happen!
?
Go, Mattsun, go!!

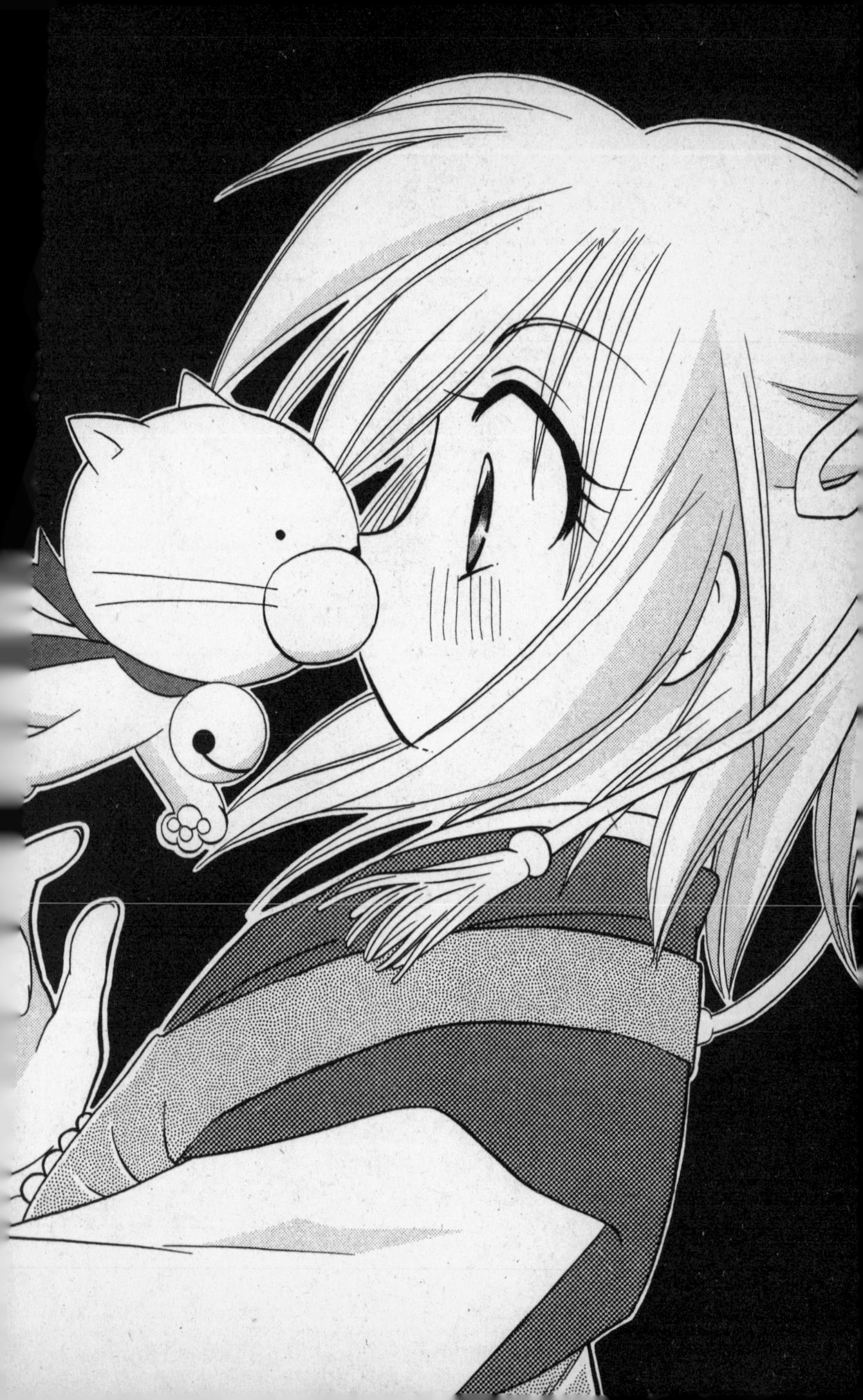

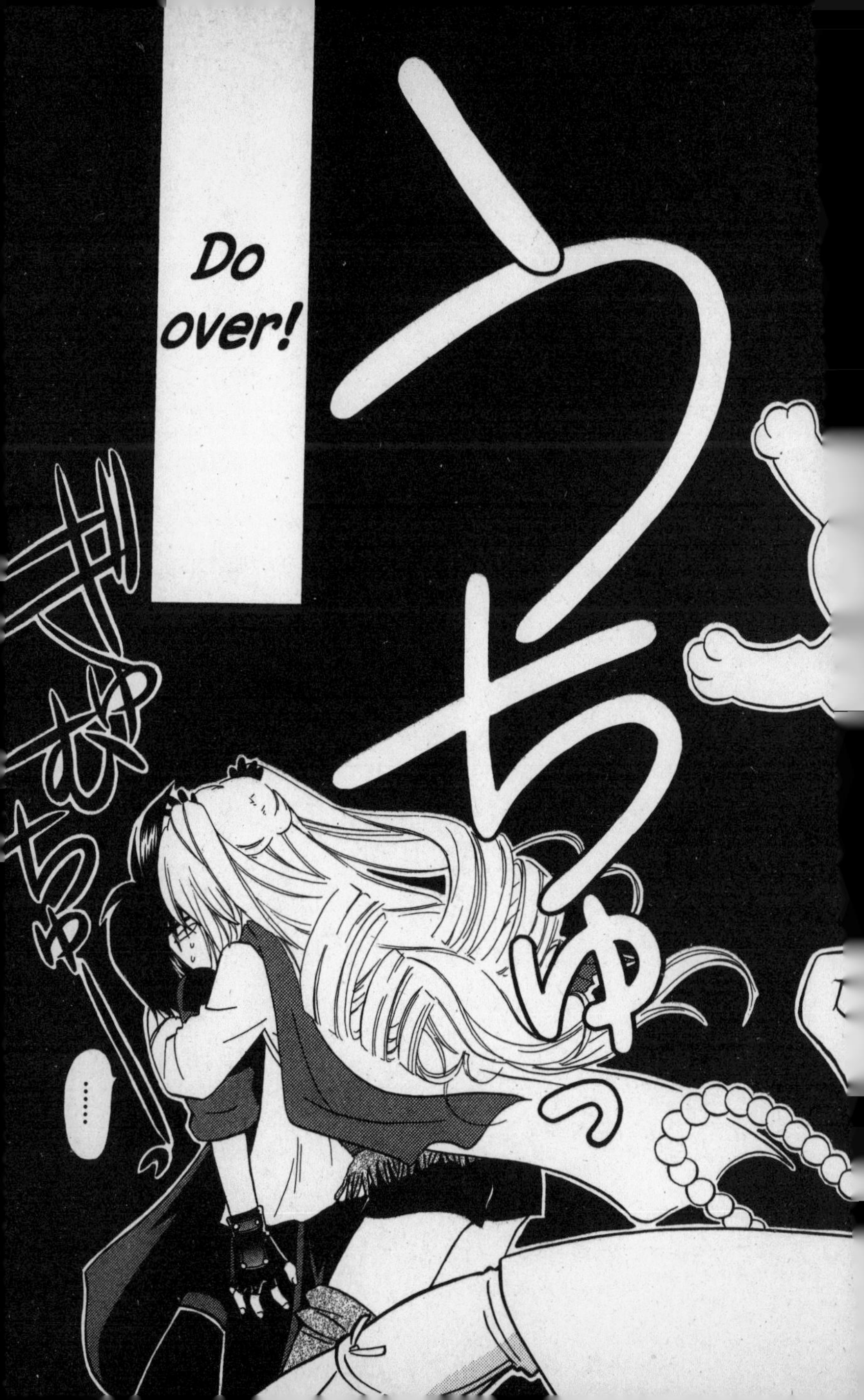
Do over!
……

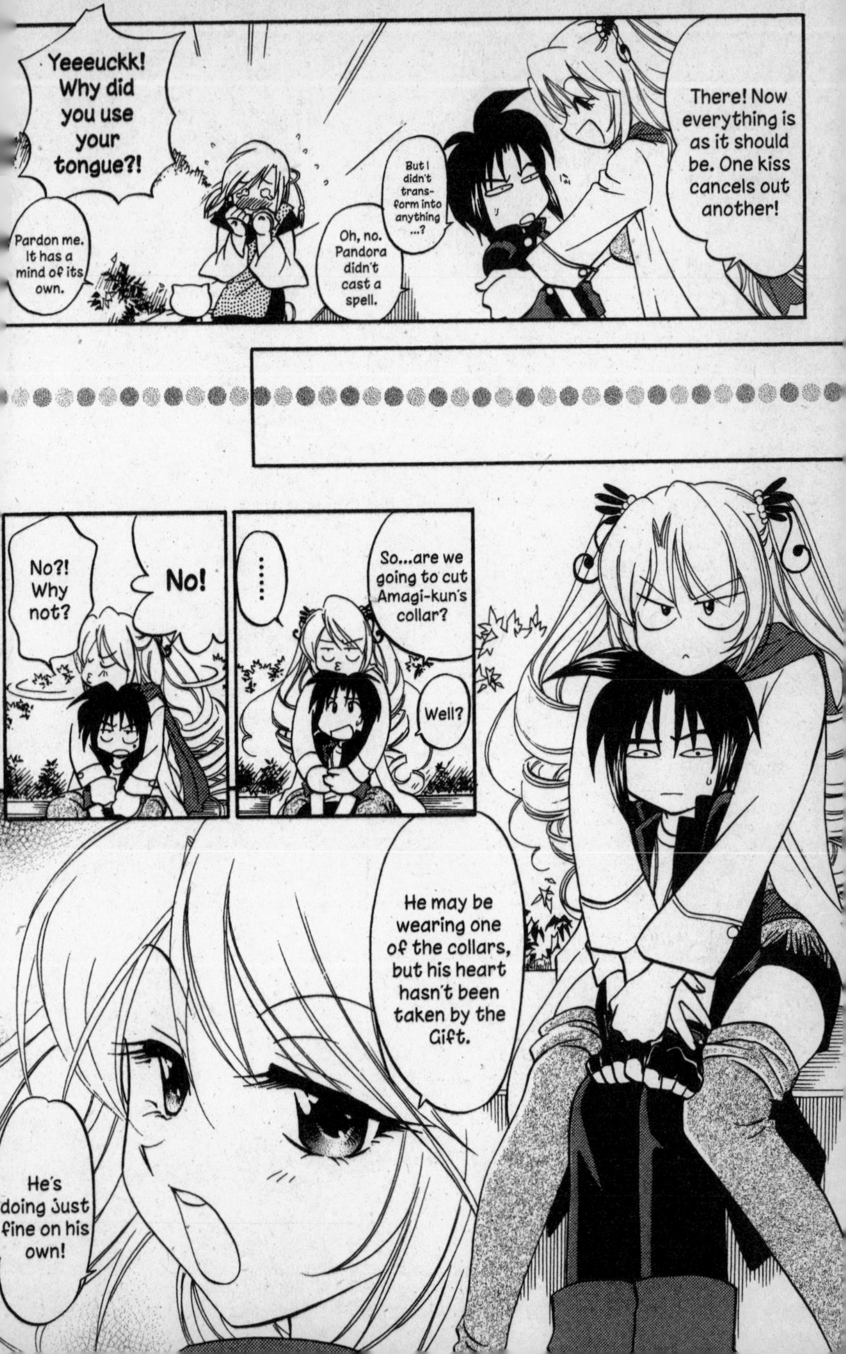
There! Now everything is as it should be. One kiss cancels out another!
But I didn't trans-form into anything ...?
Oh, no. Pandora didn't cast a spell.
Yeeeuckk! Why did you use your tongue?!
Pardon me. It has a mind of its own.
So...are we going to cut Amagi-kun's collar?
......
Well?
No!
No?! Why not?
He may be wearing one of the collars, but his heart hasn't been taken by the Gift.
He's doing just fine on his own!

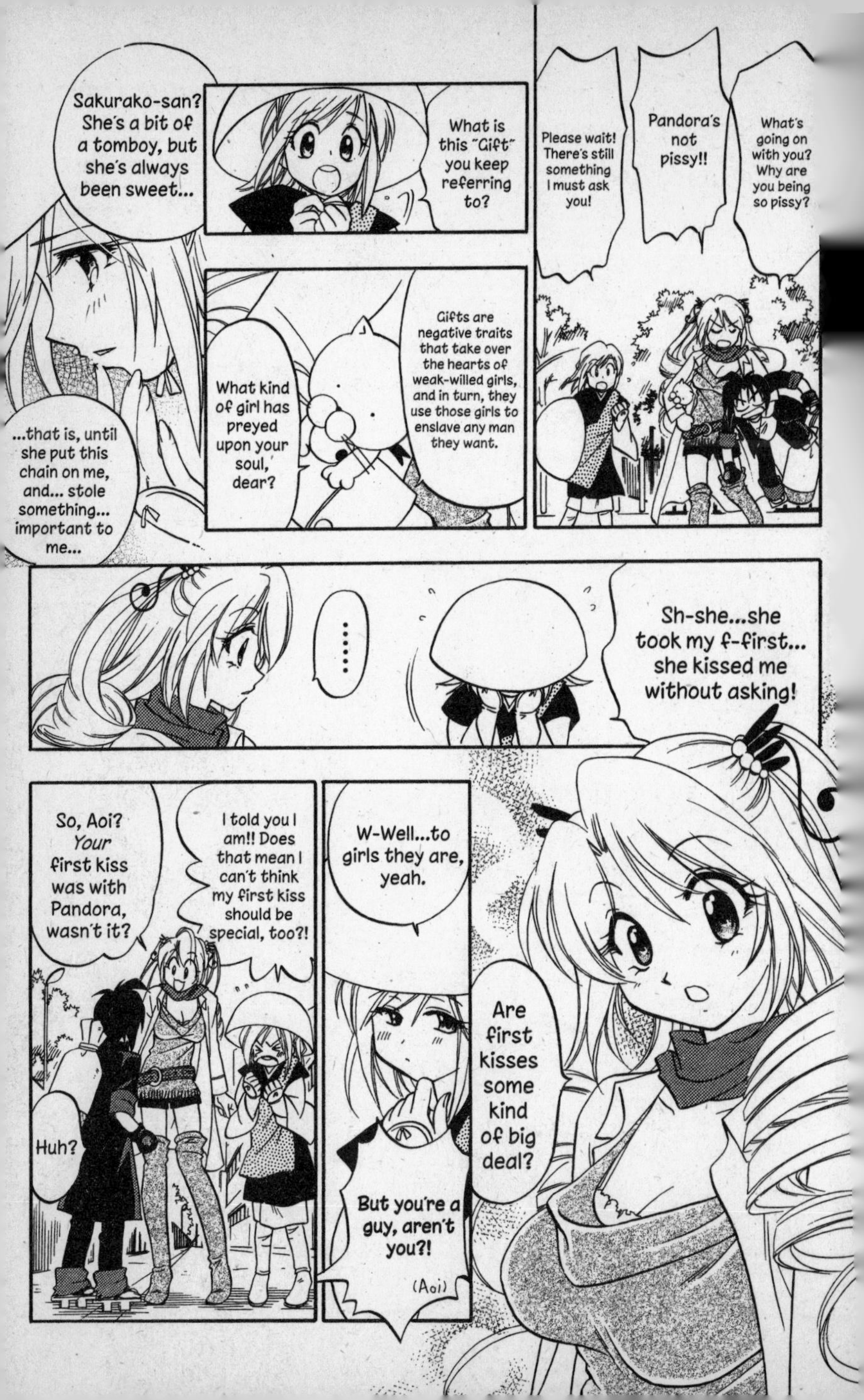
What's going on with you? Why are you being so pissy?
Pandora's not pissy!!
Please wait! There's still something I must ask you!
What is this "Gift" you keep referring to?
Gifts are negative traits that take over the hearts of weak-willed girls, and in turn, they use those girls to enslave any man they want.
What kind of girl has preyed upon your soul, dear?
Sakurako-san? She's a bit of a tomboy, but she's always been sweet...
...that is, until she put this chain on me, and... stole something... important to me...
Sh-she...she took my f-first... she kissed me without asking!
......
Are first kisses some kind of big deal?
W-Well...to girls they are, yeah.
But you're a guy, aren't you?!
(Aoi)
I told you I am!! Does that mean I can't think my first kiss should be special, too?!
So, Aoi? *Your* first kiss was with Pandora, wasn't it?
Huh?

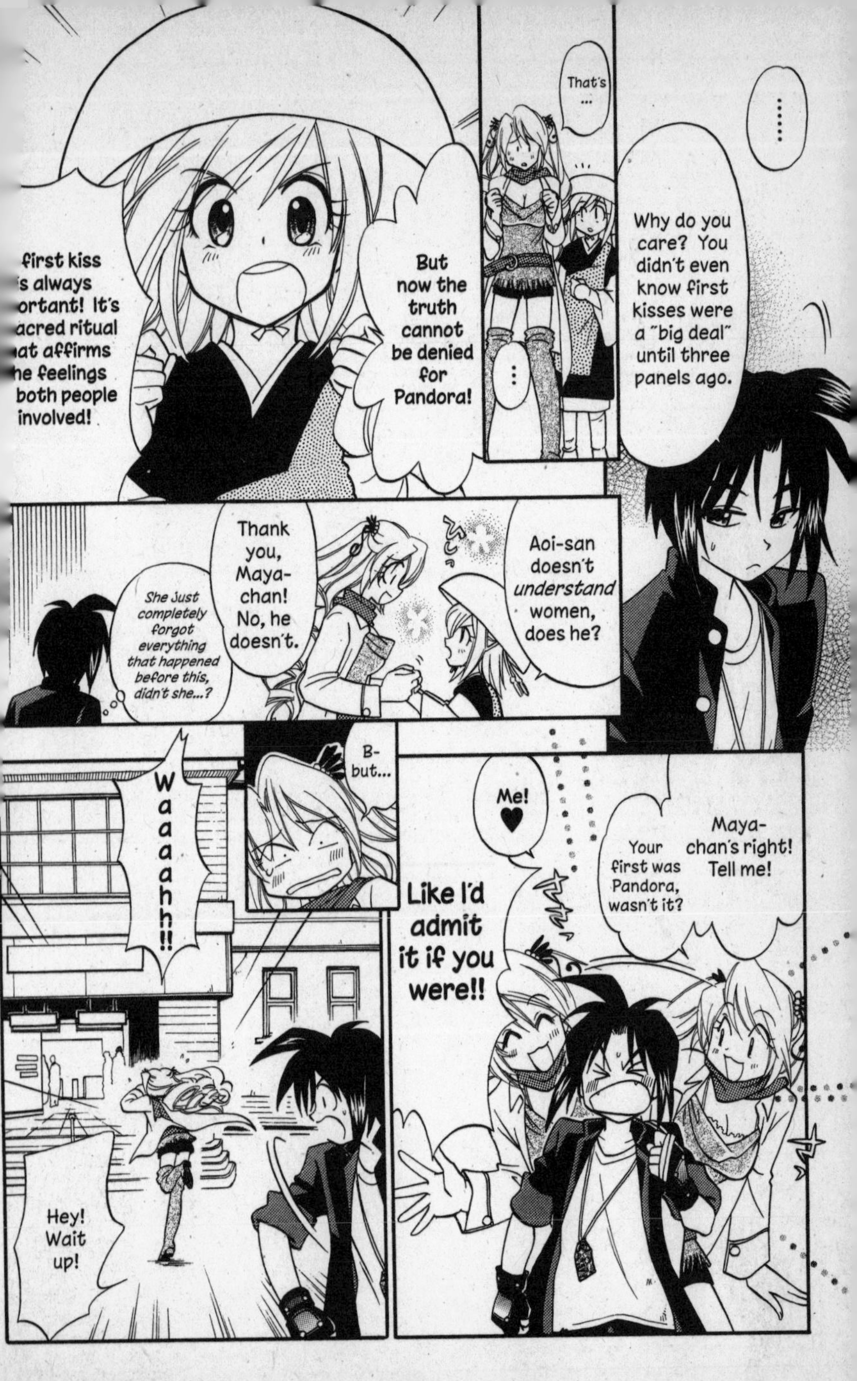
......
Why do you care? You didn't even know first kisses were a "big deal" until three panels ago.
That's ...
...
first kiss is always ortant! It's acred ritual at affirms he feelings both people involved!
But now the truth cannot be denied for Pandora!
Aoi-san doesn't understand women, does he?
Thank you, Maya-chan! No, he doesn't.
She just completely forgot everything that happened before this, didn't she...?
Maya-chan's right! Tell me!
Your first was Pandora, wasn't it?
Me! ♥
Like I'd admit it if you were!!
B-but...
Waaaahh!!
Hey! Wait up!

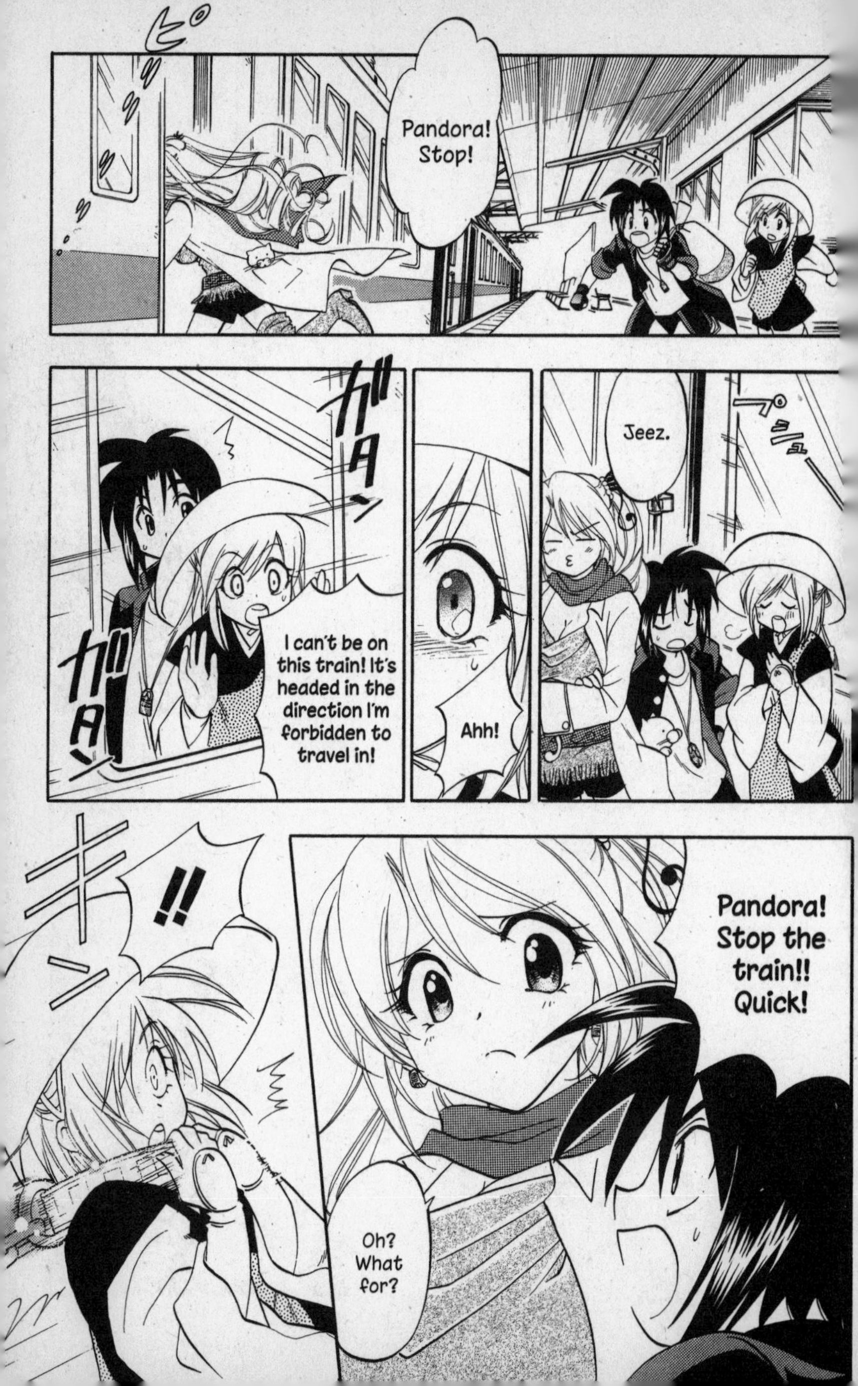
Pandora! Stop!
Jeez.
Ahh!
I can't be on this train! It's headed in the direction I'm forbidden to travel in!
Pandora! Stop the train!! Quick!
Oh? What for?
!!

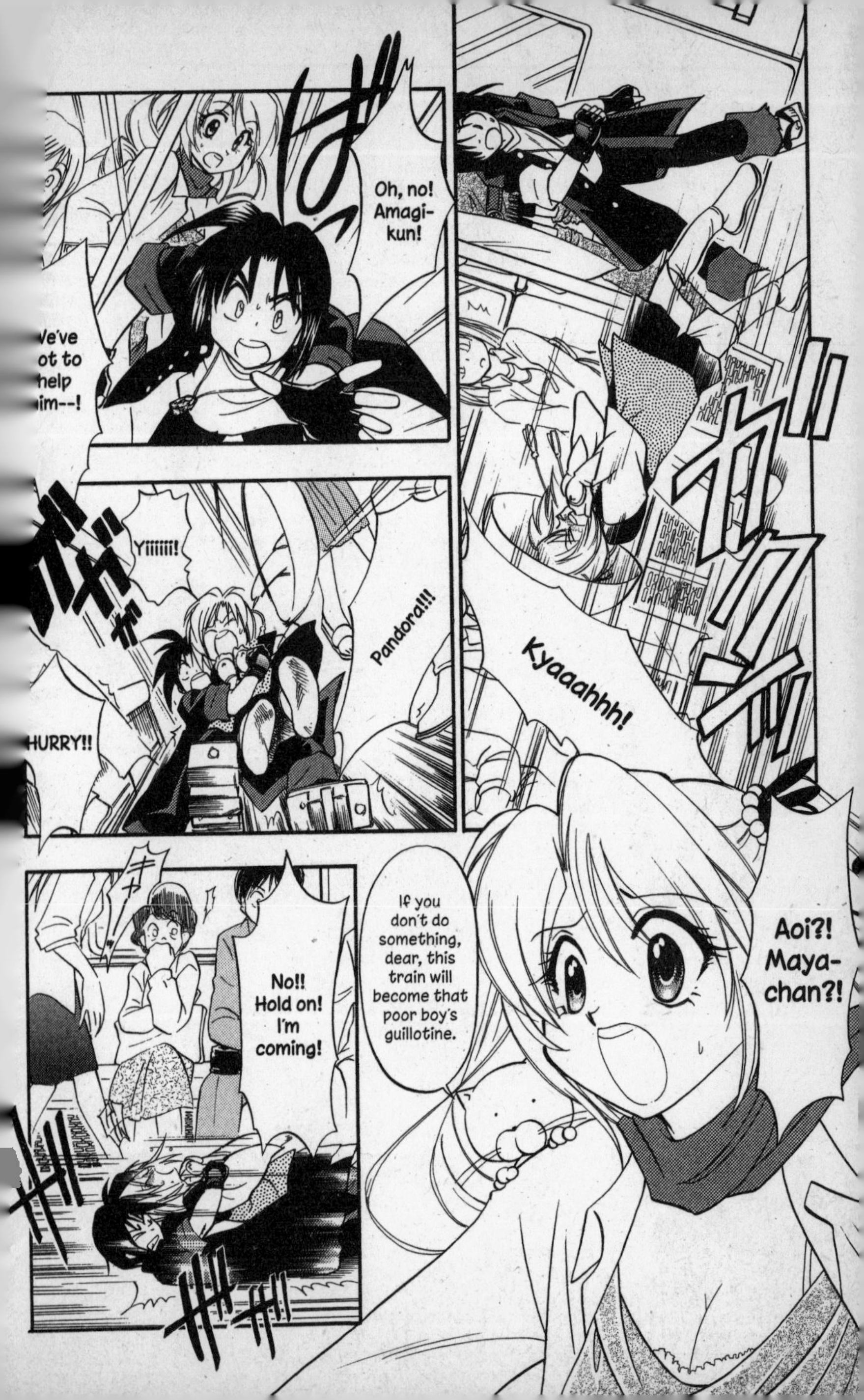
Kyaaahhh!
Oh, no! Amagi-kun!
e've ot to help im--!
Pandora!!!
Yiiiiii!
HURRY!!
Aoi?! Maya-chan?!
If you don't do something, dear, this train will become that poor boy's guillotine.
No!! Hold on! I'm coming!

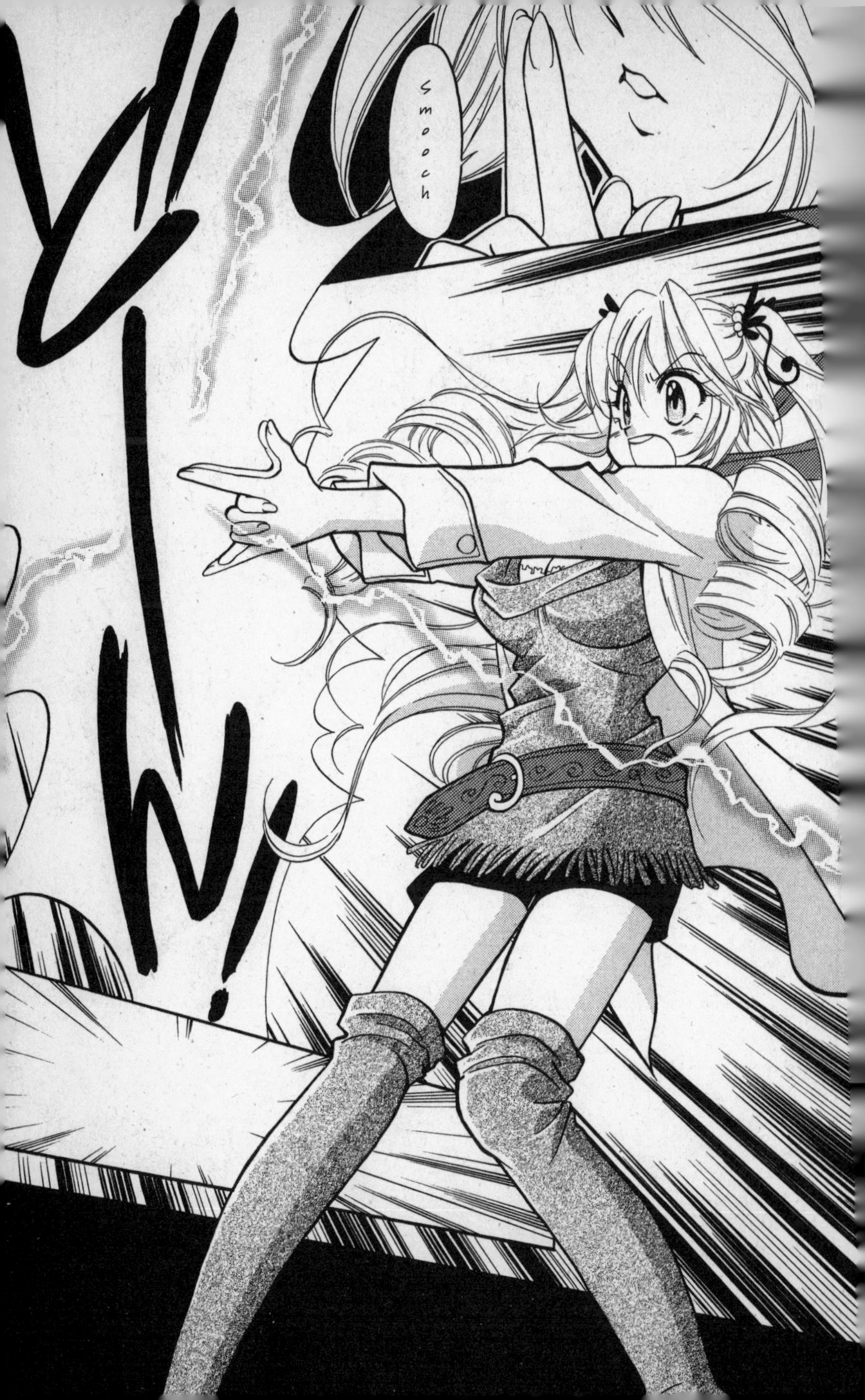
Smooch

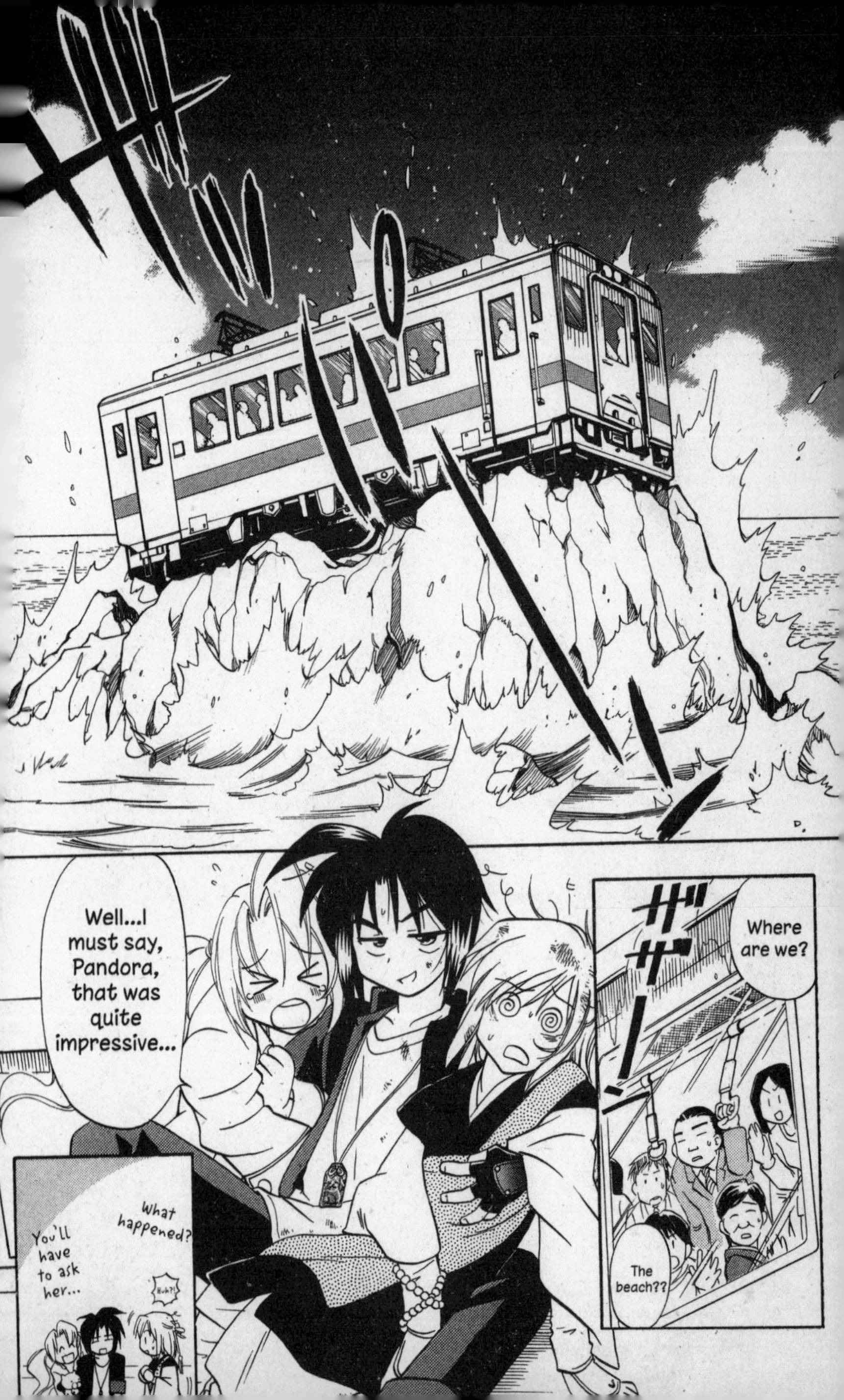
Where are we?
The beach??
Well...I must say, Pandora, that was quite impressive...
What happened?
You'll have to ask her...
Huh?!

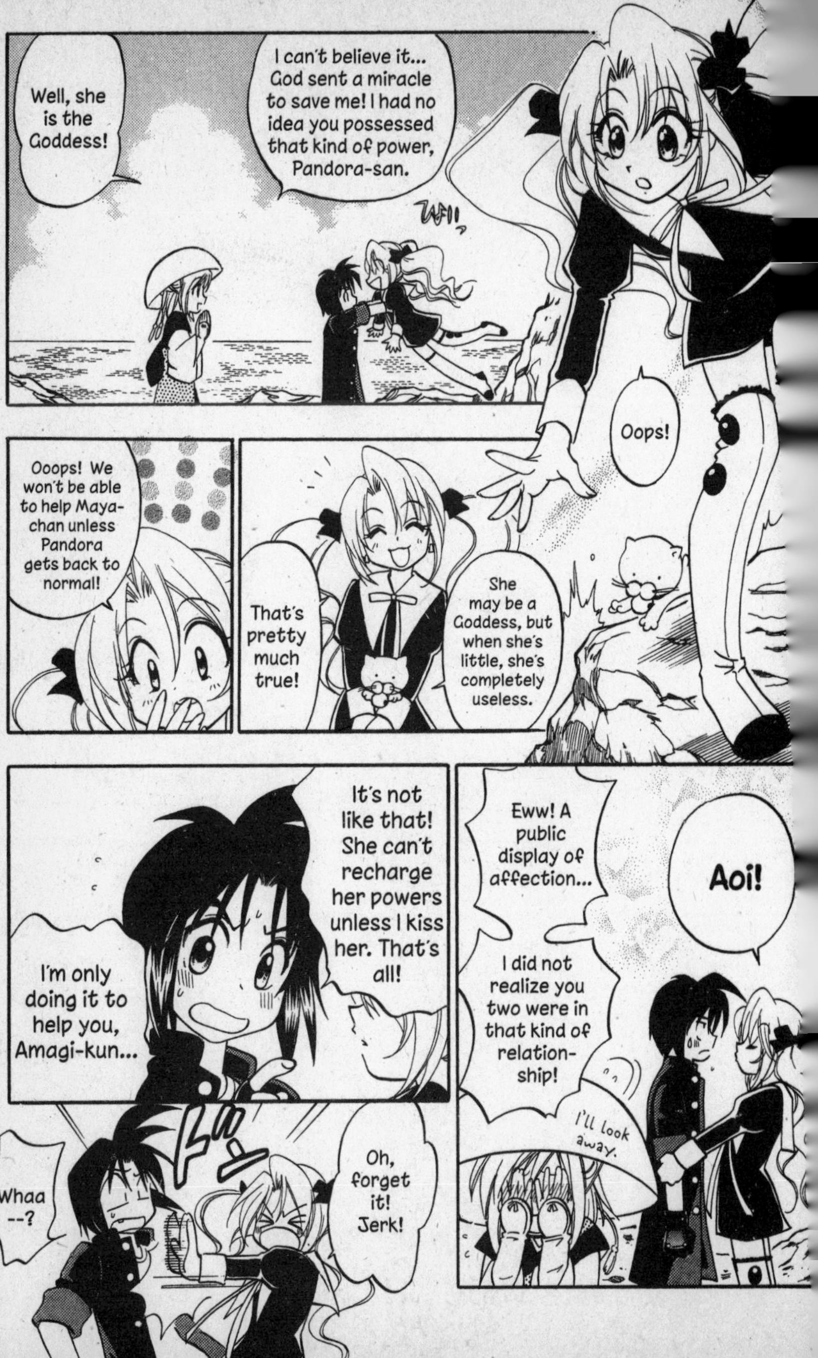

Oops!
I can't believe it... God sent a miracle to save me! I had no idea you possessed that kind of power, Pandora-san.
Well, she is the Goddess!
She may be a Goddess, but when she's little, she's completely useless.
That's pretty much true!
Ooops! We won't be able to help Maya-chan unless Pandora gets back to normal!
Aoi!
Eww! A public display of affection...
I did not realize you two were in that kind of relationship!
I'll look away.
It's not like that! She can't recharge her powers unless I kiss her. That's all!
I'm only doing it to help you, Amagi-kun...
Oh, forget it! Jerk!
Whaa --?

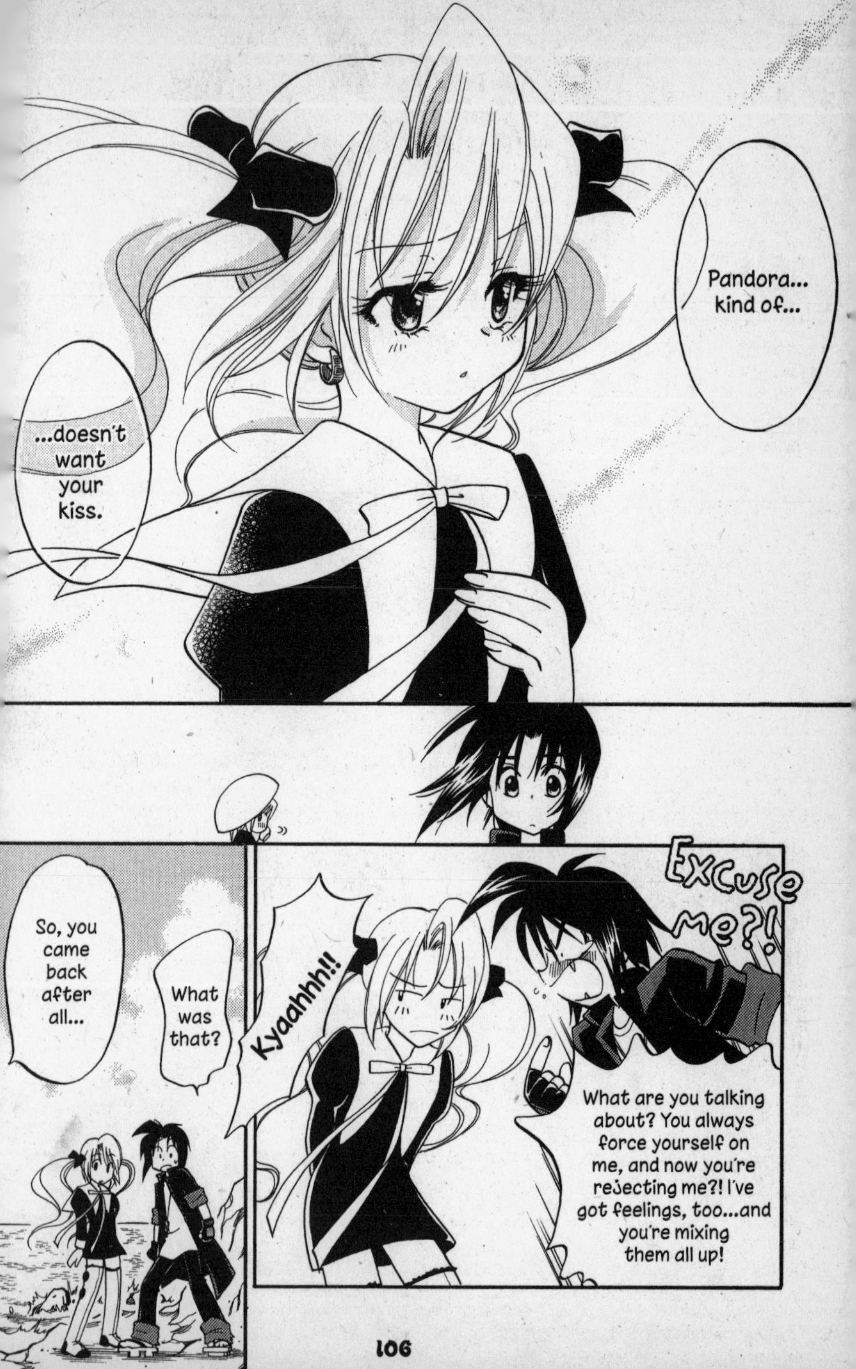
Pandora... kind of...
...doesn't want your kiss.
Excuse me?!
Kyaahhh!!
What are you talking about? You always force yourself on me, and now you're rejecting me?! I've got feelings, too...and you're mixing them all up!
What was that?
So, you came back after all...

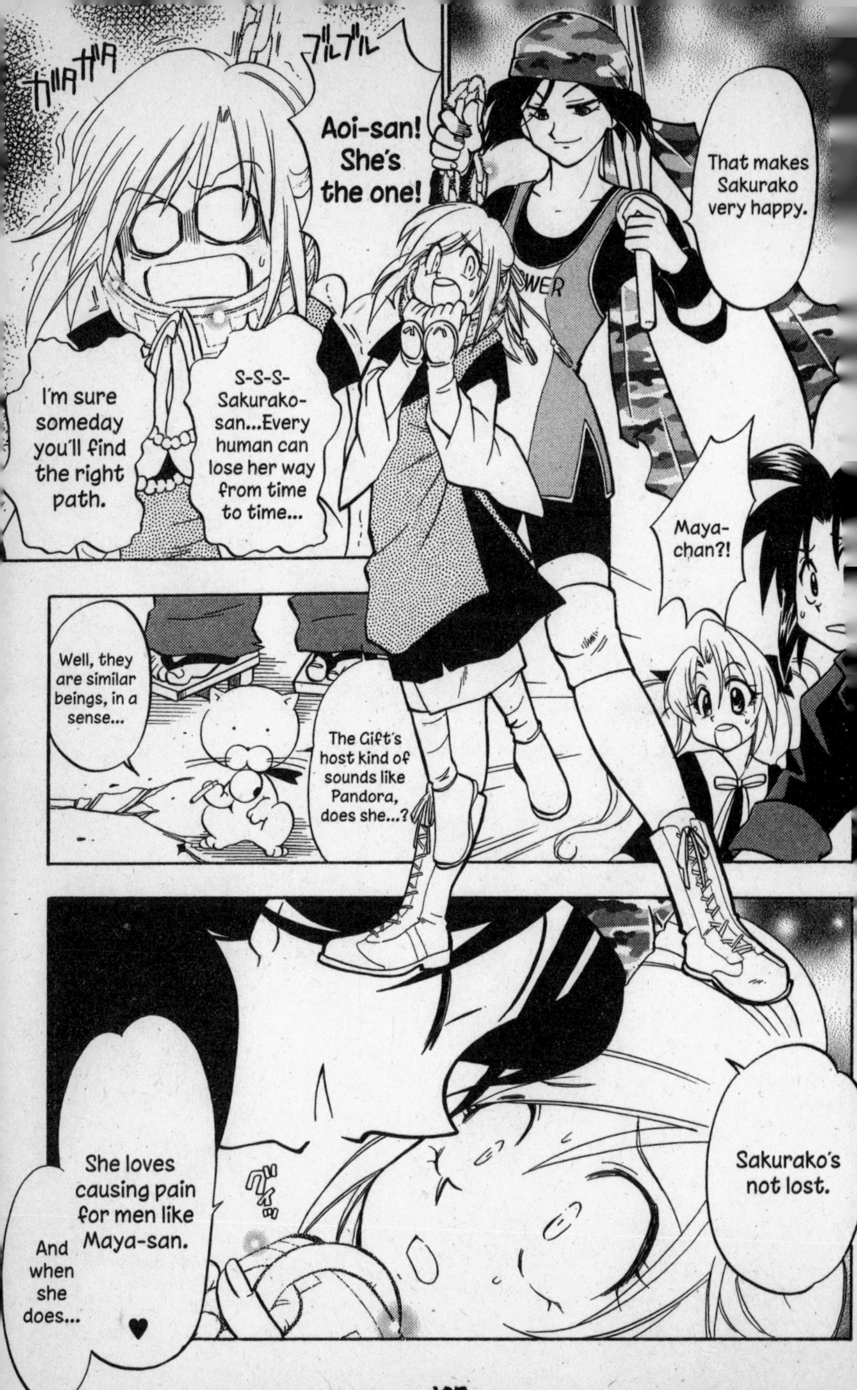
ブルブル
That makes Sakurako very happy.
Aoi-san! She's the one!
S-S-S-Sakurako-san...Every human can lose her way from time to time...
I'm sure someday you'll find the right path.
Maya-chan?!
The Gift's host kind of sounds like Pandora, does she...?
Well, they are similar beings, in a sense...
Sakurako's not lost.
She loves causing pain for men like Maya-san.
And when she does... ♥

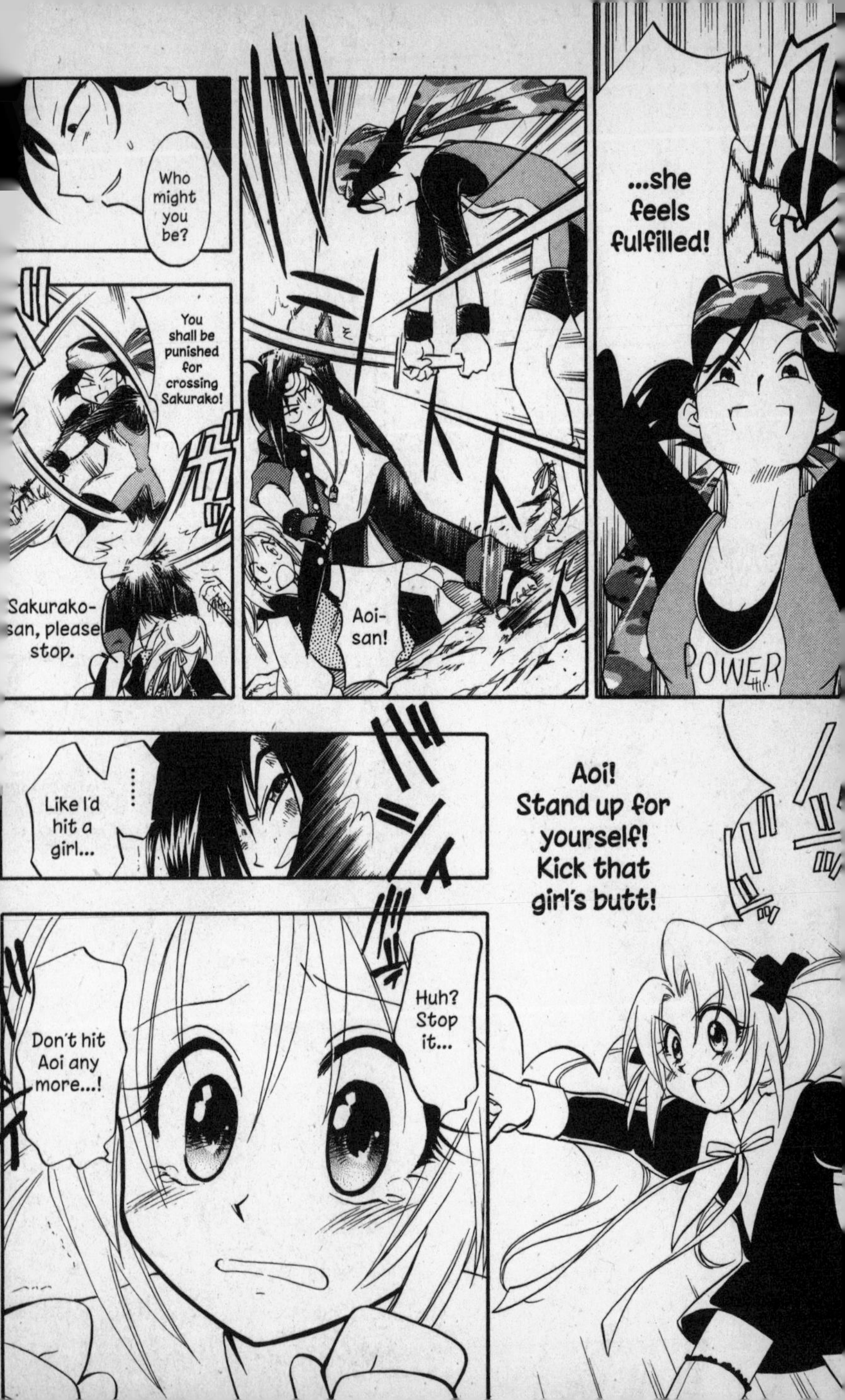
...she feels fulfilled!
POWER
Aoi-san!
Who might you be?
You shall be punished for crossing Sakurako!
Sakurako-san, please stop.
Aoi! Stand up for yourself! Kick that girl's butt!
......
Like I'd hit a girl...
Huh? Stop it...
Don't hit Aoi any more...!

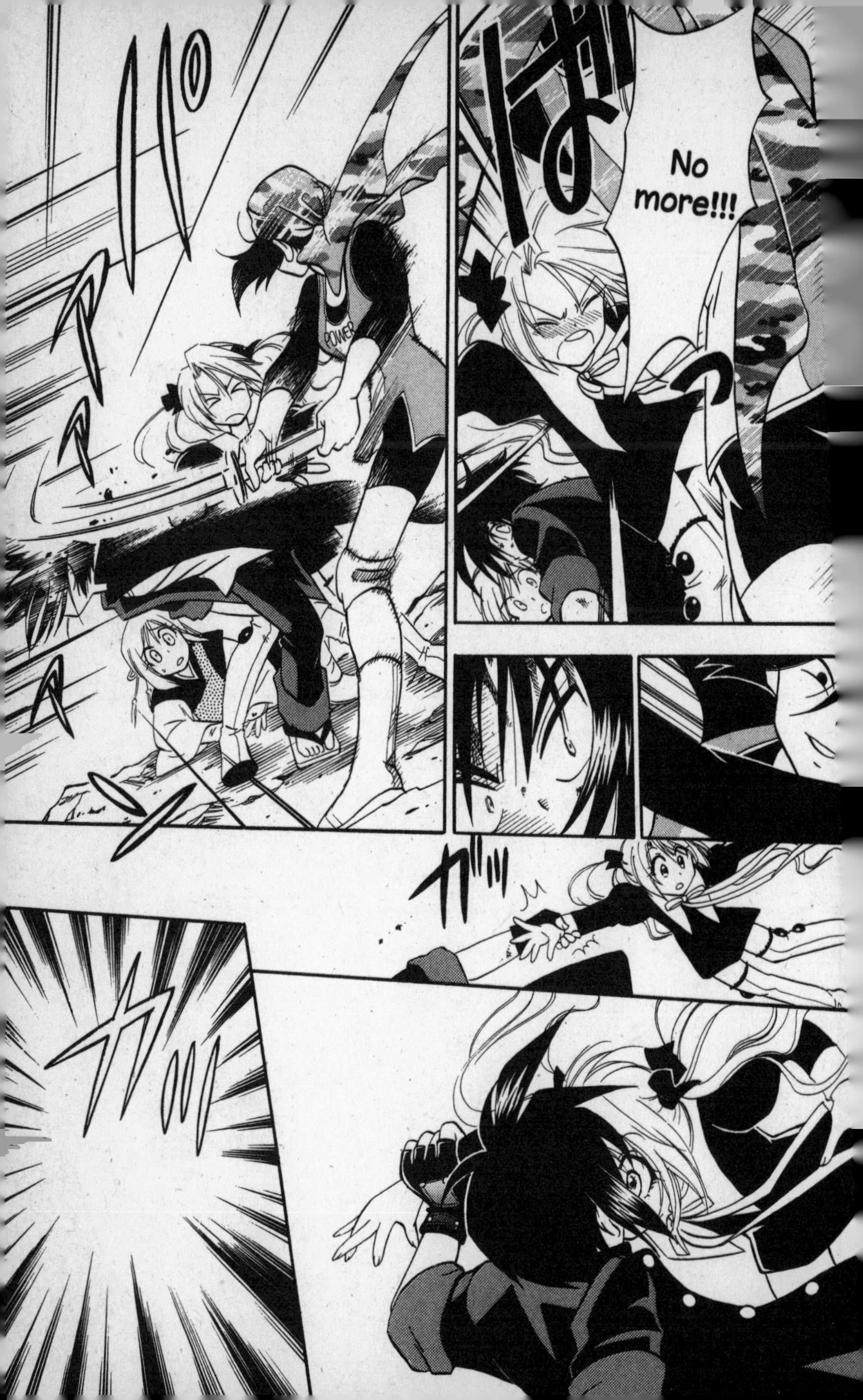
No more!!!
POWER

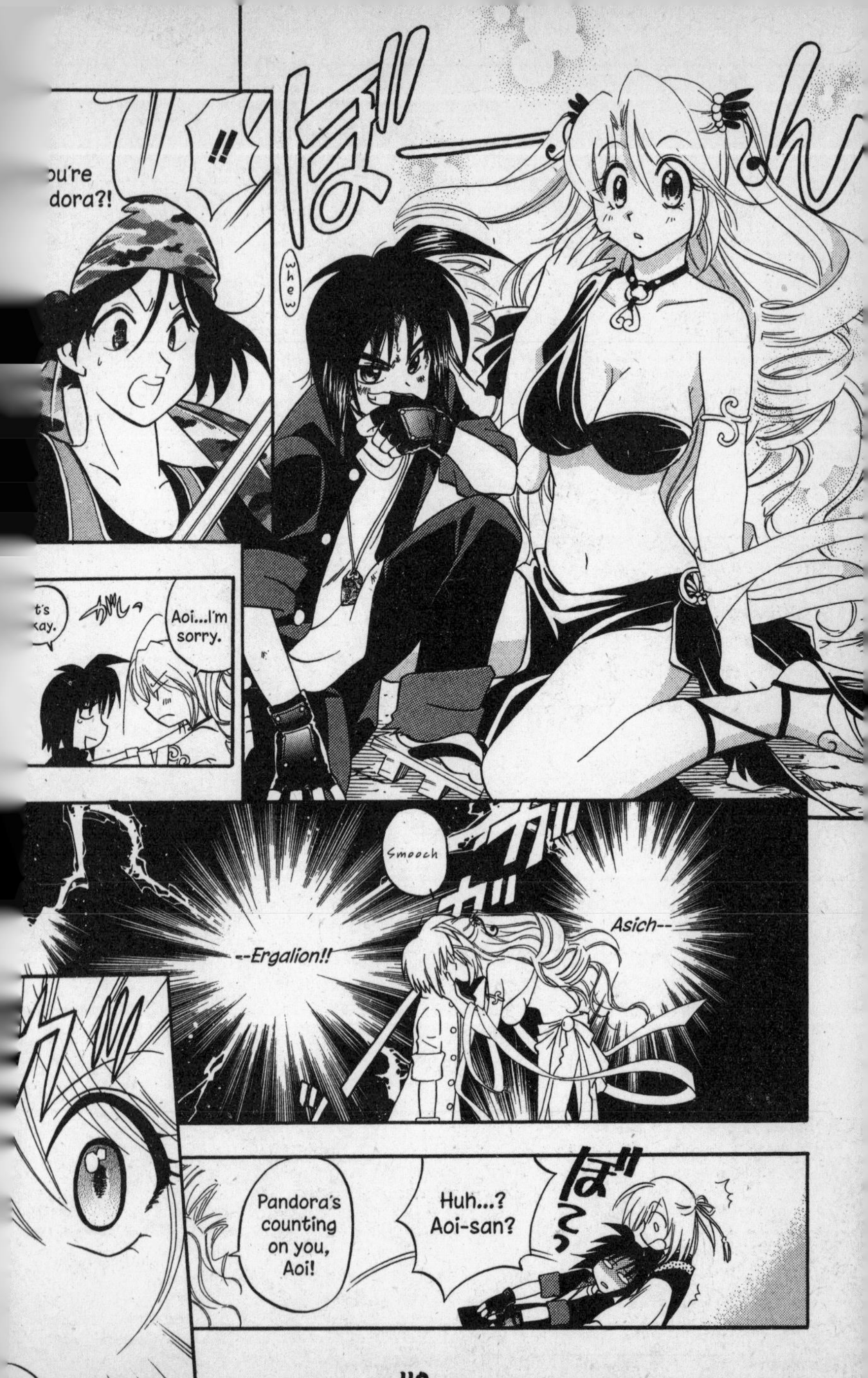
whew
ou're
dora?!
Aoi...I'm sorry.
t's
kay.
Smooch
Asich--
--Ergalion!!
Huh...? Aoi-san?
Pandora's counting on you, Aoi!

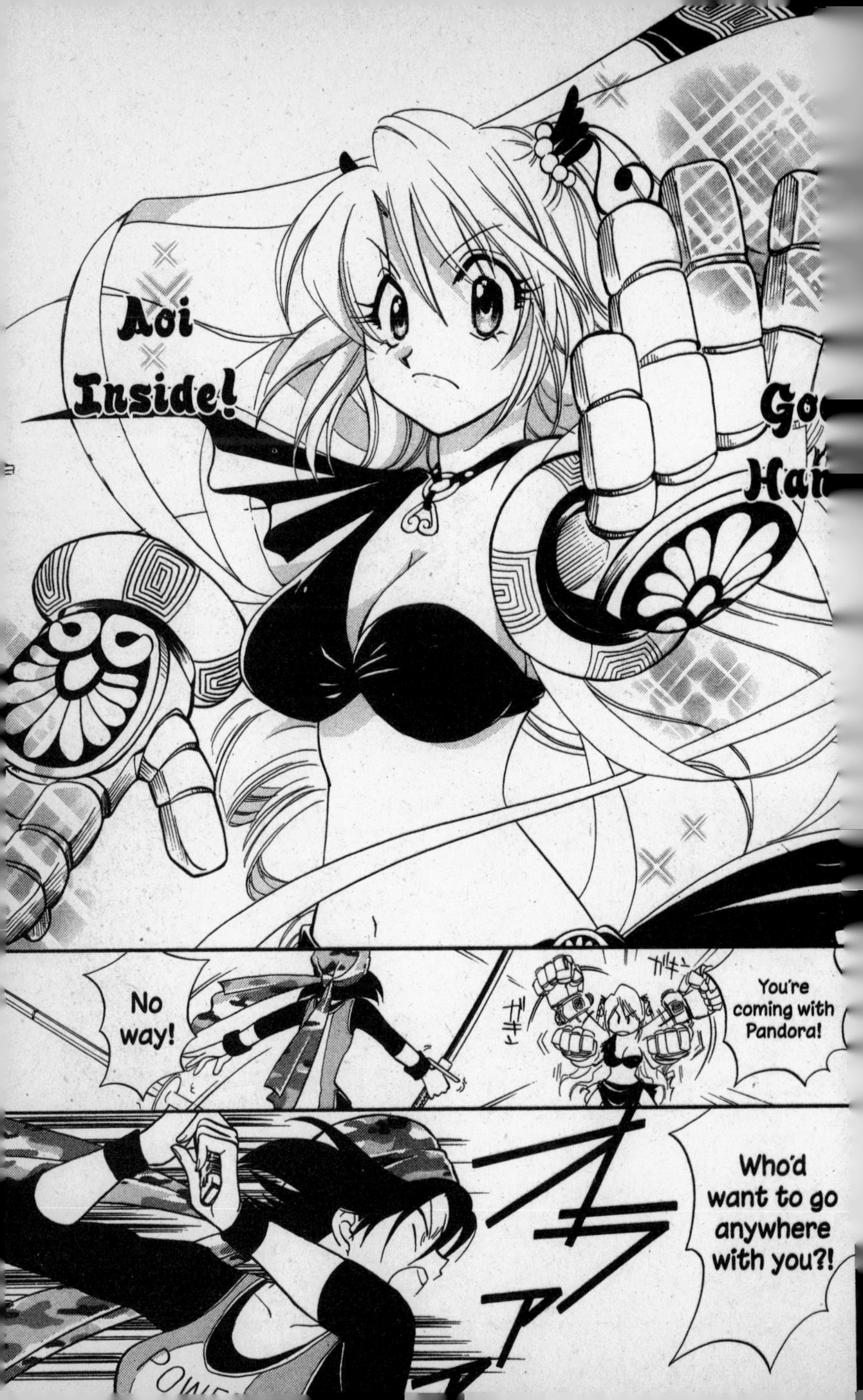
Go
Han
Aoi Inside!
You're coming with Pandora!
No way!
Who'd want to go anywhere with you?!

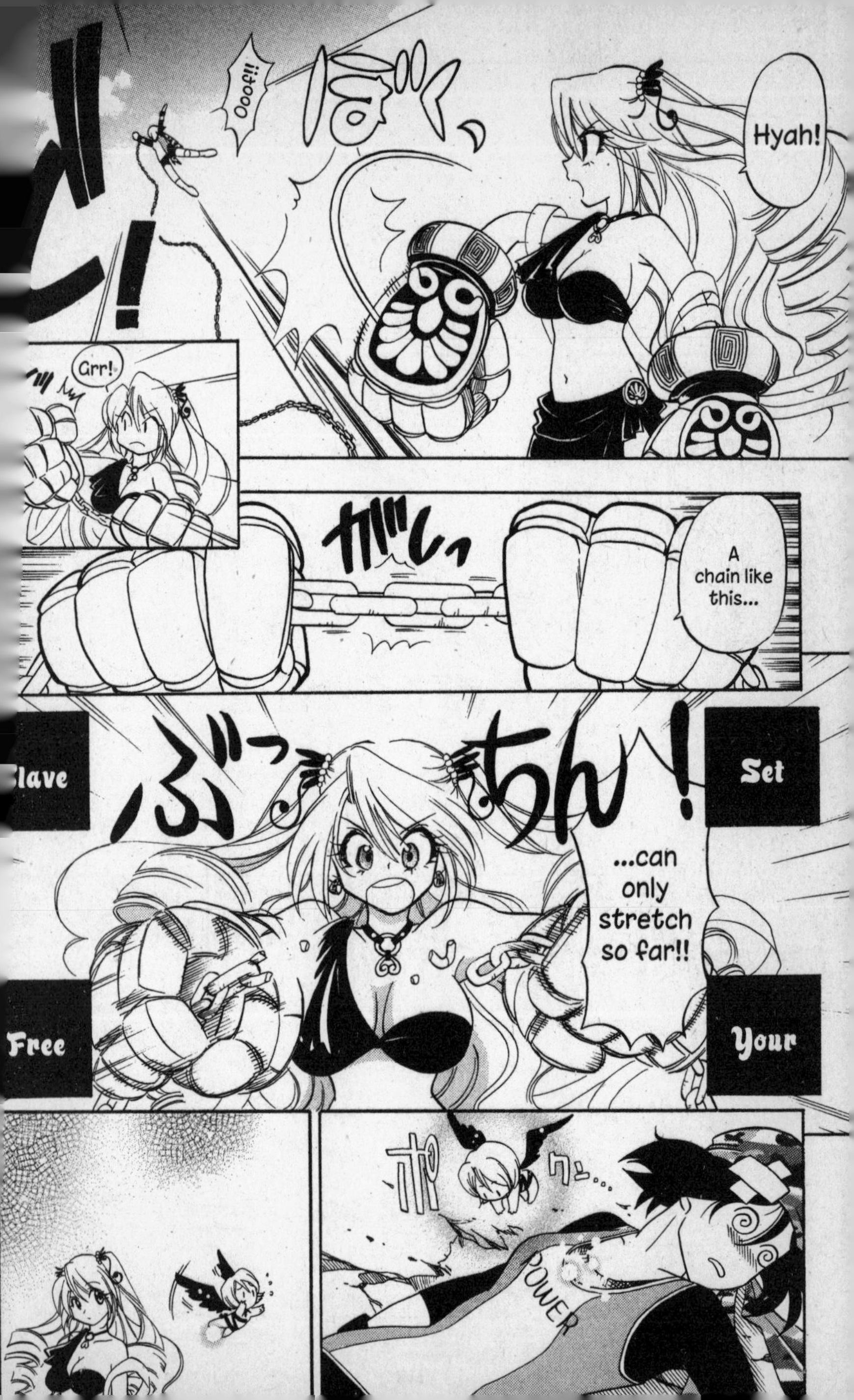

Hyah!
Oooof!!
Grr!
A chain like this...
...can only stretch so far!!
ぶっちん!
Set
Your
lave
Free
ポ
POWER

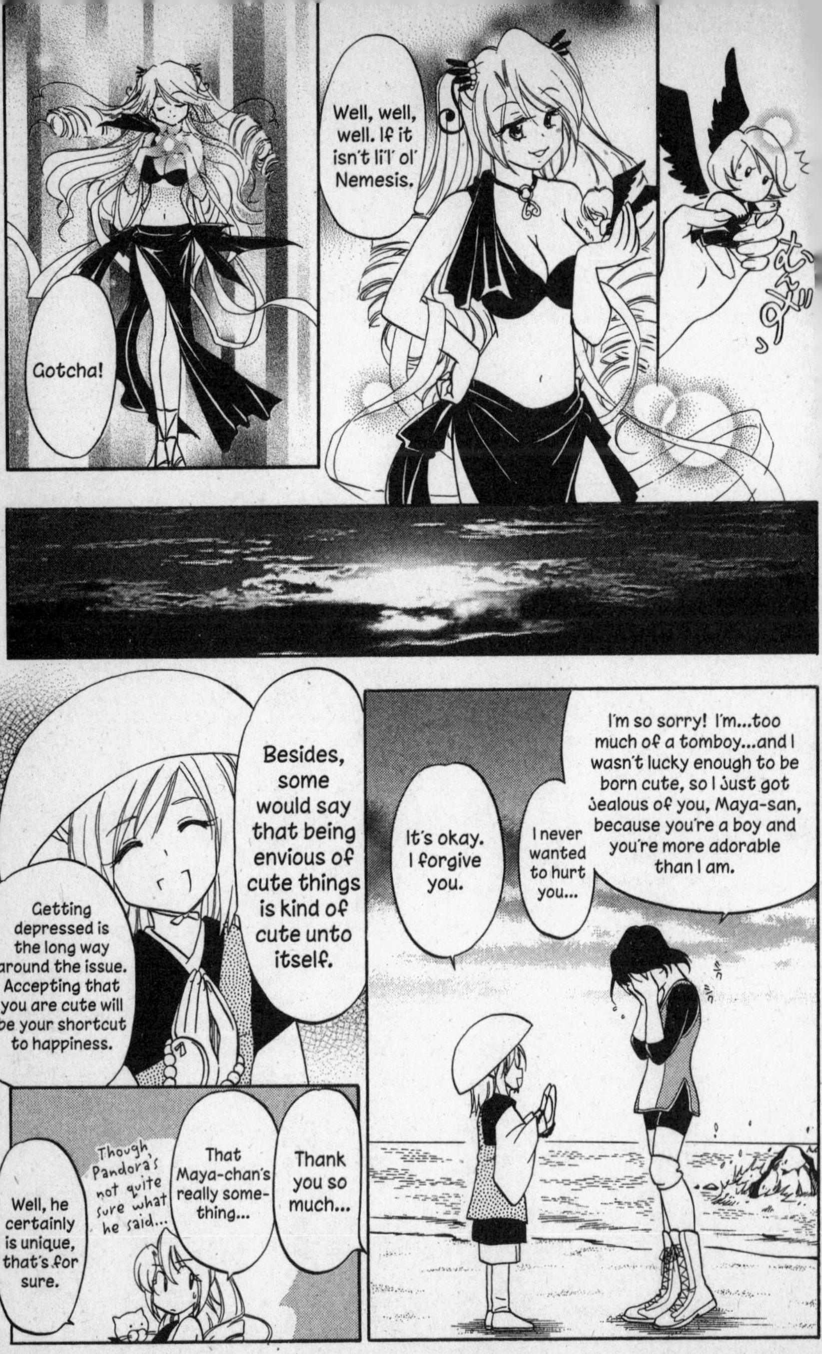
Well, well, well. If it isn't li'l' ol' Nemesis.
Gotcha!
I'm so sorry! I'm...too much of a tomboy...and I wasn't lucky enough to be born cute, so I just got jealous of you, Maya-san, because you're a boy and you're more adorable than I am.
I never wanted to hurt you...
It's okay. I forgive you.
Besides, some would say that being envious of cute things is kind of cute unto itself.
Getting depressed is the long way around the issue. Accepting that you are cute will be your shortcut to happiness.
Thank you so much...
That Maya-chan's really some-thing...
Though Pandora's not quite sure what he said...
Well, he certainly is unique, that's for sure.

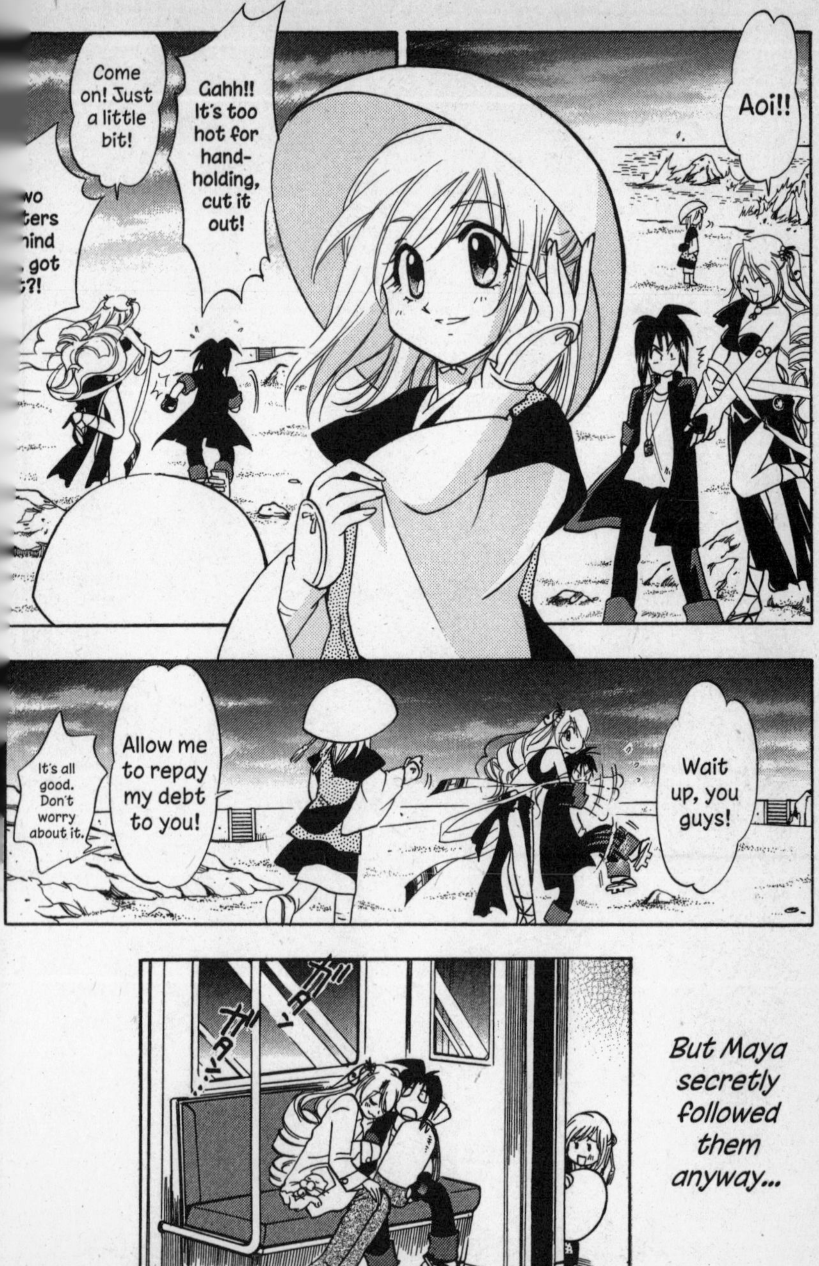
Aoi!!
Gahh!! It's too hot for hand-holding, cut it out!
Come on! Just a little bit!
Wait up, you guys!
Allow me to repay my debt to you!
It's all good. Don't worry about it.
But Maya secretly followed them anyway...

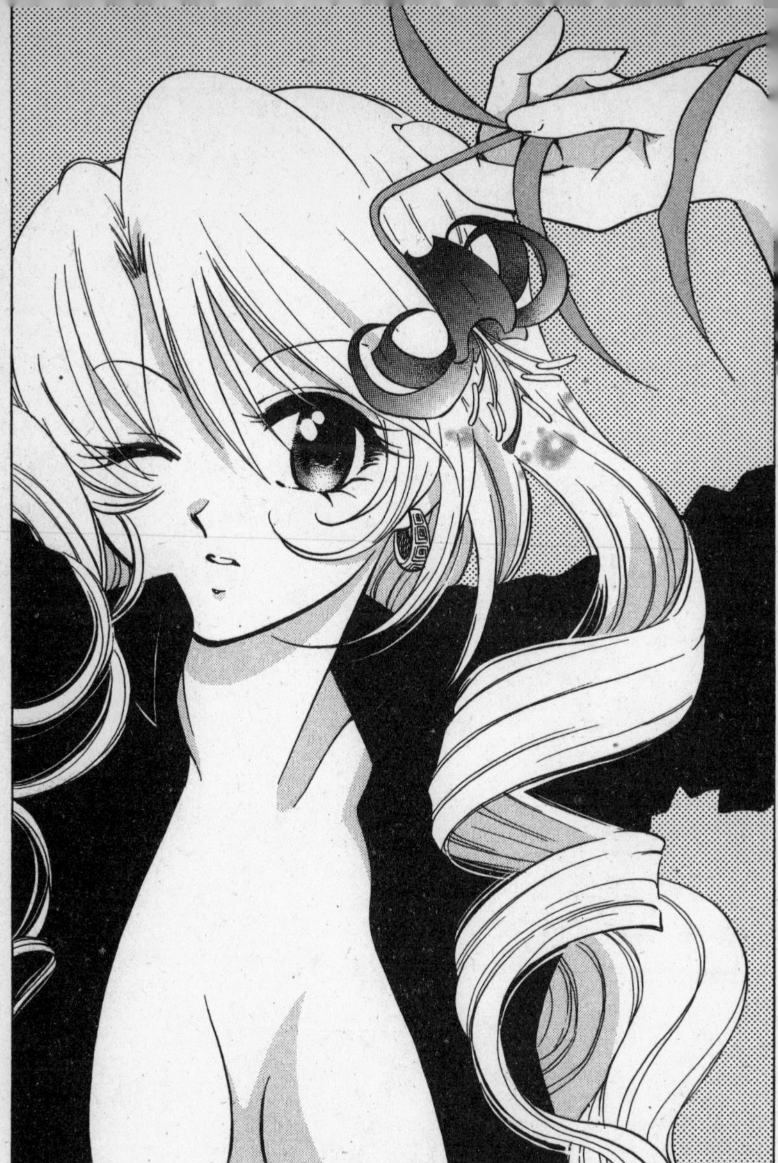

Chapter 5:
Matsuyuki's Love Lessons

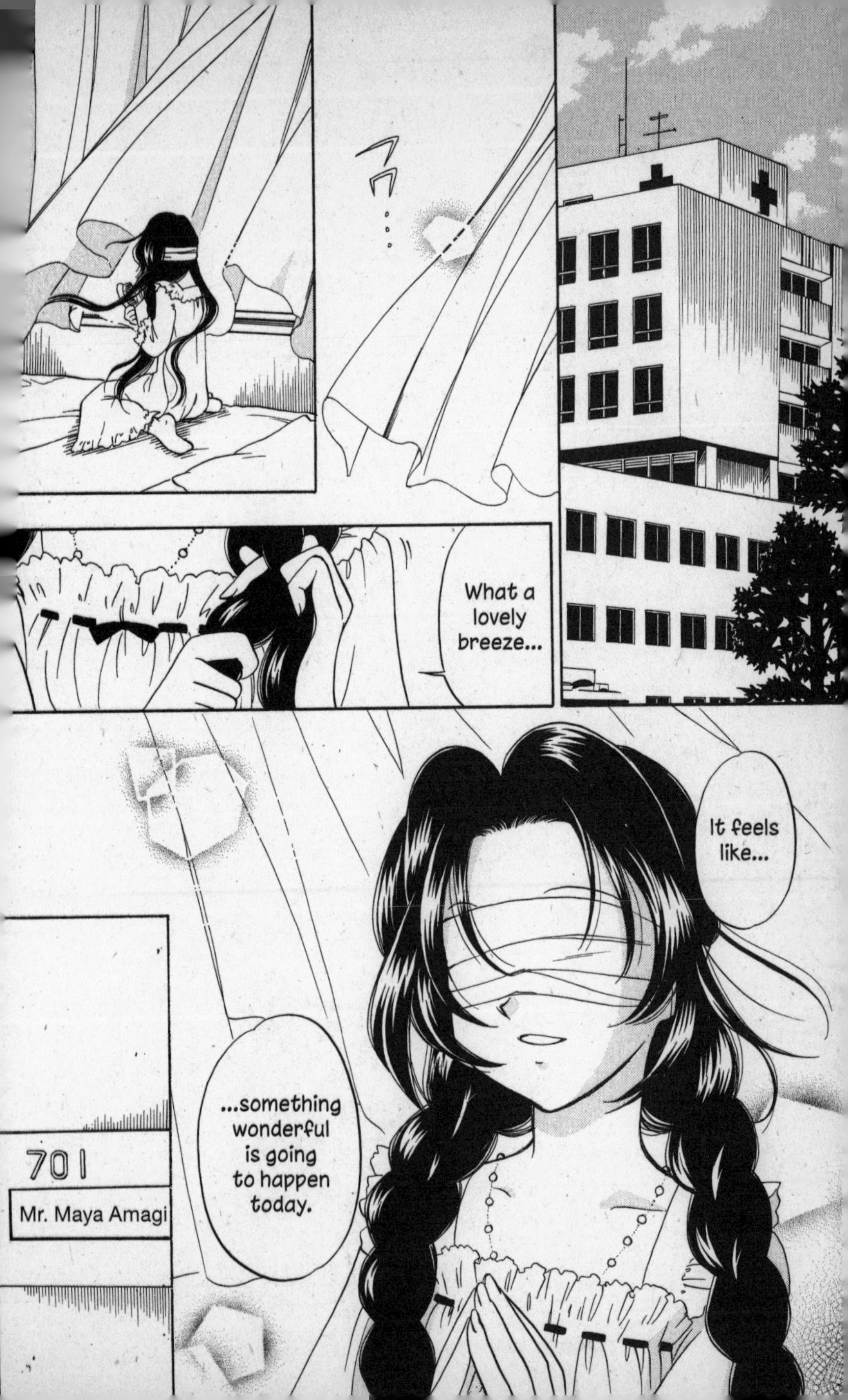
What a lovely breeze...
It feels like...
...something wonderful is going to happen today.
701
Mr. Maya Amagi

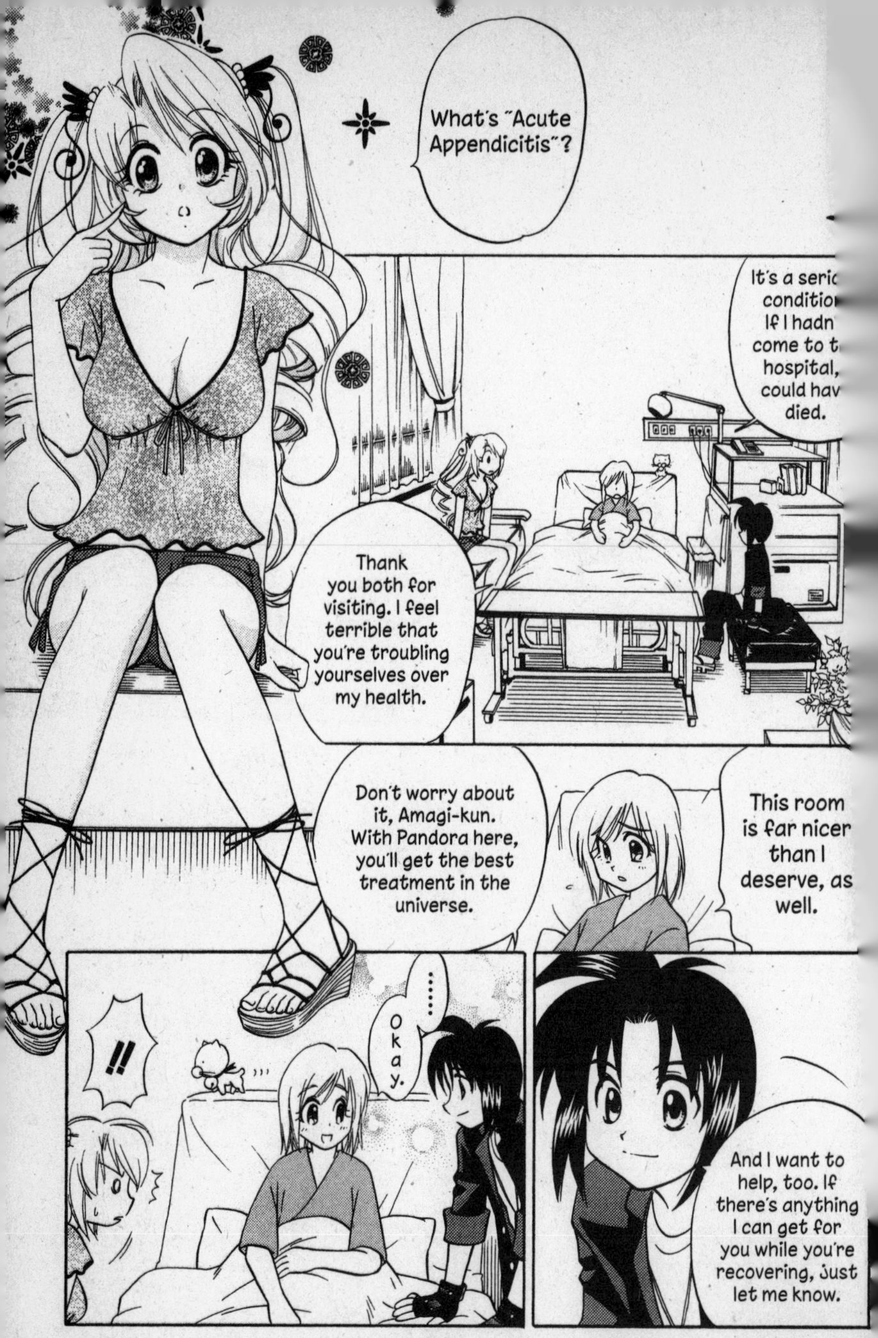
What's "Acute Appendicitis"?
It's a serio conditio If I hadn come to t hospital, could hav died.
Thank you both for visiting. I feel terrible that you're troubling yourselves over my health.
This room is far nicer than I deserve, as well.
Don't worry about it, Amagi-kun. With Pandora here, you'll get the best treatment in the universe.
And I want to help, too. If there's anything I can get for you while you're recovering, just let me know.
......
Okay.
!!

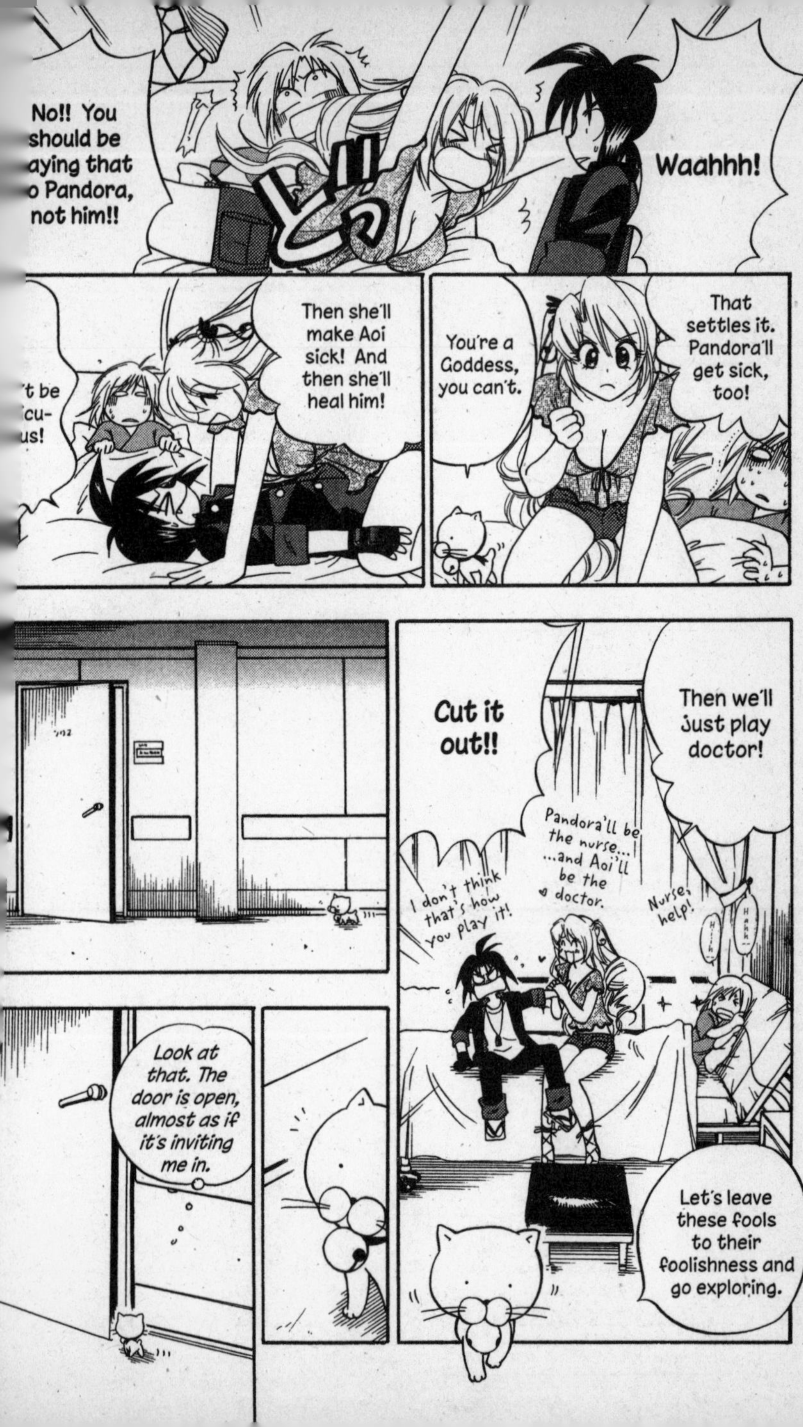
Waahhh!
No!! You should be aying that o Pandora, not him!!
That settles it. Pandora'll get sick, too!
You're a Goddess, you can't.
Then she'll make Aoi sick! And then she'll heal him!
't be cu- us!
Then we'll just play doctor!
Cut it out!!
Nurse, help!
Pandora'll be the nurse... ...and Aoi'll be the doctor.
I don't think that's how you play it!
Let's leave these fools to their foolishness and go exploring.
Look at that. The door is open, almost as if it's inviting me in.

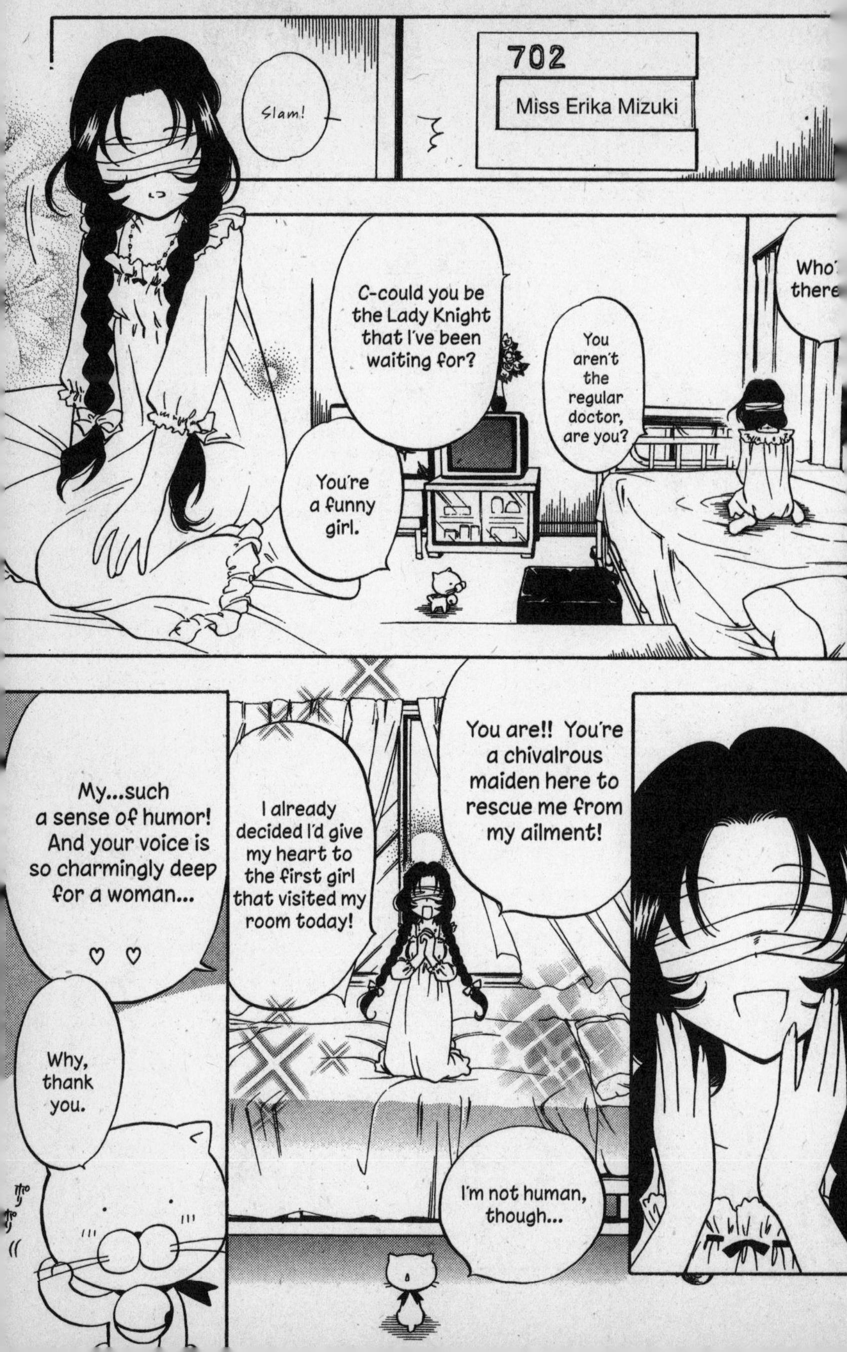
702
Miss Erika Mizuki
Slam!
Who' there
You aren't the regular doctor, are you?
C-could you be the Lady Knight that I've been waiting for?
You're a funny girl.
You are!! You're a chivalrous maiden here to rescue me from my ailment!
I already decided I'd give my heart to the first girl that visited my room today!
I'm not human, though...
My...such a sense of humor! And your voice is so charmingly deep for a woman... ♡ ♡
Why, thank you.

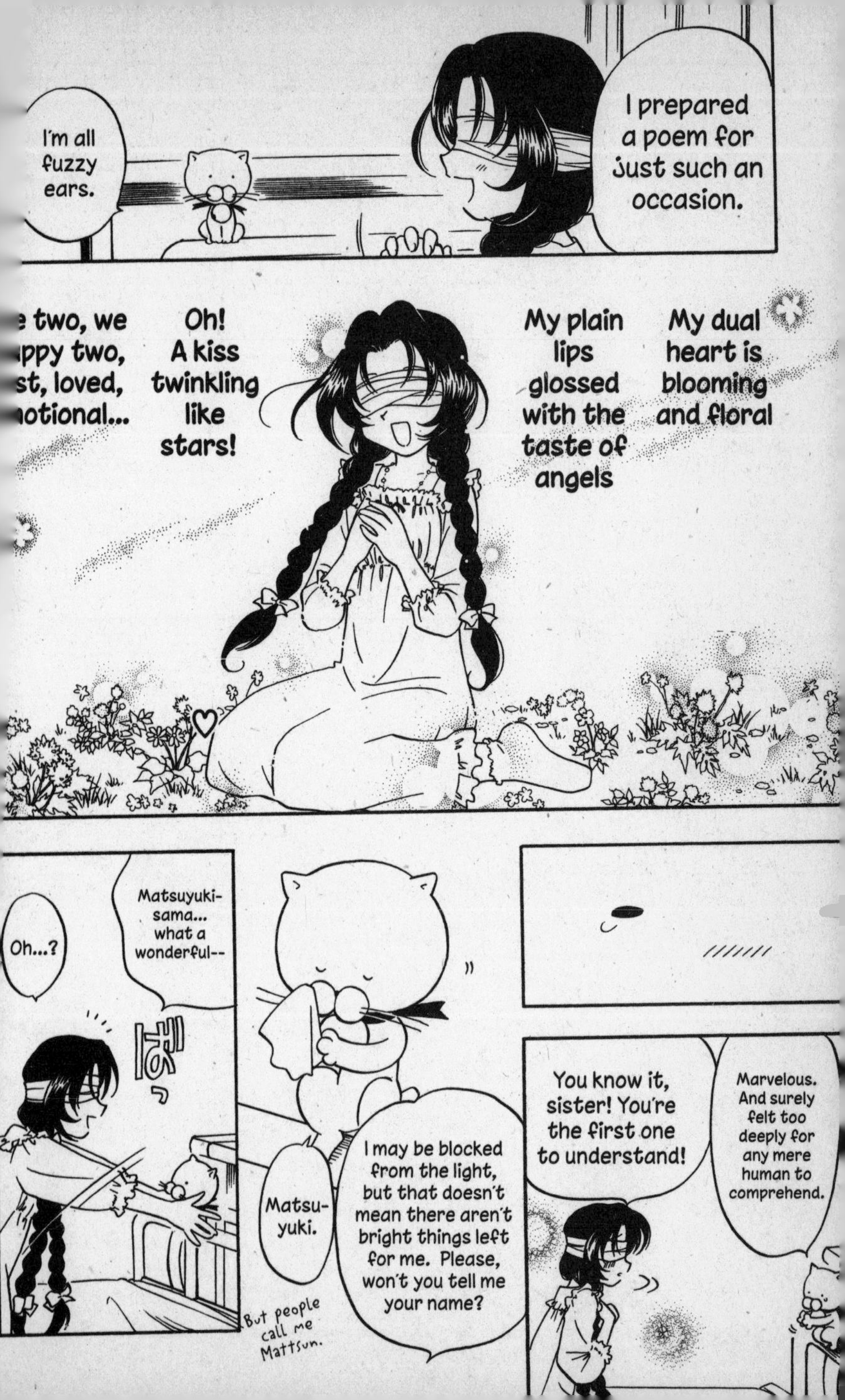
I prepared a poem for just such an occasion.
I'm all fuzzy ears.
My dual heart is blooming and floral
My plain lips glossed with the taste of angels
Oh! A kiss twinkling like stars!
e two, we
ppy two,
st, loved,
notional...
Marvelous. And surely felt too deeply for any mere human to comprehend.
You know it, sister! You're the first one to understand!
I may be blocked from the light, but that doesn't mean there aren't bright things left for me. Please, won't you tell me your name?
Matsu-yuki.
But people call me Mattsun.
Matsuyuki-sama... what a wonderful--
Oh...?
ぱっ

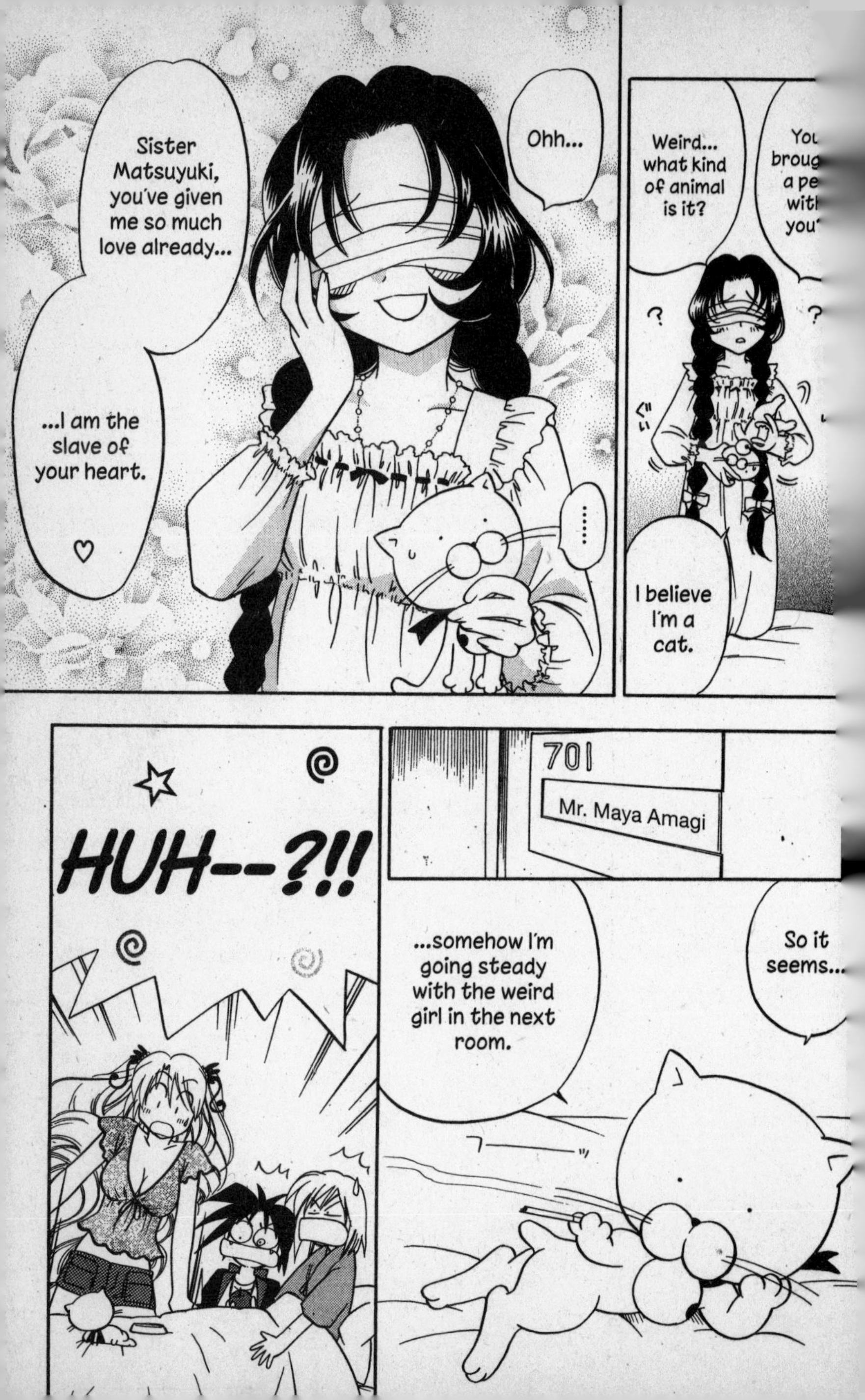
Weird... what kind of animal is it?
I believe I'm a cat.
Ohh...
Sister Matsuyuki, you've given me so much love already...
......
...I am the slave of your heart. ♡
701
Mr. Maya Amagi
So it seems...
...somehow I'm going steady with the weird girl in the next room.
HUH--?!!

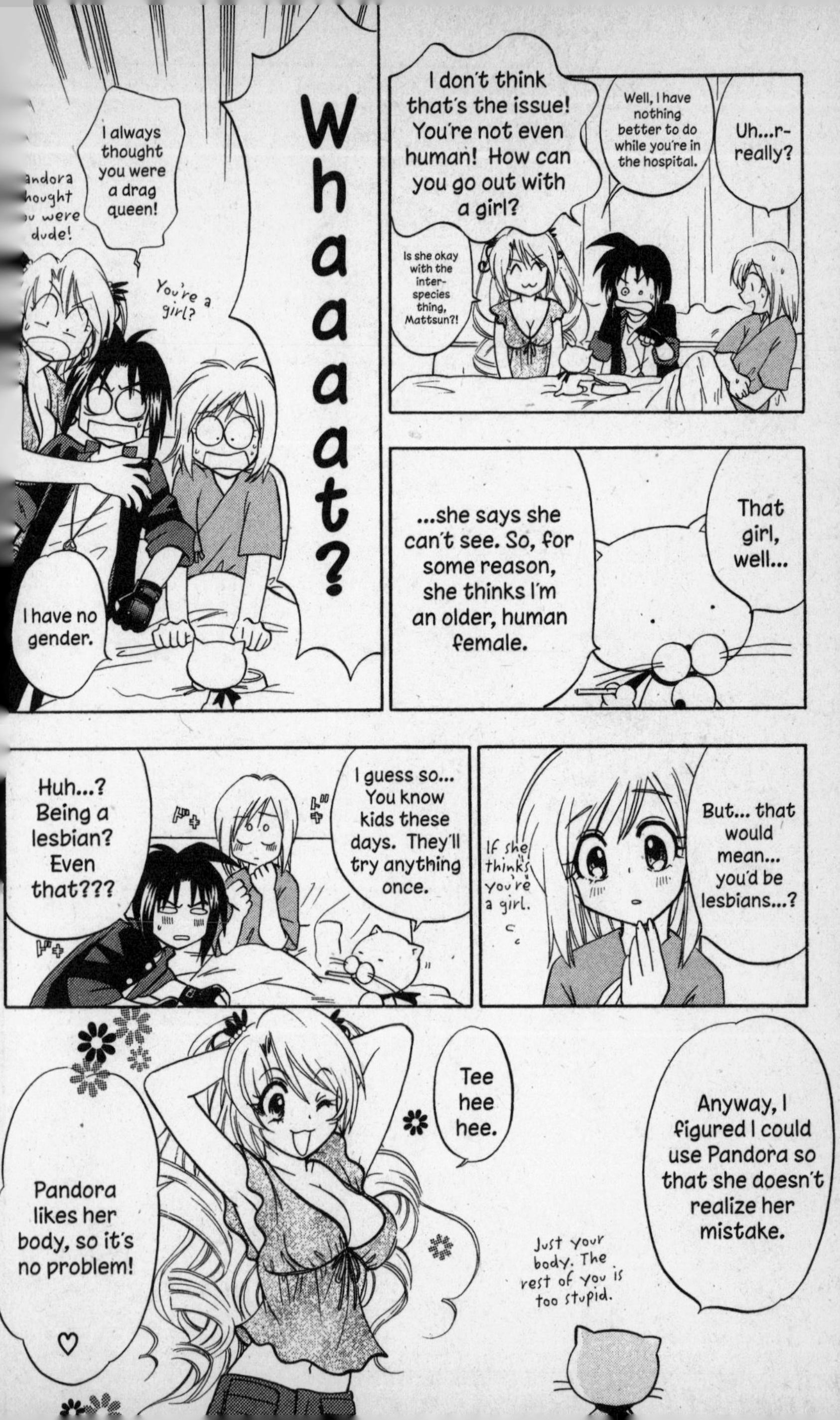
Uh...r-really?
Well, I have nothing better to do while you're in the hospital.
I don't think that's the issue! You're not even human! How can you go out with a girl?
Is she okay with the inter-species thing, Mattsun?!
That girl, well...
...she says she can't see. So, for some reason, she thinks I'm an older, human female.
Whaaaat?
You're a girl?
I always thought you were a drag queen!
andora hought u were dude!
I have no gender.
But... that would mean... you'd be lesbians...?
If she thinks you're a girl.
I guess so... You know kids these days. They'll try anything once.
Huh...? Being a lesbian? Even that???
Anyway, I figured I could use Pandora so that she doesn't realize her mistake.
Just your body. The rest of you is too stupid.
Tee hee hee.
Pandora likes her body, so it's no problem! ♡

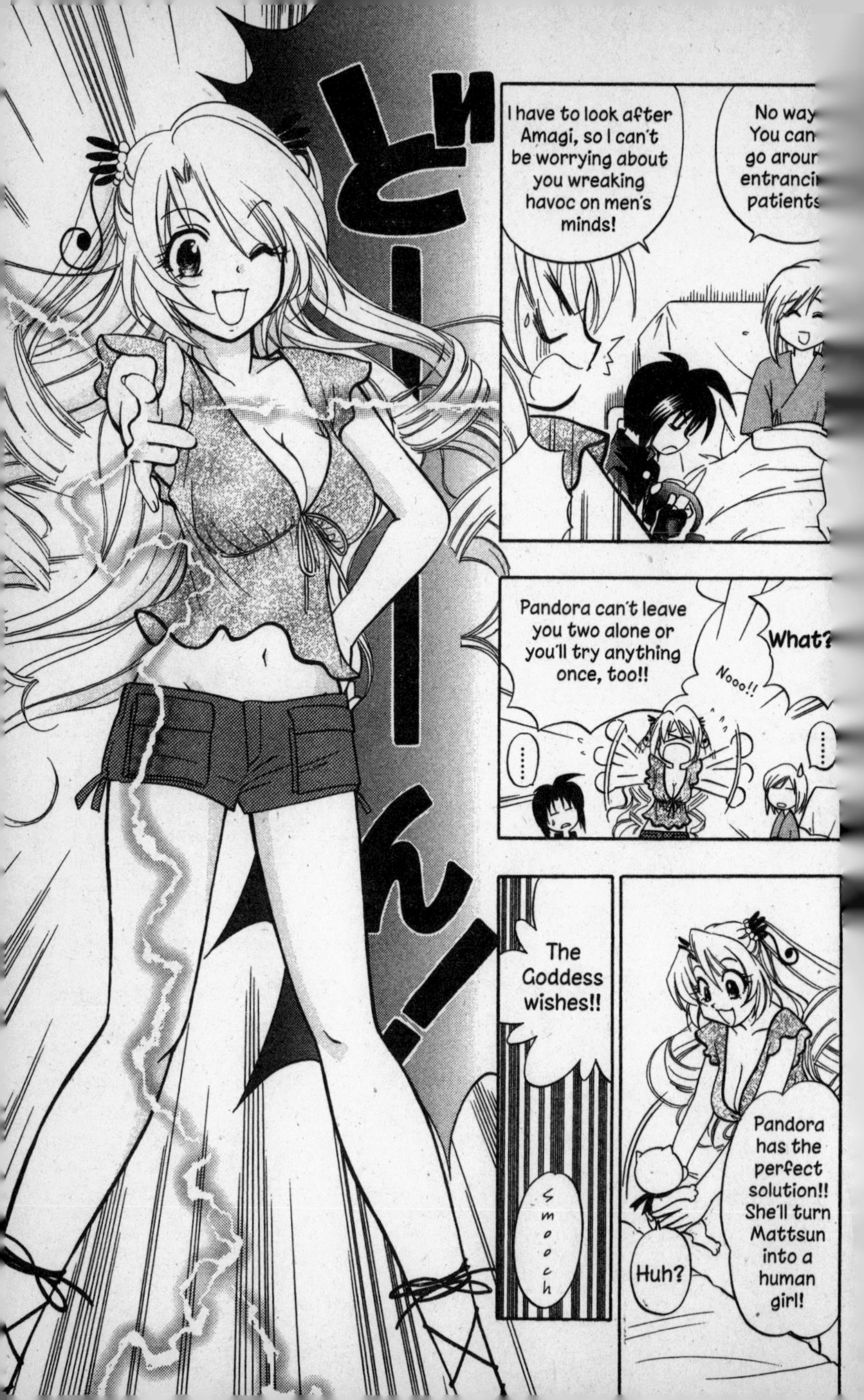
No way
You can
go arour
entrancin
patients
I have to look after Amagi, so I can't be worrying about you wreaking havoc on men's minds!
What?
Nooo!!
Pandora can't leave you two alone or you'll try anything once, too!!
......
......
Pandora has the perfect solution!! She'll turn Mattsun into a human girl!
Huh?
The Goddess wishes!!
Smooch
どーーん!!

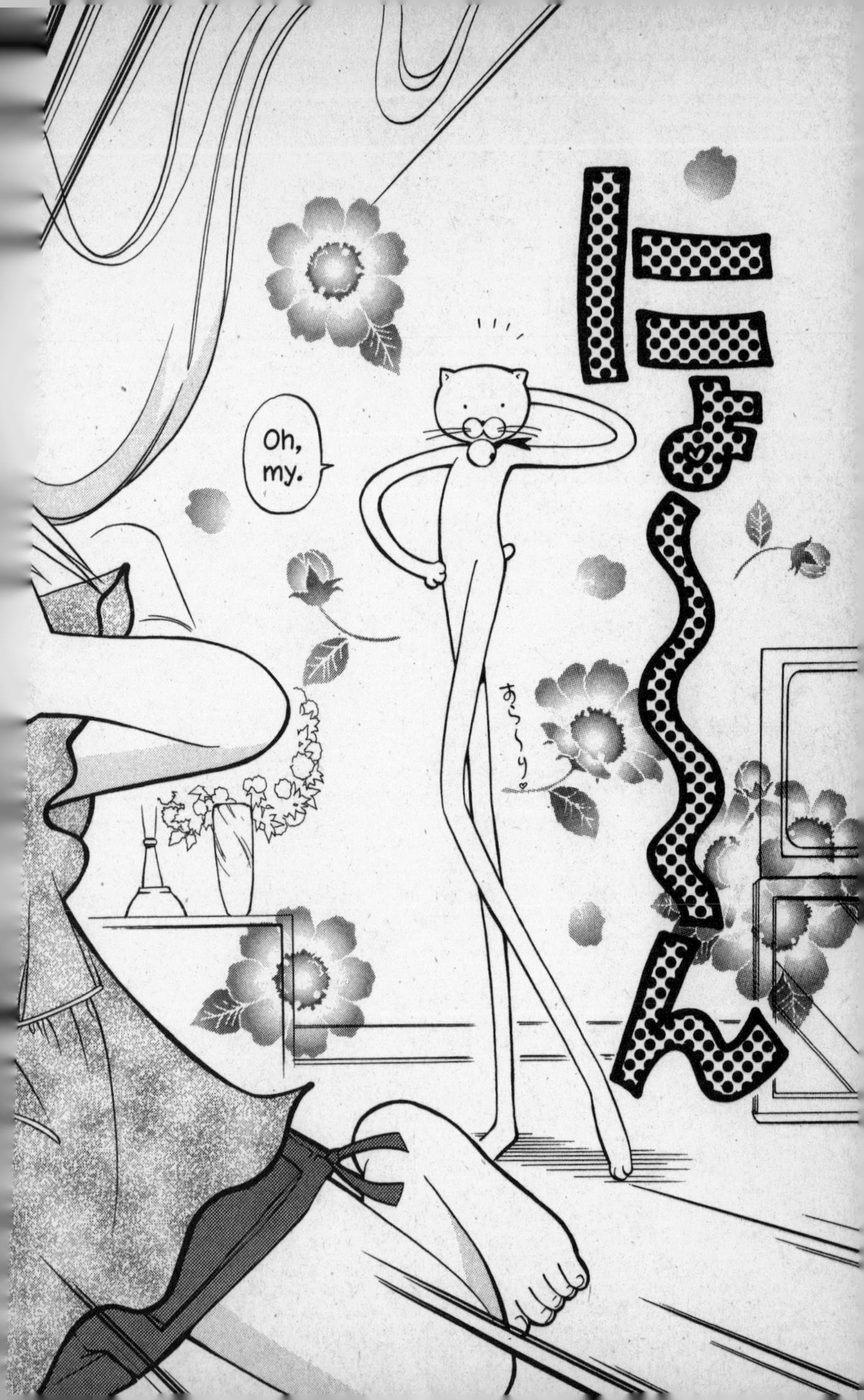
にょ〜〜ん
Oh, my.
おら〜り

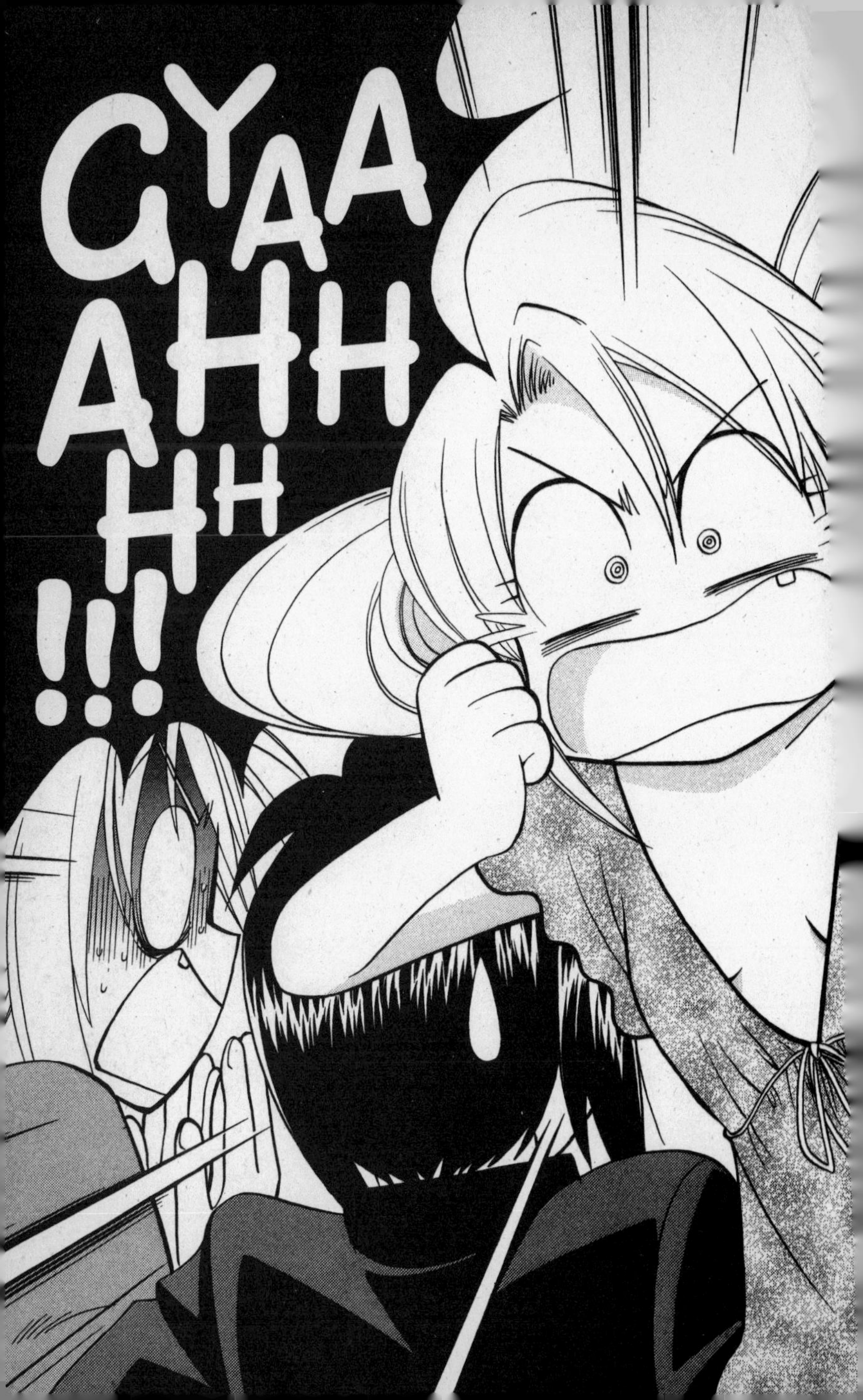
GYAAAHHHH!!!

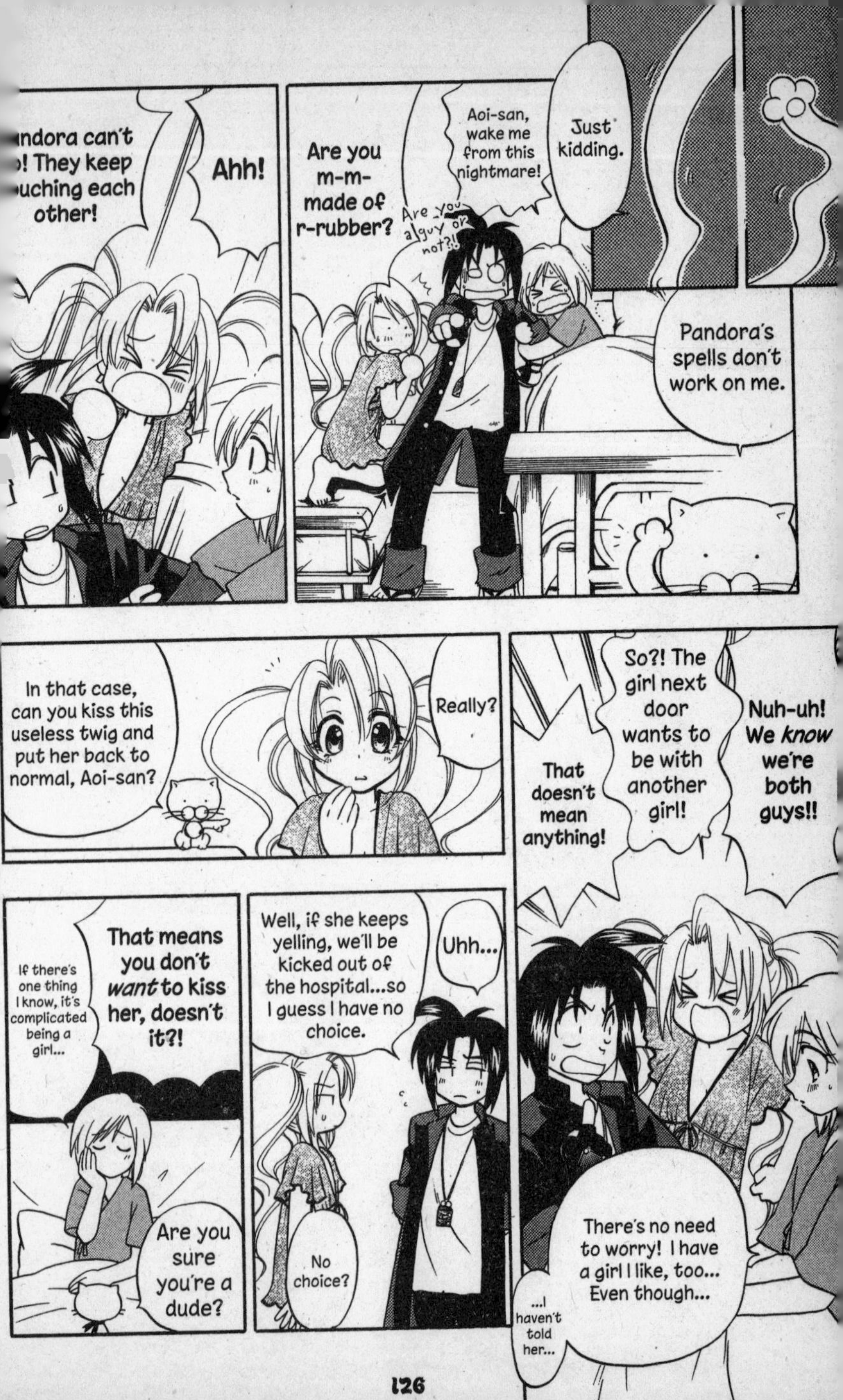
Just kidding.
Pandora's spells don't work on me.
Aoi-san, wake me from this nightmare!
Are you m-m-made of r-rubber?
Are you a guy or not?!
Ahh!
ndora can't ! They keep uching each other!
Nuh-uh! We *know* we're both guys!!
So?! The girl next door wants to be with another girl!
That doesn't mean anything!
There's no need to worry! I have a girl I like, too... Even though...
...I haven't told her...
Really?
In that case, can you kiss this useless twig and put her back to normal, Aoi-san?
Uhh...
Well, if she keeps yelling, we'll be kicked out of the hospital...so I guess I have no choice.
No choice?
That means you don't *want* to kiss her, doesn't it?!
If there's one thing I know, it's complicated being a girl...
Are you sure you're a dude?

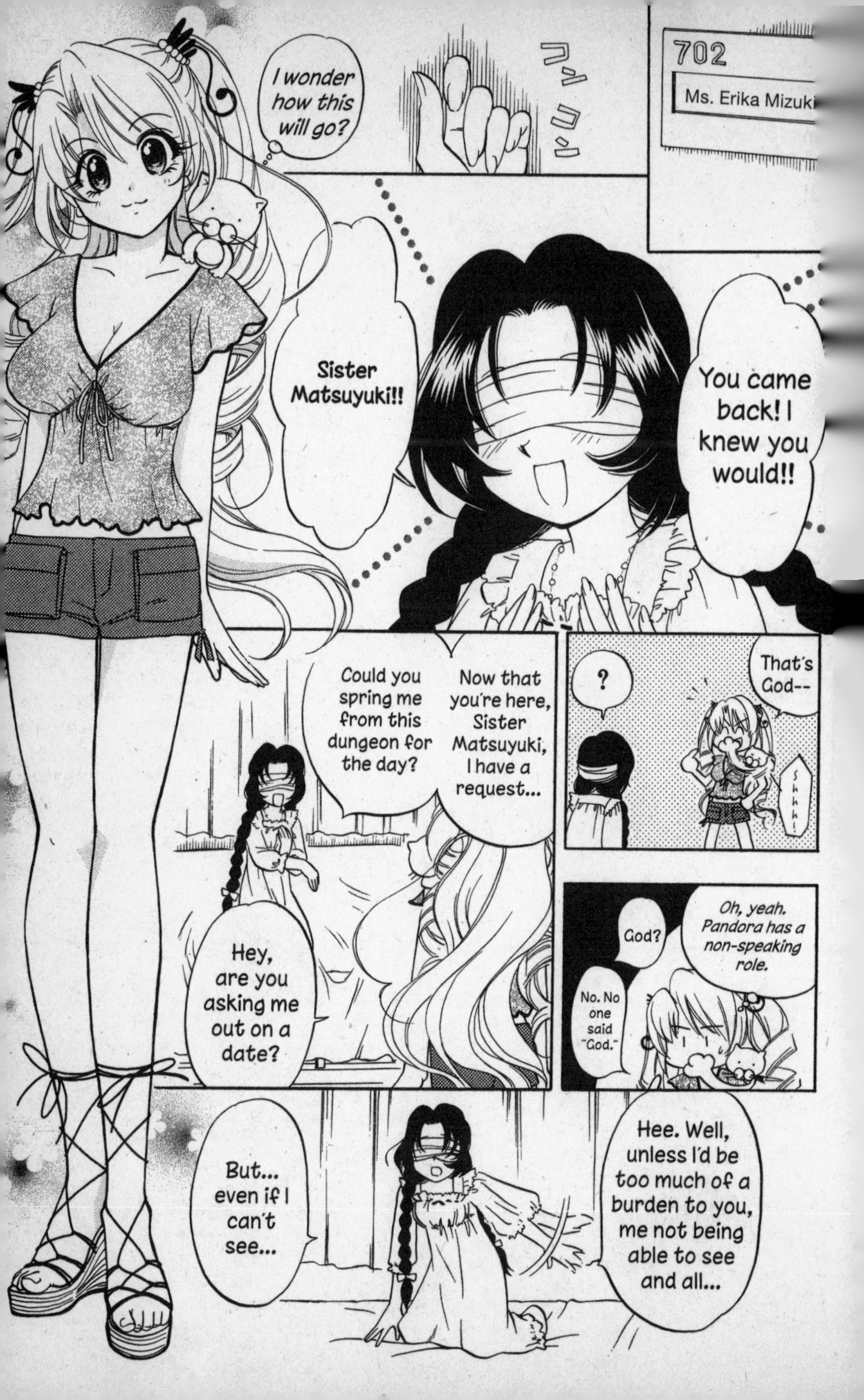
702
Ms. Erika Mizuki
コンコン
You came back! I knew you would!!
Sister Matsuyuki!!
That's God--
Shhh!
?
Now that you're here, Sister Matsuyuki, I have a request...
Could you spring me from this dungeon for the day?
Hey, are you asking me out on a date?
Oh, yeah. Pandora has a non-speaking role.
God?
No. No one said "God."
Hee. Well, unless I'd be too much of a burden to you, me not being able to see and all...
But... even if I can't see...
I wonder how this will go?

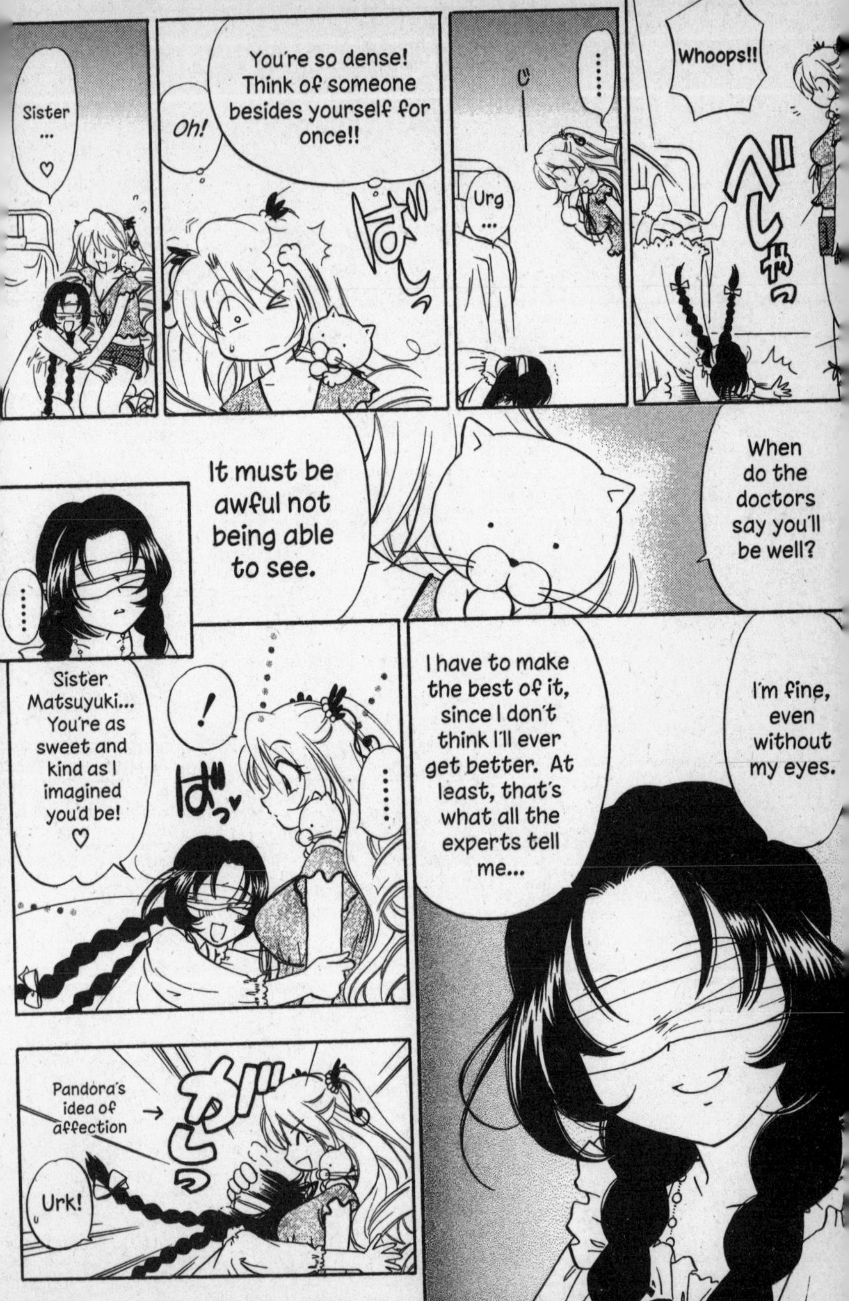

Whoops!!
べしゃっ
......
Urg ...
You're so dense! Think of someone besides yourself for once!!
Oh!
ばしっ
Sister ... ♡
When do the doctors say you'll be well?
It must be awful not being able to see.
......
I'm fine, even without my eyes.
I have to make the best of it, since I don't think I'll ever get better. At least, that's what all the experts tell me...
!
......
ばっ♥
Sister Matsuyuki... You're as sweet and kind as I imagined you'd be! ♡
がしっ
Pandora's idea of affection →
Urk!

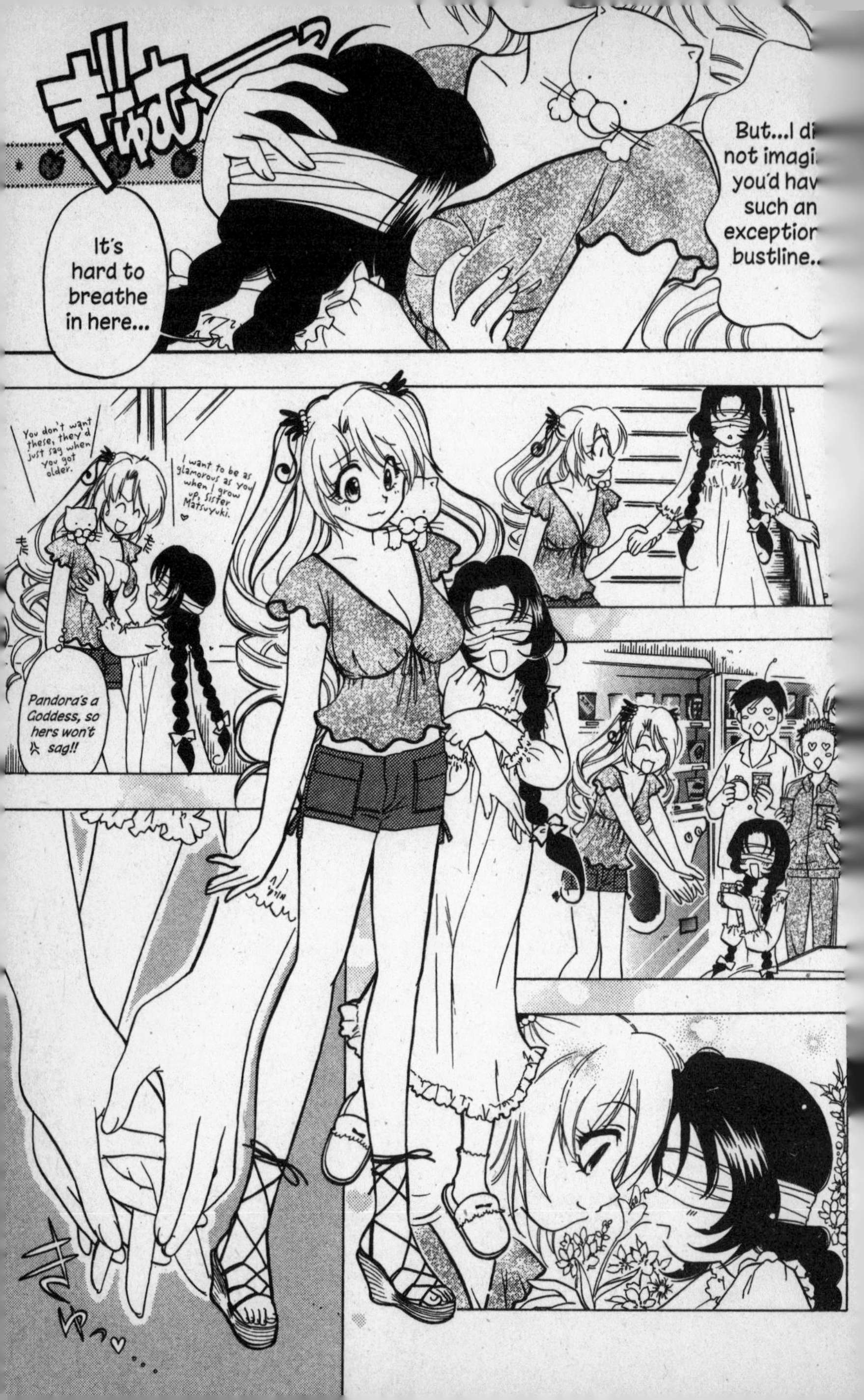

But...I di
not imagi
you'd hav
such an
exception
bustline..
ぎゅむ
It's hard to breathe in here...
I want to be as glamorous as you when I grow up, Sister Matsuyuki.
You don't want these, they'd just sag when you got older.
Pandora's a Goddess, so hers won't sag!!
きゅっ♡...

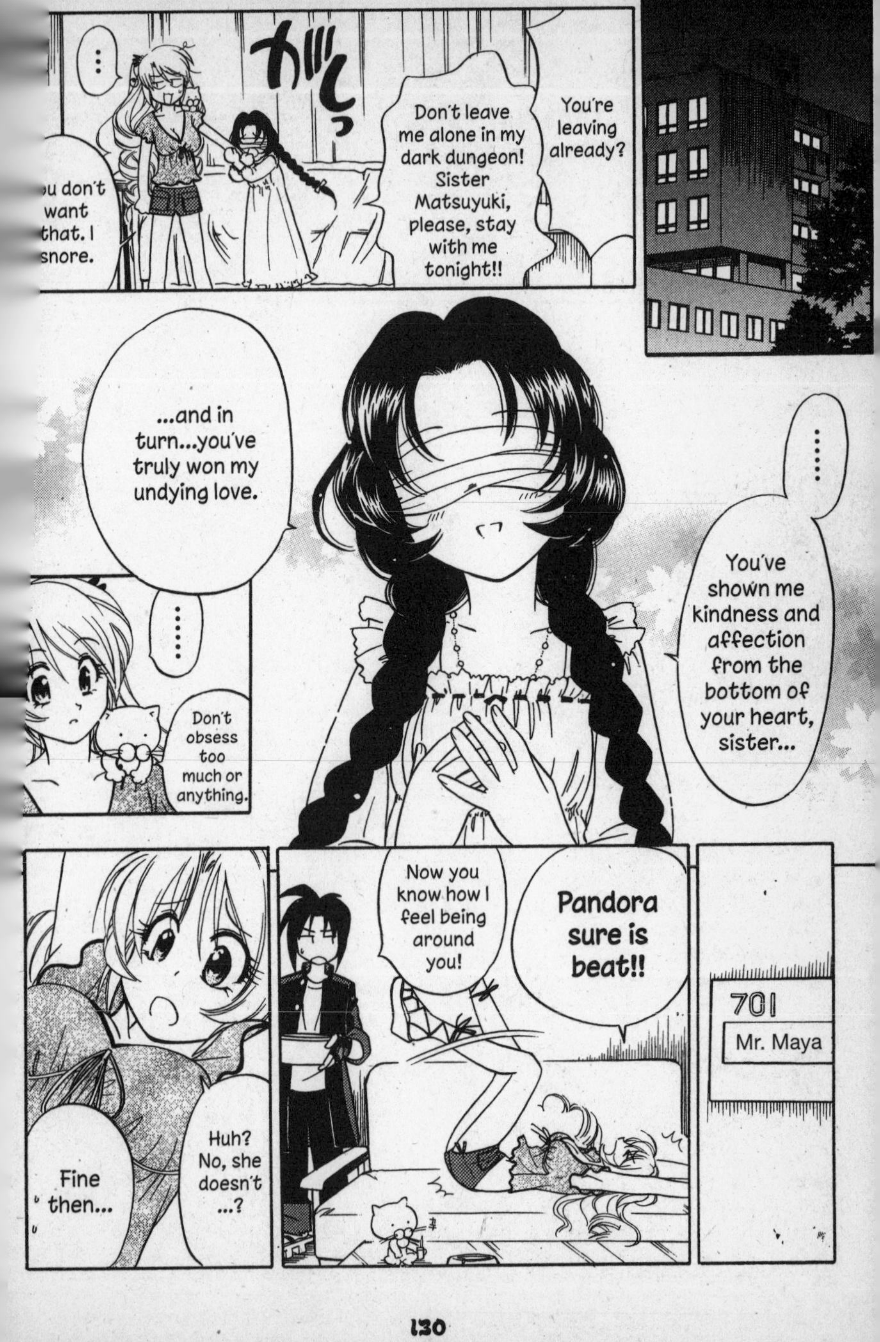
You're leaving already?
Don't leave me alone in my dark dungeon! Sister Matsuyuki, please, stay with me tonight!!
がしっ
...
u don't want that. I snore.
......
You've shown me kindness and affection from the bottom of your heart, sister...
...and in turn...you've truly won my undying love.
......
Don't obsess too much or anything.
701
Mr. Maya
Pandora sure is beat!!
Now you know how I feel being around you!
Huh? No, she doesn't ...?
Fine then...

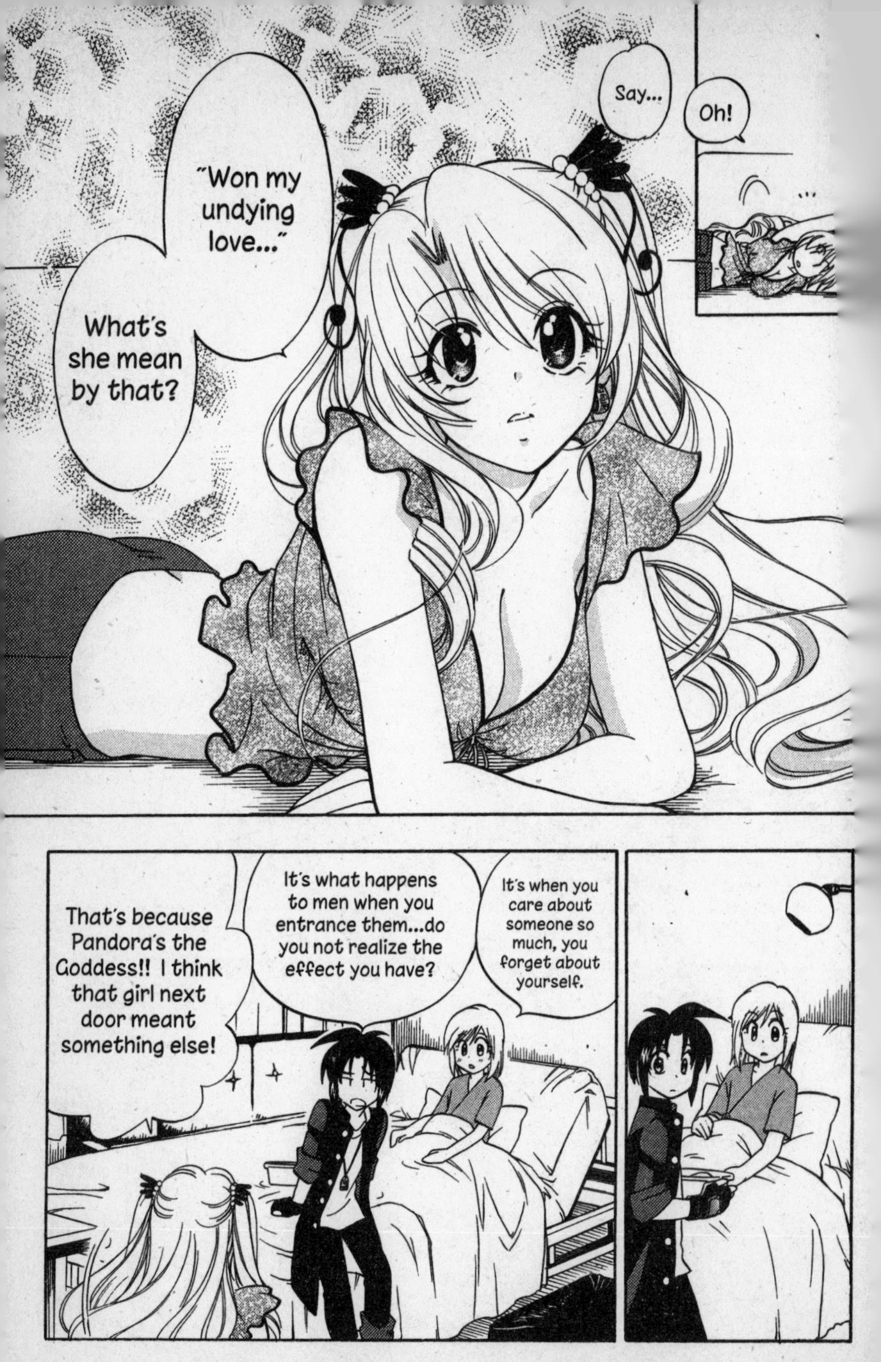
Oh!
...
Say...
"Won my undying love..."
What's she mean by that?
It's when you care about someone so much, you forget about yourself.
It's what happens to men when you entrance them...do you not realize the effect you have?
That's because Pandora's the Goddess!! I think that girl next door meant something else!

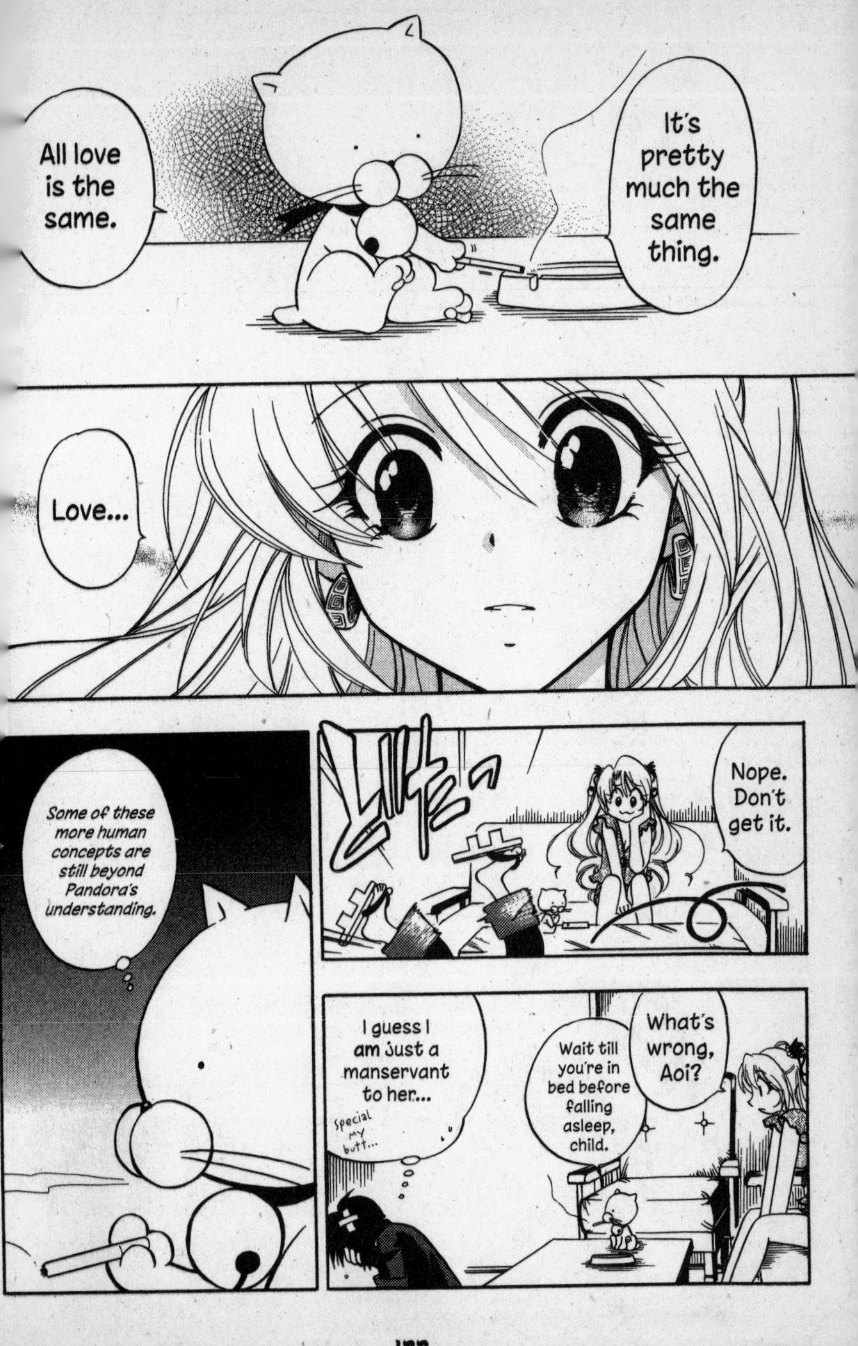
It's pretty much the same thing.
All love is the same.
Love...
Nope. Don't get it.
What's wrong, Aoi?
Wait till you're in bed before falling asleep, child.
I guess I am just a manservant to her...
Special my butt...
Some of these more human concepts are still beyond Pandora's understanding.

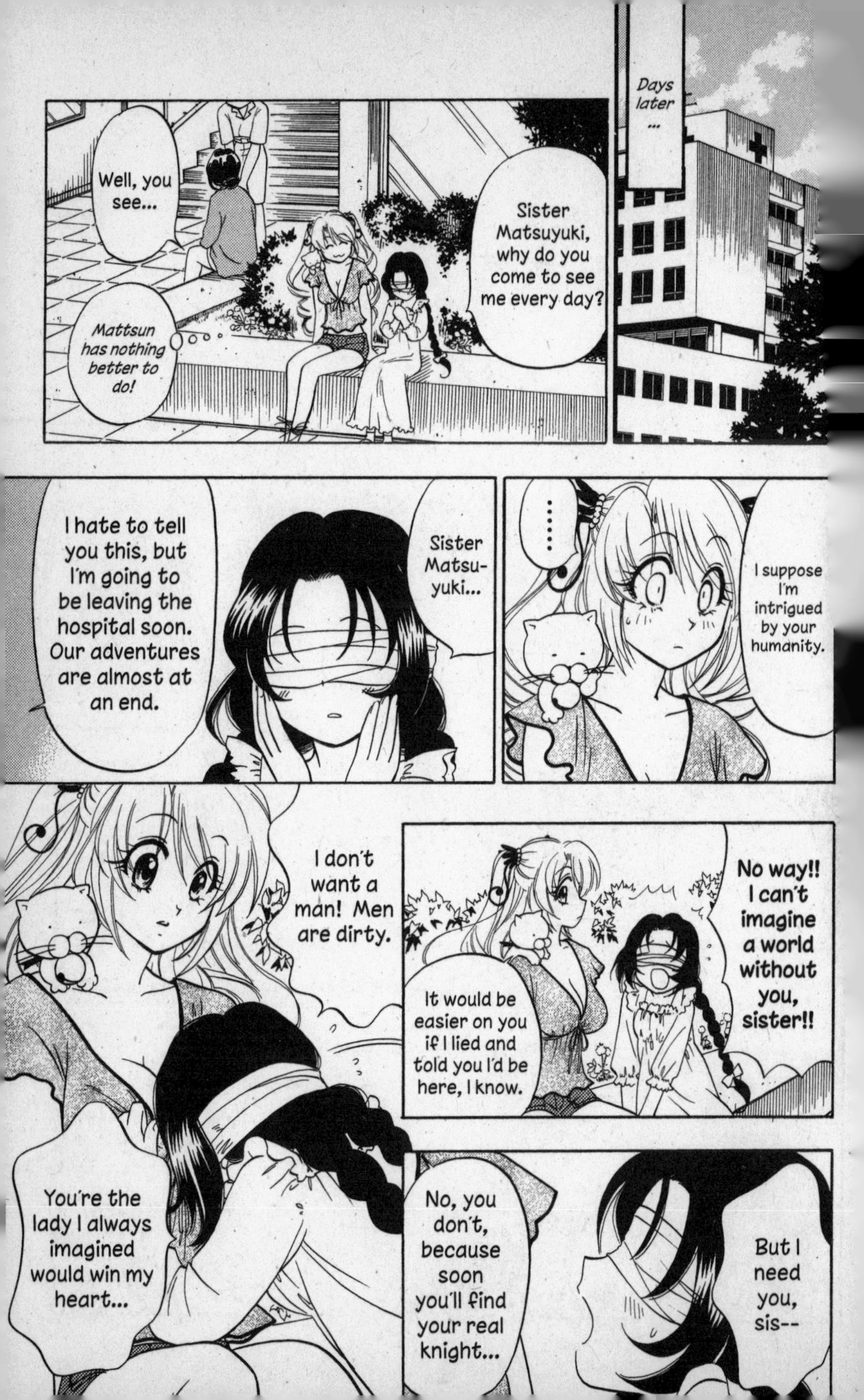
Days later ...
Sister Matsuyuki, why do you come to see me every day?
Well, you see...
Mattsun has nothing better to do!
......
I suppose I'm intrigued by your humanity.
Sister Matsu-yuki...
I hate to tell you this, but I'm going to be leaving the hospital soon. Our adventures are almost at an end.
No way!! I can't imagine a world without you, sister!!
It would be easier on you if I lied and told you I'd be here, I know.
But I need you, sis--
No, you don't, because soon you'll find your real knight...
I don't want a man! Men are dirty.
You're the lady I always imagined would win my heart...

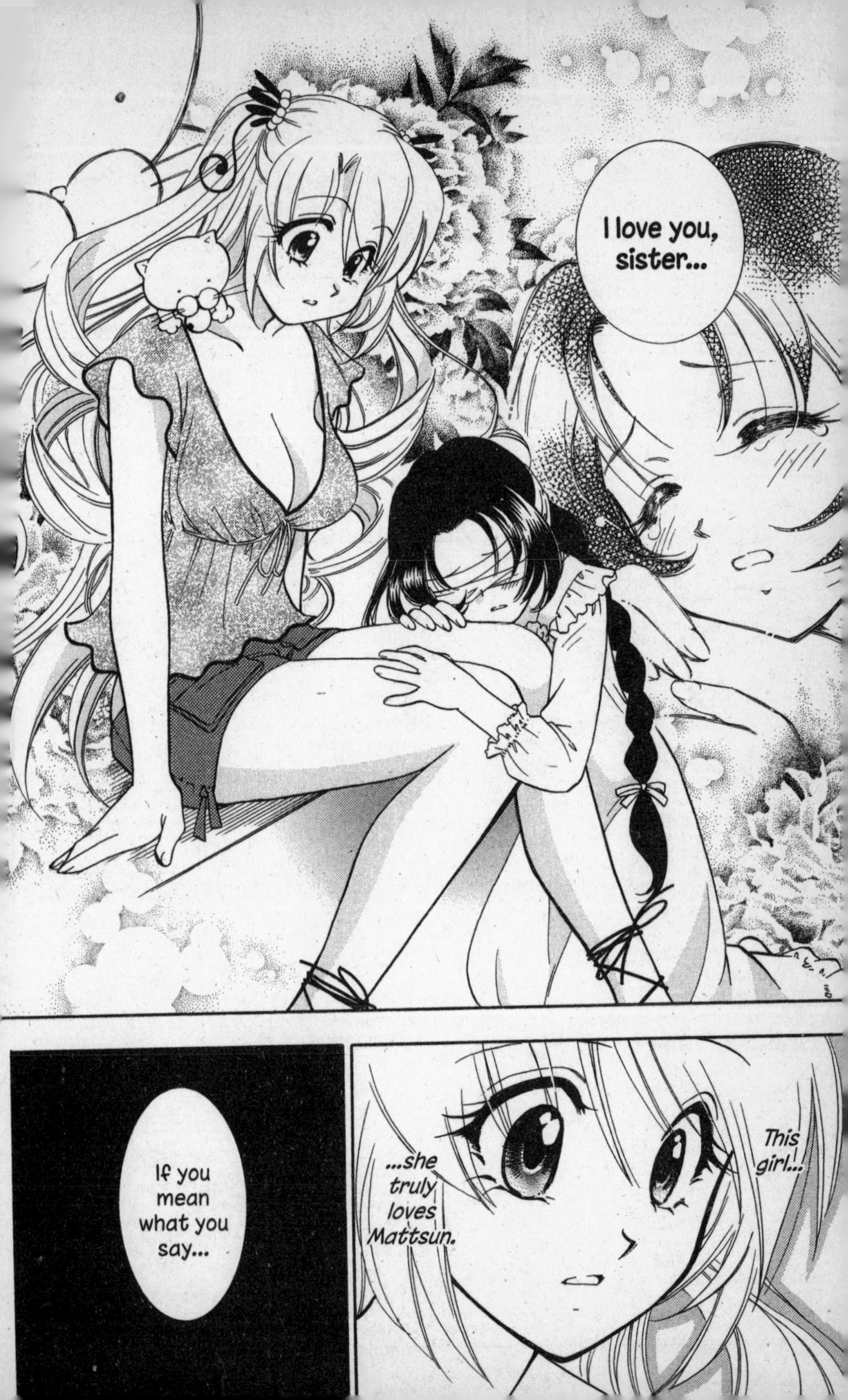
I love you, sister...
This girl...
...she truly loves Mattsun.
If you mean what you say...

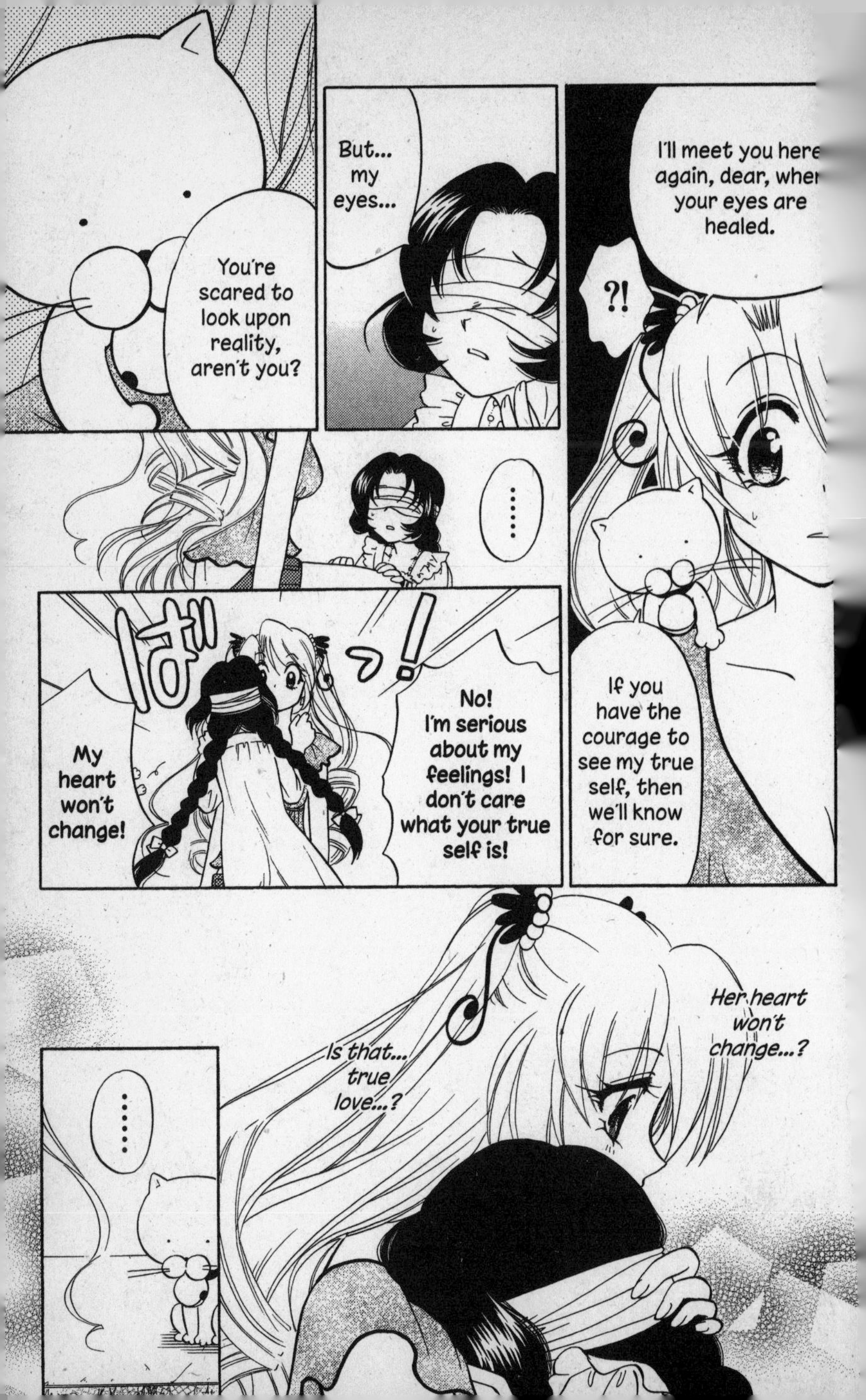
I'll meet you here again, dear, whe your eyes are healed.
?!
If you have the courage to see my true self, then we'll know for sure.
But... my eyes...
You're scared to look upon reality, aren't you?
......
ばっ!
No! I'm serious about my feelings! I don't care what your true self is!
My heart won't change!
Her heart won't change...?
Is that... true love...?
......

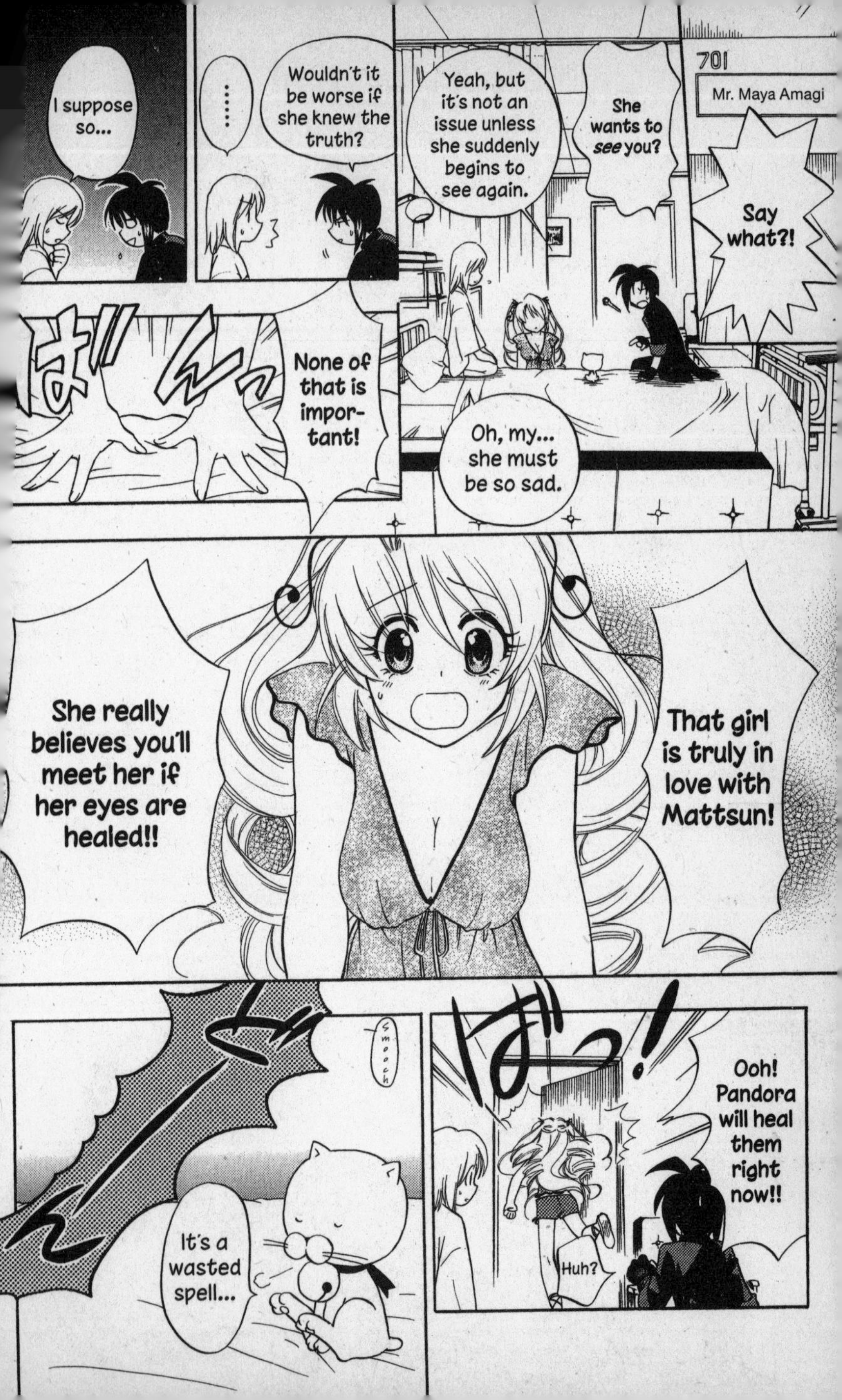
701
Mr. Maya Amagi
Say what?!
She wants to see you?
Yeah, but it's not an issue unless she suddenly begins to see again.
Oh, my... she must be so sad.
Wouldn't it be worse if she knew the truth?
......
I suppose so...
None of that is important!
ばんっ
That girl is truly in love with Mattsun!
She really believes you'll meet her if her eyes are healed!!
ばっ!!
Ooh! Pandora will heal them right now!!
Huh?
Smooch
It's a wasted spell...

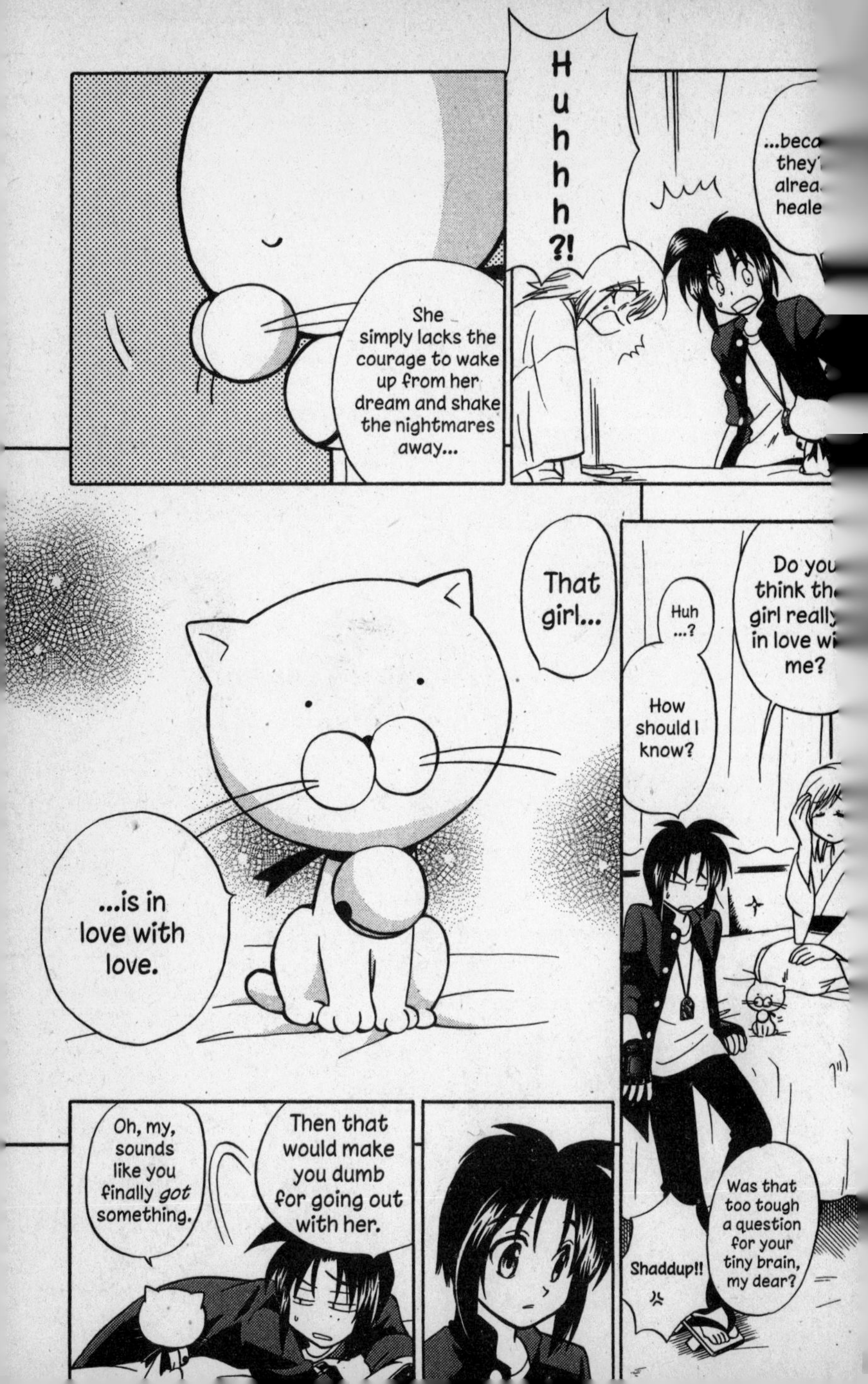
...beca they' alrea heale
Huhhh?!
She simply lacks the courage to wake up from her dream and shake the nightmares away...
Do you think th girl really in love wi me?
Huh ...?
How should I know?
Was that too tough a question for your tiny brain, my dear?
Shaddup!!
That girl...
...is in love with love.
Then that would make you dumb for going out with her.
Oh, my, sounds like you finally *got* something.

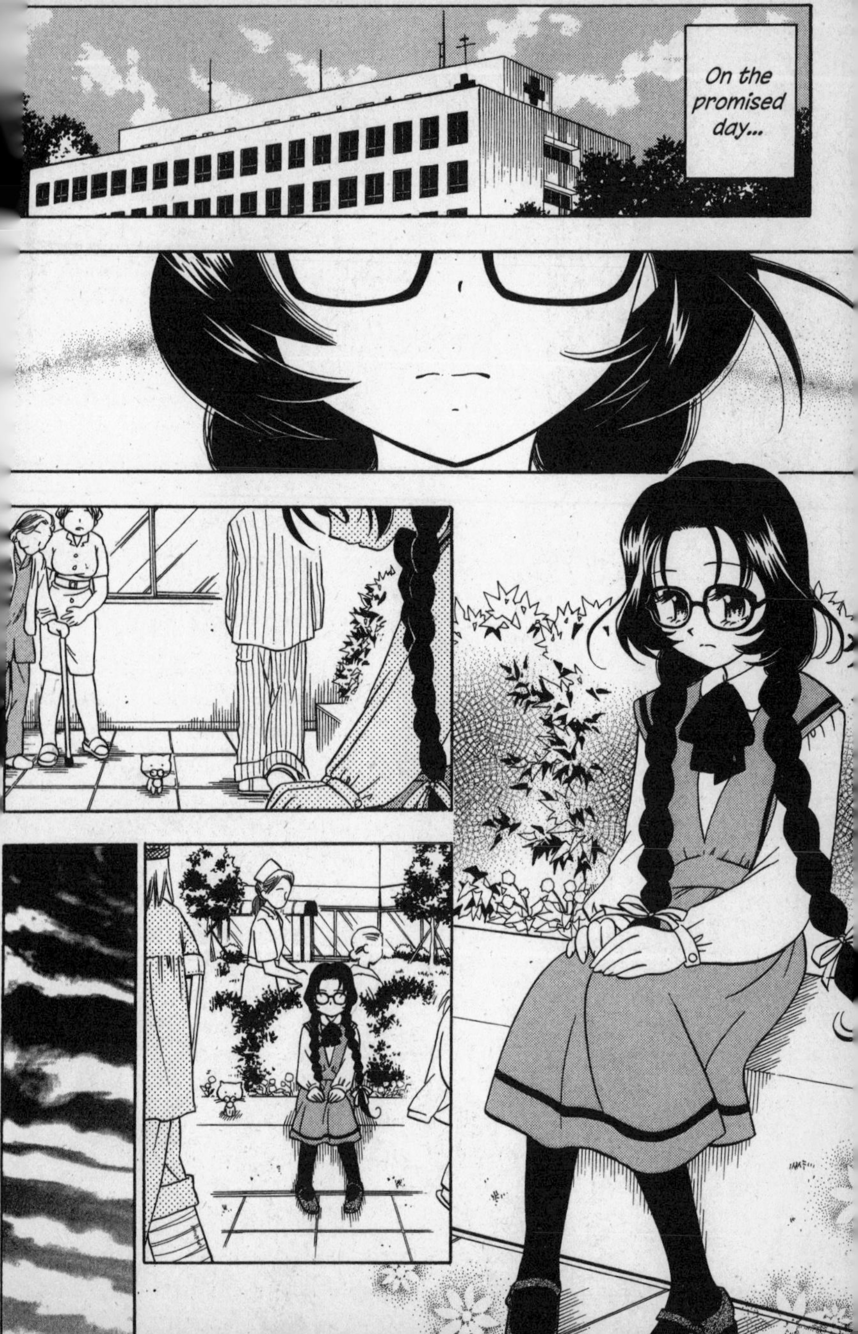
On the promised day...

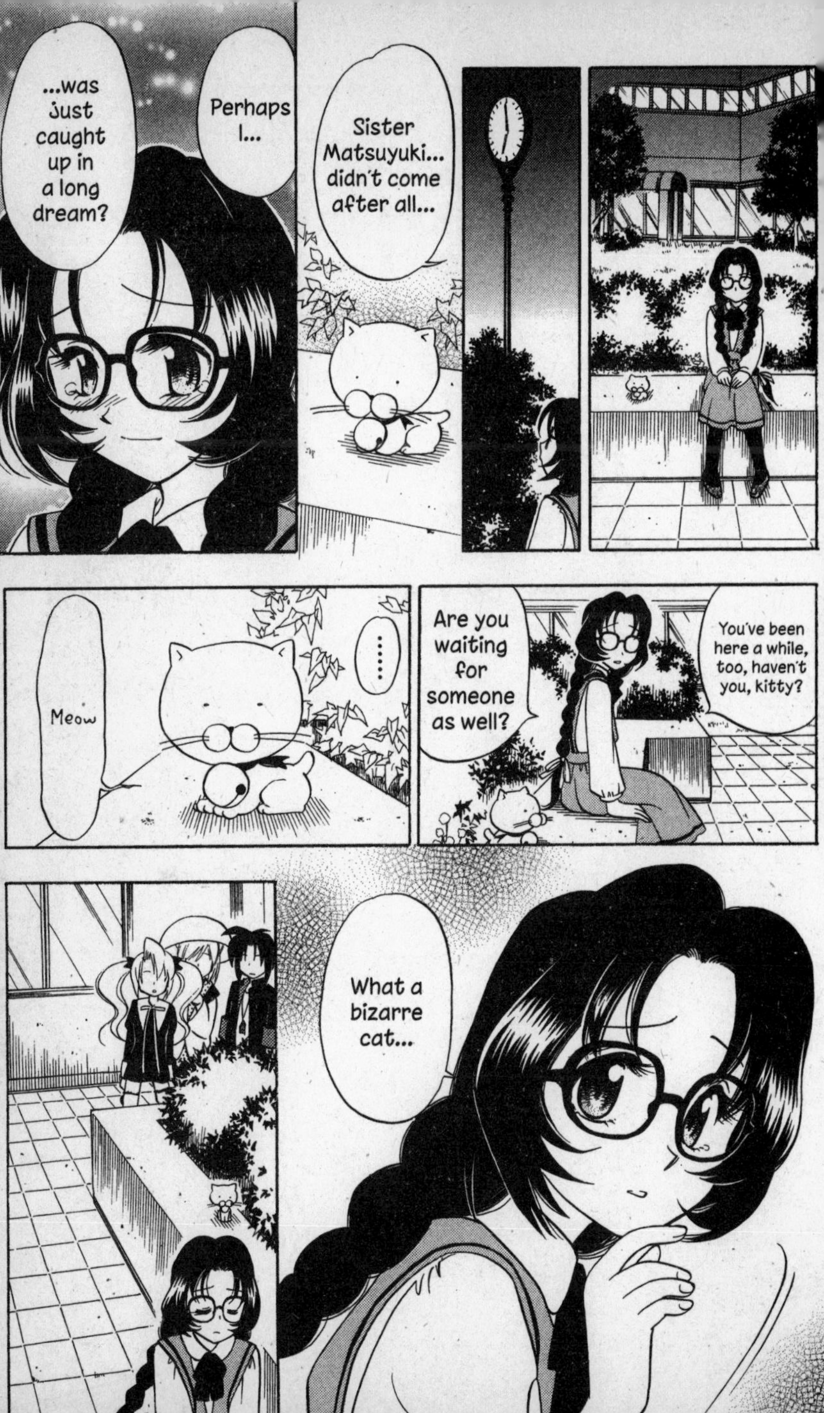
Sister Matsuyuki... didn't come after all...
Perhaps I...
...was just caught up in a long dream?
You've been here a while, too, haven't you, kitty?
Are you waiting for someone as well?
......
Meow
What a bizarre cat...

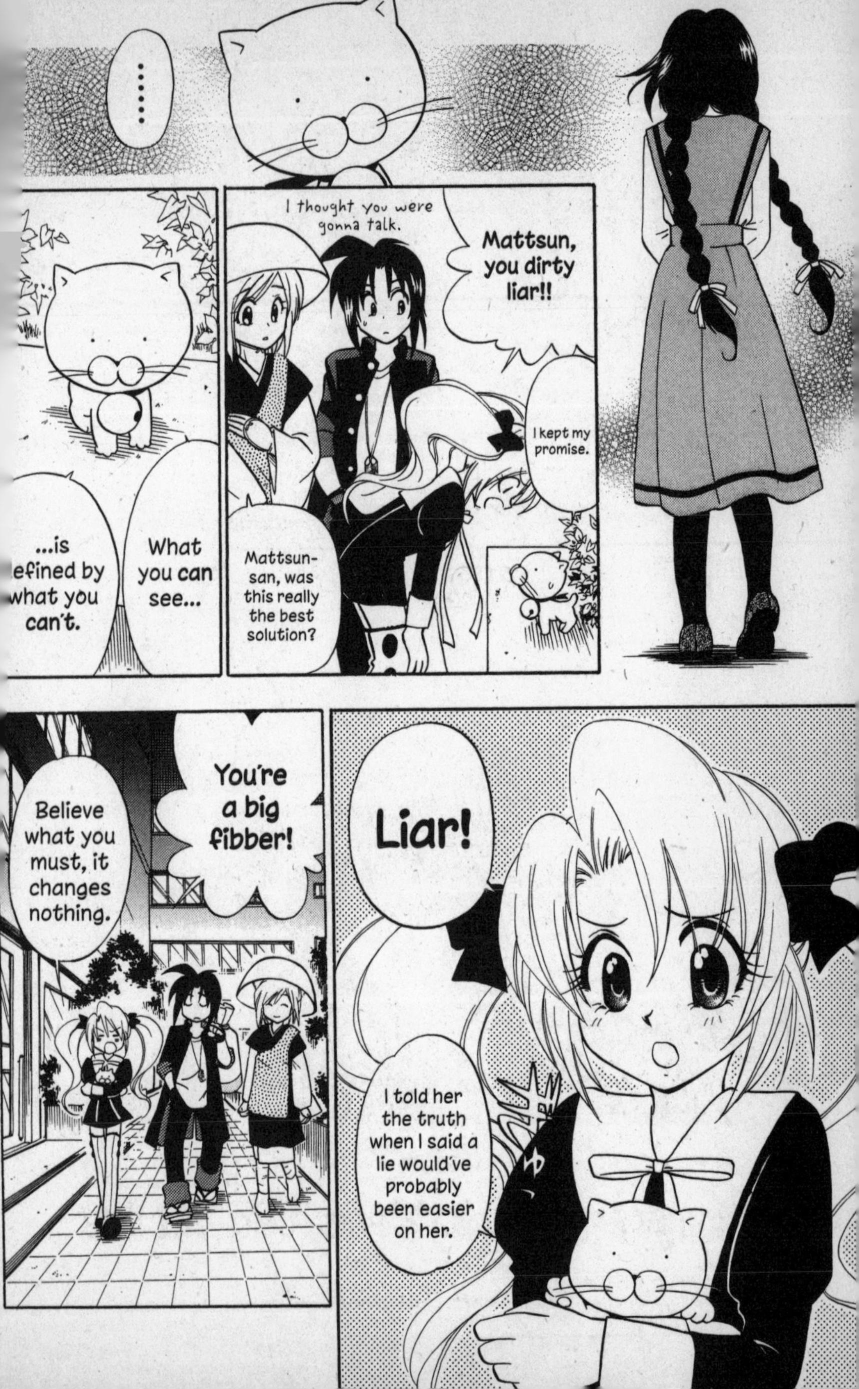
......
Mattsun, you dirty liar!!
I thought you were gonna talk.
I kept my promise.
Mattsun-san, was this really the best solution?
What you can see...
...is efined by what you can't.
Liar!
I told her the truth when I said a lie would've probably been easier on her.
You're a big fibber!
Believe what you must, it changes nothing.

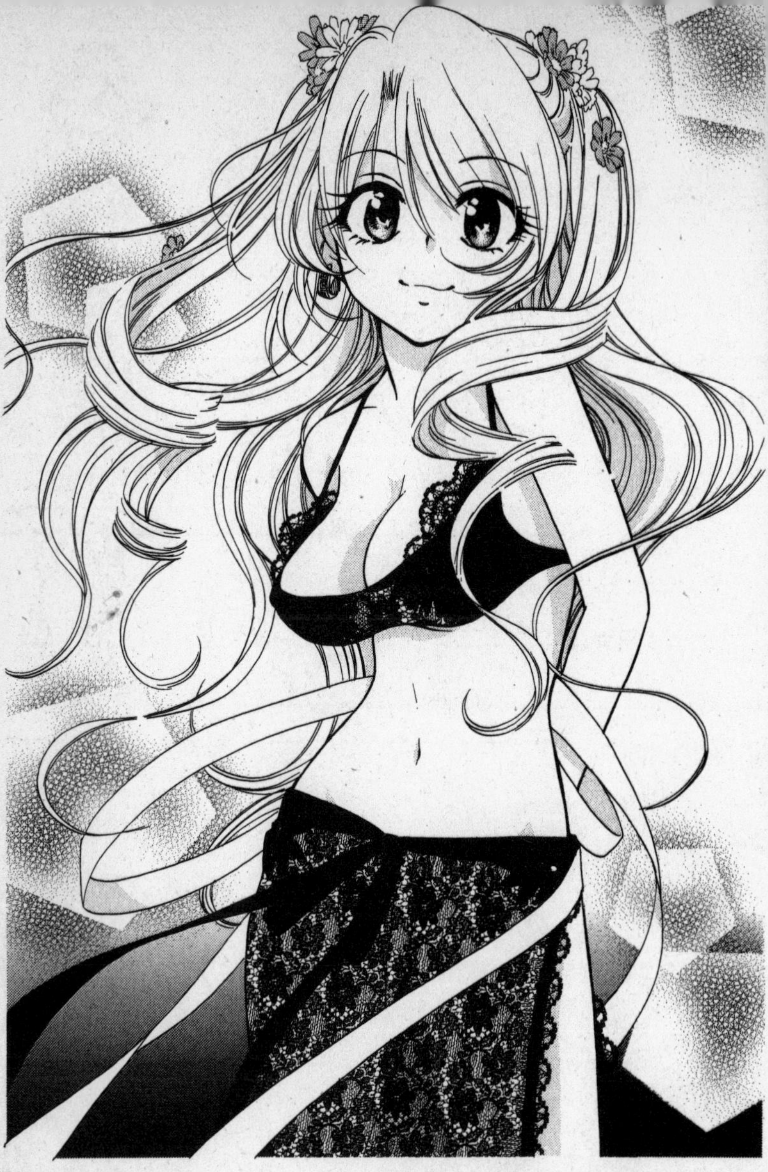

Chapter 6: A Trusting Heart

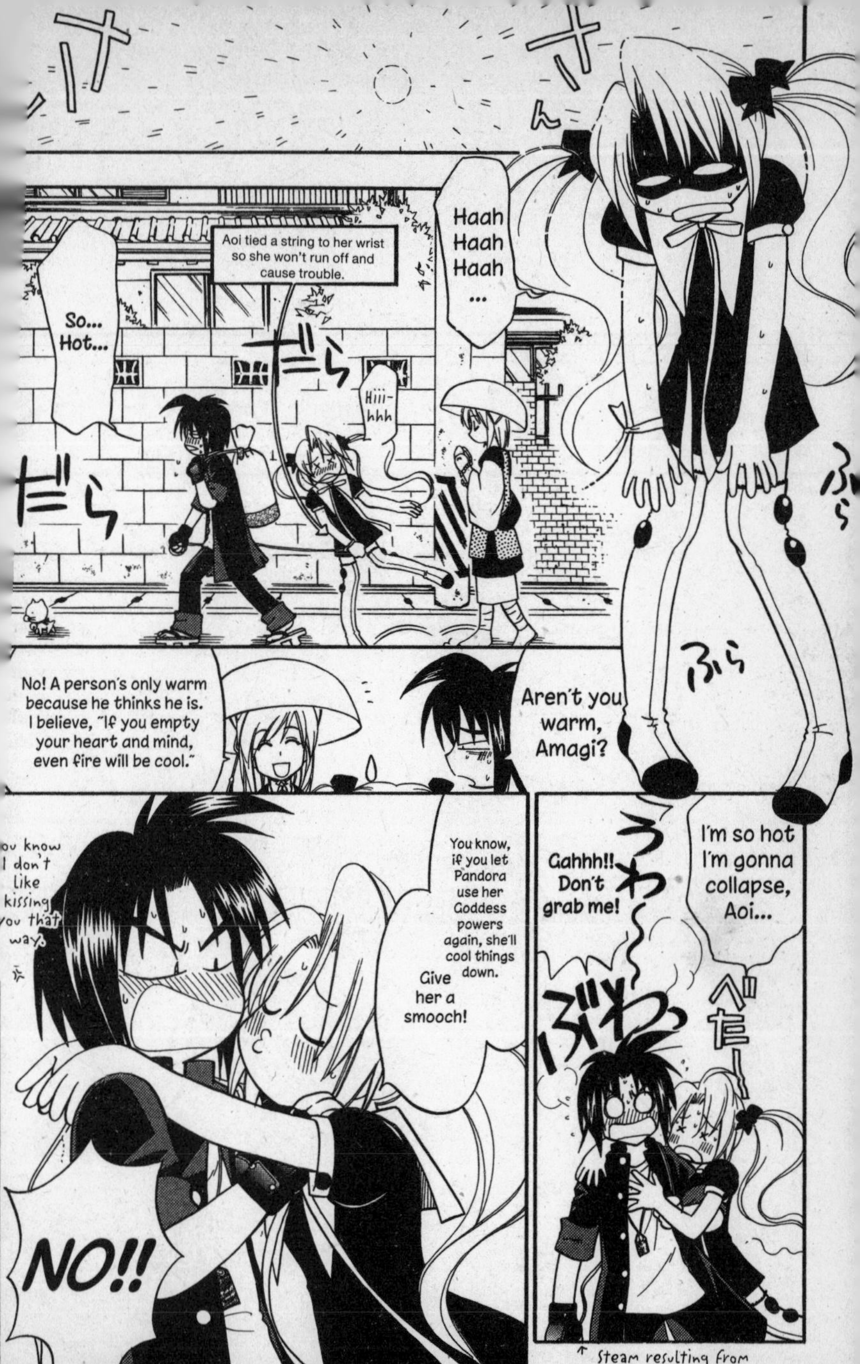
さん
ふら
ふら
Haah Haah Haah ...
Aoi tied a string to her wrist so she won't run off and cause trouble.
だら
Hiii-hhh
So... Hot...
だら
Aren't you warm, Amagi?
No! A person's only warm because he thinks he is. I believe, "If you empty your heart and mind, even fire will be cool."
I'm so hot I'm gonna collapse, Aoi...
べたー
うわ〜〜
Gahhh!! Don't grab me!
ぶわっ
↑ Steam resulting from increasing body temperature.
You know, if you let Pandora use her Goddess powers again, she'll cool things down.
Give her a smooch!
NO!!
ou know I don't like kissing you that way.

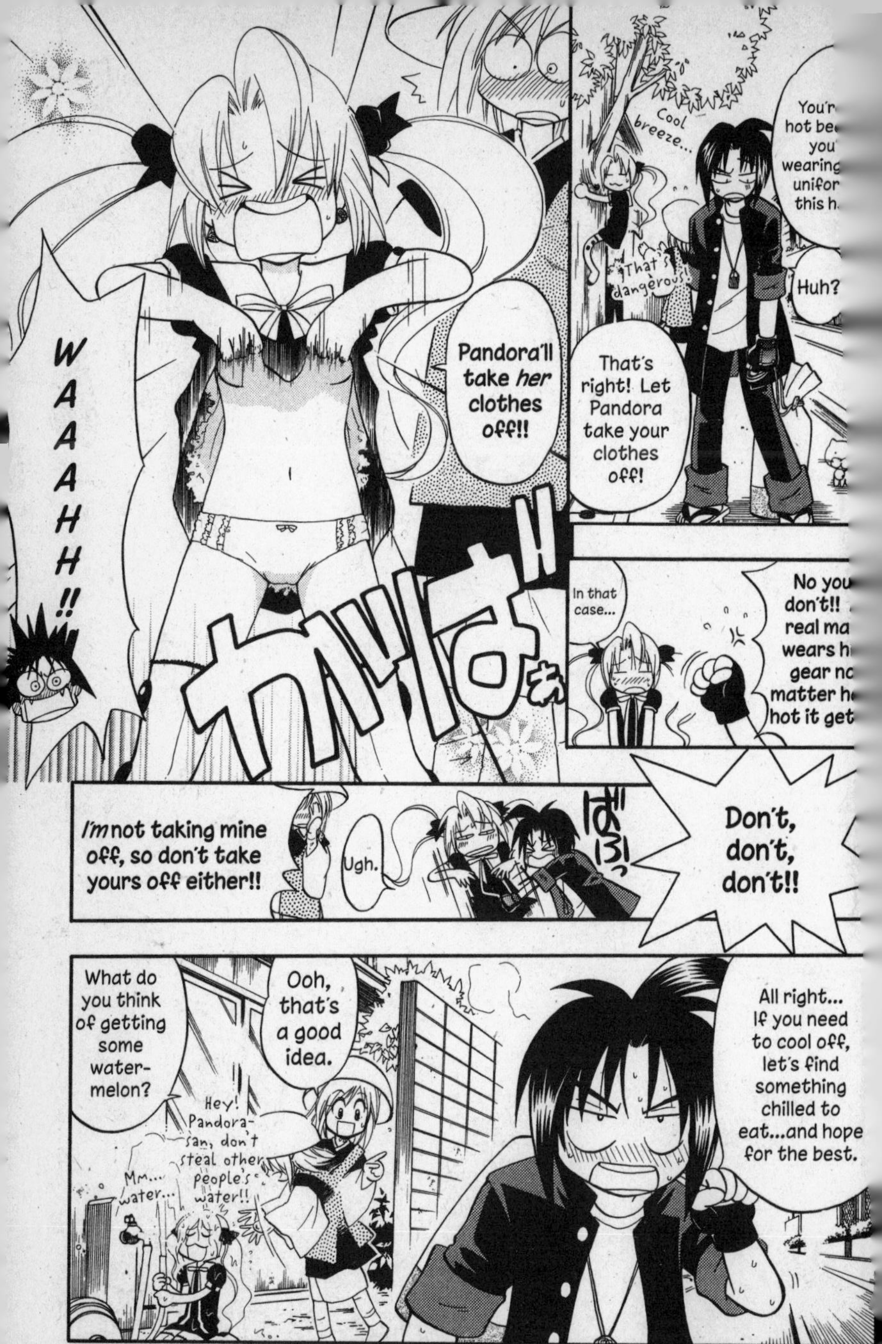

You'r hot bec you' wearing unifor this h
Huh?
Cool breeze...
That's dangerous!
That's right! Let Pandora take your clothes off!
No you don't!! real ma wears h gear no matter h hot it get
In that case...
Pandora'll take *her* clothes off!!
WAAAAHH!!
Don't, don't, don't!!
ばふっ
Ugh.
I'm not taking mine off, so don't take yours off either!!
All right... If you need to cool off, let's find something chilled to eat...and hope for the best.
Ooh, that's a good idea.
What do you think of getting some water-melon?
Hey! Pandora-san, don't steal other people's water!!
Mm... water...

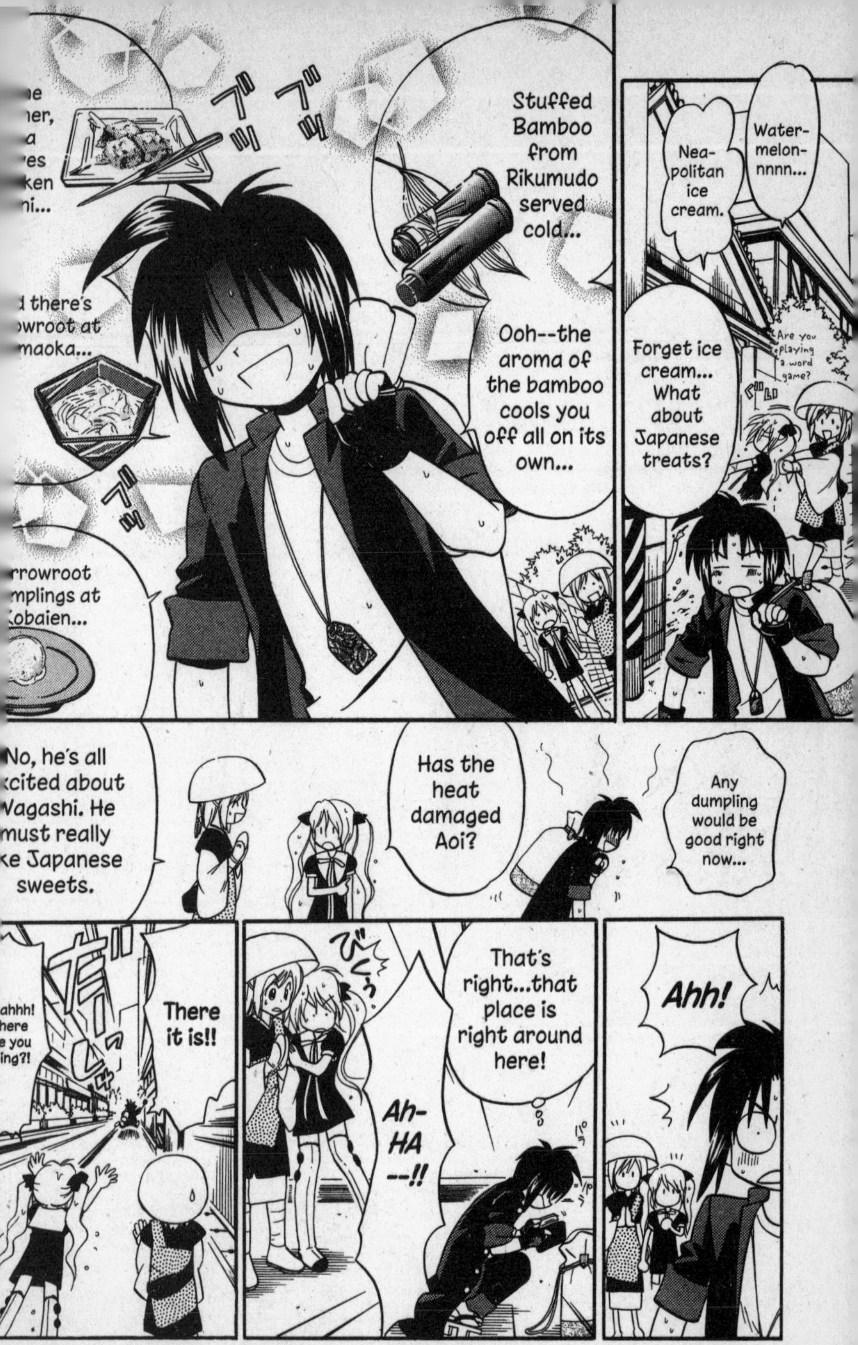
Water-melon-nnnn...
Nea-politan ice cream.
Forget ice cream... What about Japanese treats?
Are you playing a word game?
Stuffed Bamboo from Rikumudo served cold...
Ooh--the aroma of the bamboo cools you off all on its own...
he ner, a ves ken ni...
d there's owroot at maoka...
rrowroot mplings at Kobaien...
Any dumpling would be good right now...
Has the heat damaged Aoi?
No, he's all xcited about Vagashi. He must really xe Japanese sweets.
Ahh!
That's right...that place is right around here!
Ah-HA--!!
There it is!!
ahhh! here e you oing?!

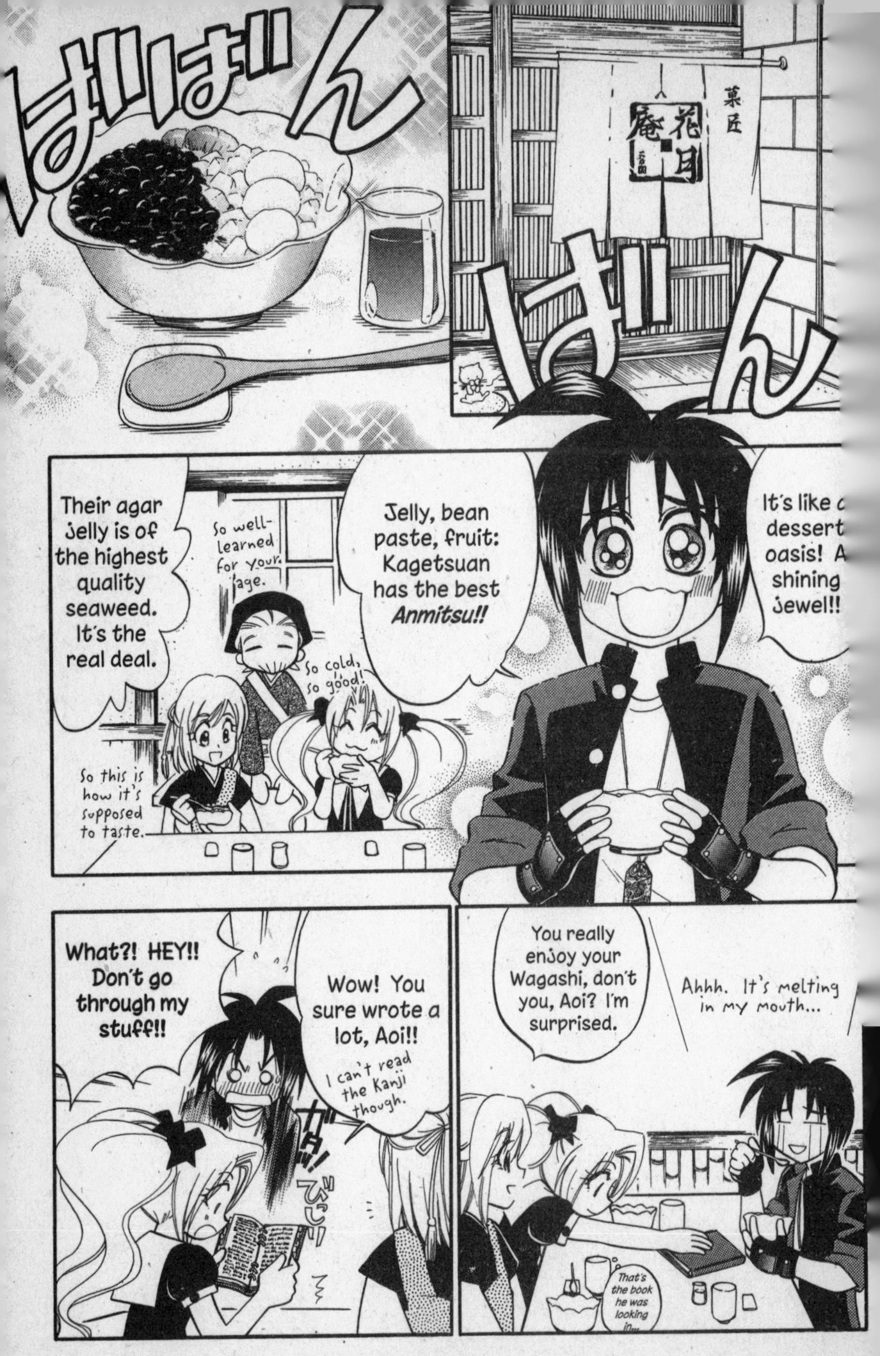
菓匠
花月庵
ばん
ばばん
It's like a dessert oasis! A shining jewel!!
Jelly, bean paste, fruit: Kagetsuan has the best *Anmitsu!!*
So cold, so good!
Their agar jelly is of the highest quality seaweed. It's the real deal.
So well-learned for your age.
So this is how it's supposed to taste.
Ahhh. It's melting in my mouth...
You really enjoy your Wagashi, don't you, Aoi? I'm surprised.
That's the book he was looking in...
Wow! You sure wrote a lot, Aoi!!
I can't read the Kanji though.
What?! HEY!! Don't go through my stuff!!
ガタッ
びくっ

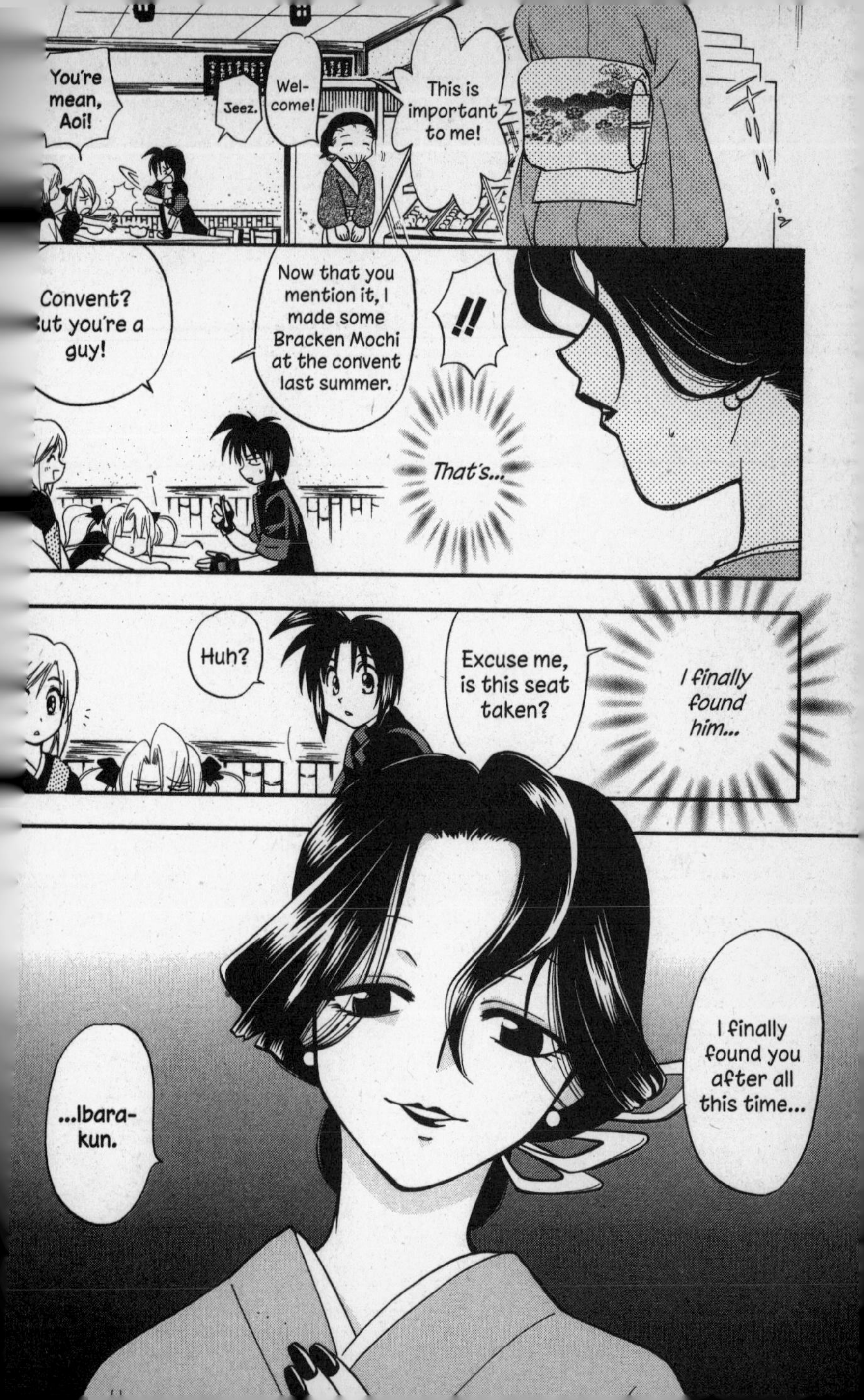
This is important to me!
Wel-come!
Jeez.
You're mean, Aoi!
!!
That's...
Now that you mention it, I made some Bracken Mochi at the convent last summer.
Convent? But you're a guy!
I finally found him...
Excuse me, is this seat taken?
Huh?
I finally found you after all this time...
...Ibara-kun.

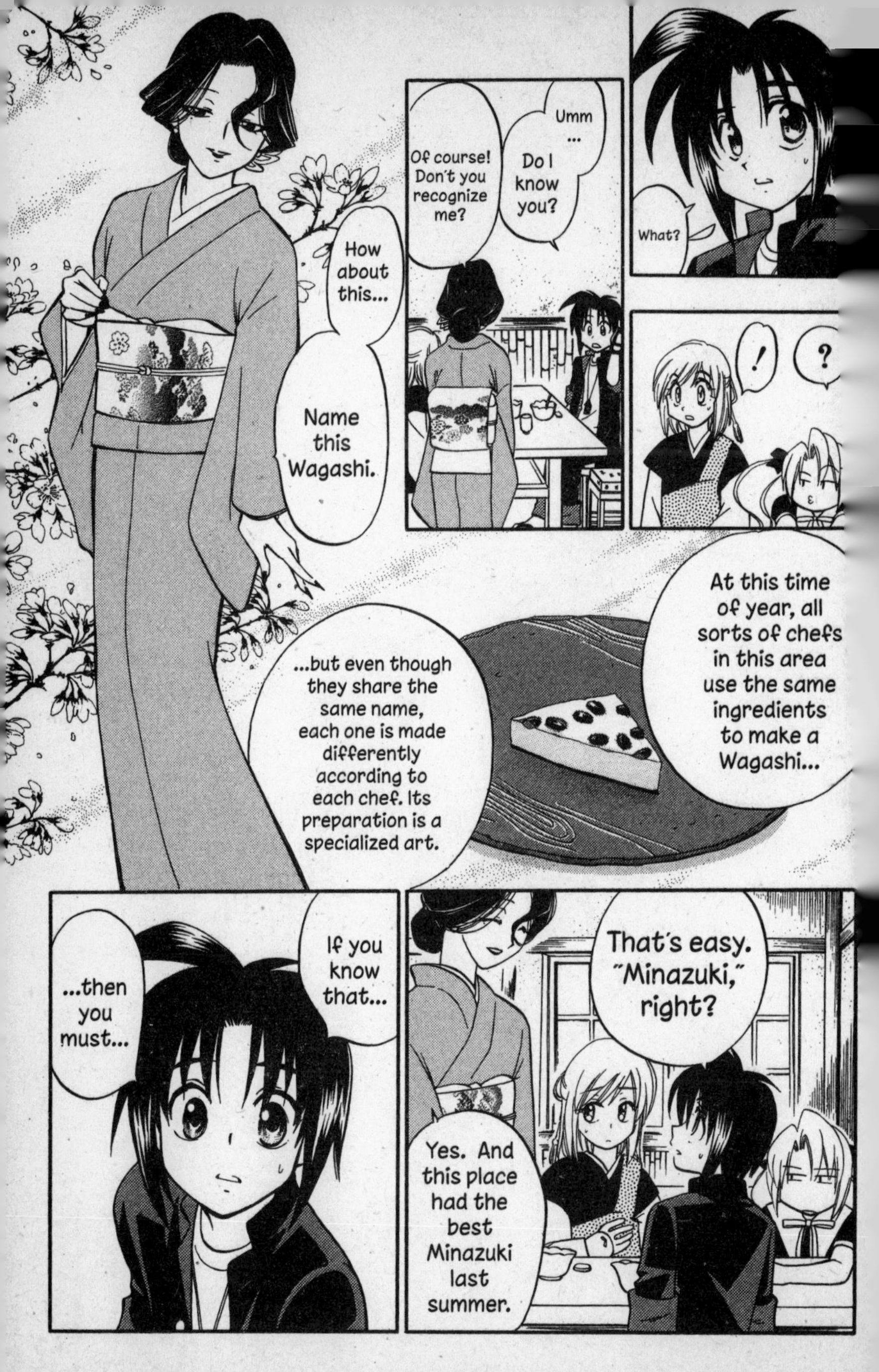
What?
!
?
Umm ... Do I know you?
Of course! Don't you recognize me?
How about this...
Name this Wagashi.
At this time of year, all sorts of chefs in this area use the same ingredients to make a Wagashi...
...but even though they share the same name, each one is made differently according to each chef. Its preparation is a specialized art.
That's easy. "Minazuki," right?
Yes. And this place had the best Minazuki last summer.
If you know that...
...then you must...

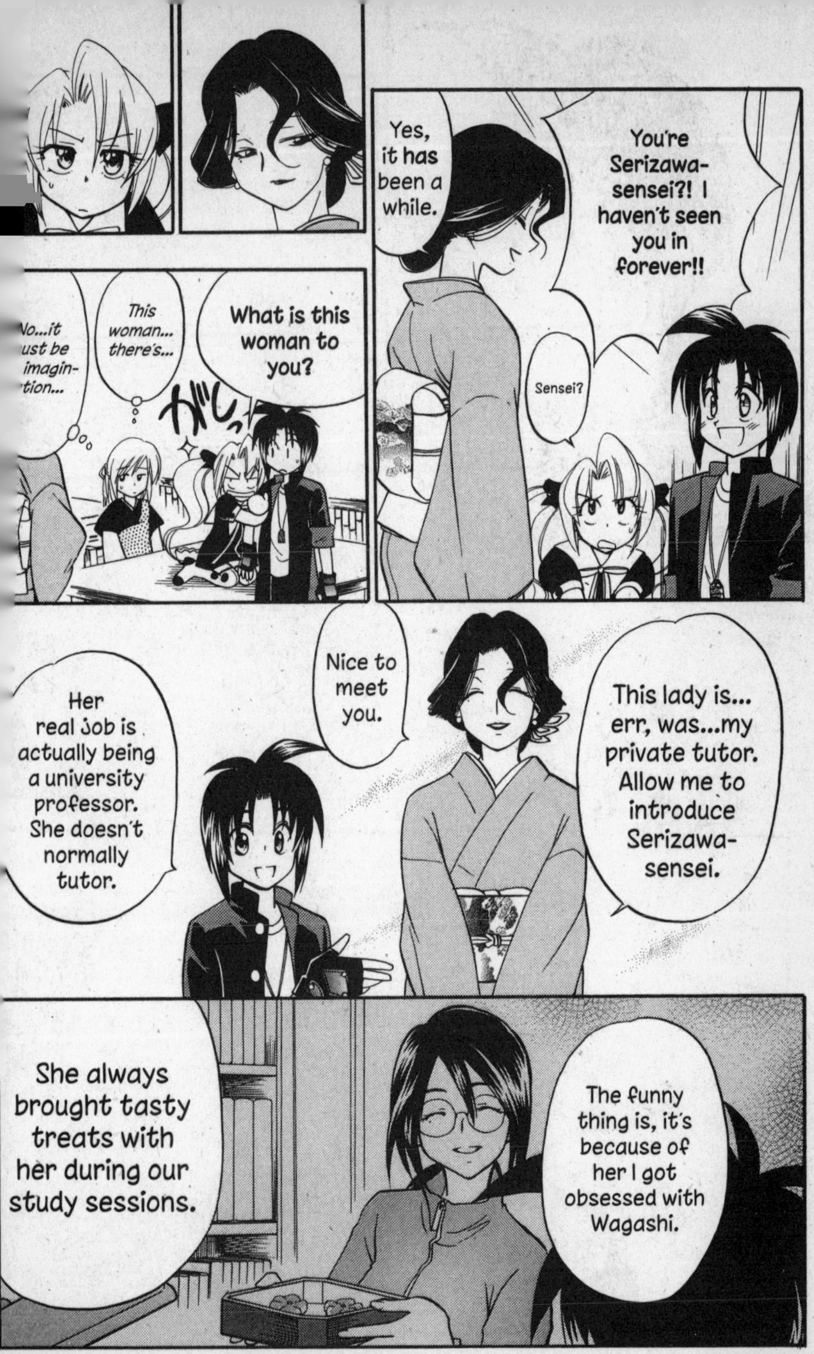
You're Serizawa-sensei?! I haven't seen you in forever!!
Yes, it has been a while.
Sensei?
What is this woman to you?
がしっ
This woman... there's...
No...it ust be imagin-tion...
This lady is... err, was...my private tutor. Allow me to introduce Serizawa-sensei.
Nice to meet you.
Her real job is actually being a university professor. She doesn't normally tutor.
The funny thing is, it's because of her I got obsessed with Wagashi.
She always brought tasty treats with her during our study sessions.

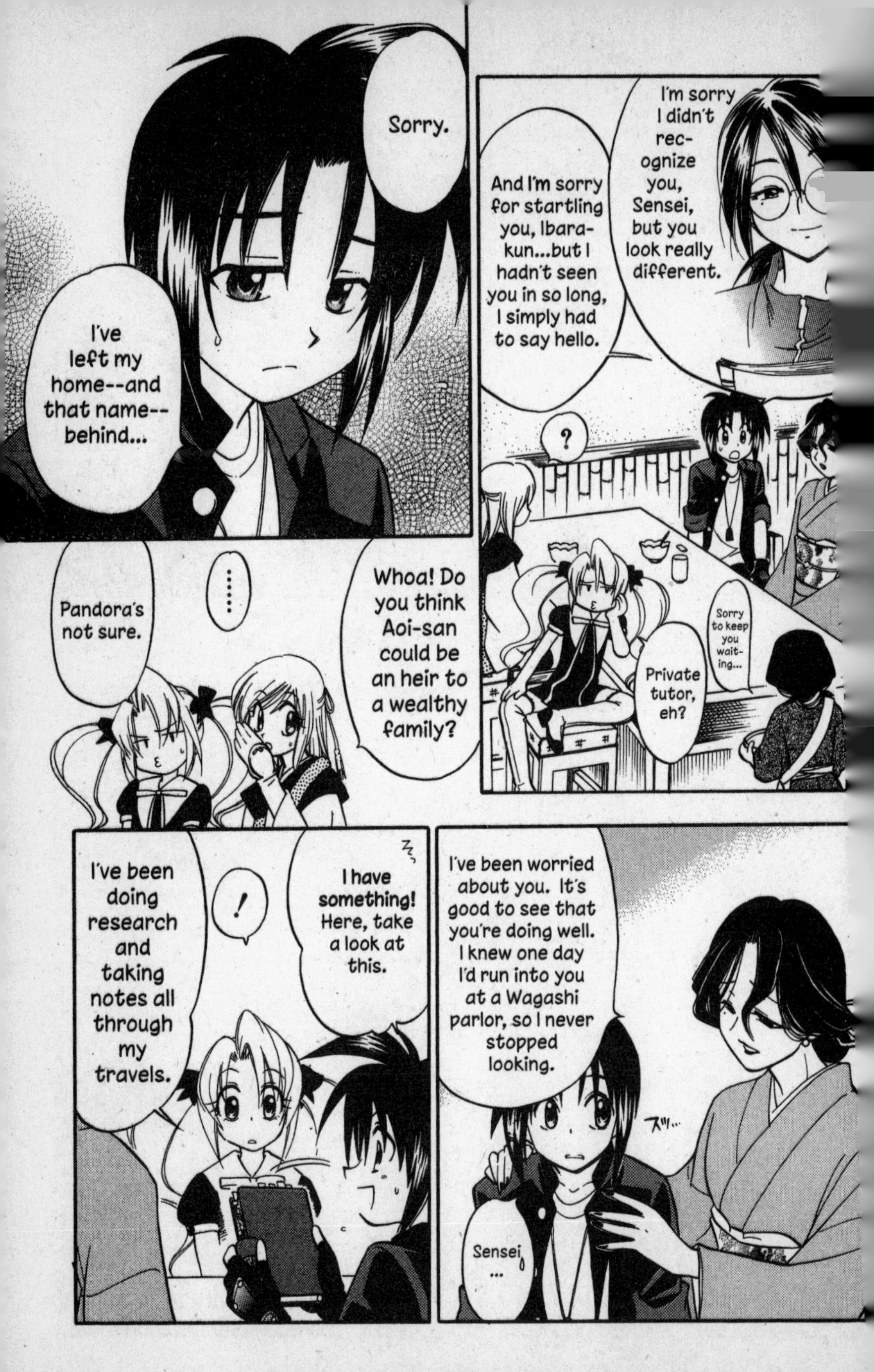
I'm sorry I didn't rec-ognize you, Sensei, but you look really different.
And I'm sorry for startling you, Ibara-kun...but I hadn't seen you in so long, I simply had to say hello.
?
Sorry to keep you wait-ing...
Private tutor, eh?
Sorry.
I've left my home--and that name--behind...
Whoa! Do you think Aoi-san could be an heir to a wealthy family?
......
Pandora's not sure.
I've been worried about you. It's good to see that you're doing well. I knew one day I'd run into you at a Wagashi parlor, so I never stopped looking.
ズッ...
Sensei...
I have something! Here, take a look at this.
!
I've been doing research and taking notes all through my travels.

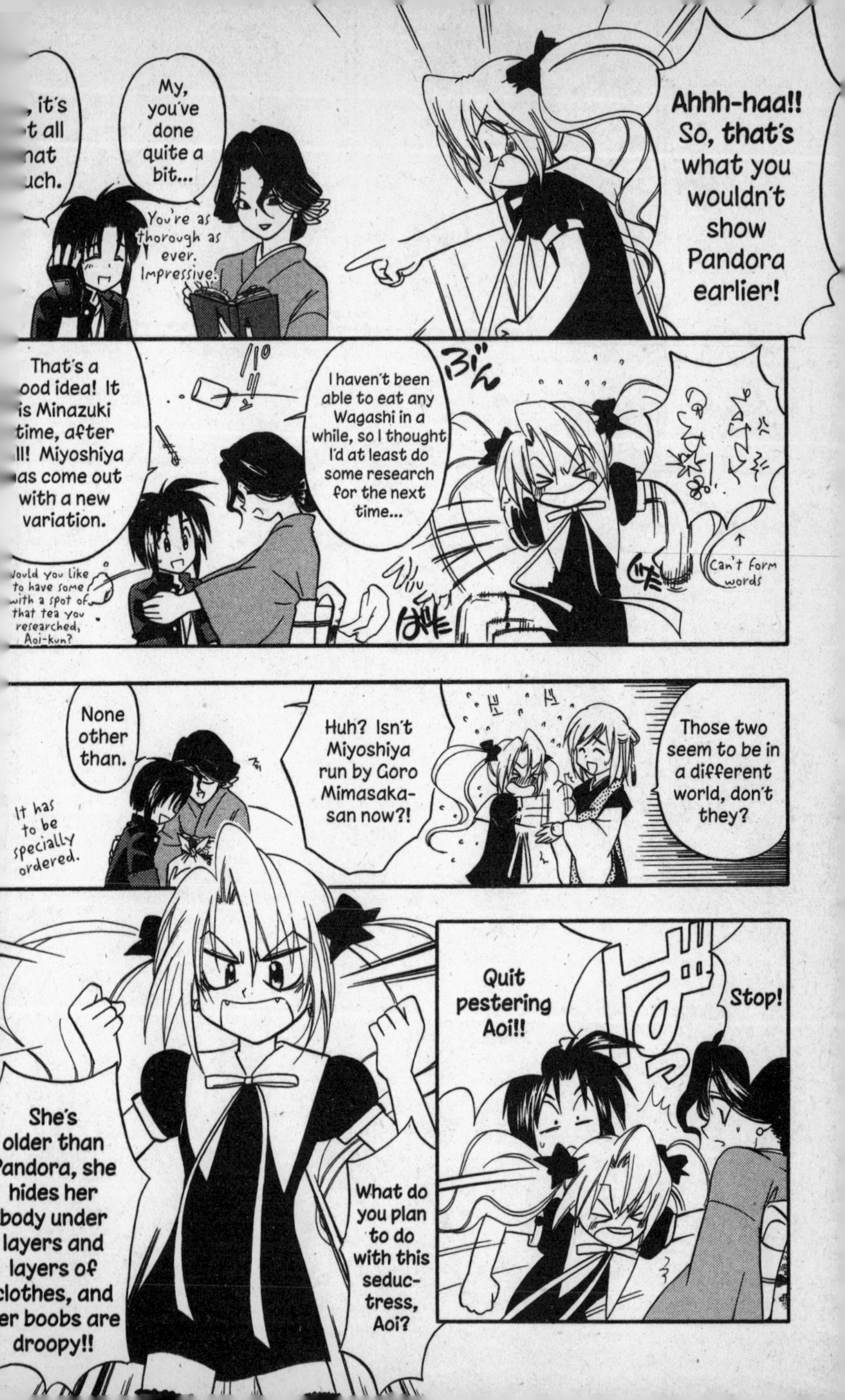

Ahhh-haa!! So, that's what you wouldn't show Pandora earlier!
My, you've done quite a bit...
You're as thorough as ever. Impressive.
Can't form words
I haven't been able to eat any Wagashi in a while, so I thought I'd at least do some research for the next time...
That's a ood idea! It is Minazuki time, after ll! Miyoshiya as come out with a new variation.
ould you like to have some with a spot of that tea you researched, Aoi-kun?
Those two seem to be in a different world, don't they?
Huh? Isn't Miyoshiya run by Goro Mimasaka-san now?!
None other than.
It has to be specially ordered.
Stop!
Quit pestering Aoi!!
What do you plan to do with this seductress, Aoi?
She's older than Pandora, she hides her body under layers and layers of clothes, and her boobs are droopy!!

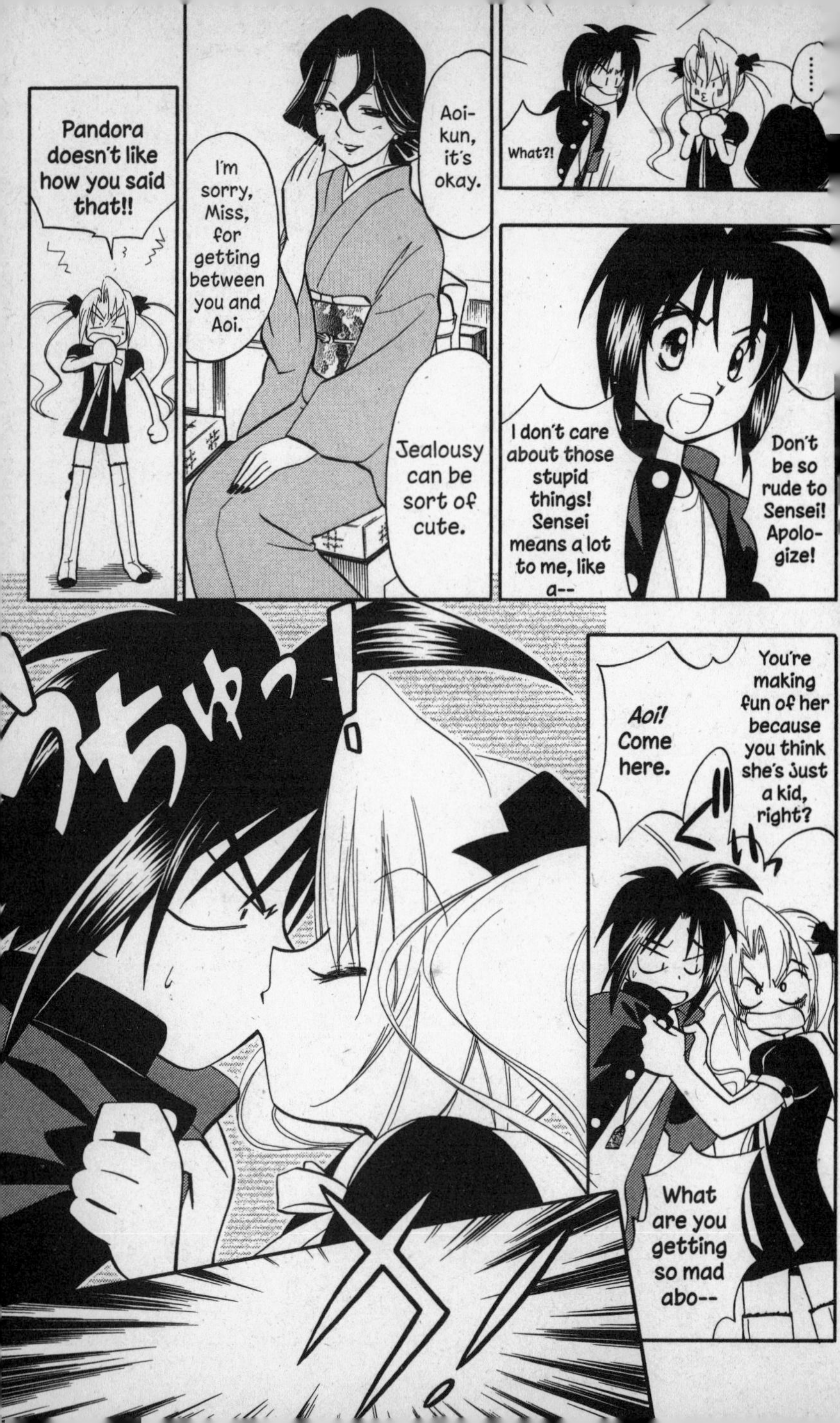
......
What?!
Don't be so rude to Sensei! Apologize!
I don't care about those stupid things! Sensei means a lot to me, like a--
Aoi-kun, it's okay.
I'm sorry, Miss, for getting between you and Aoi.
Jealousy can be sort of cute.
Pandora doesn't like how you said that!!
You're making fun of her because you think she's just a kid, right?
Aoi! Come here.
What are you getting so mad abo--
ちゅっ!

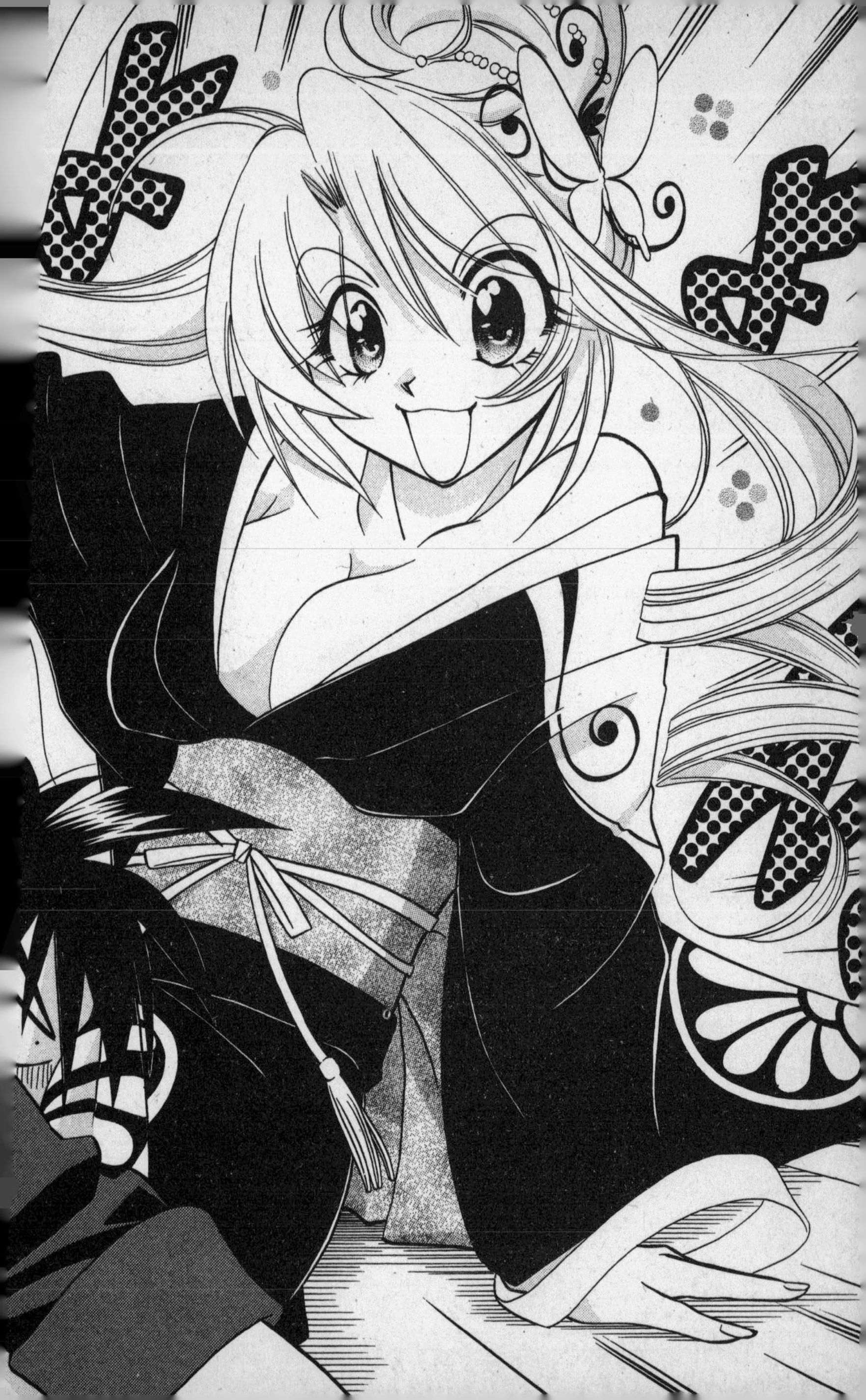

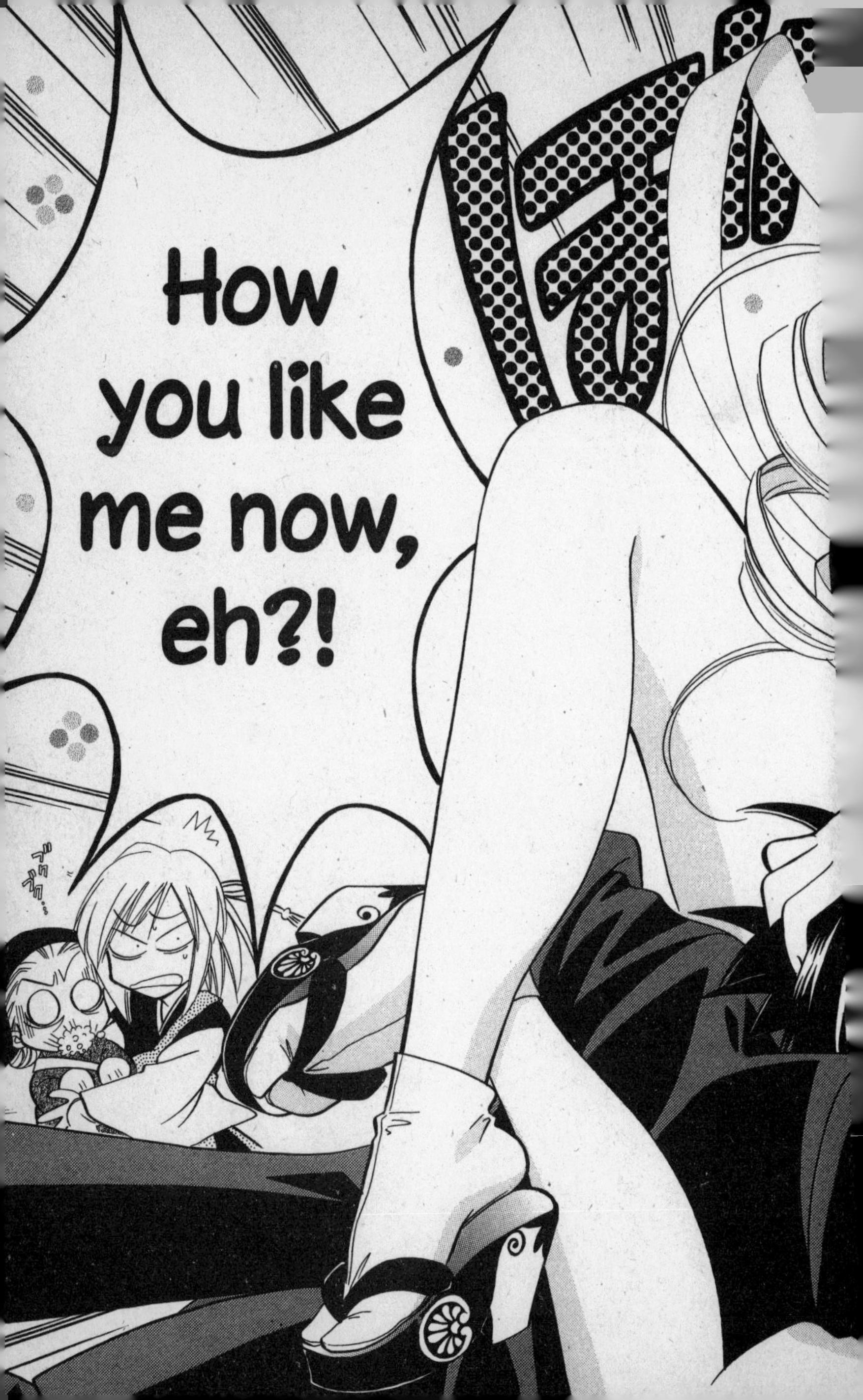
How you like me now, eh?!

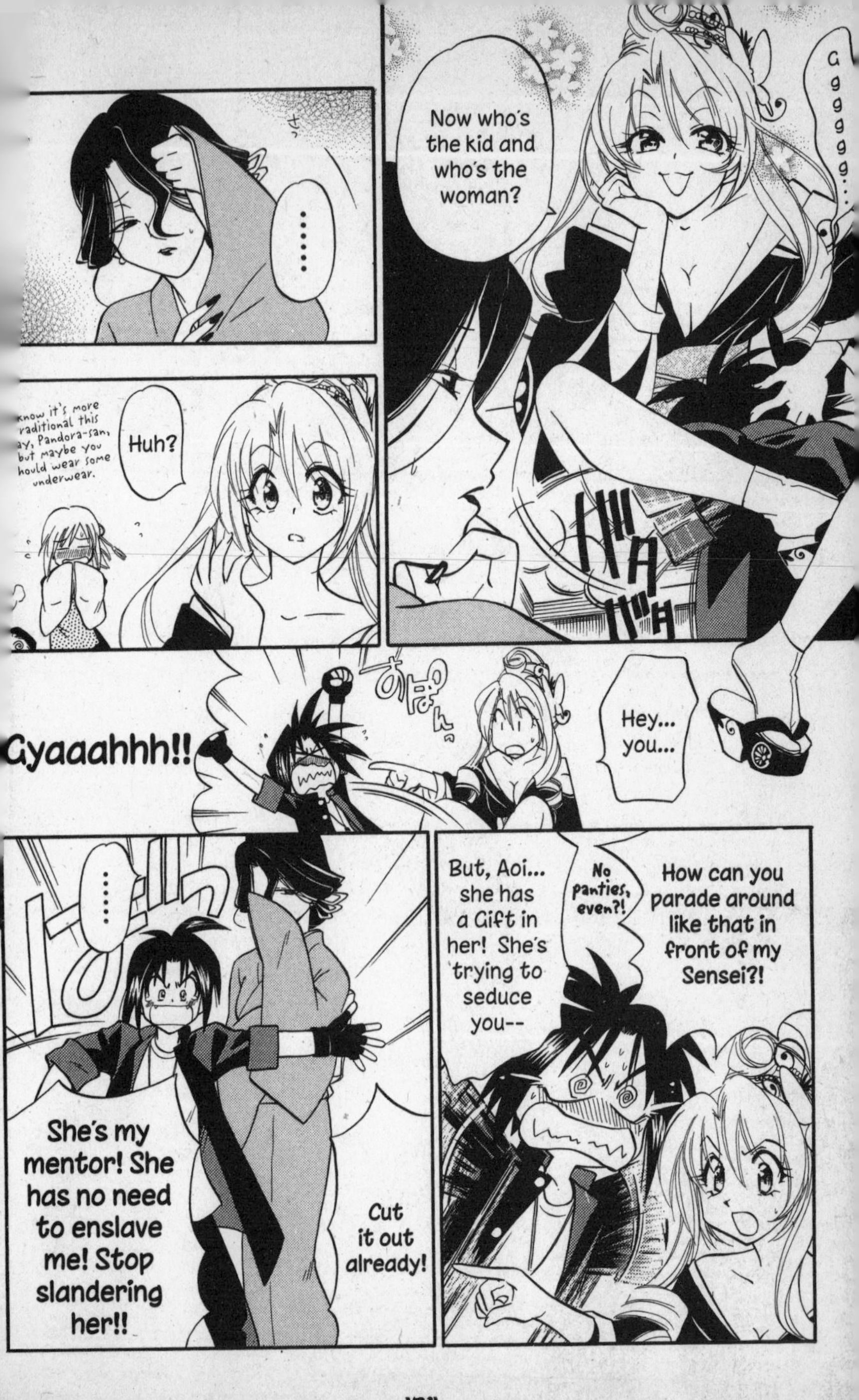

Ggggg...
Now who's the kid and who's the woman?
バタ
バタ
......
Huh?
know it's more raditional this ay, Pandora-san, but maybe you hould wear some underwear.
Hey... you...
おぱん
Gyaaahhh!!
How can you parade around like that in front of my Sensei?!
No panties, even?!
But, Aoi... she has a Gift in her! She's trying to seduce you--
......
Cut it out already!
She's my mentor! She has no need to enslave me! Stop slandering her!!

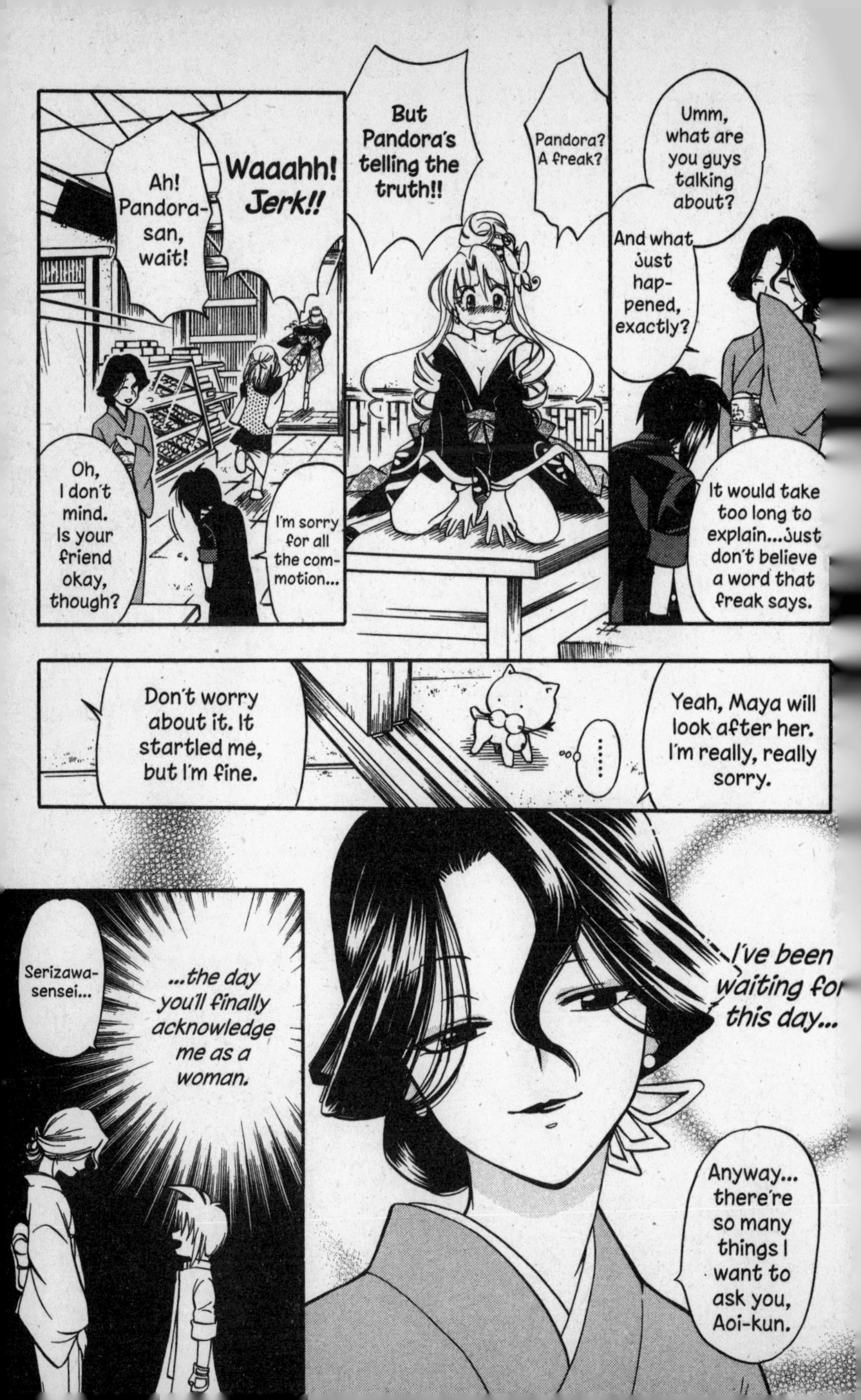
Umm, what are you guys talking about?
And what just happened, exactly?
It would take too long to explain...Just don't believe a word that freak says.
Pandora? A freak?
But Pandora's telling the truth!!
Waaahh! Jerk!!
Ah! Pandora-san, wait!
I'm sorry for all the commotion...
Oh, I don't mind. Is your friend okay, though?
Yeah, Maya will look after her. I'm really, really sorry.
......
Don't worry about it. It startled me, but I'm fine.
I've been waiting fo this day...
...the day you'll finally acknowledge me as a woman.
Serizawa-sensei...
Anyway... there're so many things I want to ask you, Aoi-kun.

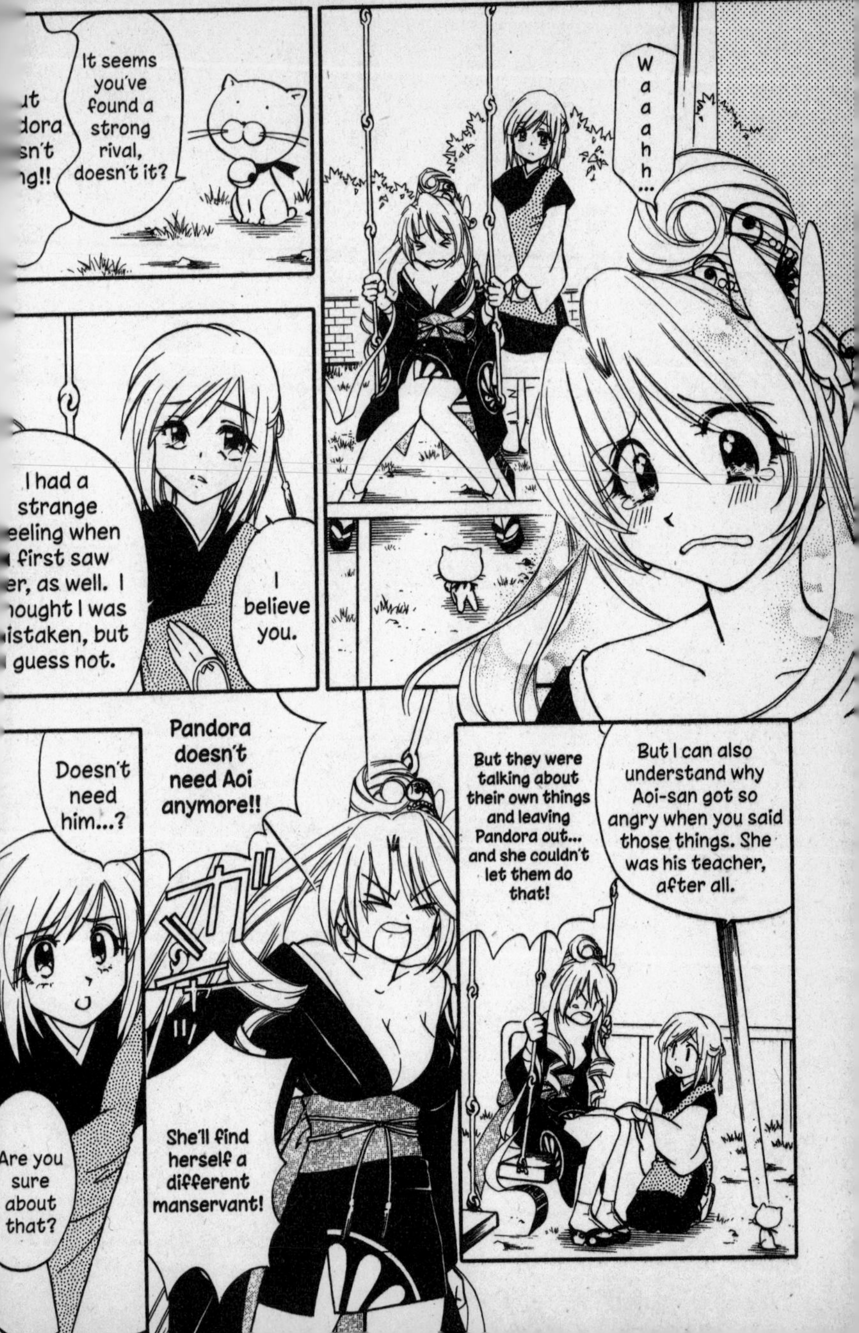
Waaahh...
It seems you've found a strong rival, doesn't it?
ut dora sn't ng!!
I believe you.
I had a strange eeling when first saw er, as well. I hought I was istaken, but guess not.
But I can also understand why Aoi-san got so angry when you said those things. She was his teacher, after all.
But they were talking about their own things and leaving Pandora out... and she couldn't let them do that!
Pandora doesn't need Aoi anymore!!
Doesn't need him...?
She'll find herself a different manservant!
Are you sure about that?

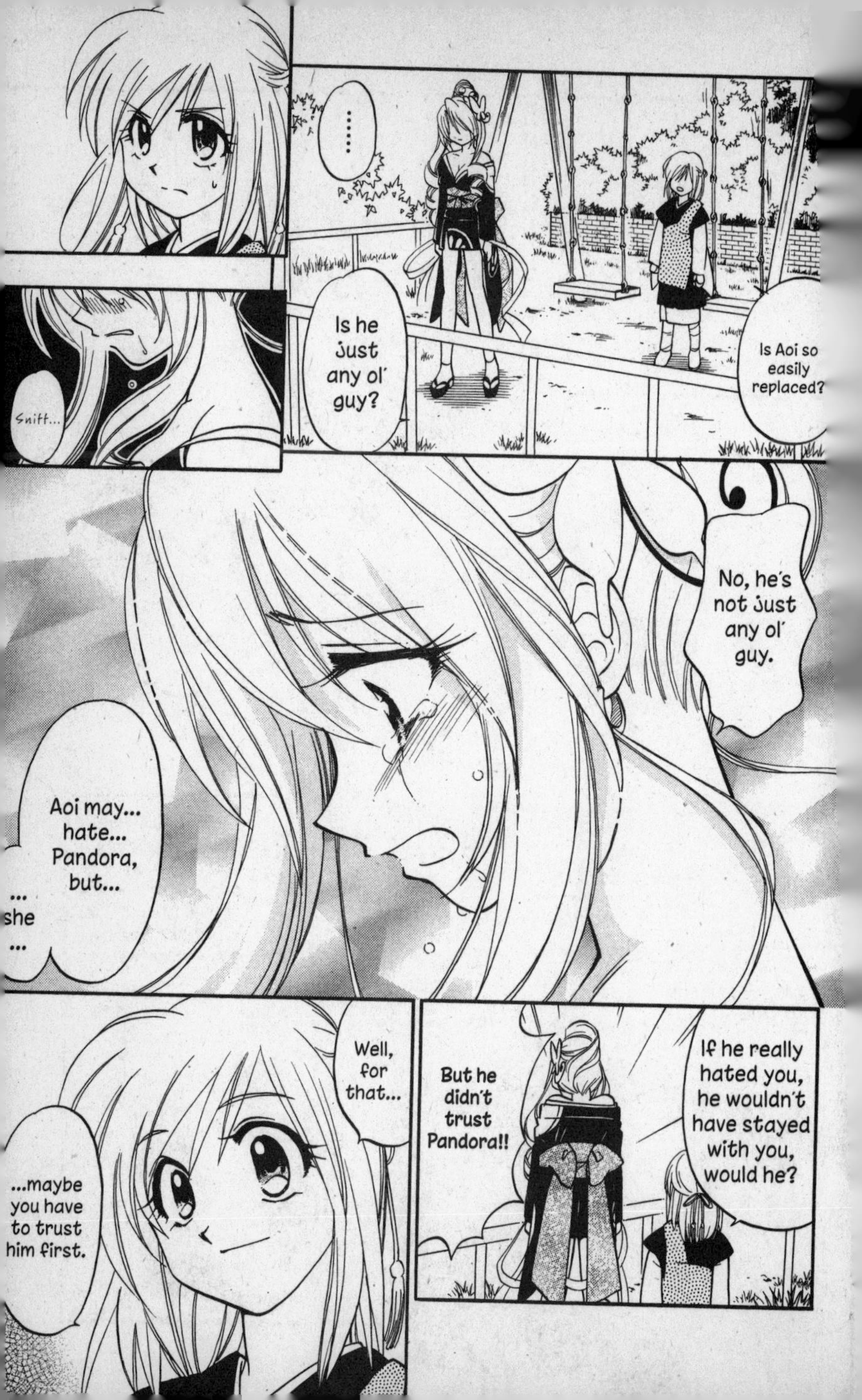
......
Is Aoi so easily replaced?
Is he just any ol' guy?
Sniff...
No, he's not just any ol' guy.
Aoi may... hate... Pandora, but...
... she ...
If he really hated you, he wouldn't have stayed with you, would he?
But he didn't trust Pandora!!
Well, for that...
...maybe you have to trust him first.

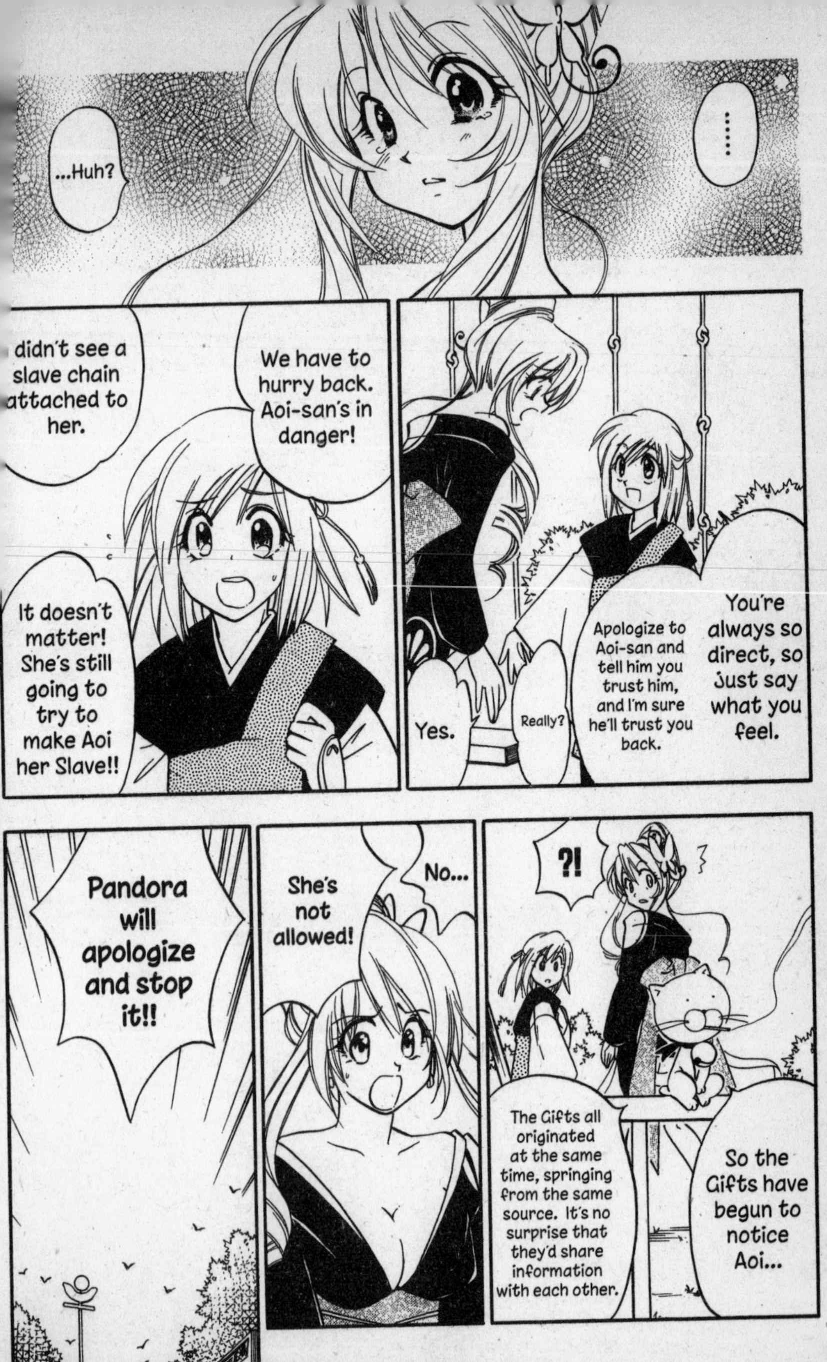
......
...Huh?
You're always so direct, so just say what you feel.
Apologize to Aoi-san and tell him you trust him, and I'm sure he'll trust you back.
Really?
Yes.
We have to hurry back. Aoi-san's in danger!
didn't see a slave chain attached to her.
It doesn't matter! She's still going to try to make Aoi her Slave!!
?!
So the Gifts have begun to notice Aoi...
The Gifts all originated at the same time, springing from the same source. It's no surprise that they'd share information with each other.
No...
She's not allowed!
Pandora will apologize and stop it!!

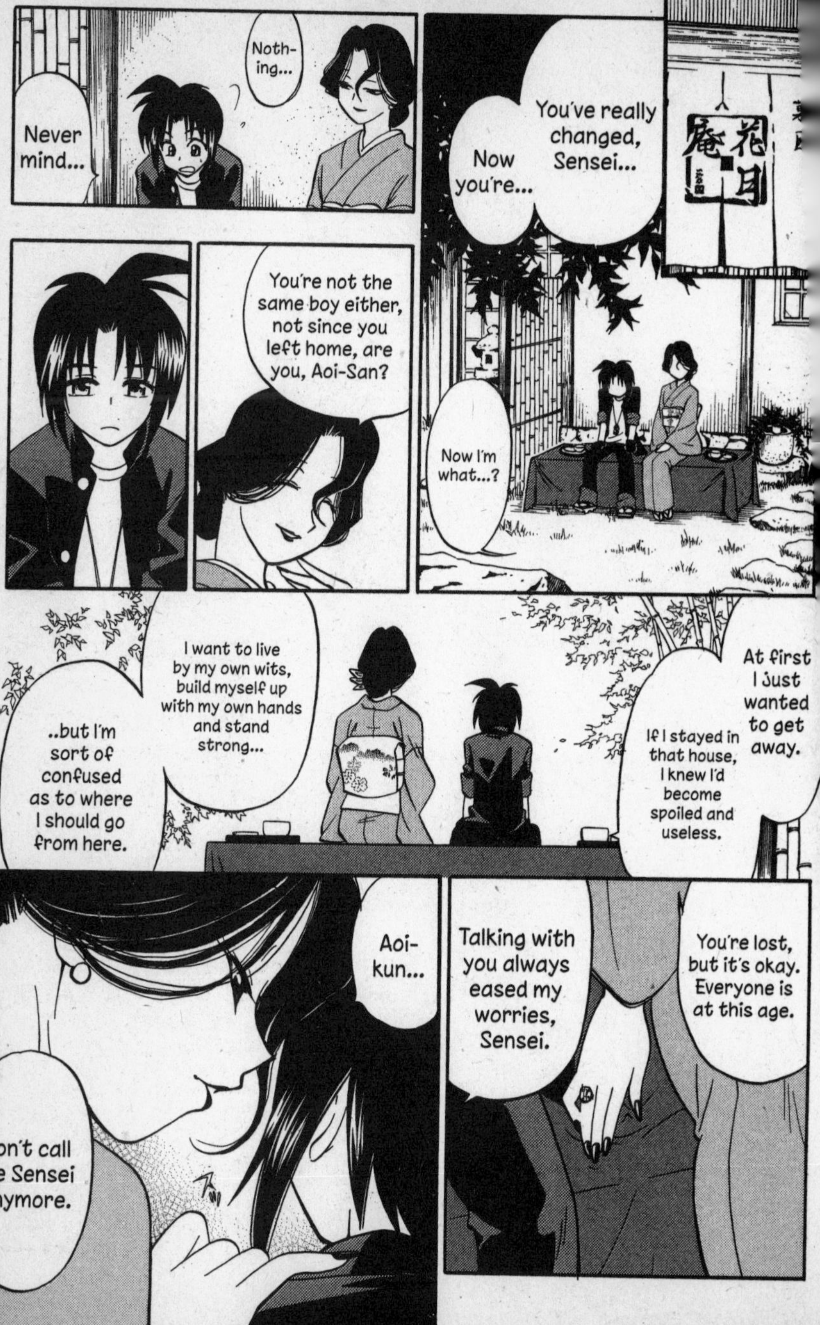
花月庵
You've really changed, Sensei...
Now you're...
Now I'm what...?
Noth-ing...
Never mind...
You're not the same boy either, not since you left home, are you, Aoi-San?
At first I just wanted to get away.
If I stayed in that house, I knew I'd become spoiled and useless.
I want to live by my own wits, build myself up with my own hands and stand strong...
..but I'm sort of confused as to where I should go from here.
You're lost, but it's okay. Everyone is at this age.
Talking with you always eased my worries, Sensei.
Aoi-kun...
Don't call me Sensei anymore.

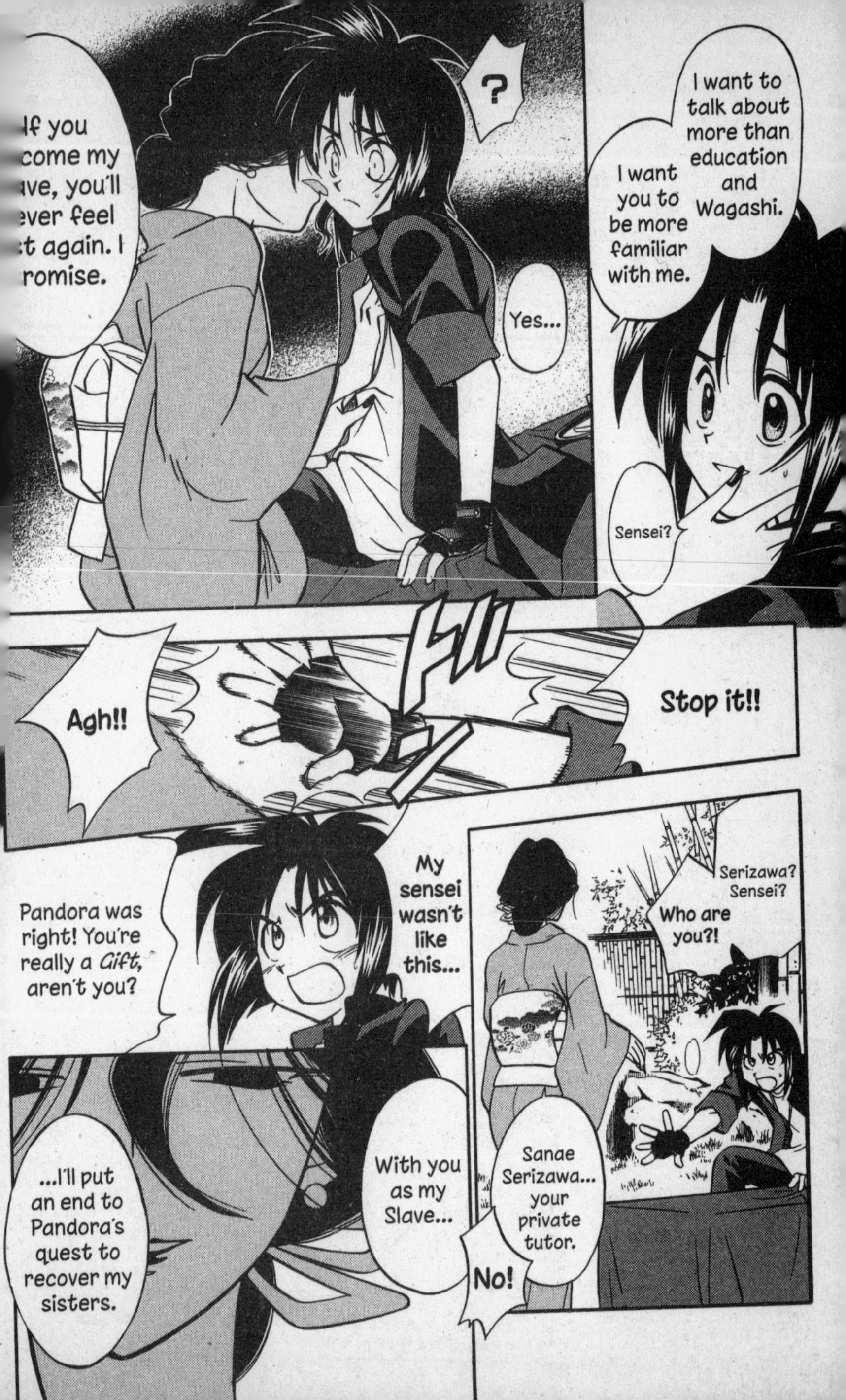

I want to talk about more than education and Wagashi.
I want you to be more familiar with me.
Sensei?
?
If you come my ave, you'll ever feel t again. I romise.
Yes...
Stop it!!
Agh!!
Serizawa? Sensei?
Who are you?!
Sanae Serizawa... your private tutor.
No!
My sensei wasn't like this...
Pandora was right! You're really a *Gift*, aren't you?
With you as my Slave...
...I'll put an end to Pandora's quest to recover my sisters.

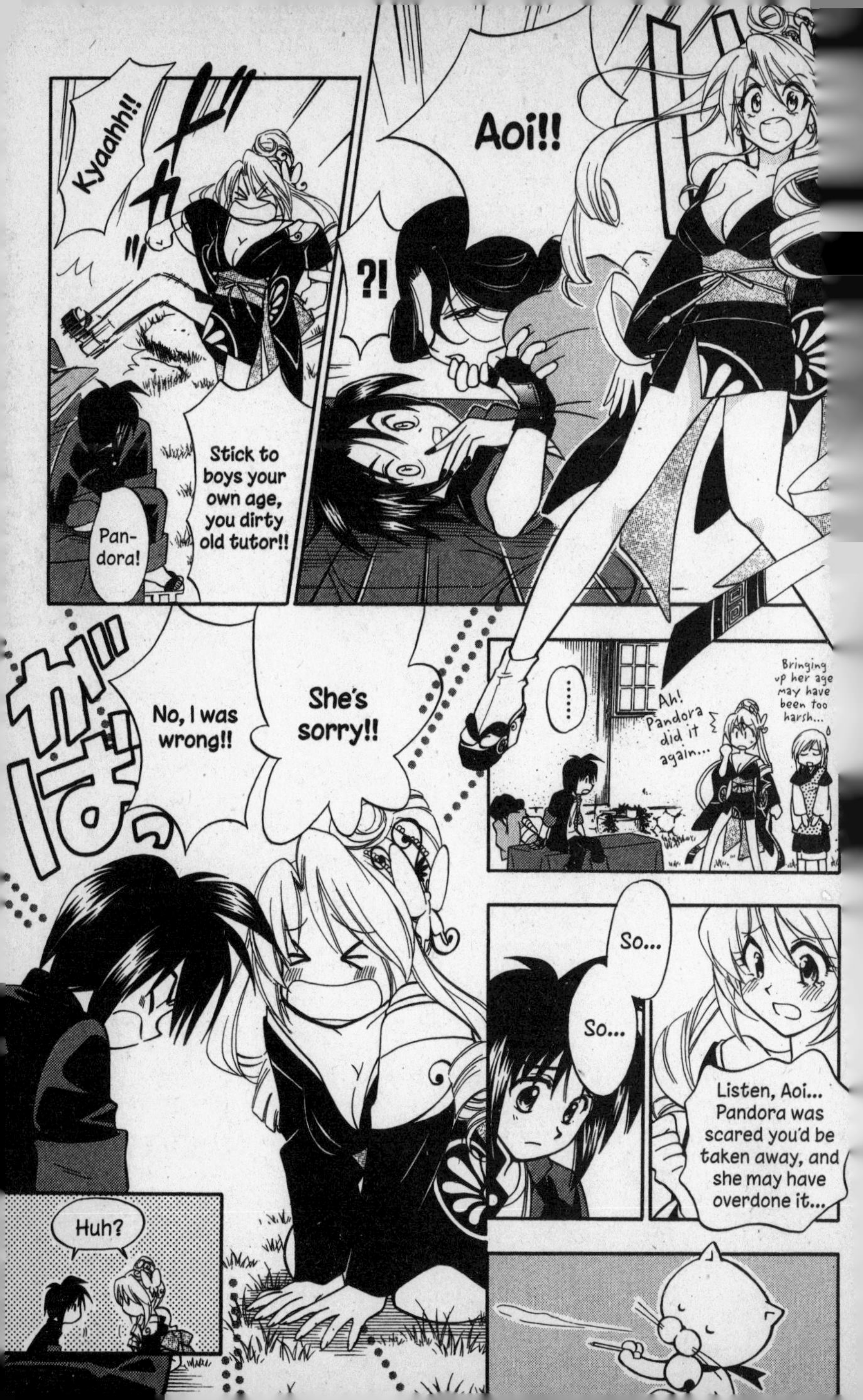

Aoi!!
?!
Kyaahh!!
ドガ
Stick to boys your own age, you dirty old tutor!!
Pan-dora!
......
Bringing up her age may have been too harsh...
Ah! Pandora did it again...
Listen, Aoi... Pandora was scared you'd be taken away, and she may have overdone it...
So...
So...
She's sorry!!
No, I was wrong!!
がばっ
Huh?

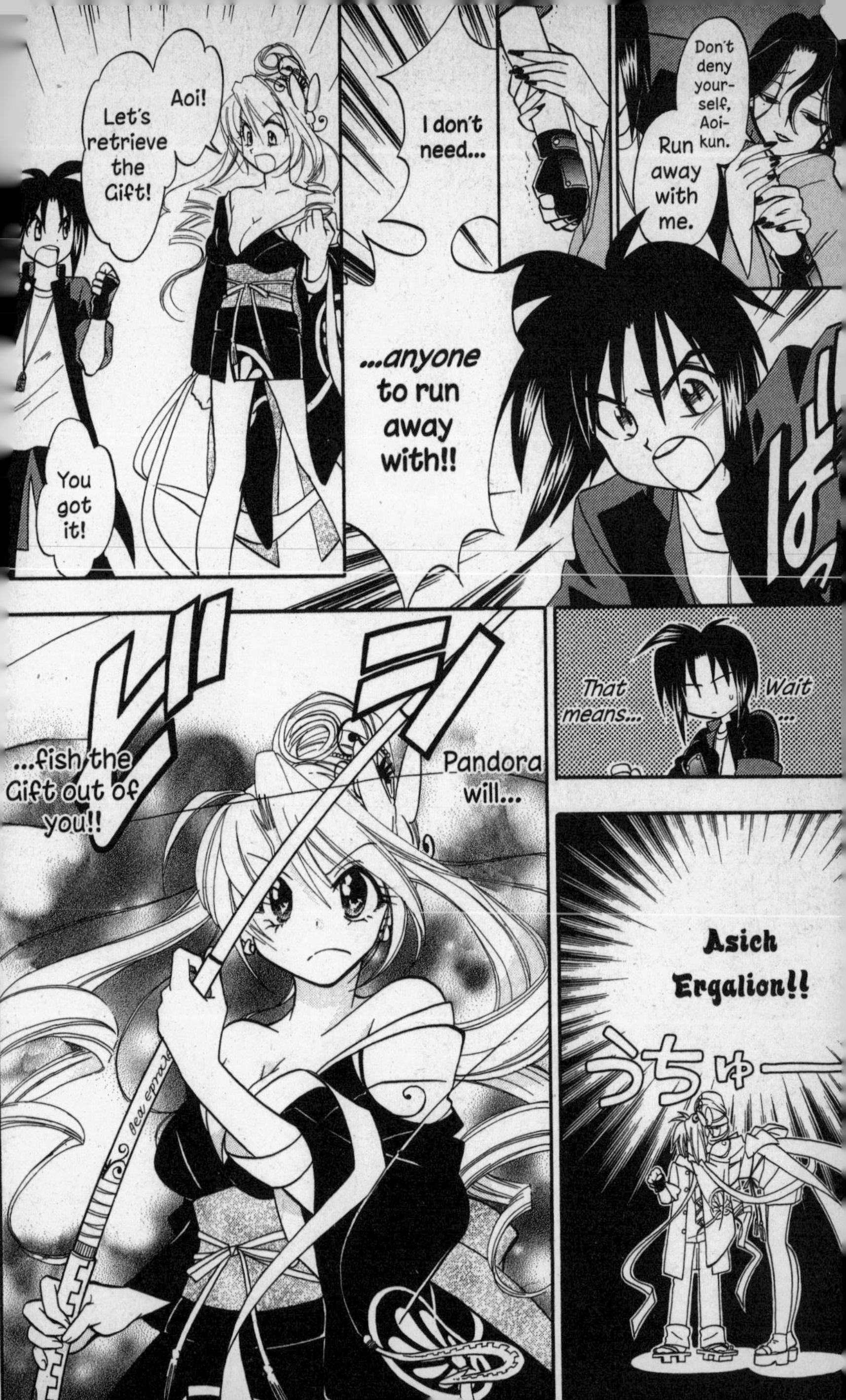
Don't deny your-self, Aoi-kun.
Run away with me.
I don't need...
...anyone to run away with!!
Aoi! Let's retrieve the Gift!
You got it!
Wait...
That means...
Asich Ergalion!!
うちゅー
Pandora will...
...fish the Gift out of you!!

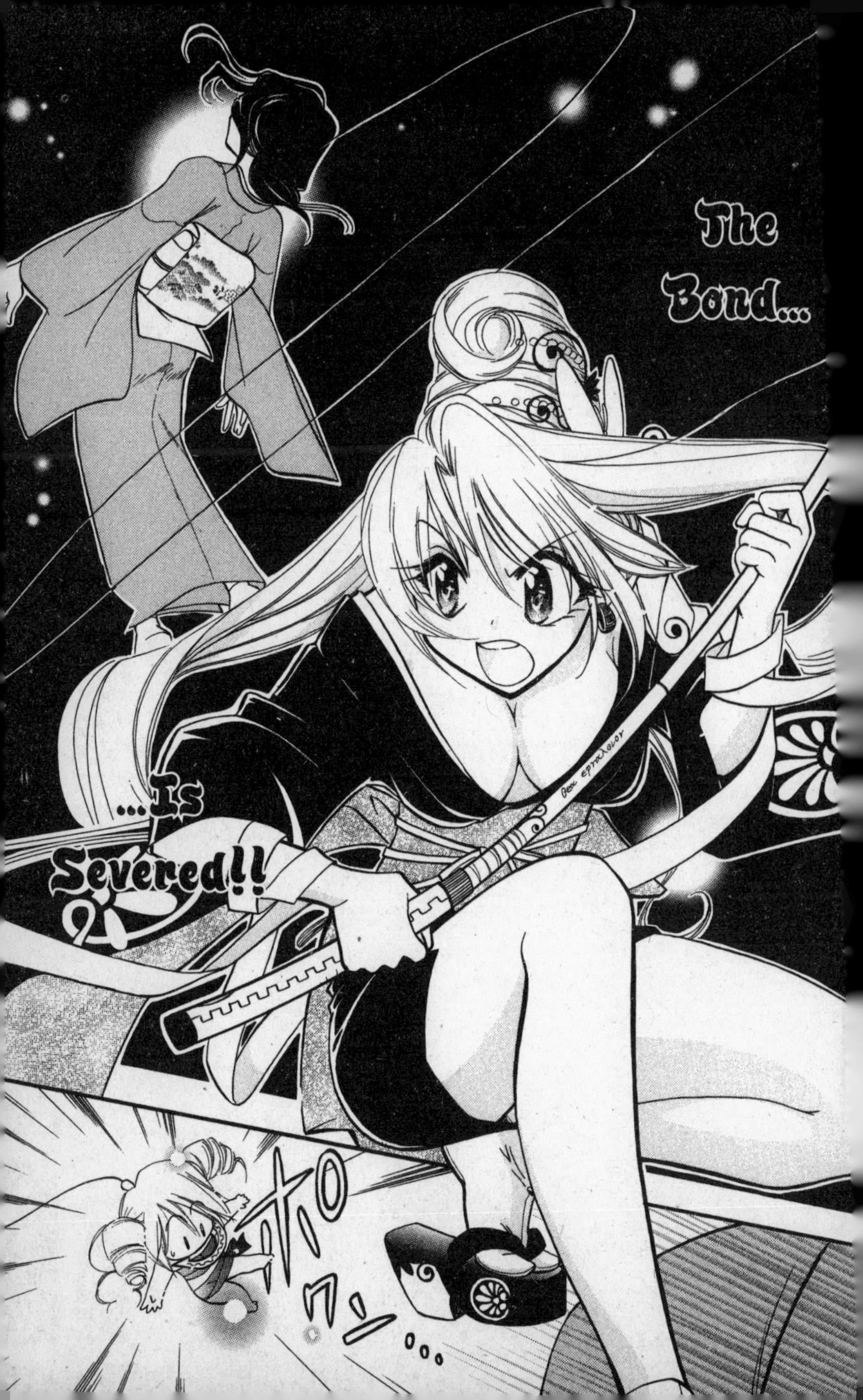
The Bond...
...Is Severed!!

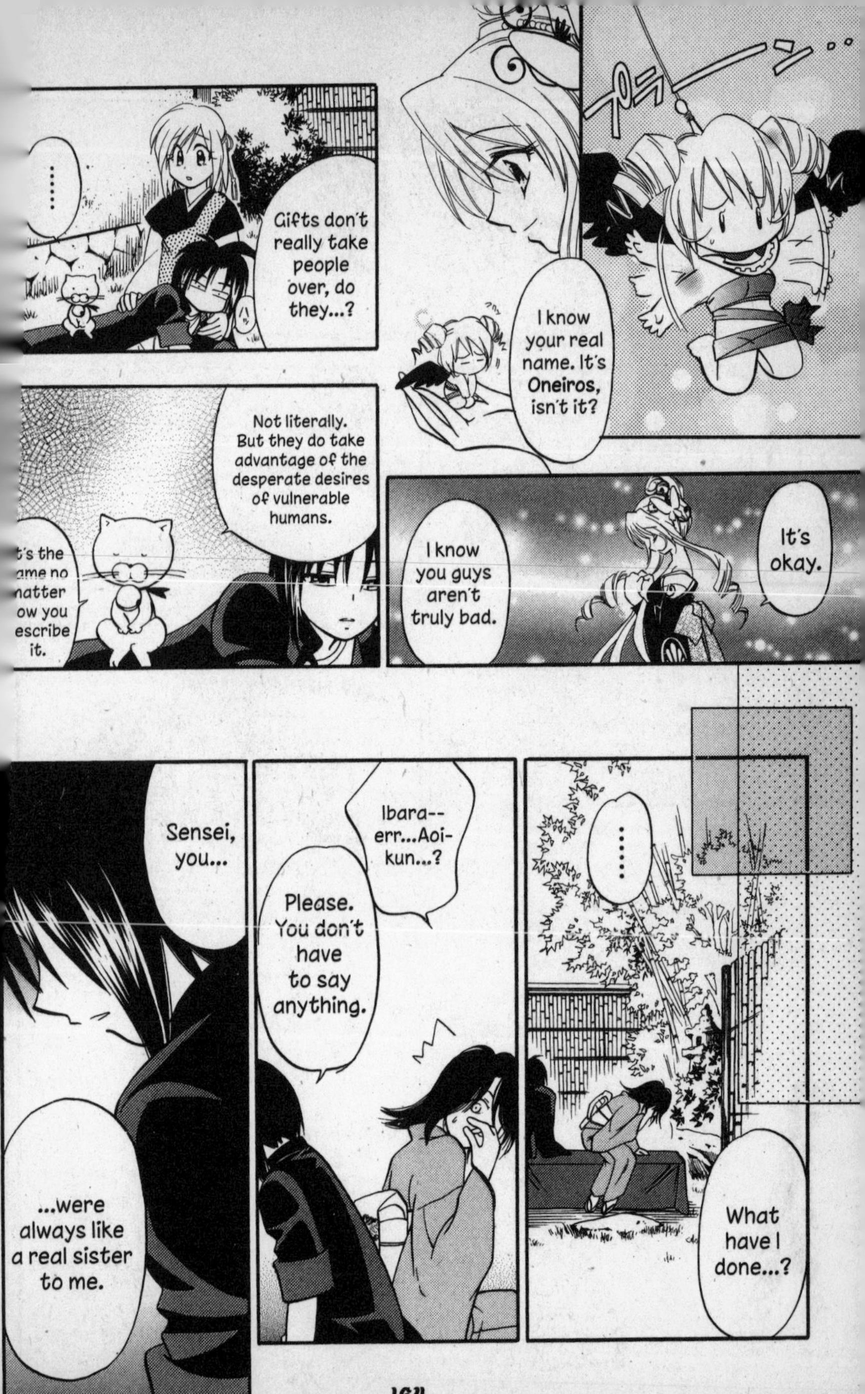
I know your real name. It's Oneiros, isn't it?
It's okay.
I know you guys aren't truly bad.
......
Gifts don't really take people over, do they...?
Not literally. But they do take advantage of the desperate desires of vulnerable humans.
t's the ame no natter ow you escribe it.
What have I done...?
......
Ibara-- err...Aoi-kun...?
Please. You don't have to say anything.
Sensei, you...
...were always like a real sister to me.

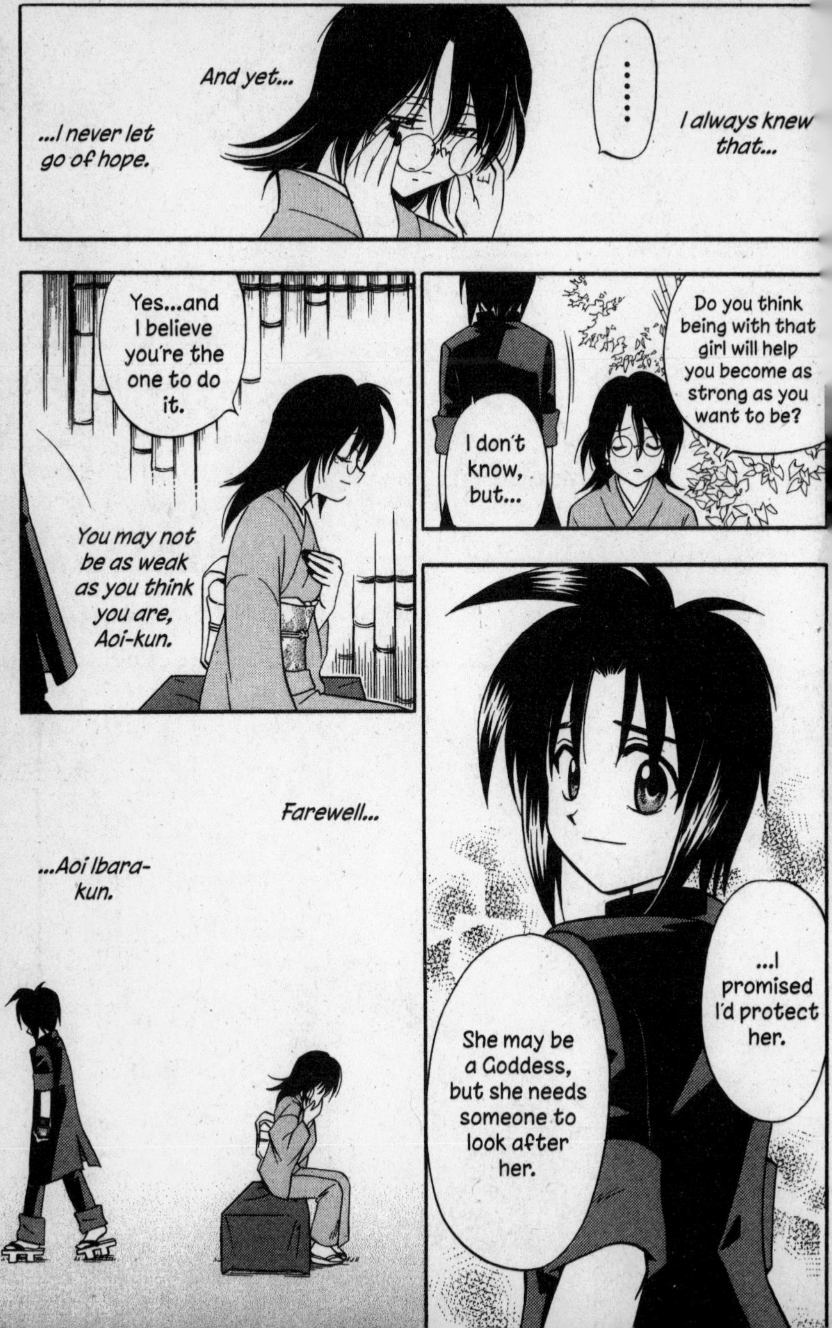
I always knew that...
......
And yet...
...I never let go of hope.
Do you think being with that girl will help you become as strong as you want to be?
I don't know, but...
...I promised I'd protect her.
She may be a Goddess, but she needs someone to look after her.
Yes...and I believe you're the one to do it.
You may not be as weak as you think you are, Aoi-kun.
Farewell...
...Aoi Ibara-kun.

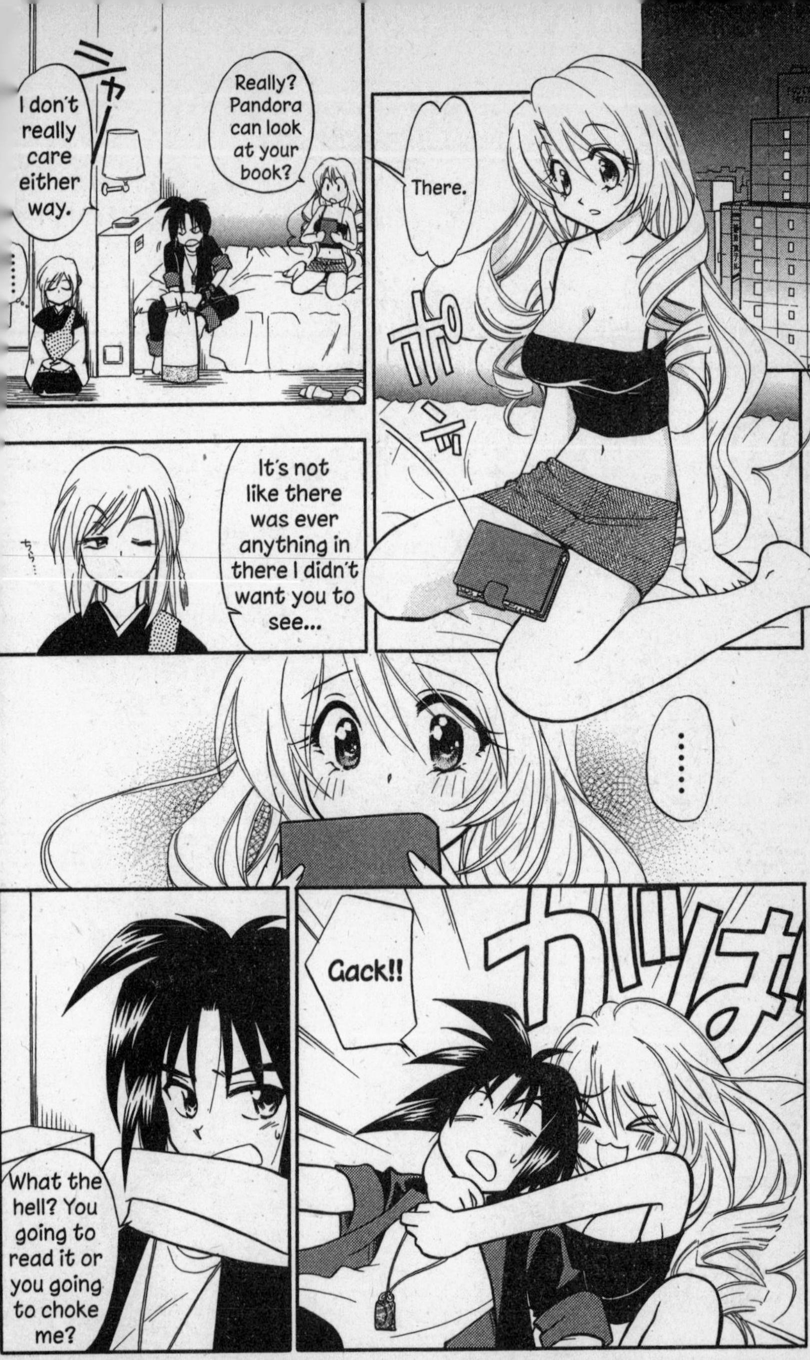
There.
Really? Pandora can look at your book?
I don't really care either way.
......
It's not like there was ever anything in there I didn't want you to see...
......
Gack!!
What the hell? You going to read it or you going to choke me?

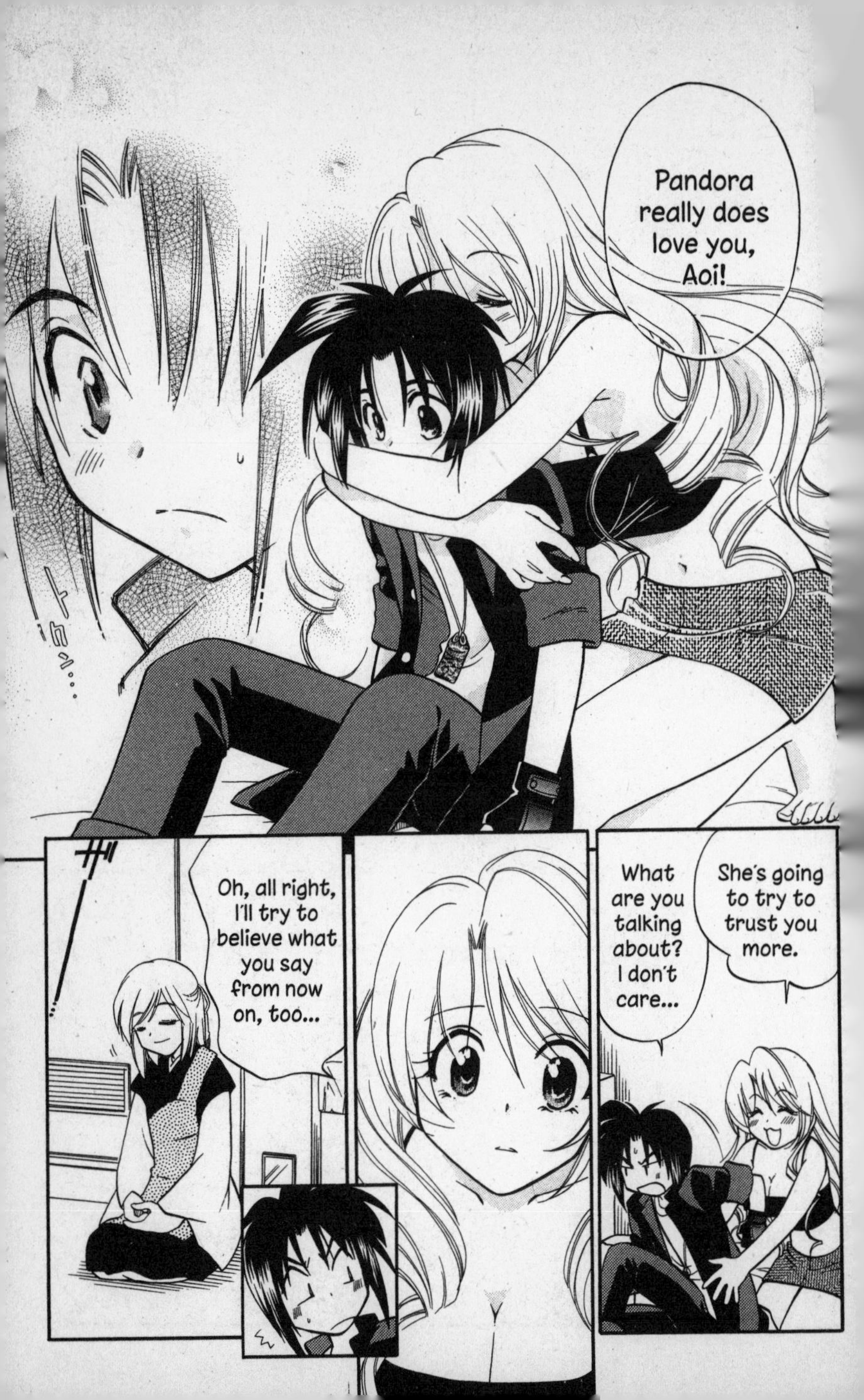
Pandora really does love you, Aoi!
She's going to try to trust you more.
What are you talking about? I don't care...
Oh, all right, I'll try to believe what you say from now on, too...

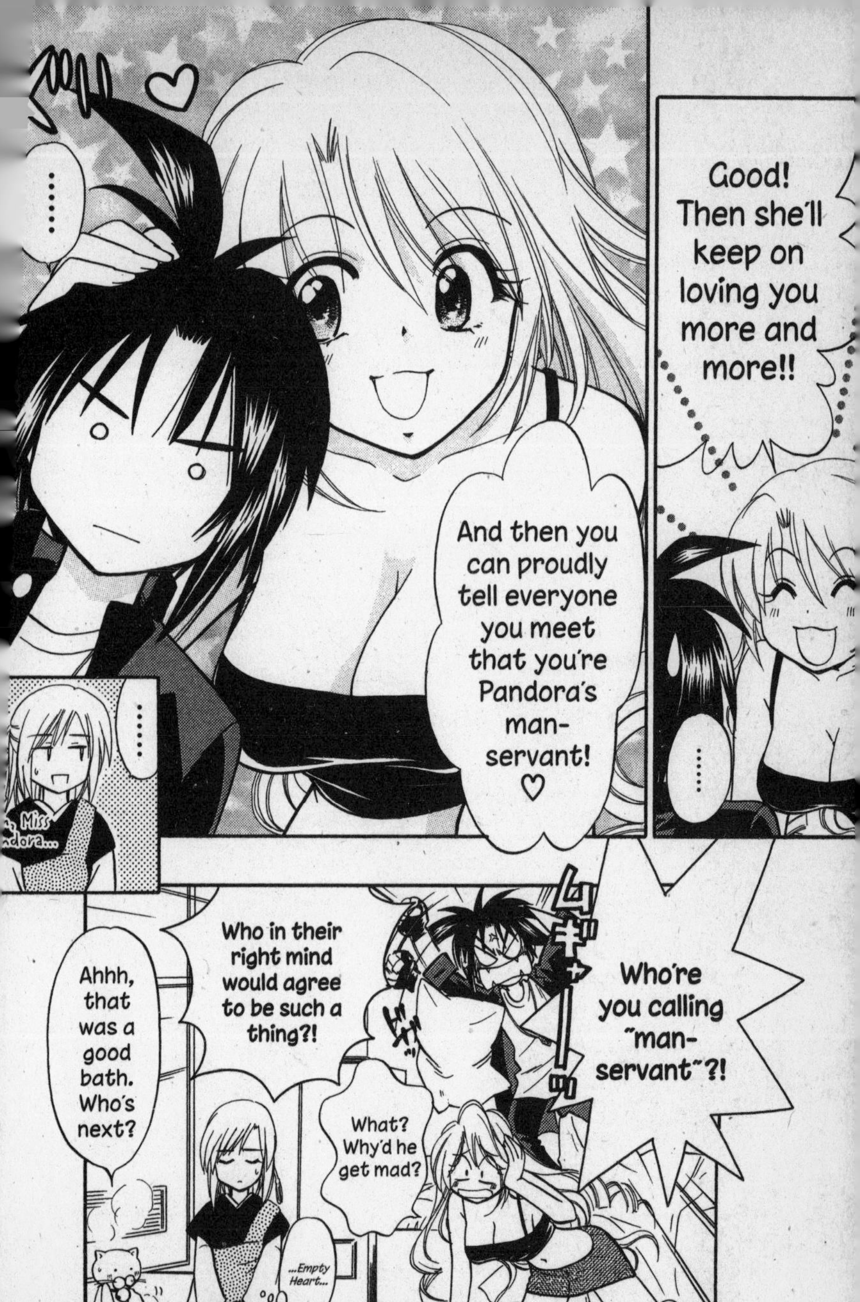
Good! Then she'll keep on loving you more and more!!
......
......
And then you can proudly tell everyone you meet that you're Pandora's man-servant! ♡
......
Miss
Who're you calling "man-servant"?!
Who in their right mind would agree to be such a thing?!
What? Why'd he get mad?
Ahhh, that was a good bath. Who's next?
...Empty Heart...

神様だもの

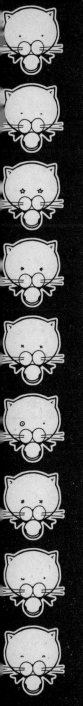

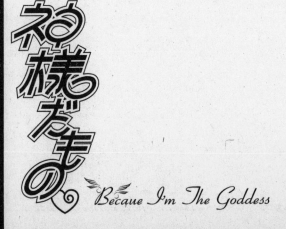

Becaue I'm The Goddess

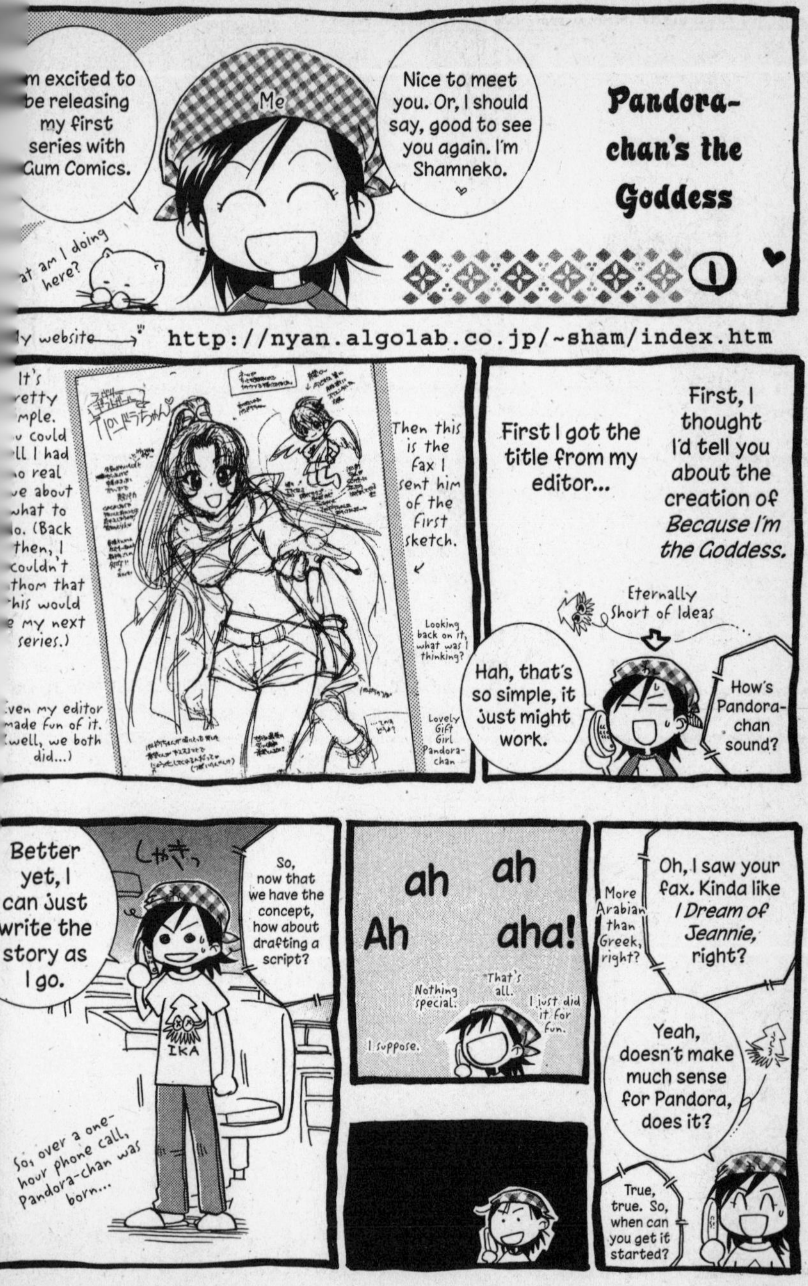

Pandora-chan's the Goddess 1
Me
Nice to meet you. Or, I should say, good to see you again. I'm Shamneko.
m excited to be releasing my first series with Gum Comics.
at am I doing here?
ly website
http://nyan.algolab.co.jp/~sham/index.htm
First, I thought I'd tell you about the creation of *Because I'm the Goddess.*
First I got the title from my editor...
Eternally Short of Ideas
How's Pandora-chan sound?
Hah, that's so simple, it just might work.
Then this is the fax I sent him of the first sketch.
It's retty mple. u could ll I had o real e about what to o. (Back then, I couldn't thom that his would e my next series.)
Looking back on it, what was I thinking?
Lovely Gift Girl Pandora-chan
ven my editor made fun of it. well, we both did...)
Oh, I saw your fax. Kinda like *I Dream of Jeannie,* right?
More Arabian than Greek, right?
Yeah, doesn't make much sense for Pandora, does it?
True, true. So, when can you get it started?
ah ah Ah aha!
That's all.
Nothing special.
I just did it for fun.
I suppose.
So, now that we have the concept, how about drafting a script?
しゃきっ
Better yet, I can just write the story as I go.
IKA
So, over a one-hour phone call, Pandora-chan was born...

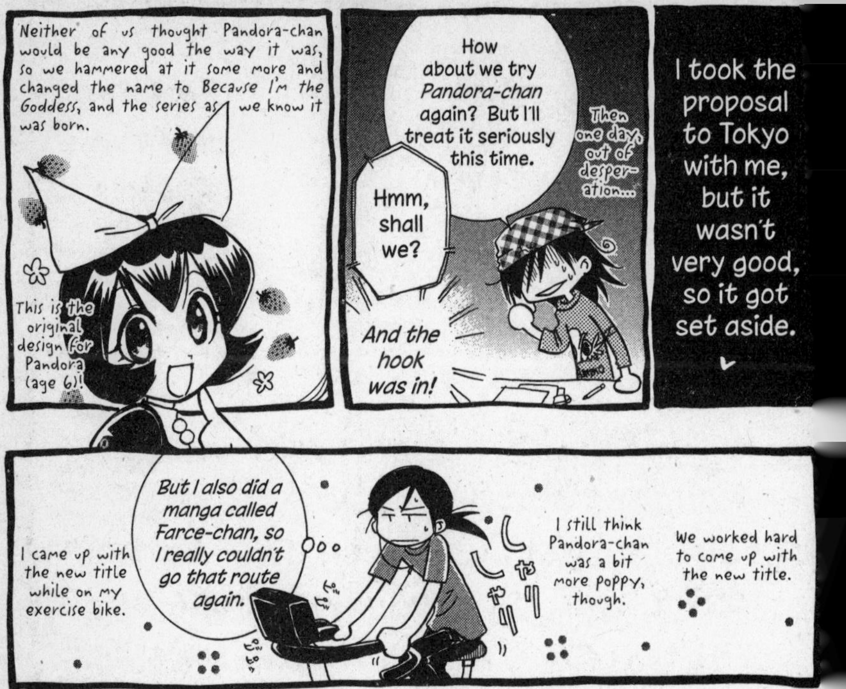
I took the proposal to Tokyo with me, but it wasn't very good, so it got set aside.
Then one day, out of desperation...
How about we try Pandora-chan again? But I'll treat it seriously this time.
Hmm, shall we?
And the hook was in!
Neither of us thought Pandora-chan would be any good the way it was, so we hammered at it some more and changed the name to Because I'm the Goddess, and the series as we know it was born.
This is the original design for Pandora (age 6)!
We worked hard to come up with the new title.
I still think Pandora-chan was a bit more poppy, though.
But I also did a manga called Farce-chan, so I really couldn't go that route again.
I came up with the new title while on my exercise bike.

✿STAFF✿ Ide-cchi ✿ Kodo-chan ✿ Miss Fujita ✿ Miss Umanami ✿ and my editor (Ume): Thank you lots!!

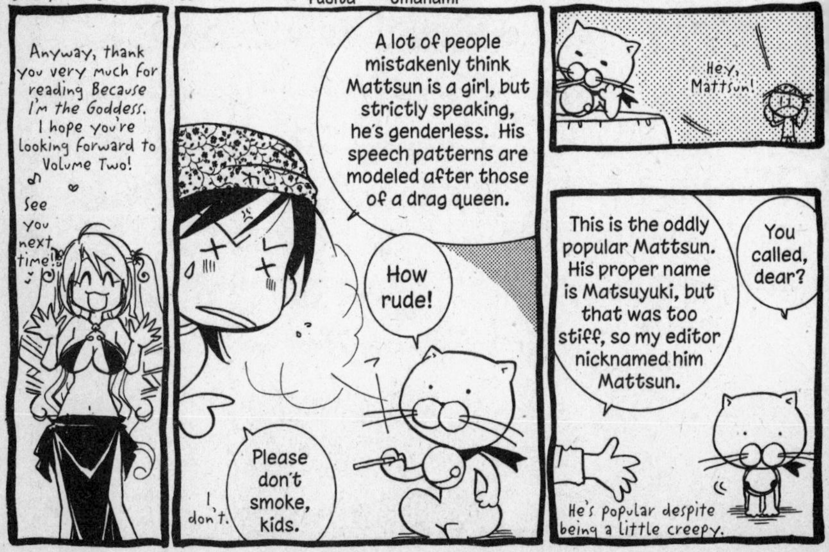
Hey, Mattsun!
You called, dear?
This is the oddly popular Mattsun. His proper name is Matsuyuki, but that was too stiff, so my editor nicknamed him Mattsun.
He's popular despite being a little creepy.
A lot of people mistakenly think Mattsun is a girl, but strictly speaking, he's genderless. His speech patterns are modeled after those of a drag queen.
How rude!
Please don't smoke, kids.
I don't.
Anyway, thank you very much for reading Because I'm the Goddess. I hope you're looking forward to Volume Two!
See you next time!

In the next volume of

The Gifts fight back! While Pandora and Aoi embark on a quest for the best Japanese sweets, Aoi is confronted by a maid from the family he ran away from. But the maid is actually a vessel for a Gift and her driver is the Slave! Pandora shows up in time to prevent Aoi from being dragged off to his old home, but finds herself embroiled in a battle with a Gift capable of the powerful Asich Ergalion spell! Will the ditzy goddess meet her makers?

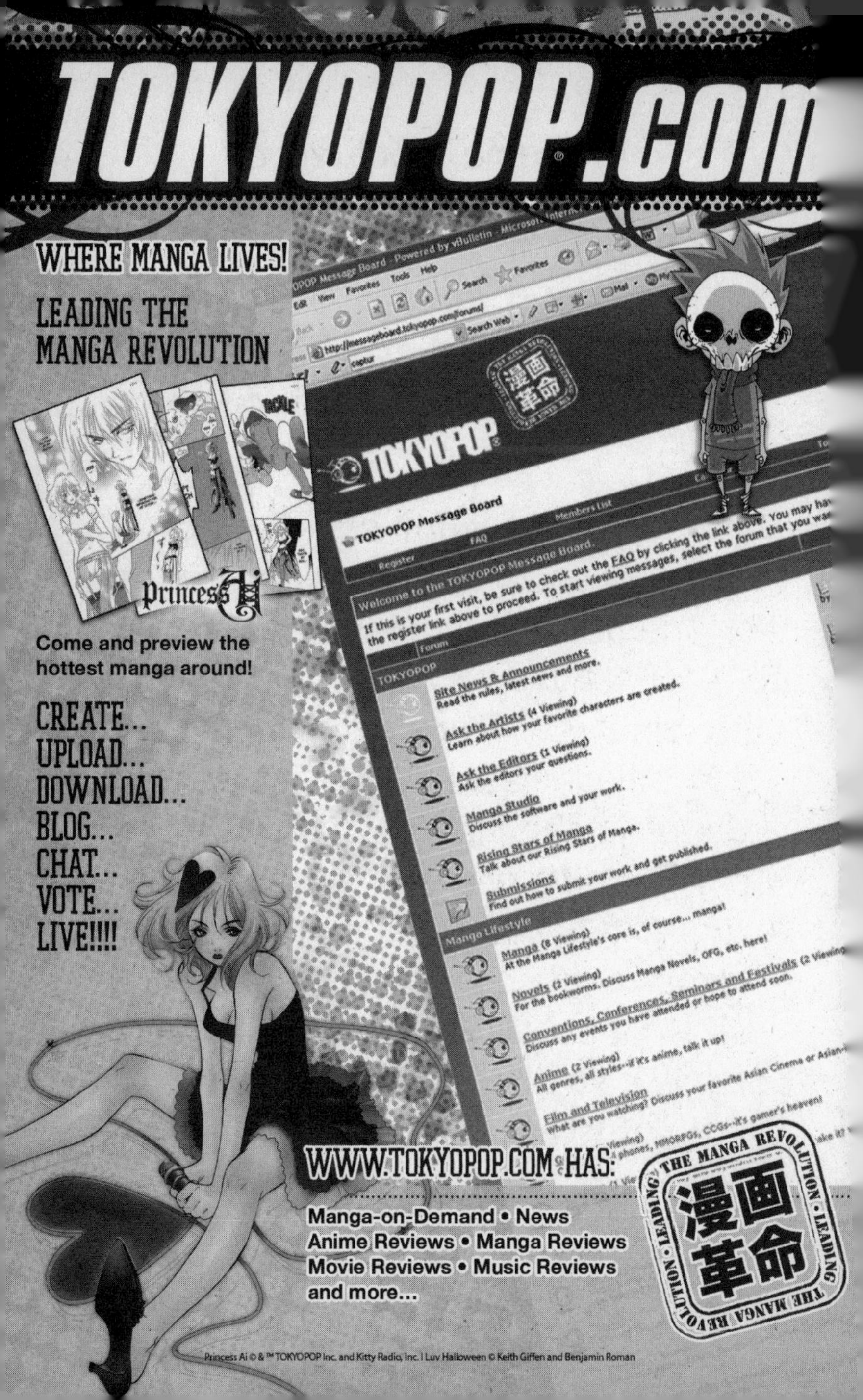
TOKYOPOP.com
WHERE MANGA LIVES!
LEADING THE MANGA REVOLUTION
Princess Ai
Come and preview the hottest manga around!
CREATE...
UPLOAD...
DOWNLOAD...
BLOG...
CHAT...
VOTE...
LIVE!!!!
TOKYOPOP
TOKYOPOP Message Board
Site News & Announcements
Ask the Artists
Ask the Editors
Manga Studio
Rising Stars of Manga
Submissions
Manga Lifestyle
Manga
Novels
Conventions, Conferences, Seminars and Festivals
Anime
Film and Television
WWW.TOKYOPOP.COM HAS:
Manga-on-Demand • News
Anime Reviews • Manga Reviews
Movie Reviews • Music Reviews
and more...
LEADING THE MANGA REVOLUTION
漫画革命
Princess Ai © & ™ TOKYOPOP Inc. and Kitty Radio, Inc. I Luv Halloween © Keith Giffen and Benjamin Roman

STOP!

This is the back of the book.
You wouldn't want to spoil a great ending!

This book is printed "manga-style," in the authentic Japanese right-to-left format. Since none of the artwork has been flipped or altered, readers get to experience the story just as the creator intended. You've been asking for it, so TOKYOPOP® delivered: authentic, hot-off-the-press, and far more fun!

DIRECTIONS

If this is your first time reading manga-style, here's a quick guide to help you understand how it works.

It's easy... just start in the top right panel and follow the numbers. Have fun, and look for more 100% authentic manga from TOKYOPOP®!